The Old Lie

THE OLD LIE

The Great War and the Public School Ethos

PETER PARKER

hambledon
continuum

First published in Great Britain 1987
by Constable and Company Limited
This paperback edition published by Hambledon Continuum
The Tower Building, 11 York Road, London, SE1 7NX, UK
Suite 704, 80 Maiden Lane, New York, NY 10038, USA
Copyright © 1987 by Peter Parker
Set in Monophoto Poliphilus 12pt by
Servis Filmsetting Ltd, Manchester
Printed in Great Britain by
MPG Books Ltd, Cornwall

ISBN 1 84725 0440

Contents

THIS BOOK IS DEDICATED

TO MY PARENTS

IN MEMORY OF

THEIR FATHERS:

6827 Pte. A.R.N. Parker H.A.C.

Capt. F.R. Sturridge M.C. R.A.M.C.

Illustrations

'Jesu, Lover of my Soul' (*Bamforth & Co.*)
'The White Comrade'
Officers' Christmas dinner at the Front, 1915 (*Illustrated War News*)
Charles Hamilton Sorley (*Marlborough College Archive*)
Rupert Brooke (*Imperial War Museum*)
Alec Waugh
Edward Lyttelton (*Illustrated War News*)
The Cavalry: *Young England's* vision
The Cavalry: In training (*Illustrated War News*)
Etonians unloading supplies at Didcot (*Illustrated War News*)
'The Playing Fields of Eton, 1917' (*Eton College Library*)
Classical War memorial: South Africa (*Illustrated War News*)
Chivalric War memorial: Westminster (*Westminster School Library*)

Eighteen, by Jove! You've timed your lives wonderfully, my boys. To be eighteen in 1914 is to be the best thing in England. England's wealth used to consist in other things. Nowadays you boys are the richest thing she's got. She's solvent with you, and bankrupt without you. . . . Eighteen years ago you were born for this day. Through the last eighteen years you've been educated for it. Your birth and breeding were given you that you might officer England's youth in this hour. And now you enter upon your inheritance.

Ernest Raymond

They died for great ideals

Leighton Park War Memorial

Acknowledgements

Without the co-operation of a certain number of schools, this book would have been impossible. For unfailing help, not only in directing me towards the relevant shelves, but also in showing me around the schools and providing duplicates and photocopies, I would like to thank the following: Mr Paul Quarrie of the College Library at Eton; Mr G. Kempson, former Archivist, and Mr. W. Latham, Librarian, at Marlborough; Mr A. Childs, former Librarian at Sherborne; Mr James Lawson, Librarian at Shrewsbury; and Mr John Field, Librarian at Westminster. For further assistance, and for answering letters, I would like thank Mr Patrick Strong, the Archivist at Eton; Ms Felicity O'Sullivan and Mr Michael Davis at Marlborough; Mr John Warmington, Librarian at Sherborne; Mr Donald Boyd of the Downs School, Colwall; and Mr Andrew Sims of the New Beacon School, Sevenoaks.

I have also received invaluable assistance from a number of archivists and librarians at assorted institutions during the course of my researches. In particular I am most grateful to Mr Roderick Suddaby of the Department of Documents at the Imperial War Museum, whose knowledge saved me a great deal of time, and who kindly negotiated permission to use material from the collection. I would also like to thank other members of staff in the Department of Documents, staff in the Department of Printed Books, and Mr Paul Kemp of the Department of Photography. The staff at the University of London Library, Maida Vale Library, the British Library, and University College London Library have all given me welcome assistance, often digging out recondite books from depositories. I must also record my gratitude to various members of staff at the Public Records Office at Kew for helping me in what turned out to be an interesting, but finally fruitless search for material relating to the War Office and the public schools, and also thank staff at the Mansell Collection.

I am extremely grateful to the families of the men whose letters and diaries are kept in the Department of Documents at the Imperial War Museum for permission to quote certain passages. I am indebted in particular to Mrs Desmond Allhusen, and to Mr Anthony Bond (on behalf of the estate of Revd T.S. Nevill). It has not been possible to trace the copyright-holders of all the material I have quoted, and I would be pleased to hear of any copyright-holders whose permission I have not been able to obtain. In particular I would like to thank the family of Captain Arthur Gibbs, and hope that this acknowledge-ment goes some way towards substituting for formal permission. I am also extremely grateful to Mrs Virginia Sorensen Waugh and Captain Andrew Waugh RN for permission to quote from papers relating to Alec Waugh's *The Loom of Youth*, donated by the author to Sherborne School Library.

Mr Timothy d'Arch Smith generously gave me the run of his collection of boys' fiction and allowed me to borrow (often for extended periods) a number of rare books and magazines. He also answered numerous questions, and even accompanied me to Lord's one unsettled May morning so that I could view cricketing pictures. I am forever in his debt. I would also like to thank the following people who gave, loaned, or otherwise acquired for me books and other material: Mr Geoffrey Elborn; Ms Alison Hennegan; Mr Ron Hill; Mr Philip Hodson; Ms Sarah Long; Mr St John Pope; Mr Jonathan Rich; Mr Graeme T. Steel.

A number of people kindly provided me with information of one sort or another and I would like to record my gratitude to: Mr C.T.A. Beevor; Mr H. Lewis Bugbee; Mr Simon Burt; Sir Rupert Hart-Davis; Major P.G.E. Hill; Mr Martin Middlebrook; Mr Richard O'Sullivan; the Rt Hon the Earl of Stockton; Mrs M. Thomas; Major A.D.I. Wall; and four former pupils of the Downs School who wrote to me with their reminiscences of life at Quaker preparatory and public schools during the Great War: Mr G.W. Cadbury, Mr F.H. Gillett, Mr David More, and Mr R. Lestor Steynor, who also provided me with a copy of his unpublished typescript, 'Memories of the Downs School 1916–1919'.

A large amount of the poetry I have quoted is still in copyright and I must express my gratitude to those copyright-holders who gave me permission to quote, often extensively, from such material. In particular, I should like to thank Mr George Sassoon and Mrs Bridget Painter for their generosity. Herbert Asquith's 'The Volunteer' (from *Poems 1912–33*) is reproduced here with the permission of Sidgwick & Jackson Ltd.; the extract from Laurence Binyon's 'For the Fallen, 1914' is reproduced by kind permission of Mrs Nicolette Gray and the Society of Authors on behalf of the Laurence Binyon Estate; the extracts from Robert Graves's 'Goliath and David' (from *Fairies and Fusiliers*, Heinemann 1916) are reproduced by permission of A.P. Watt Ltd on behalf of the Executors of the Estate of Robert Graves. Extracts from Robert Nichols's 'Fulfilment' (from *Ardours and Endurances* (1917)), from Wilfred Owen's 'The Ballard of Purchase Money' (from *Wilfred Owen* by Jon Stallworthy (1974)) and from *The Poems of Wilfred Owen* (edited by Jon Stallworthy, Hogarth Press 1985) are reproduced by kind permission of Chatto & Windus; the poems of Jessie Pope are reprinted by kind permission of her great-niece, Mrs Bridget Painter; the extracts from Herbert Read's 'My Company' (from *Collected Poems* published by Faber & Faber 1946) are reprinted by permission of David Higham Associates Ltd.; extracts from the works of Siegfried Sassoon are reproduced by kind permission of George Sassoon.

The lyrics of 'Keep the Home Fires Burning' by L.G. Ford ((c) 1914 Ascherberg, Hopwood & Crew Ltd.) are reproduced by permission of Chappell Music Limited London; the lyrics of 'I'll Make a Man of You' by Arthur Wimperis ((c) 1914 Francis Day & Hunter Ltd.) are reproduced by permission of EMI Music Publishing Ltd, London WC2H oLD.

For permission to reproduce material from the archives of the schools, I should like to thank the Provost and Fellows of Eton College; the Master of Marlborough College; Mr R.D. Macnaghten, M.A., Headmaster of Sherborne; the Chairman and the Governing Body of Shrewsbury School; and the Governing Body of Westminster School.

The letter from John Murray on p. 208 is reproduced by kind permission of John Murray Ltd.

For illustrations, I would like to thank Hills & Saunders of Eton, and Cecil and Jean Woolf, who kindly provided a print of the photograph of Sorley. The photograph of Brooke is reproduced by permission of the Imperial War Museum. The photograph of Alec Waugh is reproduced by kind permission of Captain Andrew Waugh. Photographs from the *Illustrated War News* are reproduced by kind permission of the *Illustrated London News*. The postcard of 'Jesu, Lover of My Soul' is reproduced by permission of Bamforth & Co. Ltd.

Mr Paul Taylor spent a great deal of time reading my manuscript and discussing it with me, and there is no doubt that the book has greatly benefitted from his advice. I am extremely grateful to him and to Mr Christopher Potter and Mr Jonathan Rich, who also read the manuscript and made suggestions. That I did not always act upon these does not mean that I was not very glad of them; the responsibility for any errors of fact or judgement remain my own.

My most long-standing debt is to Mr Dan Jacobson, who, as an inspiriting tutor at University College London, encouraged me along the road which eventually led to this book. I would also like to thank Ms Elfreda Powell for her early enthusiasm. Mr Bill Hamilton at A.M. Heath persuaded me to write rather than talk about the book and offered help and criticism throughout. At Constable & Co. Mr Robin Baird-Smith has been a sympathetic and patient editor and I have also received invaluable assistance from Ms Clare Derrick.

Finally there are personal debts, most difficult to itemise but impossible to have done without. In particular, I would like to thank Christopher Potter and Thomas Blaikie. My parents gave considerable support and never asked when I was going to get a proper job. This book is for them.

PETER PARKER
London, 1986

Introduction
to the 2007 edition

*T*he *Old Lie* is not the work of a professional historian. Having given up on history while still at school, I first had the idea of writing the book while studying the literature of the First World War as part of an English degree at university. As I explain in the original Introduction, this literature is largely one of disillusion, and in order to be disillusioned one has to have illu- sions in the first place. Reading these poems, novels and memoirs for the first time, I was immediately struck by the similarity between the ideals and values these writers were rejecting and those that were promoted in the Victorian and Edwardian public schools at which many of them had been educated. Encouraged by my tutor to pursue this idea, I spent the next eight or so years happily reading social and military history and delving into assorted archives.

At the time *The Old Lie* was first published, what is now regarded by some historians as 'the myth of the First World War' was largely unquestioned. The First World War, it was generally agreed, was an unmitigated tragedy in which callous and incompetent generals, comfortably situated in grand chateaux well behind the line, conducted a uniquely costly and futile war of attrition. The 'plan of attack', as Siegfried Sassoon sarcastically called it in one of his poems, was to send wave after wave of young men over the top to be mown down by German machine guns. The *locus classicus* of this myth was the first day of the Battle of the Somme, 1 July 1916, in which a massive assault upon the German front line failed at the cost of 60,000 British casualties. It was, and remains, without question the worst single day in the history of the British army. In spite of this the battle continued until November, by which time the British had gained a few miles of shattered ground in exchange for a total cost of 419,654 casualties, many of whom simply disappeared. Edwin Lutyens' vast Memorial to the Missing of the Somme at Thiepval lists 73,357 names of soldiers whose bodies were never recovered or identified, including those of the writer H. H. Munro ('Saki') and the composer George Butterworth.

Although it would be hard to find any redeeming feature in the Battle of the Somme, or indeed many of the other major battles, military historians have begun to challenge widespread popular ideas about the First World War. These 'myths', they protest, are founded not upon history but upon literature, in particular upon 'a small and unrepresentative group of junior officers' known collectively as the War Poets[1]. Perhaps the most persuasive and articulate of these 'revisionists' is Gary Sheffield, whose *Forgotten Victory* (2001) is subtitled 'The First World War: Myths and Realities'. 'It would be wrong to deny that poetry represents a valid expression of a particular individual's experience,' Sheffield admits, 'but one should no more rely solely or even primarily on literary sources to understand the First World War than base one's entire knowledge of fifteenth-century Anglo-French relations on Shakespeare's *Henry V*.'[2] Worse still, the revisionists grumble, the skewed contribution of such soldier-poets as Wilfred Owen, Siegfried Sassoon, Robert Graves and Edmund Blunden has been promulgated in subsequent popular accounts of the war: the play and film *Oh! What a Lovely War*, novels such as Sebastian Faulks' *Birdsong* and Pat Barker's *Regeneration* trilogy, and the television comedy *Blackadder Goes Forth*. As the title of his book suggests, Sheffield argues that the prevailing view of the conflict apparently overlooks the fact that Britain and her allies did eventually win the war. The German Spring Offensive in March 1918 may have recaptured the ground the British gained at such terrible cost during the Battle of the Somme, but it was the last throw of the dice. During the rest of that year, the British achieved remarkable gains, the result of improvements in both strategy and the artillery that had so signally and disastrously failed to destroy the German defences in June 1916. The Germans finally surrendered in November, but to the annoyance of some military historians Britain's 'spectacular victories' took place in battles that scarcely anyone can name: 'The British have become fixated with the Somme and Passchendaele and these battles which are seen as disasters. There hasn't been a great deal of interest until very recently in examining the victorious battles. We have got the First World War firmly stamped on our collective memory as being a disaster'[3].

---

[1] Gary Sheffield, *Forgotten Victory* (Headline, 2001), p.18.
[2] Ibid., p.19.
[3] *Thing We Forgot to Remember*, presented by Michael Portillo, BBC Radio 4 (3 December 2006.)

The revisionists are not of course the first people to have made this observa-tion. As long ago as 1941, in his famous essay 'England, Your England', George Orwell noted that most British people 'do not retain among their historical memories the name of a single military victory.' He went on to remark that:

English literature, like other literatures, is full of battle-poems, but it is worth noticing that the ones that have won for themselves a kind of popularity are always a tale of disasters and retreats. There is no popular poem about Trafalgar or Waterloo, for instance. Sir John Moore's army at Corunna, fighting a desperate rearguard action before escaping overseas (just like Dunkirk!) has more appeal than a brilliant victory. The most stirring battle-poem in English is about a brigade of cavalry which charged in the wrong direction. And of the last war, the four names which have really engraved themselves on the popular memory are Mons, Ypres, Gallipoli and Passchendaele, every time a disaster. The names of the great battles that finally broke the German armies are simply unknown to the general public.[1]

It is no accident that the First World War is the subject chosen to illustrate dif-ferent ways of looking at historical events in Alan Bennett's play about edu-cation, *The History Boys* (2004). As the revisionists frequently complain, in Britain the War Poets have become a core text of the National Curriculum, instilling schoolchildren with an 'unbalanced' view of the conflict. Bennett has said that Irwin, the young teacher who goes on to be a television pundit, is partly inspired by 'the new breed of historians … who all came to promi-nence under Mrs Thatcher and share some of her characteristics. Having found that taking the contrary view pays dividends, they tend to make this the tone of their customary discourse'[2]. One of the historians Bennett names is Niall Ferguson, whose *The Pity of War* (1999) takes a provocatively contrarian view of the First World War, though not one that necessarily coincides with that of revisionist historians such as Gary Sheffield and Huw Strachan. In Bennett's play what might be described as the poets' view of the war is set up against the revisionists' one. 'So we arrive eventually at the less-than-startling conclusion that so far as the poets are concerned, the First World War gets the thumbs down,' Irwin announces to the class of boys he is coaching for the Oxbridge entrance examination.[3] He invites them to list what the revisionists

[1] George Orwell, *Inside the Whale and Other Essays* (Penguin, 1962), pp.68–9
[2] Alan Bennett, *The History Boys* (Faber, 2004), p.xxiv.
[3] Ibid., p.23.

would call the 'myths' of the war, and they happily oblige: 'Trench warfare', 'Barrenness of strategy', 'Stupidity of the generals [...] Haig in particular', and so on. When Irwin responds by saying such notions will simply bore an Oxbridge examiner, one boy protests: 'But it's all true'. 'What has that got to do with it?' replies Irwin before outlining a different and distinctly contrarian view of the war.[1] He goes on to say, as revisionist do, that in spite of what they wrote in their poems Sassoon and Owen were good officers, both of whom were determined to return to the trenches after sick leave in order to lead their men. The boys are not convinced. 'You can't explain away the poetry, sir,' one says. 'No, sir,' chimes another. 'Art wins in the end'. By way of illustration, the boys recite Philip Larkin's poem 'MCMXIV'. 'How come you know all this by heart?' asks the 'baffled' Irwin.[2]

A similar sense of bafflement assails the revisionist historians, who in com-plaining, however justifiably, about the ascendancy of literature over history occasionally give the impression that they are involved in some sort of turf war. However often and however convincingly they explain that the First World War was both necessary and just, the poets' view of the war prevails: art does indeed win in the end. Except that it is surely possible to acknowledge many of the facts pointed out by military historians while at the same time recognising the essential truth of those reports from the front line provided by poets, novelists and memoirists. Whatever you might think of the military strategies pursued by the generals *qua* strategies, you would not necessarily want to be spearhead-ing them in the trenches. Some revisionists nevertheless argue that General Haig in particular has been badly treated by history. In 1965, the writer and editor J. R. Ackerley (who had been in the trenches on 1 July 1916 and became one of the 60,000 casualties of what he described as 'General Haig's masterly operation') noted that a bottle of Haig whisky was one shilling cheaper than any other brand. He affected to believe that this was a direct result of the enduring disgrace the Earl had brought to that name.[3] Indeed, an advertising catchphrase for this whisky, 'Don't' be vague: ask for Haig' was at one point adapted for historical-satirical use: 'Don't be vague: blame General Haig'. Leading figures in the attempt to rehabilitate Haig remind us that the day of his funeral, 3 February 1928, was a day of national mourning. Crowds gathered on the streets of London to watch the coffin being taken by gun carriage to

[1] Ibid., p.23.
[2] Ibid., p.24–5.
[3] J.R. Ackerley, *My Father and Myself* (Bodley Head, 1968), p.56; Peter Parker, *Ackerley* (Constable, 1989), p.24.

Westminster Abbey, and at level crossings to doff their hats as it made its way by rail to Edinburgh. While admitting that even in 1928 Haig was a not uncontroversial figure, Dan Todman goes on to suggest that the funeral was 'a moment of symbolic mourning for all the dead who hadn't had a funeral', apparently forgetting that this moment had already been provided some seven years earlier by the funeral of the Unknown Warrior.[1] In truth it would have been rather more remarkable if the public had stayed away from so grand a state event.

More persuasive is Gary Sheffield's argument that 'Haig's army played the leading role in defeating the German forces in the crucial battles of 1918. In terms of the numbers of German divisions engaged, the numbers of prisoners and guns captured, the importance of the stakes and the toughness of the enemy, the 1918 "Hundred Days" campaign rates as the greatest series of victories in British history.'[2] This may be true, but Haig did not help his reputation by issuing high-flown rallying cries that seemed to have little regard for the soldiers under his command. 'Every position must be held to the last man,' he famously declared during the German Spring Offensive: 'there must be no retirement. With our backs to the wall and believing in the justice of our cause each one of us must fight to the end.'[3] It is hardly surprising that people have wondered precisely which wall Haig's back was up against: certainly not the wall of a trench. Even if one accepts that generals cannot conduct wars from the front line and that windy rhetoric of this sort was genuinely intended to raise morale, there still remains the uncomfortable fact pointed out by John Keegan in his classic 1998 account of the war: in the general's 'public manner and private diaries no concern for human suffering was or is discernible [...] He seemed to move through the horrors of the First World War as if guided by some inner voice, speaking of a higher purpose and a personal destiny'.[4] Sheffield nevertheless goes on to argue that:

Even the Somme (1916) and Passchendaele (1917), battles that have become by-words for murderous futility, not only had sensible strategic rationales but qualified as British strategic successes, not least in the amount of attritional damage they inflicted on the Germans. No one denies that the British Expeditionary Force (BEF) had a bloody learning curve, or that

[1] *Things We Forgot to Remember, op. cit.*
[2] Gary Sheffield, 'The Western Front: Lions Led by Donkeys?', BBC History website: www.bbc.co.uk/history/worldwars/wwone/lions_donkeys (1 March 2002).
[3] John Terraine, *Douglas Haig: The Educated Soldier* (Hutchinson, 1963), p.433.
[4] John Keegan, *The First World War* (Hutchinson, 1998), p.311.

generals made mistakes that had catastrophic consequences. However, before dismissing the generals as mere incompetent buffoons, we must establish the context.[1]

Even when one has established a context that to some extent exonerates the generals from irrational or ill-informed blame, the fact remains that even for the professional soldiers on the front line – let alone the civilian volunteers and conscripts – the bloodiness of this particular learning curve was not merely metaphorical. *The Old Lie* is precisely about the gulf between metaphor and actuality, between noble causes and battlefront realities, between 'the glorious dead' and those blown to irrecoverable bits by high explosives or left to die slowly in the mud and filth of No-Man's-Land.

Revisionist military historians, like the generals themselves, are chiefly concerned with overall strategy, sometimes acknowledging but generally choosing not to dwell at length on its human consequences at trench level. Unlike the professional soldiers who had fought in previous wars, the majority of the men in the front line between 1914 and 1918 were civilian volunteers or conscripts, many of whom were highly articulate. These soldiers needed no Kipling, who had sympathetically articulated professional soldiers' grumbles in such 'Barrack Room Ballads' as 'Tommy'; they wrote about their experiences of warfare themselves. It is hardly surprising, therefore, that the war has entered the national consciousness from the bottom up, as it were. Political and military history can tell us why and how the war was fought and what it was about, but it doesn't tell us what it was like. It is an unfair contest. No amount of rational argument about the justice of the cause can match the immediacy of a poem written in the trenches. No carefully considered review of the military strategies that brought about an eventual victory for the British and their allies can stand up against the memoirs of those who spent months in the front line.

When providing a biographical note for the dustjacket of the first edition of this book, I quite deliberately left the details of my education vague. Some people regarded this as merely coy, but it was in fact strategic. I didn't want any reader to assume that the book was in some way, at however far a remove, 'about' my own educational experience or a critique of public schools in the latter half of the twentieth century. I was in fact educated at a fairly traditional public school, although it was not founded until after the First World War. In

---

[1] 'The Western Front: Lions Led by Donkeys?', *op. cit.*

answer to Charles Sorley's question, there was indeed still a folly called the Corps at this school, although a certain degree of 1960s liberalism had penetrated even the Combined Cadet Force (as it was then known), and it was no longer strictly compulsory to join. Historically (or simply temperamentally) a child of that period, I would tell anyone foolish enough to ask that the chief value of attending an English public school was that it taught you that those in authority were not necessarily right, and that it gave you something to rebel against. No doubt some of those feelings fed into this book, and although I might have written it differently today, I would not in any way alter its central thesis. After the book was published, my editor wondered aloud what I'd think of it in years to come, adding: 'It's very much a young man's book.' My answer is that this is perhaps as it should be: it was, after all, a young man's war.

PETER PARKER
London, 2007

Introduction

I

IN 1968 Vera Brittain was asked to contribute to a volume which was to be published to commemorate the fiftieth anniversary of the Armistice. Although she had served as a nurse in the Voluntary Aid Detachment in London, France and Malta, it was not the hospitals she recalled, but a scene from what seemed to her an irrecoverable past:

> What does the date, August 4, 1914, immediately bring back to me? . . . The huge figures of the war casualties and the cost of war expenditure vanish in a phantasmagoria of human scenes and sounds. I think, instead, of names, places, and individuals and hear, above all, the echo of a boy's laughing voice on a school playing field in that golden summer.
> And gradually the voice becomes one of many: the sound of the Uppingham School choir marching up the chapel for the Speech Day Service in July 1914, and singing the Commemoration hymn . . . There was a thrilling, a poignant quality in those boys' voices, as though they were singing their own requiem – as indeed many of them were.

The echo of that anonymous boy's laughing voice sounded throughout the Great War and beyond it, a touchstone of the innocence, the excellence and the promise that was to perish. Since the beginning of the century the public schools had grown in power and influence, the final blossoming of a process which had been taking place since the mid-nineteenth century. The schools were the subject of both serious debate and popular fiction, so that by the time the Great War started, the image of the English Public School and the sort of boy who would be educated in one had entered the national consciousness. How this came about, and what its effect was upon people's response to the War, is the subject of this book.

II

Isn't it luck for me to have been born so as to be just the right age and in just the right place?

Julian Grenfell

The Fourth of June celebrations in 1914, 'A Pageant of Youth, Beauty and Tradition', as the *Daily Graphic* described them, were particularly notable, since amongst the boys taking part was George V's third son, Prince Henry. A royal, if not particularly bright, Etonian was news and the press was out in force to record the celebrations, which took place under the cloudless skies forever associated with that summer. Two months later, to the day, England declared War on Germany. To understand the effect of the Great War upon a school like Eton, it is necessary to give some substance to the casualty figures. If we imagine every single boy who was a member of the school on that June day simply vanishing we can get some idea of what people meant when they spoke of the death of a generation. Eton at that time had an average of 1,100 pupils; 1,157 Old Etonians were killed in the War.[1] If we now visualise the scene once again and imagine one in every five boys vanishing, we arrive at an even more devastating picture. Of those who died almost twenty per cent left Eton between 1914 and 1917; almost all of them would have been taking part in the festivities that day.

At schools with a military tradition the figures were even worse. Wellington had an average of 500 pupils before the War; 699 Old Boys were killed in action. At Haileybury one in three of the boys who entered the school between 1905 and 1912 died in the War. Elsewhere the numbers mount with almost unimaginable profusion: Shrewsbury, 322; City of London, 350;

[1] Compare this with the figures from the Second World War: 4,958 Old Etonians served, of whom 748 died, some 15 per cent. In the Great War, of the 5,650 Old Etonians who served, some 20.5 per cent were killed.

Uppingham, 447; Malvern, 457; Winchester, 500; Dulwich, 518; Harrow, 600; Cheltenham, 675; Charterhouse, 686; Marlborough, 733. At Westminster six pairs of brothers have their names recorded on the Roll of Honour, alongside three of the sons of the Bishop of Exeter. At Marlborough John Bain wrote a poem in memory of three brothers called Shaw. Shrewsbury lost five masters, Marlborough lost seven. A wall painting at St George's, Harpenden commemorates seven School Captains, six of whom held the post in succession. Eighty per cent of the members of the Public Schools Club in Albemarle Street had enlisted by November 1914. During the War the Club went into liquidation: there simply weren't enough members left to keep it going – by the Armistice, 800 had been killed.

Recalling the death of an individual soldier, Wilfred Owen had asked in a poem written in May 1918: 'Was it for this the clay grew tall?' Many people, even as late as the last summer of the War, might have replied 'Yes' to Owen's rhetorical question. It was believed that the clay of a generation of young men had grown tall and been moulded to be proved in the fires of war. The long-cherished notion that the Great War burst unexpectedly upon the golden summer of 1914 has the basic core of truth and the subsequent accretions of romance which typify myth. Whilst few people can have been prepared for the nature of the War, there is no doubt that one section of the community was ready to meet the challenge: the English Public Schools. This is not to say that young gentlemen all over the country were spoiling for a fight, despite the fact that writers of boys' fiction did their best to encourage belligerence under the guise of chauvinistic adventurousness. However, educated in a gentlemanly tradition of loyalty, honour, chivalry, Christianity, patriotism, sportsmanship and leadership, public-school boys could be regarded as suitable officer material in any war. Those who spoke of men as the *product* of a public school were more acute than they perhaps realised. There is some justice in the accusation that the intention – or at any rate the achievement – of the public-school system was to 'melt the boys down and run them all out of the same mould like bullets'. Like bullets, they were in great demand in August 1914. In order to officer a vast new volunteer army it was necessary to recruit young men who, with the minimum of training, would prove worthy of commissions. These schoolboys, remarkable as a phenomenon, were not necessarily remarkable as individuals, however much obituaries were to make of their 'outstanding qualities'. Thousands of them whose names would never have appeared on the Honours Board achieved lasting fame on the War Memorial. The Class of 1914 had been prepared both implicitly, by the codes

[17]

to which the schools subscribed, and explicitly, by the junior branch of the Officers' Training Corps, for the eventuality of war. What they had not been prepared for was this particular war, which brutally exposed the inadequacy both of an outmoded set of ideals and an archaic and optimistic concept of warfare.

From their medieval foundations as 'grammar schools' intended to provide a literate clerical class to conduct the country's business, the public schools had undergone considerable transformation, so that by the second decade of the twentieth century they were turning out an officer class to lead the country's army. The emergence of the public-school boy as a subaltern in the making was a result of the reforms in private education which took place during the second half of the nineteenth century. These reforms stemmed largely from Dr Thomas Arnold, headmaster of Rugby, whose ideals were disseminated and distorted by a zealous miscellany of former pupils and colleagues. A best-selling novel by Thomas Hughes, *Tom Brown's Schooldays*, popularised the aims and achievements of Rugby in particular and public schools in general. As well as serving as propaganda, the novel founded the fictional genre of the school story. Novels set entirely within schools represent a literary phenomenon peculiar to England, and one that proved immensely successful. The emergence and proliferation of boys' magazines in the last quarter of the nineteenth century provided a new forum for the public-school story, and consequently for the public-school ethos. The popularity of such stories led to the ideals and codes of the schools reaching a far wider audience than the privileged minority who were educated in them. The spread of the ethos to other sections of society was also seen in the founding of Boys' Clubs and similar philanthropic organisations such as the Boy Scouts.

With this background it is scarcely surprising that when war was declared volunteers from all levels of society queued at the recruiting stations. Instilled with the public-school ethos and encouraged to follow in the footsteps of story-book heroes, young men from all classes were ready to march off to glory. The propagandists' groundwork had already been done for them.

III

[The public-school system] has fairly helped, you may say, to get us out of the mess of August 1914. Yes, but it contributed heavily to get us into it! . . .

The last gleams of this particular chivalry and the grim old square chins who fought in Crimea and at Lucknow have wellnigh passed. It cannot, unassisted, save the Allies of 1917, though it has fought as bravely and unreservedly as of old.

Thomas Seccombe (Preface to The Loom of Youth)

The importance attached to the image of the public-school boy during the War can be judged from the outcry which greeted Alec Waugh's autobiographical novel, *The Loom of Youth*, rejected by six publishers before finally being accepted by Grant Richards in 1917. Richards realised that the book was likely to cause a sensation and to ensure that it did so commissioned a combative Preface from Thomas Seccombe, a Sandhurst historian. The novel provoked reams of journalism and at least two books in reply to it: *A Dream of Youth* ('An Etonian's reply to *The Loom of Youth*') by Martin Browne, and the pseudonymous *Heart of a Schoolboy* by 'Jack Hood'.

Most school stories were written in the same celebratory vein as *Tom Brown's Schooldays* by similarly devoted Old Boys. The schools had capitalised upon the nostalgia of Englishmen for the lost days of their youth in creating the concept of the Old Boy, a sentimental alumnus whose tie or blazer proclaimed his place of education, whose donations to assorted appeals proclaimed his belief in the future of his old school, and whose lachrymose displays of emotion upon hearing the School Song betrayed his attachment to its past. Around this sorrowful figure, forever mourning his exile from the magic garden of his youth, the lushly romantic setting of many of the schools, and the industry of praise and commemoration of *Alma Mater*, grew up what amounted to a religion. The schools represented places of worship, with headmasters and their staff (frequently in holy orders in any case) representing the priests, uniforms and old school ties provided vestments, and the verses of the 'Eton Boating Song' or 'Forty Years On' serving as hymns. The entire proceedings were wreathed in the incense fumes of nostalgia and the mystique of privilege. By the late-nineteenth century the public schools had become bound up in the ideals of Class and Empire. John Galsworthy provided a Creed in 1907:

I believe in my father, and his father, and his father's father, the makers and keepers of my estate, and I believe in myself and my son and my son's son. And I believe that we have made the country, and shall keep the country what it is. And I believe in the Public Schools, especially the Public School I was at. And I believe in my social equals and the country house, and in things as they are, for ever and ever, Amen.

[19]

Given this background, it is hardly surprising that anything which dared to criticise the public-school system was considered sacrilegious. In fact, a volume of criticism had been growing before the War, culminating in Arnold Lunn's *The Harrovians* (1913). However, the much-lauded response of public-school men to the War put all such criticism beyond the pale. E.C. Mack, author of a monumental two-volume study of *Public Schools and British Opinion*, was unable to find 'a significant criticism' between August 1914 and the spring of 1916, and after that what criticism there was was more apologetic than attacking. Mack considered *The Loom* as influential as *Tom Brown's Schooldays*.

The novel's subsequent reputation, partially encouraged by Waugh himself, as the first public-school story to deal explicitly with homosexuality is unmerited. Its contemporary *succés* was very much *de scandale*, but apart from *Health & Strength* which felt that, 'If anywhere it fails in making a sharp enough point of self-abuse in schools', few of the reviewers made much of the book's attitude towards sex. What caused such a furore was that a book attacking the public-school system should be published during a war in which the schools were proving themselves and vindicating their ethos in the trenches. When Edward Lyttelton, delivering the most famous attack upon the book in the *Contemporary Review*, asserted that 'there is no reason why we should read such novels and there are many reasons why in war-time we should not buy them', he was not merely referring to paper shortages. Lord Dartmouth, at the climax of two months of heated exchange in the *Spectator*, insisted:

> But the war has given us a picture of the pleasanter side of the Public School 'in fact'. Quite recently there appeared in one of the evening papers a pathetic little paragraph which tells how in 1914 384 boys, the representative marksmen of 43 of our leading Public Schools competed for the Ashburton Shield at Bisley. Three years after, of the 384 boys 66 have given their lives and 79 have been wounded in their country's cause. To-day every school-boy, past and present, is proud of his own school's 'Roll of Honour'. It does not seem quite the best time to choose to throw stones at a system, whatever its faults may be, that has produced so splendid a record.

Waugh challenged Dartmouth's assertion that there was anything pleasant about this picture and accused him of making copy out of the dead. The *Spectator*, perhaps wisely, closed the correspondence at this point.

Lyttelton found the book 'uniformly dull, occasionally unpleasant, and, in my judgement at least, almost wholly untrue'. Lyttelton's judgement was notoriously unreliable and his article was both intemperate and confused. Although he claimed that the novel was 'so remote from the truth that there is no probability of anybody believing it', he found it necessary to write seven pages' worth of indignant refutation. Seccombe's complaint that the public-school system was overrated and outmoded, turning out insular young men whose ignorance was only matched by their complacency, should be addressed not to schoolmasters, Lyttelton felt, but to parents. If there was no stimulus within the home, 'then the soil in which an interest in history can be planted is not laid'. Presumably there was little discussion of Greek authors in most homes, but this had not prevented Lyttelton from attempting to teach Classics at Eton.[1] Taken to its logical conclusion, Lyttelton's argument would do away with public schools altogether, or at any rate the academic side of them. Lyttelton put his faith in other 'advantages belonging to the Public School system which are not often clearly discerned and are in danger of extinction from rash-reforming ventures. The social training is far more effective than the educational.'

This, really, is the crux of the controversy. Nobody would have minded if Waugh had confined his criticism to the curriculum, but to attack the 'social training' which was at that time producing splendid young officers was unforgivable. Browne's case rests principally on the suggestion that 'when the crisis of this war came upon England it was the leadership of the Public School men that chiefly saved the situation.' He praised the system for its inculcation of 'a sense of duty (the duty of English gentlemen) and a strength of purpose given by love for the school'. In contrast to this, Waugh's novel seems positively seditious. A boy who revisits 'Fernhurst' (an instantly recognisable portrayal of Waugh's own school, Sherborne) after he has enlisted, says to the hero:

> I suppose you have seen a good many ideals go tumbling down. All our generation has been sacrificed; of course it is inevitable. But it is rather hard. The older men have seen some of their hopes realised; we shall see none. I don't know when this war will end; not just yet, I think. But whenever it does, just as far as we are concerned the days of roses will be over. For the time being art and literature are dead. Look at the rotten stuff that's being written to-day. At the beginning we were deceived by the tinsel of war; Romance dies hard. But we know now. We've done with fairy tales. There

[1] Lyttelton's skills as a teacher were not renowned. Geoffrey Madan, an affectionate pupil, recalled: 'Whether in classics or theology, his teaching was positively corrosive of sound learning and only less so of religion: but there was no failure of effort on his own part.'

is nothing glorious in war; no good can come of it. It's bloody, utterly bloody. I know it's inevitable, but that's no excuse. So are rape, theft, murder.

This was scarcely the message that those interested in the prosecution of the War wanted to hear, or have broadcast. If the ethos of the schools was shown to be worthless, how could public-school boys be expected to fight for the honour of *Alma Mater*? Until the publication of *The Loom* the schools had been bathed in an even more glorious light than ever. Here was the thin beam of a torch aimed at the less edifying nooks and crannies of the system, casting frightening shadows on the wall. There is a sense that people would rather not have known, just as they would rather not have heard about the real conditions at the Front.

Waugh, who had been drafted to France within days of the book's publication, felt that some of its success was simply a matter of timing: '*The Loom* could not have appeared at a luckier time. It had immediate news value. There was a boom in soldier-poets . . . Here was a soldier-novelist, the first, and in his teens.' The timing was even more fortuitous than Waugh realised. 'There was a spirit of challenge and criticism in the air. The war after three years was still "bogged down" and public opinion attributed to allied failings in the field to mismanagement in high places.' Indeed, on the day *The Loom of Youth* was published, 20 July 1917, Siegfried Sassoon was attending a medical board because he had sent a letter to his commanding officer in which he explained why he no longer intended to 'perform any further military duties. I am doing this as a protest against the policy of the Government in prolonging the War by failing to state their conditions of peace.' Whilst reviews of *The Loom* were filling the columns of every paper, Sassoon's famous declaration was circulating amongst journalists, writers, editors and Members of Parliament. On 30 July the statement was read out in the House of Commons, and published in *The Times* the following day.

Meanwhile, in Derbyshire, Repton was being 'radicalised' by two young masters. Upon arriving at the school in 1916, Victor Gollancz made two important discoveries. The first was that the boys were essentially 'good', blessed with 'original virtue' rather than cursed with 'original sin'. The second was that they had nonetheless grown up with all the prejudices of their class and had become 'intolerant, class-ridden, narrow, self-righteous, smug, superior, ignorant; grotesquely ignorant, in particular, of conditions on their own doorstep and in the world outside.' With a history master, David Somervell,

Gollancz set out to change this, and to that end set up a Civics class in which topical issues were discussed freely. Gollancz was appalled that the boys were 'going out to be wounded or killed, and to wound or kill others: and yet none of them had the foggiest idea of what, in terms of historical perspective and a mature understanding, the catastrophe was about.'

Once the boys had learned they began to rebel against a simplistic, nationalistic view of history, and against the received notions of their education. The two masters were clearly flying in the face of tradition, represented by one of their colleagues who announced: 'It is our solemn duty to instil into the boys such a hatred of the Hun that for the rest of their lives they'll never speak to one again.'

The fruits of the Civics class were made public in June 1917 when the first edition of *A Public School Looks at the World* was published. Affectionately known as 'The Pubber', this magazine was modelled upon *The Nation*, but was 'Edited by Members of Repton School', as its title-page proudly proclaimed. It was supported officially by the headmaster, Geoffrey Fisher, and financially by local advertisers. All copy was submitted to Fisher for approval and, although some of the articles were radical by public-school standards, there was nothing to cause the liberal headmaster disquiet.

Opponents of the magazine bided their time until the autumn term when the November issue of the magazine carried an article on 'Patriotism', in which the young writer suggested that true patriotism was not based upon competition but upon a love of humanity as a whole. Even this might have been acceptable had not the editor, a boy called Amyas Ross, weighed in with a piece entitled 'State Your Terms', in which he echoed Sassoon and called for negotiations towards a peaceful conclusion to the War. The Enemy persuaded an athlete known as 'Ox' to write to the official school magazine to protest about a certain 'cosmopolitan influence' which was sapping the 'healthy patriotism' of the school. Fortunately, this anti-semitic libel was blocked before it got into print, but from that moment 'The Pubber' was required to carry a disclaimer ('Nothing in this Paper is to be taken as representing the views of the School as a whole.'), as well as a 'balancing' editorial written by a more 'conservative' pupil.

Unfortunately, the March 1918 edition of the magazine was advertised as 'Published by the Repton School Book Shop Ltd. and Henderson & Sons, 44 Charing Cross Road.' Henderson's was a radical bookshop commonly known as 'The Bomb Shop' because of its supposed anarchist tendencies. 'Published' in this context meant 'available from', but the link between the magazine and Henderson's confirmed the worst suspicions of the War Office, which had been keeping a wary eye on both. A few days before the beginning of the summer term 1918, Gollancz received notification that he had been sacked. No one seems to know quite what happened, but the W.O. certainly put pressure upon Fisher to get rid of Gollancz. Assorted rumours suggested that the W.O. had threatened to outlaw the Repton Officers' Training Corps or even refuse commissions to any of its members unless Gollancz went. How the W.O. could have effected this without causing a major scandal is unclear; perhaps they simply hoped that Fisher would not call their bluff.

Fisher requested that there should be no more 'political discussion' within the school. Somervell refused to accede to this and although 'The Pubber' no longer appeared, unofficial Civics classes continued, where *The Nation* was circulated behind closed doors. During half-term another letter from the W.O. arrived on Fisher's desk. When the boys returned, a prefects' meeting was held during which Fisher and Amyas Ross argued about the propriety of 'political activity' in the school. Fisher insisted that it should cease. Ross walked out of the school a week later in protest. Fisher then approached Somervell once more, asking him to give his word that there would now be 'silence on all political matters'. Somervell refused and agreed to resign. The Old Guard breathed a sigh of relief. 'Well, we've had a long fight,' one of them said to his Army Class, 'but we've won. We've got rid of the last of the traitors.' This particular 'traitor' took a job with Churchill in the Ministry of Munitions; all the pupils who had been involved with 'The Pubber' enlisted and fought in the War.

By this time Alec Waugh was in a prisoner-of-war camp and Siegfried Sassoon was back in France with his Battalion. The enemies within had been successfully dealt with.

IV

But the youth we have lost in these dread years has not perished in vain; if 'the spring has gone out of the year', as Pericles lamented, yet we are immeasurably the richer for the spirituality they have bequeathed to us, of which the poems in this book are an enduring expression.

E.B. Osborn (Introduction to The Muse in Arms)

Waugh's novel did not prove, as one critic had predicted, 'the *Uncle Tom's Cabin* of the public school system', any more than Sassoon's declaration altered the course of the War or the attitude of civilians. 1917 was no more a pivot than 1916. If there was rebellion in the air there was also complacency. Historical perspective has persuaded some critics to hinge the War neatly at July 1916 when the Battle of the Somme took place. Whilst the Somme was a major catastrophe for the British Army and a terrifying example of misjudgement and mismanagement, much of this was played down at the time. Wildly optimistic reports about the success of the 'Big Push' on 1 July, in the course of which the British suffered some 60,000 casualties and gained next to nothing in return, were published in the newspapers. To some extent this offset the dismay people felt when the casualty lists began to appear. In fact the Somme was less of a disaster for the officers than for the other ranks, particularly if one compares it with the Battle of Loos in September 1915, during which 2,031 officers became casualties. During 1915 officer casualties were running at nearly double those of other ranks. This is significant because, with some important exceptions (Isaac Rosenberg is the most obvious), most of the literature of the Great War was written by officers. Consequently the (in any case untenable) theory about changes in attitude reflected in the literature of the War would be more convincing if 1915, rather than 1916, was taken as the turning point.

In considering the literature of the War it is instructive to remember that, despite the raised voices of those we now regard as *the* war poets, it was Brooke, Grenfell and the scores of other young (and preferably dead) poets, now forgotten, who were considered representative during and just after the War. Sassoon was widely read, but not as widely as Robert Nichols. Owen and Rosenberg remained virtually unknown and unpublished until after the War. Sorely achieved some posthumous success during the War, but this was largely because he had, as he wrote of Brooke, 'conformed to [*The Morning Post's*] stupid axiom of literary criticism that the only stuff of poetry is violent physical exercise, by dying on active service.' E.B. Osborn's *The Muse in Arms* was one of the most popular war-time anthologies. It first appeared in November 1917, reprinted immediately, and again in February 1918: 'The object of this Anthology is to show what passes in the British warrior's soul when, in moments of aspiration and inspiration, before or after action or in the busy days of self-preparation for self-sacrifice, he has glimpses of the ultimate significance of warfare.' There is a good deal more aspiration than inspiration in the volume and the tenor of the book can be gauged from the fact that Sassoon's glimpses of the ultimate significance of warfare are restricted to 'Absolution' and 'The

Rear-guard'. No one, it seems, wanted to hear about what passed in the British Warrior's soul in moments of despair and anger.[1] No wonder that R.B. Talbot Kelly told his son that 'the poems that were closest to the world he remembered were Rupert Brooke's "The Soldier", and Julian Grenfell's "Into Battle".' It comes as something of a shock to find Robert Nichols described as 'the greatest of the poets as yet published' in Osborn's *The New Elizabethans* (1919).

Another characteristic volume is A. St John Adcock's *For Remembrance: Soldier Poets Who Have Fallen in the War* (1918; revised and enlarged 1920). Adcock emphasises a poetic heritage that is reminiscent of *Lyra Heroica*. He claims that the majority of war poetry written before 1914 was written by civilians rather than soldiers, which suggests that his book will include poetry which reflects the reality of the War:

> There is a wide world of difference between those romantic old war lyrics that our patriotic civilians used to write and the grim realism or high spiritual significance of those that were written in the mud and squalor of the trenches, in dug-out or billet, just before going into action, just after coming out of it, in the quiet of a rest-camp or while the writers were lying wounded in hospital.

But there is not as much difference as there is between *Lyra Heroica*, or indeed much of the poetry Adcock reproduces, and the poems of Sassoon, Owen and Rosenberg. Of course, none of these poets would have been eligible for Adcock's book, since Sassoon was certainly, and the others probably, alive when the first edition was compiled. However, readers will look in vain for E.A. Mackintosh's 'Recruiting', or his poem which trounces 'The Charge of the Light Brigade' (a romantic old war lyric if ever there was one), although this poet is represented.[2] Instead there is rather too much of what Mackintosh characterised as 'Washy verse on England's need'.

England's need during the War was reassurance that young men were laying down their lives gladly for a just cause, that the old public-school traditions of chivalry, self-sacrifice, fair-play and selfless patriotism were being maintained on the field of battle. England's need immediately after the War

---

[1] Osborn wrote a favourable review of *The Old Huntsman* and had such poems as 'Blighters', 'They', 'The Hero' and 'The Redeemer' from which to make his selection for *The Muse in Arms*.

[2] See pp 181–2 for 'Recruiting'. Part of the other poem reads: 'Into the mouth of hell,/ Sticking it pretty well,/Slouched the six hundred.'

was reassurance, in the face of more than a million deaths, that it had all been worthwhile. Such needs do not admit the poetry of Sassoon, Owen or Rosenberg.

The poets of the First World War are an immensely diverse group, held together by history rather than ideology. Those we now regard as the foremost amongst them are, by and large, those who conform to our notions about the War. Because Brooke is remembered for his 'war poetry' his reputation as a poet is constantly under threat. 'As a War Poet Brooke hardly begins to exist', wrote one of the authors of *Fifty Works of English Literature We Could Do Without*, which included the '1914' sonnets. Brooke is compared to Owen and, whilst this might seem unjust, it is no more pointless than speculation as to whether or not, had he lived, Brooke's view might have changed. This is a crucial point: although Owen is demonstrably a better poet than Brooke – the complexity of his language and imagery and the subtlety and inventiveness of his rhymes are infinitely superior – it is Brooke's *attitude* which really damns him. Owen is the better poet in the first instance because he was 'right' about war. It is this sense of what is appropriate that brings us up short when we read 'Peace' or 'Into Battle'. For in such poems the ideals of a generation are expressed without irony, and if they are somewhat self-regarding, they are nonetheless sincere. By investigating these ideals and tracing their sources we can gain a valuable perspective on the literature of the Great War, which should illuminate rather than limit. Vera Brittain wrote that 'The work of Sassoon and his contemporaries was one long cry of protest precisely because they were the products of an extraordinarily fortunate social era.' It is a cry of disillusion, and it is this process of disillusion which gives much of the literature of the Great War its impetus, its power, its poignance and its dominant mode of irony. Irony is a way of assimilating the unpalatable and the unthinkable; it is not merely an adequate response, but at times the only response possible. To be disillusioned it is necessary to have illusions in the first place. A major source of those illusions was the English Public School System.

PART ONE

[1]

Schools for Subalterns

1 Answering the Call

DURING the last week of July 1914 boys from the public schools of
England were congregating in Summer Camps organised by the
Officers' Training Corps. Some 10,000 diminutive soldiers took part in
parades and manoeuvres in an atmosphere that was less relaxed than in
previous years. Rumours buzzed as thick as flies in the warm summer air. The
first inklings that something was amiss came when the cooks, supplied to these
amateurs by the regular army, began packing up early to return to their
regiments. On 1 August orders were given that the camps were to disband
several days early. Westminster's magazine, *The Elizabethan*, reported that 'it
was a great pity that Fate cut short a Camp which, in point of numbers at any
rate, was the most successful this Contingent had enjoyed.' The magazine's
correspondent, without, it seems, any sense of irony, informed those boys 'who
had not been to Camp before, that the last three days (which they missed this
year) are usually the most enjoyable, and Camp is apt to be more pleasant when
gloomy rumours, such as prevailed at Mytchett, are not rife.' S.P.B. Mais,
writing of Sherborne, also felt that the War had rather spoiled the 'colossal
picnic' of Camp: 'It was in the midst of one of these great social gatherings', he
recalls, 'that the bomb of war burst.' In fact, despite the cries of 'Spoilsport!'
from the *Elizabethan* and Mais, the declaration of war could hardly have come
at a better time as far as recruitment was concerned. The boys were keyed up,
well-drilled and already in training; it must have seemed as though the picnic
would go on for some time. Certainly there was little gloom at Aldershot,
where Etonians were in the midst of their Camp. One participant, Desmond

[31]

Allhusen, recalled 'scenes of wild enthusiasm'. The boys were taken back to Eton and then sent home, where Allhusen found his elder brother Rupert 'sharpening his sword'. Despite being an 'incredibly inefficient' member of the OTC, Allhusen applied for a commission in the Devonshire Regiment on the day war was declared. On 15 August he was gazetted as a second lieutenant, and on the 24th, the day after his eighteenth birthday, he joined his battalion for training at Plymouth.

Younger Etonians could not secure commissions as easily, but nonetheless enlisted and, by a series of ruses, went into battle. Brian Riverdale Osborne, aged fifteen, enlisted as a trumpeter in the West Kent Yeomanry in the first week of the War. A year later he marched off with his regiment, but was prevented from boarding the departure train. Undeterred he contrived to get sent to Gallipoli, where his deception was overlooked and he was considered a credit to his old school. Hoodwinking the authorities was notoriously simple, particularly at the beginning of the War. A horribly cynical cartoon in *Punch* depicts 'a boy of thirteen who, in his effort to get taken on as a bugler, has given his age as sixteen'. The recruiting officer asks: 'Do you know where boys go who tell lies?' 'To the Front, sir,' the boy replies. Osborne finally got his commission, went to the Front, and was killed within a month at Warringer-le-Petit on the same day as Wilfred Owen, 4 November 1918.

Similar eagerness was to be found at other schools, many of which produced special 'War Issues' of their magazines, which listed all the Old Boys who were serving in the forces. The *Salopian* announced in October 1914 that some 400 were already in uniform. The Old Westminsters' Football and Cricketing Club, in the knowledge that its members were likely to play the game, sent out pamphlets at the beginning of December in which 504 serving members were listed. Eleven of them had already been killed. In the first three months of the War casualty figures at other schools were even more alarming: Eton had lost 65 Old Boys, Wellington 38, Charterhouse and Harrow 21 each, Rugby 20, Clifton 19 and Haileybury 18. Such a toll did not seem to deter more and more boys from enlisting. Nine months later the October 'War Number' of the *Elizabethan* in 1915 ran to twenty-nine pages, listing 930 Old Westminsters serving or already killed: 'It is a record of which we may be justly proud, for it should be remembered that Westminster, which has contributed more than three times its own size, is the smallest of the great Public Schools, and that not more than about eighty Old Westminsters were in the Regular Army when war was declared.' So many Old Etonian joined up that a *List of Etonians on Active Service* was published as a separate book every year of the War. Each school had its proud boast, not only in England, but also in the Empire. Few English schools could claim, as did St Andrew's Aurora, Toronto, that 98 per cent of its Old Boys fought in the War. However, the most extreme example of devotion to school and country must be that of the Old Suttonian who 'travelled 3,600 miles by a dog train to enlist'.

What set the Great War apart from all previous wars, and what gives it in retrospect its special interest and poignancy, was that it was a civilians' war. Previously wars had been fought by the small but well-trained army of professional soldiers which Britain maintained. Lord Kitchener, appointed Minister of War as soon as war was declared, foresaw that the regular army and its reserves would be insufficient for a conflict of some duration. When she signed the *Entente Cordiale* in 1906 Britain had pledged a force of 60,000 men to support France in the event of her involvement in a war in Europe. This number, although tiny by European standards, left a large hole in the regular army, which in 1914 was some 250,000 strong. Many of these troops were many miles away, guarding the outposts of the Empire. There was a further reserve of about 213,000 to draw upon, and a volunteer, part-time force of 63,000 Territorials. The Territorials, like the OTC, had been founded as a result of the Army Reforms introduced by R.B. Haldane in 1907. Knowing that the Territorials were primarily a Home Defence force and that in any case they could not be compelled to serve abroad, Kitchener decided to form an entirely new army and, with the sceptical assent of the Cabinet, decided that one million men should be recruited 'for three years of the duration' of the War. His call for what came to be known as 'The First Hundred Thousand' was published on 6 August 1914, and the response was extraordinary. By the end of the year Kitchener had got his million men: 1,186,375 men, to be precise. Another one and a quarter million men volunteered in 1915.

However, even these vast numbers were insufficient to feed the fires of this war. The initial burst of enthusiasm began to wane and there were renewed calls for conscription. Because of her geographical circumstances, Britain had always relied upon her navy as the first line of defence, maintaining her small army for action overseas. However, after the near-disaster of the Boer War, it was felt by many that conscription should be introduced, a case vociferously argued by the saviour of that war, Lord Roberts, and the National Service League. Most other European countries had large conscripted armies: France had some four million trained men in 1914; Germany had around five million. But conscription went against the liberal traditions of Britain in general and the philosophy of the Liberal Party, who were in power, in particular. It was felt that a vast campaign of propaganda and moral coercion was preferable to conscription. As the War dragged on into its second year with no end in sight, even those who had believed in the sanctity of a voluntary system began to have their doubts. Lord Roberts's old school, Eton, perhaps reacting to the sinister rumours that officer casualties were running at double those of other ranks, thought that some people were clearly not pulling their weight. The *Eton College Chronicle* stated in October of that year:

> The opposition felt by a large proportion of the lower classes to compulsory service must be overcome. England is a Democracy; her people must therefore be led and not driven, and the lead must be taken by the upper classes. In this matter of military service the upper classes need no compulsion; they have given the flower of their manhood to the service of their country and they have done it voluntarily. But for the sake of their weaker brethren they must declare themselves ready to do, under compulsion, that which formerly they did voluntarily, and what better place could there be in which to begin this further sacrifice than the greatest of England's great Public Schools? . . . we maintain that the nation should be plainly shown of what vital importance Compulsory Service is and that it might prove extremely helpful to such an education if the lower classes were to see the sons of the so-called 'idle rich' compelled to undergo a course of military training at the Public Schools.

The War Office also felt that the public schools were in a unique position to give a lead to the masses. Although the initial response in 1914 was gratifying, it caused considerable problems of organisation. The Territorials had, almost to a man, volunteered for immediate service overseas, without the six months training programme to which they were entitled. It was difficult enough to find uniform, arms and accommodation for the eager new recruits, but the main problem was in finding enough officers. About 500 Indian Army officers, home on leave, were instantly commandeered, and 2,000 'young gentlemen' on the War Office's files received invitations to apply for immediate commissions on the day that war was declared. It was felt that these young public-school and university men would have the right background and sufficient training in the OTC to be able to command men without more ado. Within the first fifteen months of the War ten times as many young gentlemen with OTC experience had been granted commissions, enough to officer over 570 battalions. Quite how adequate their training had been is open to question. Accounts of the

OTC before the War suggest that few boys were really serious about the corps. At Winchester the only people who took the corps seriously were 'a few prospective army candidates and here and there a lonely, earnest soul who appeared to deem cadetship rather a form of moral callisthenics fitting the individual for citizenship than a training in field combat'. Although some pupils strove hard to pass their exams and become officers in the corps, Robert Nichols recalled that 'proficiency . . . provoked no discussion and leadership . . . carried no prestige'. Indeed, although boys were expected to take proficiency tests, in practice such exams were not always as daunting as they seemed on paper. Charles Sorley and a group of fellow-Marlburians were taken to Devizes Barracks for a three-part examination in Musketry, Company Drill and Tactical in December 1911:

> Twenty questions I was asked, and I looked sheepish and I said 'Don't know' to each one. Then he said, 'Is there anything you do know?' and I gave him the two pieces of knowledge I had come armed with – the weight of a rifle and episodes in the life of a bullet from the time it leaves the breech till it hits its man. Then I saluted really smartly, and the gentleman gave me 60 out of a hundred. Company Drill came next which merely consisted in drilling a Company (as you might think) of most alarmingly smart regulars. For this I got 70 (every one got 70) – and then I went off to Tactical. Tactical was equally a farce. I was told to send out an advance-guard, lost my head, sent out a flank guard, scored 70 per cent.

At the end of the day 'only three people had been ploughed – they must have been bad.'

Nonetheless, whether or not the young gentlemen were proficient, they were aware of the honour that was being conferred upon them: 'The public school class now saw the particular form of its duty in the national emergency more plainly before it, and the 2,000 vacancies were very quickly filled from this source.'

Those who missed this opportunity had to report for further training and were frequently dismayed by what they found. Guy Chapman, although 'loath to go' and without 'romantic illusions' was nevertheless 'shocked by [his] first contact with the New Army' in December 1914: 'It was not so much the circumstances; the dull little south coast watering-place in winter; the derelict palazzo, the headquarters, facing on one side the tumbling sea and on the other an unkempt field; it was not the men in shabby blue[1] clothes and forage caps with their equipment girt about them with bits of string: it was the obvious incapacity and amateurishness of the whole outfit which depressed.' One can imagine the dispiriting effect of this picture upon someone more keen to march off to glory than Chapman.

In spite of Sorley's account of OTC exams, many young men felt that they knew it all and resented the endless parades when they might have been at the Front having a crack at Jerry. Many of them, like George Sherston, found that 'being in the Army was very much like being back at school'. Old Rugbeian John Nettleton, who called the first chapter of his war memoirs 'The New School', thought that enlisting with the Artists' Rifles was like transferring to another school: 'One had to learn a new set of rules and, ridiculous though they might be, they were really no more ridiculous than the rules one had learned to live with at one's last school.' Alec Waugh found much of the training he underwent with the Inns of Court OTC drearily familiar from exercises at Sherborne. Sorley was bored rigid by the whole process. It was not only the fact that his regimental colours were the same as his House colours ('Most affecting!') that reminded him of Marlborough. In military training he discerned the conformity against which he had rebelled at school: 'War in England only means putting all the men of "military age" in England into a state of routinal coma, preparatory to getting them killed', he complained. 'You are being given six months to become conventional: your peace thus made with God, you will be sent out and killed. At least if you aren't killed, you'll come back so unfitted for any other job that you'll have to stay in the Army'.

There was no doubt that in some ways a public-school education prepared a young man for the living conditions and routine of army training. Basil Willey felt that it was particularly hard for him to accept military life because, 'never having had the normal boarding-school contacts with vice, prurience, snobbery, brutality, and worldliness, I was aghast at the sort of men these seemed and at the things they said and thought and did.' Other things Willey might have gained from a public-school education were lacking in his attitude to the army: 'For me, there was absolutely nothing – no pride, pomp and circumstance of glorious war, no desire to excel in smartness or efficiency, no eagerness for promotion, honourable mention, or medals – just nothing whatever to mitigate the loathsomeness of military training.'

[1] Charles Carrington also recalled the 'rather gaudy blue uniforms' at the beginning of the War when there wasn't enough khaki to clothe all the new recruits.

Sorley's remarks, although written partially to shock a schoolfriend, were not that wide of the mark. The essence of military training was like the tuning of an engine: the recruit had to be stripped down, then built up again to become an efficient machine. Whilst it may be impossible to create an army of 200,000 identical soldiers, the erosion of individuality was one of the main aims of training, as it had been in the past. Even though the raw material was rather different than previously, old army methods died hard, if at all, and the men of Kitchener's Army underwent the same routine as men who had joined the forces as a career. In some ways the training *was* a hideous parody of a public-school upbringing, in which the individual became subservient to and subsumed by the institution. Uniform, when available, was intended to destroy physical individuality and to identify a group, just as at school. Recruits were taught to conform and to obey the orders of their superiors, however absurd or inimical these orders might seem. They were stripped of their possessions, separated from their families and forced into a communal existence from which privacy was totally eliminated. At the same time they were indoctrinated with a corporate pride, a sense of traditions to which they were the (sometimes reluctant) heirs. This was particularly true of the grander regular regiments, such as the Royal Welch Fusiliers, in which Graves and Sassoon served. 'In the First and Second Battalions, throughout the war, not merely the officers and the non-commissioned officers knew their regimental history', Graves wrote. 'The men had learned far more about Minden, Albuhera, and Waterloo, and the Battle of the Pyramids, than they had about the fighting on the other fronts, or the official causes of the war.' A young man fresh from his public school, accustomed to a spartan, monastic existence in which he strove for the common weal, was urged to conform and was instilled with a sense of tradition and history, would find little that was entirely new in this process. In the army, as at school, the entire edifice was supported by a system of punishment, frequently applied.

Not all military training was as severe as this suggests, however, particularly during the first chaotic months of the War. In fact the standard of training for young officers and their even less experienced men could be extremely haphazard. Desmond Allhusen's recollections of the 3rd Battalion of the Devon Regiment which underwent its training at Exeter, are a testimony to enthusiastic amateurism during this period. His company was commanded by 'a nice old man of the county parson type' called Snow, whose 'previous military training consisted of two or three summer trainings in the militia [a forerunner of the Territorials] during the South African War. His military activities had been confined to one large field near Topsham, which he pointed out regularly whenever we passed.' Even as unseasoned a soldier as Allhusen recognised that Snow, however charming, was 'hardly fit to command 280 very keen recruits'. These men had neither uniform nor equipment, and spent their time drilling on a cricket pitch under the instruction of six NCOs detailed from a regular battalion. They were assisted by elderly veterans 'who had been in the Army generations before', and who were dug out of the ranks and made sergeants. 'Everybody taught their men anything and everything they could remember or invent,' Allhusen recalled, 'and by degrees the company began to take shape.' Particularly enjoyable, after the drilling, were field exercises. These, 'under the direction of our Crimean Company Commander, consisted in marching out to some farm and having a free meal and unlimited cider,' after which there was a display of 'a modern battle as pictured by Snow'. This ended with the old gentleman charging a hedge, cheered on by patriotic and enthusiastic farm-hands, after which the company drank more cider, then marched back to barracks. Allhusen concludes that there was 'no discipline at all, but an immense good will. Snow never punished a man, and the subalterns weren't allowed to tell them off.'

Anthony Eden found his officers' training course 'strenuous', but when he joined his battalion he was 'acutely conscious of how little I knew'. One field exercise involved driving a herd of deer across Duncombe Park from one enclosure to another through a gateway. The entire battalion, in open order with mounted officers, advanced upon the deer who walked as far as the gate, then turned and 'leapt the extended line of astonished riflemen and galloped swiftly into the park of their choice'. Sometimes this amateurism had devastating consequences. Eden, Blunden and Graves all report stupid accidents involving explosives in which there were fatal injuries.

There was another reason, beyond rudimentary OTC experience, why officers were recruited from public schools. The realisation that the regular army was insufficient for the job of defeating the Germans was a blow to the morale of Sandhurst. This blow was somewhat softened by giving commissions to young men whose education, if it had not made them soldiers, at least proclaimed them gentlemen. Of course, as the War dragged on and casualties mounted, men rose through the ranks to become officers for the duration and thus 'temporary gentlemen'. In fact, during the War, the Sandhurst experience did not amount to very much, according to Allhusen, who went on from Captain Snow's gentle regime to the Royal Military Academy: 'I can't recollect having learned anything there, but the time passed very pleasantly. I found some of my Eton friends there. The Old Etonian coterie was apparently exempt from most of the orders and regulations, and we amused ourselves without much interference.' Allhusen's Commanding Officer concentrated upon under-officers whilst 'the remaining forty odd cadets . . . used to amuse themselves by throwing fircones at each other while the five elect worked out some elaborate scheme.' Allhusen concludes: 'I don't think the CO knew very much worth knowing, so this arrangement was quite satisfactory.' It was not until a year after gaining his commission, that Allhusen received any useful training, with regular soldiers at Sheerness. In October he sailed for France.

That obtaining a commission was largely a matter of class can be seen from the experience of R.C. Sherriff, the future author of *Journey's End*, who strolled confidently into the recruiting office to offer his services: 'An officer, I realised, had to be a bit above the others, but I had had a sound education at the grammar school and could speak good English. I had had some experience of responsibility. I had been captain of games at school. I was fit and strong. I was surely one of the "suitable young men" they were calling for.' Apparently not. The adjutant was apologetic, but he explained that: 'our instructions are that all applicants for commissions must be selected from the recognised public schools, and yours is not among them.' Another veteran, Herbert Hall, remembered getting similar short shrift when he applied for a commission: 'I only had the one question: "What school did you go to?" So I told him: "The State school". He said, "I think you'd better work your way up through the ranks."'

Compare this with the experience of Peter Davies, the publisher and a contemporary of Allhusen at Eton, destined for Trinity College, Cambridge. Even though he had not yet started at university, the adjutant of the Cambridge OTC sent him a circular informing him that it was his duty to enlist forthwith. Davies obediently reported to Winchester with his elder brother, George, who was asked:

'Where were you at school?'
'Eton, sir.'
'In the corps?'
'Yes, sir, Sergeant.'
'Play any games? Cricket?'
'Well, sir, actually I managed to get my eleven.'
'Oh, you did, did you?'

The Colonel, who had played for Eton himself in his day, now became noticeably more genial, and by the time he had ascertained that George was the Davies who had knocked up a valuable 59 at Lord's (which knock he had himself witnessed with due appreciation) it was evident that little more need be said.

'And what about you, young man?' he asked, turning to me.

'Please, sir, I'm his brother,' was the best I could offer in the way of a reference.

'Oh, well, that's all right, then. Just take these forms and fill them in . . .' So easy was it, in August 1914, to obtain the King's commission in the Special Reserve of the 60th Rifles.

2 *The Clarendon Commission*

In order to understand why the public schools were widely regarded as excellent sources for the supply of officers, it is necessary to examine their development during the nineteenth century. The most thorough investigation of the public schools was the Clarendon Commission, set up in 1861 in response to widespread criticism of the system. Most of the criticism was that of friends, and none the less astringent for that. Few voices had been raised demanding the abolition of the schools; what was desired was reform, and reform from within. The most vociferous critics were not idealistic educational theorists, but pragmatic men of the world. Matthew Higgins, who wrote a series of influential letters to *The Cornhill* in the early 1860s, signed himself 'Paterfamilias', which suggested a sensible, concerned parent, rather than some cranky, radical social reformer. He simply accused the schools of failing to fulfil the needs of those who paid to have their sons educated in the system. Boys emerged from the schools, their minds dulled by poorly-taught Classics, unable to pass the examinations which would lead to careers in the forces, law or civil service. He wanted the curriculum improved, not because of any notions about a broad, liberal education, but because modern languages and mathematics would prove useful. In short, he accused headmasters of running schools for their own profit, rather than for the benefit of the pupils. Schools had become a poor investment with little return for the capital outlay.

Higgins's letters instigated further criticism as well as more sinister accusations of embezzlement. This is not the place to investigate arguments about the finances of the schools, but the Clarendon Commission was set up partially as a response to accusations of financial mismanagement.

The Clarendon Commission, like most parliamentary commissions, if not actually a whitewash was hardly as rigorous as critics of the schools would have liked. Gladstone emphasised that the Commission would take the form of an enquiry, not an attack, and to this end the Commissioners appointed were not the sort of men who wished to abolish the schools. Although Clarendon himself had been educated privately, all but one of his colleagues had been to top public schools: Eton, Winchester, Westminster and Rugby. They were not, however, a very good advertisement for the system in the eyes of their chairman, who described them variously as 'weak', 'pedantic', 'idle', 'quirky' and 'mad'.

Although there were recommendations concerning financial irregularities and curricular reform when the Report was published in 1864, it was thought that the schools should be allowed to put their own houses in order rather than suffer the indignity of direct governmental interference. Furthermore, for all the criticisms levelled at the schools in the Report, the Commissioners felt that these were far outweighed by the system's ability to mould character:

On the general results of public-school education as an instrument for the training of character, we can speak with much confidence. Like most English institutions – for it deserves to rank among English institutions – it is not framed upon a preconceived plan, but has grown up gradually . . . The organisation of monitors or prefects, the system of boarding houses and the relation of tutor and pupil have arisen and been developed by degrees. The magnitude and the freedom of these schools make each of them, for a boy of from 12 to 18, a little world, calculated to give his character an education of the same kind as it is destined afterwards to undergo in the world of business and society . . . It is not easy to estimate the degree in which the English people are indebted to these schools for the qualities on which they pique themselves most – for their capacity to govern others and control themselves, their aptitude for combining freedom with order, their public spirit, their vigour and manliness of character, their strong but not slavish respect for public opinion, their love of healthy sports and exercise. These schools have been the chief nurseries of our statesmen; on them, and in schools modelled after them, men of all the various classes that make up English society, destined for every profession and career, have been brought

[41]

up on a footing of social equality, and have contracted the most enduring friendships, and some of the ruling habits, of their lives; and they have had perhaps the largest share in moulding the character of an English gentleman.

One feels, upon reading this, that the lamentable failure observed in the classroom (where 'only about one half of the boys could, on examination, answer easy questions in grammar or construe or write even tolerable Latin') was of small matter compared to the real business of the schools as it was now conceived. This summary is an admirably concise checklist of the elements that went to make up the public-school ethos in the 1860s.

There is approval of the organic development of the schools, 'not framed upon a preconceived plan', for this would smack of professionalism. There is pride in the traditional, gentlemanly amateurism of the process of growth and development. The end result of what amounted, in plainer language, to trial and error, was 'a little world' consisting of 'all the various classes that make up English society', by which the Commissioners mean the aristocracy, the gentry and the middle classes. In this microcosm of the world beyond the school gates the English gentleman, that repository of national values, acquires everything he needs to take his place in society. Of particular note are the qualities of self-control and 'the capacity to govern others' (even if it required a crammer to get a boy through the necessary examinations).

It will be seen that the other things a pupil acquires are, if anything, even more vague. This is all part of the mystique of the gentleman, something to which certain classes of society were apparently born and which the schools were able to consolidate. Those unfortunate enough to have missed out on this birthright now had the chance to acquire it, thanks to the expansion of the schools. Amongst the nebulous ingredients that went to make up an English gentleman were such things as 'public spirit' and 'vigour and manliness of character', qualities one would be hard put to define with any degree of precision. The combination of 'freedom and order' was something which had been maintained, after a fashion, by headmasters before Arnold, but since his reforms it could be argued that the former was largely sacrificed to the latter. It could also be argued that if the respect for public opinion (by which is meant opinion within the school community not that expressed in the radical press) was strong in the 1860s, it was very soon to become slavish. Conformity became one of the most deadening forces within the schools, embodied in such notions as 'good form', 'honour' and 'house feeling'. This conformity was emphasised by the universal 'love of healthy sports and exercise', a love often extracted under duress,[1] and in marked contrast to the hours of freedom in which formerly boys rambled around the countryside. The dangers inherent in the cult of games (not in its infancy; the Harrow Philathletic Club had been in existence for eleven years) passed the Commissioners by.

A new note was sounded in the suggestion (difficult to substantiate, one would have thought) that a public-school education prepared a boy for a future in 'the world of business'. How many of the rising bourgeoisie, one wonders, were encouraged to send their sons to public schools as a result of these glad tidings? The yoking together of business and society also suggested an emergent respectability for the professional classes. However, the stigma of 'trade', a term which covered a wide spectrum of occupations but carried with it a suggestion of shop counters ('Tradesmen's Entrance'), remained. For example, when Cheltenham College was founded in 1841, local residents were invited to become shareholders. But: 'no person should be considered eligible who should not be moving in the circle of gentlemen. No retail trader being under any circumstances to be considered.'

Finally the schools were praised for providing their pupils with 'the most enduring friendships, and some of the ruling habits of their lives'. When a system of education is exclusive, available only to a small minority, it has the effect of making its pupils aware of their similarity with their fellows and their difference from the rest of society. This sense of exclusiveness persists throughout life, with the result that the Old Boy Network has been this country's most powerful freemasonry. The tribal experiences undergone by boys at public schools resulted in the emergence of a pattern of behaviour and attitude, an ethos which seemed applicable to the world beyond the school gates and which was shared by former pupils however far they might disperse after the end of their final term. The rituals, the argot, the songs and anthems, and the uniform (even if reduced to an old school tie) reinforced this sense of solidarity, and are characteristic of sections of the community that have been set apart from the majority. Societies kept old boys informed about each other's exploits and promoted reunions. Nostalgia for and loyalty to one's old school and schoolfellows had become a dominant force in society and politics.

That so cohesive an ideology was created owes much to earlier reforms of the public-school system pioneered by Arnold at Rugby. During the eighteenth century the schools which had originally been founded for the benefit of the poor, had been colonised by the wealthy. Such pupils were an attractive

---

[1] Alec Waugh, writing of Sherborne in 1913, compares the methods used for 'dragooning the less athletic-minded into conformity' with those later employed by the Nazis.

prospect, since the fees they paid for board and lodging helped to supplement the unrealistic incomes of masters which had been fixed by the founders' charters and never altered. More and more paying pupils were admitted so that before long the schools had become overcrowded and out of hand. In the last three decades of the eighteenth century Winchester, Rugby and Eton had suffered a spate of rebellions, some so severe that the militia had been summoned and the Riot Act read. In an attempt to forestall such incidents a system had been introduced by which senior boys were enlisted to help maintain order. Unfortunately the majority of these 'praeposters' or 'prefects' abused their new positions of authority.

By the beginning of the nineteenth century the schools were in a deplorable state, as alien to the modern public school as to the sort of school envisaged by their founders. Discipline, such as it was, was maintained by mass floggings and summary expulsions. However, even these threats did not prevent a standard of conduct more associated with the early navy than with schoolchildren. When not terrorising the neighbourhood by acts of vandalism, poaching and brawling, the young gentlemen of these schools spent their time drinking, gambling, and bullying and sexually assaulting their fellow-pupils. There were numerous incidents in which boys were physically maimed and even murdered. Conditions within the schools were scarcely conducive to civilised behaviour. Drastic overcrowding in classrooms, dormitories and even beds meant that neither the intellects nor the morals of the pupils were much advanced. Food, even by the standards for which schools have been, and continue to be, notorious, was inadequate in both quantity and quality. The increased funds supplied by the boarding fees were frequently embezzled by masters.

Clearly something had to be done about the state into which the schools had fallen. How the privileged youth of England was tamed during the nineteenth century is a fascinating story, a story encapsulated in the first and most famous public school novel. It is the story of the triumph of Tom Brown over Flashman.

3 A Legend and a Legacy

The Provost of Oriel's declaration in 1827 that if Thomas Arnold was appointed headmaster of Rugby he would 'change the face of education all through the public schools of England' has generally been quoted as a prophecy rather than as an opinion. Often presented in messianic colours, Arnold enjoyed the *posthumous* career of a religious leader, but during his life he performed few miracles. Nonetheless, two evangelists, A.P. Stanley and Thomas Hughes, penned gospels, whilst other disciples went forth into the world to spread the word, teaching in, transforming and founding other schools. The development of the public schools in the nineteenth century sometimes has the appearance of the acts of the apostles, and it is these men, rather than Arnold himself, who were responsible for what we now think of as a Victorian public school.

Arnold's qualifications for effecting so important a programme of reform were at best vague. His motives had more to do with souls than with scholarships and he was more interested in reforming society than he was with reforming the public-school system. Ten years as a private tutor and a shorter period as a parent had failed to acclimatise Arnold to the natural rowdiness of children. Could it be that he had forgotten his own schooldays at Winchester where he had ragged with the best of them? Further pranks had taken place at Oxford, but Arnold was not haunted by a nostalgia for his youth; he was haunted by the spirit of rebellion. He was a radical who put his faith in reform rather than in revolution. The history of public school criticism throughout the nineteenth century is dominated by similar motivation. Arnold did not want to see society restructured; he wanted to see it stabilised. He believed in the ruling class but felt that it was profligate and consequently losing the respect due to it from other sections of the community. The French Revolution had acted as an awful warning of what could happen in such circumstances. Not only were the great public schools the training ground, by intention or default, of the future leaders of society, they were also a microcosm of that society, and as such presented a worrying picture. Were not the young aristocratic praeposters at Eton and Harrow as despotic and dissolute as those French nobles who had been hauled off to the guillotine? Had not the pupils of Rugby, when they rose against Dr Ingles in 1794, piped about the Rights of Boys? Had not *Floreat Seditio* been chalked upon the walls of Eton as recently as 1818? By training the future administrators of society in truly Christian conduct Arnold would not only be saving their souls but also saving English society.

Hitherto the education of England's future statesmen had been both morally and intellectually haphazard, as may be seen from the reign at Eton (1809–1834) of Dr John Keate. Although barbaric by modern standards, Keate's regime appears to have been popular with his students. It has come down to us

[45]

in anecdotal form via the forgiving memoirs of his pupils. Keate was an extraordinary figure, not unlike a contemporaneous autocrat across the Channel. About five feet tall, swathed in a greatcoat, his head topped with a cocked hat, he was a stockier, more powerful Bonaparte. It was said that any Etonian could cut or draw his silhouette (examples of which could be found anywhere in the world 'where English gentlemen were forced to kick their heels'), and he has been reduced to a caricature by history. The floggings for which he was famous, with Keate flailing about indiscriminately with a birch whilst being jeered at and pelted with eggs by onlooking pupils, have been transmuted to slapstick. Feared and revered in about equal measure, Keate was the only nineteenth-century headmaster who achieved anything like the fame of Arnold, and he did so without, as he no doubt would have seen it, vulgar advertisement. He retired, much loved, loaded with gifts and a testimony from his pupils to 'the High sense they entertain[ed] . . . of the Firm yet Parental Exercise Of his Authority Which has conciliated the Affection While It Has Commanded the Respect Of His Scholars'.

This is not the sort of admiration which would have counted for much with Arnold. Far from exercising parental authority over his charges, he put his faith in spiritual authority. Whilst at Oxford he had experienced religious doubts. These doubts, we are given to understand, were intellectual, and overcome by the rigorous application of prayer. Thereafter prayer guided his life and emotion dominated his intellect. He re-embraced Christianity with all the fervour of a convert, weeping in the pulpit as he read of the Crucifixion. In 1828 piety was not a natural state for a schoolboy and chapel services were constantly interrupted by pet mice, and even snakes, let loose amongst the congregation. Preachers droned on, scarcely heard above the continual chatter of pupils. Arnold was as aware as anyone of the natural impiety of boys, but regarded it as something to be eradicated. By personal example, and the example of a chosen élite amongst the boys, Arnold hoped to create an atmosphere of hushed reverence, not only in Rugby chapel but in the whole school.

Discipline under Arnold became less a simple case of crime and punishment than a moral question of sin and redemption. A boy discovered in some misdemeanour was not merely breaking a school rule; he was profaning the law of God. With so impressive a partner Arnold should have had few problems in running a public school which had already undergone reforms in the previous century. 'There has been no flogging yet,' he wrote to a friend one month after he had taken up his appointment, '(and I hope there will be none), and surprisingly few irregularities. I chastise at first by very gentle impositions, which are raised for a repetition of offences – flogging will be only my ratio ultima – and *talking* I shall try to the utmost.' Talking – or 'jawing' as generations of schoolboys called it – did not prove as efficacious as the Doctor had hoped. Boys were expelled and the *ratio ultima* of flogging was resorted to all too frequently. Much has been made of Arnold's public apology to a boy whom he had flogged unjustly, but since Arnold had lost his temper and delivered an unprecedentedly savage eighteen strokes upon a weak child who suffered from a hernia, apologising was the least he could do. One also suspects that Arnold's display of humility would not be altogether distasteful to a man given to weeping in the pulpit.

Arnold's chief instrument of discipline was his prefects; indeed, he has often been credited with inventing the prefect system. As we have seen, monstrous youths with sidewhiskers had been tyrannising their juniors for some time, receiving little interference from headmasters. Arnold transformed these older boys into an inner circle of responsible, pious deputies whom he trusted and in whom he confided, making them the instruments of his will. This, at any rate, was the ideal. Arnold's absolute belief in his Sixth Form élite remained unshaken even by incidents such as a poaching episode in 1833. A keeper who had been pitched into the river by Rugbeians made a formal complaint and Arnold set his prefects to discover the culprits. They failed to do so probably because, in spite of his efforts, loyalty to one's schoolfellows still outweighed a loyalty to the Truth. Arnold was forced to resort to an identity parade, after which six boys were expelled on the spot, an act which almost caused a riot. Arnold's view of the incident is clear from the speech he made to the school after the poachers had been removed: 'It is not necessary that this should be a school of three hundred, or one hundred, or of fifty boys; but it is necessary that it should be a school of Christian gentlemen.' It is to be doubted, as this incident shows, that Arnold ever achieved this goal.

What he did achieve was an inner circle of high-minded youths with a propensity for piety, whom he groomed to be his representatives. More mystagogue than pedagogue, Arnold was concerned chiefly with the souls of his elect; the prose of the lower forms could safely be left in the hands of his assistant masters. His constitutional dislike of children made it more congenial for him to delegate authority and distance himself from his younger charges until they had got over the distasteful process of attaining maturity. He created a forcing-house in which children were hurried towards the adult state, when they could be treated as fellow-beings, alert and receptive to his doctrines. His defensive claim that, 'I never disguise or suppress my opinions, but I have been

[47]

and am, most religiously careful not to influence my boys with them', was perhaps true in the case of the majority of his pupils. In the case of such Sixth Formers as A.H. Clough, A.P. Stanley and C.J. Vaughan this was clearly untrue; but then they were no longer boys, but had pupated, emerging from the chrysalis as Christian men.

How much the pupils benefited from this is open to question. It has been suggested that Clough, who staggered into Balliol under a dead weight of prizes and moral scruples, never really recovered from his experience as a member of the 'high Arnold set'. Once at Oxford he failed to achieve either of his goals: a First or a Balliol Fellowship. His poems reflect much spiritual wrangling and it is doubtful whether many of them would have found favour with Arnold. Indeed, in *Dipsychus*, a poetic dialogue between the spirit and the flesh, there are barbed references to Arnoldian ideals.

Vaughan seemed a better advertisement, becoming headmaster of Harrow, then resigning and refusing assorted bishoprics with a humility that even Arnold might have envied. However, it was later revealed that this paragon of Rugby had been blackmailed into resigning from Harrow after writing love letters to one of his pupils. Dr Symonds, whose son John Addington had betrayed the confidence of the letters' recipient, threatened Vaughan with exposure every time he appeared to be tempted by the offer of an important see.

Any disappointment Arnold might have felt about these star pupils (or his own son, whose shilly-shallying between Canterbury and Rome showed an un-Arnoldian lack of purpose) would have been more than compensated for by Stanley. A son of the Bishop of Norwich, Stanley appeared to have some form of spiritual insulation and professed himself amazed at the comparatively innocuous accounts of Rugby high jinks in *Tom Brown's Schooldays*. He was perfect material for Arnold's Sixth Form and soon pupil and headmaster had embarked upon a relationship of apparently unshakeable mutual admiration. Like all such relationships, this one was tinged with self-congratulation. When Stanley won the Balliol Scholarship Arnold thanked him publicly at the school's Speech Day. Stanley more than repaid the compliment and was, with Thomas Hughes, chief architect of the Arnold legend.

He was frank enough to admit that: 'Loving Arnold and admiring him as I do to the very verge of all love and admiration that can be paid to a man, I fear I have passed the limits and made him my idol, and that in all I may be serving God for man's sake.' No biography written under such conditions is likely to err on the side of objectivity. Indeed, Stanley embarked upon his work as both a memorial to and a defence of his old headmaster. After the shock of Arnold's sudden death – Stanley had been obliged to take to his bed upon hearing the news – there seemed a danger that the controversies in which the Great Man had been embroiled would obliterate his achievements at Rugby. Some of these controversies, most of them concerned with local politics, were played down or simply omitted from Stanley's *Life and Correspondence of Thomas Arnold*: there is nothing, for example, about the case brought against Arnold and the Rugby Trustees which was heard in Chancery and in which it was suggested that there had been a misuse of some funds. The book, published within two years of Arnold's death, received a favourable press and enjoyed good sales well into the twentieth century. Its author went on to become Dean of Westminster, a living example of the Arnold Ideal.

However, it was *Tom Brown's Schooldays* (1857) which provided the popular image of 'the Doctor' and proved the more influential book. During its first year of publication it sold some 11,000 copies and by the time Hughes died in 1896 it was in its seventieth edition. Although issued as fiction, it was clearly propagandist in intent. It strove after authenticity, its anonymous author styling himself merely as 'An Old Boy'. It opened up the hitherto closed world of the public school to public scrutiny and despite scenes of bullying, and Stanley's exclamations of astonishment, it presented an enticing picture of school life in which good triumphed exultantly over evil. Although the book has been much mocked over the years, it must be said in fairness to Hughes that he understood boys in a way that someone like F.W. Farrar (author of *Eric, or Little by Little*) never did. He was able to include incidents which may have shocked some Old Rugbeians, but which served to leaven the moral dough of his story and make it much more palatable for the young reader.

Hughes also paid a great deal of attention to games. 'I know I'd rather win two School-house matches running than get the Balliol scholarship any day', announces Brooke, the popular Head of House, amidst 'frantic cheers'. Hughes approves of this, but it is doubtful whether Arnold would have done. The Balliol Scholarship, after all, is what Stanley achieved, and Clough after him. Rugby, of course, was famous for the 'invention' of a new type of football when William Webb Ellis 'with a fine disregard for the rules of football as played in his time' picked up the ball during a game of soccer. This happened in 1823 during the reign of Wooll. One doubts whether Arnold would have hallowed such behaviour, if indeed he had taken any interest at all, for games bored him. Even in *Tom Brown's Schooldays* he only manages to watch half an hour of the great match. One can hardly imagine the venerable figure bellowing encouragement from the sidelines when confronted with such a display of riotous youth. However, the conjunction of Ellis and Hughes led people to believe that Arnold himself started the games cult which raged through the schools during the second half of the nineteenth century and which led to the tyranny of the athlete.

More significantly Hughes was responsible for setting forth the aims of a public-school education as he conceived it in a speech much quoted and very properly ridiculed. Squire Brown's famous statement about the education of his son says more perhaps about the expectations of nineteenth-century parents than about the aims of Dr Arnold:

Shall I tell him to mind his work, and say he's sent to school to make himself a good scholar? Well, but he isn't sent to school for that — at any rate, not for that mainly. I don't care a straw for Greek particles, or the digamma; no more does his mother . . . If he'll only turn out a brave, helpful, truth-telling Englishman, and a Christian, that's all I want.

In fact the Squire's ideal is rather more laudable than that of many parents. Rugby, after all, was founded by a grocer, not a king, and its traditions had always been middle-class. The sons of the gentry and the clergy were Dr Arnold's staple and, unregenerate as boys tended to be, at least his came from respectable backgrounds. Arnold's denigration of the aristocracy appealed to his comparatively humble prospective parents. Had he not advised the Duchess of Sutherland to send her son to Eton rather than Rugby, so that he should be among his own kind? Lesser headmasters would have encouraged any duchess to have her son educated in their school to act as a honeypot for the flies of the rising middle class.

The public schools, contrary to their popular image of being immovably resistant to change, have always been astute at adapting, or seeming to adapt, to new circumstances. The expansion of the schools during the Victorian period was not entirely due to the idealistic zeal of Arnold's disciples; there was an entrepreneurial spirit in the air. The political power of the land traditionally lay with the landed classes and it was their sons who were educated in public schools, after which they inherited the estate, went into the army or got ordained, in that order. If clever they might also enter the law. Industrial expansion had led to an emergent plutocracy, generally regarded as a threat to the landed classes' supremacy. Alongside this was a growing bureaucracy which required administrators at home and abroad. Tradition dictated that any attempt by a new, wealthy class to infiltrate the ancient haunts of young gentlemen should be disdainfully resisted. However, administrators were needed and it was clearly in everyone's interests to have gentlemen in such positions. Consequently the bourgeois were gradually admitted to the schools where it was hoped that they would become impregnated with the ethos of the English Gentleman. This move also drove a wedge between the rising middle class and the working class; any threat of revolution (that spectral presence hovering behind so much Victorian social philosophy) was lessened by such an annexation. Furthermore, as the schools grew, and the demand for them grew, the need for funds increased and so this new money was put to good use. By educating and absorbing the cream of the bourgeoisie the landed classes ensured that they retained supremacy.

The *nouveaux riches* were delighted at this boost to their upward mobility. They were keen that their sons should benefit from an education that they themselves had been denied. It was also socially desirable that they should acquire the habits of gentlemen and thus enter Society where they might eventually marry well and thus consolidate their power. By attending Eton and similar establishments it was possible for the sons of industrialists to mix with the sons of the nobility. This would not only prove advantageous to the sons, but also to the fathers who might benefit from the commercial patronage of the aristocracy.[1]

However, the status of 'gentleman' carried with it certain moral obligations, duties as well as privileges. The new piety observable in public schools was partly Arnold's legacy, but was also a reflection of the indoctrination of the middle classes with the ethos of the upper. A squire, such as Tom Brown's father, would have been a spiritual as well as a social figurehead, rather as the Queen was head of the Church of England. Sitting in their own pew in full view of a congregation largely made up of tenants and employees, the Squire's family embodied a tradition of Godliness and Good Works. One way of demonstrating one's social standing was in moral excellence and acts of charity. A confusion between good breeding and good behaviour led to an alliance between social and moral snobbery.

In H.A. Vachell's Harrow novel, *The Hill* (published in 1905 and a repository of late-Victorian public-school mores), the villain of the piece, Scaife, is the grandson of a shipping magnate who rose from the slums of

---

[1] A later example of this occurs in Cyril Connolly's merciless parody of Brian Howard, *Where Engels Fears to Tread* (first published in 1937). Howard was an Eton contemporary of Connolly. His father was an American of possibly Jewish but certainly misty origins, called Gassaway. He was an art dealer and the advantages of his son acquiring patrons at Eton were obvious. In Connolly's parody the father is a bookie, given to such expressions as : 'And don't forget, my boy, a tenner for every little nob you bring home with a handle to his name.'

Liverpool (and never quite lost his taste for them). The heroes of the novel are landed and titled. Schematically nicknamed 'the Demon', Scaife is both morally and socially suspect. Indeed his 'otherness' is immediately, even anthropologically, apparent amidst the young gentlemen of Harrow. He is 'dark, almost swarthy of complexion, with strongly-marked features'. As the languid 'Caterpillar' Egerton remarks to the book's hero after poor Scaife has mispronounced 'inestimable' and 'connoisseur': 'You've noticed his hands – eh? *Very* unfinished! And his feet – short, but broad.' (Egerton, of course, has 'long, slender feet'.) Scaife drinks and gambles and is such a poor sport that even an *Etonian* is seen to behave better, congratulating the boy who bowled him out at Lord's rather than scowling. As the Caterpillar observes: 'That Eton captain is cut out of whole cloth; no shoddy there, by Jove!', a distinction which even 'urchins of thirteen' are able to recognise. The other bad character, the son of a footwear manufacturer and sporting a bogus-sounding double-barrelled name, is even worse than Scaife. Obese and spotty, he indulges in forgery and – Vachell delicately suggests – sexual harassment of little Lord Kinloch.

Nonetheless, even if Vachell's Harrovians were able to sniff out murky social origins, others believed that 'class' was there for the asking, and the middle classes were eager to assume the mantle of pious benefactor as an emblem of their newly acquired status of English Gentlemen. Thus the pupils of the public schools had become, over the centuries, the dispensers rather than the beneficiaries of charity. All this applied only to those with new wealth. The few local boys who were still educated free of charge at some of the schools were frequently differentiated by (sometimes absurd) dress from their fee-paying fellows, and were frankly regarded as social pariahs. Eventually this unsatisfactory system was abolished by the expedient of introducing an entrance examination, preparations for which required the sort of resources unavailable to the poor.

Not content with merely acquiring gentlemanly habits and connections, the middle classes began to suggest that the schools should adapt themselves to their new circumstances, hence the criticism of men like Higgins, which led to the Clarendon Commission. Arnold had asserted that, 'What we must look for [at Rugby] is, first, religious and moral principle; secondly, gentlemanly conduct; thirdly, intellectual ability.' However, in the wake of his reforms, gentlemanly conduct began to achieve ascendancy over religious and moral principle; intellectual ability remained a poor third. Although Arnold would have been horrified at the way the schools had developed away from his Christian ideal, he remained a revered figure who was credited with the creation of the Victorian public school. In numbers, if not in influence, those who had worked under or been taught by Arnold played a considerable role in the expansion of the schools. In the scramble to acquire a gentlemanly education, demand soon outstripped supply and so more public schools were founded and more old grammar schools were transformed.[1] Into these schools flooded the alumni of Rugby. Pious boys fuelled by an admiration of Arnold, and masters who had served under him and had reason to be grateful to him,[2] set about a programme of expansion and reform. During the nineteenth century Harrow, Marlborough, Sherborne, Cheltenham, Lancing, Haileybury, Berkhamstead, Felsted, Bromsgrove, Monkton Combe and, of course, Rugby itself (to name only the best known of the schools) all had Old Rugbeian headmasters. The man who introduced compulsory games to the schools, Cotton of Marlborough, had been an assistant master under Arnold at Rugby, as were Prince Lee (King Edward's Birmingham) and Herbert Hill (Warwick). It has been argued (notably by J.R.deS. Honey in *Tom Brown's Universe* (1977)) that a great many of these teachers had little influence upon the development of the public schools in the nineteenth century. It is also fair to say that reforms were taking place within the schools independent of what was happening at Rugby. Nonetheless, there is no doubt at all that Stanley and Hughes between them fixed Rugby and Arnold in the public imagination, presenting them as standards by which other schools and headmasters might be judged. They became, and still are, the archetypes of their world, and the war in which the post-Arnold public-school ideals were put to the test and found wanting was within six months of its end before their progenitor came under the sceptical and dissenting eye of Lytton Strachey in his *Eminent Victorians*.

4 Training for Empire

An important influence upon the public-school system which has nothing to do with Arnold and his followers was the British policy of expansionism. Just as the old grammar schools were bought up and transformed into public

---

[1] The Clarendon Commission considered only nine schools. In order to protect the system from further governmental interference, Thring of Uppingham formed the Headmasters' Conference in 1869. By 1873 seventy-one schools were considered eligible for membership.

[2] Amongst Arnold's achievements was the improvement of the social and financial status of schoolmasters. Within his term of office the salaries of assistant masters at Rugby doubled.

schools, so in the world outside Britain was gobbling up distant lands and colonising them. Britain needed to look overseas to find new markets for her goods and also to find raw materials from which to make those goods. In order to maintain her economic power, she had to compete with other European countries, such as France and Germany, which were also expanding. What was in fact an undignified, competitive scramble for colonies was often presented as an exercise in altruism. There was talk of Britain's 'civilising mission' to other countries, and the fair exchange of social progress for exported goods. By the 1880s an Imperialist Ideal had emerged, supported by such influential books as J.R. Seeley's *The Expansion of England* (1883). Imperialism became invigorated by an ardent patriotism and invested with a mysticism akin to that which shrouded the concept of the English Gentleman. The gentlemanly ideals of service to the community (estate workers, parish paupers and so on) was expanded to service for British properties abroad. The spiritual benefits which landowners supposedly brought to their tenants along with the material ones were similar to those brought to 'uncivilised' countries by imperialists. The almost religious aura which surrounded both the gentleman and the ideals of imperialism was also a necessary camouflage for what otherwise might have appeared entirely an exercise in self-interest.

It is easy to see how a nineteenth-century public-school education prepared boys for service to Empire. The more ennobling features ascribed to Imperialism were already dominant within the schools. The subordination of self to the community, personal striving for the common weal, the upholding of traditions and loyalty to the community, all acted as training for the administration of Empire. Other circumstances were also useful preparation. The separation of boys from their families and from female society, for example, was a preparation for long, lonely and chaste years in remote parts.[1]

It was administration rather than soldiering overseas that this education worked towards. Before the Boer War the interests of schools lay in the games-field rather than the battlefield. Boys were patriotic, of course, but their loyalty was concentrated more upon their immediate community than upon the concerns of their country. However, they could be expected to cheer the soldiers of the Queen should they encounter them. At Eton William Johnson Cory would rise from his desk at the sound of soldiers in the street and lead his classes

---

[1] There is also a parallel between the failure of the ideal at school and abroad. Just as some boys would find the monasticism of boarding-school life too much to endure and so indulge in homosexual activities with fellow-pupils, so lone Englishmen would occasionally 'go native' and take indigenous mistresses.

outside with the rallying cry: 'Brats, the British Army!' Indeed, the attitude of the schoolboy at this time seems to have been the same as that of Housman in his poem 'The street sounds to the soldiers' tread': that of uninvolved well-wishing.

It was Cory's colleague Edmond Warre who was to press for an increase in militarism within the schools. He founded the Eton Volunteers, a rifle corps which, although not compulsory, became popular under his patronage. Warre's influence at Eton was considerable, long-lived and largely malign. Before he was appointed headmaster in 1884, he acted as a forceful deputy to Hornby. Both men were unashamedly philistine, apparently colluding in the mysterious dismissal of Cory. Warre had been an Eton contemporary of Swinburne, whom he considered then and ever after a disgrace to the school. He was a skilled and ardent sportsman who inflicted his own enthusiasms upon his pupils, so that Eton began to resemble Harrow, already groaning under the tyranny of athleticism. If he had been less of a philathlete he would no doubt have made the Volunteers compulsory, but it was felt (as it was to be in other schools) that this would interfere with the real business of Eton: rowing, cricket and rugby. Warre built a drill hall, spent his holidays in barracks, and paraded the Volunteers at every possible opportunity. The Boer War was the climax of his career, and he took satisfaction from the astonishingly high number of officers provided by Eton: 1,326. However, as if writing a report, Warre claimed that Britain 'could have done better' had military training in the schools been compulsory. He gave a lecture on this subject ('The Relation of Public Secondary Schools to the Organisation of National Defence') to the United Services Institute in the summer of 1900, and began lobbying parliament for an act to make military training compulsory for public-school boys over fifteen. This provoked a flurry of debate in the columns of *The Times*, but no action by the government.

Until the Boer War the number of public-school boys entering the forces was surprisingly small; their duty to the Empire was less belligerently expressed.[1] A survey of 'eminent men' of Victoria's reign, published in 1900, showed that a mere 16 per cent of the army sample had attended a public school, compared with 71 per cent of the government sample. Colonial and

[1] Etonians flooded the diplomatic service. Until 1918 entrants for this service had to move in the correct, moneyed circles. It was necessary to have a personal recommendation, either by the Secretary of State himself or one of his acquaintances, and to guarantee a private income of not less than £400 per annum. The result was that 67 per cent of all attaché-ships between 1908 and 1913 were given to Old Etonians.

government administration was the favoured career of a large proportion of public-school men. The schools were just not equipped to provide an education suited to a boy who wanted to enter the armed forces. This is not, of course, to say that boys from these schools did not bring added lustre to the Guards, but the route from school to regiment was often circuitous. Some schools had Army and Modern 'Sides', but these were often frankly used as dumping-grounds for the least intelligent pupils. Most boys who wanted to enter the army – the Harrovian Winston Churchill amongst them – were siphoned off into special military crammers.[1]

There were schools with a military bias which catered for the sons of army officers. Wellington, founded in memory of the martial Duke by public subscription in 1859; Haileybury, set up in the disused East India Company College in 1862; and Cheltenham, founded in 1841 for the sons of the numerous colonial servants who had retired to the spa, all sent a large number of boys to Sandhurst and Woolwich. Kipling's school, the United Services College at Westward Ho, was founded for the sons of indigent army officers who could not afford the fees charged by the other three schools, and was a rather different establishment, as we shall see.

It is not militarism as such that we find in the schools of the nineteenth century, but an espousal of values which promoted local and national patriotism: house, school, country, in that order. Indeed some Imperialist critics of the system complained that fanatical devotion to a school was too narrow a patriotism and, far from serving as a model for real patriotism, engaged boys' loyalties in a distracting way. Apologists for the schools' imperial endeavours include Sir Henry Newbolt who invested School and Empire with a quasi-religious mystique. Newbolt was an early pupil at Clifton, which had been founded in 1862, taking Rugby as its model. The first headmaster, John Percival, had been an assistant master at Rugby and was eventually to return there as headmaster. In his memoirs, Newbolt recalled Percival's view of life and school, the 'impulses and influences which were to animate us all'. This was a combination of Arnoldian and Classical virtues:

> It was a Roman Rule, particularly fitted to the needs of the English schoolboy, presented to us by a man of fine character and magnificent presence, demanding of us the virtues of leadership, courage and

[1] Between 1858 and 1861 a mere 122 of the 1,976 candidates who applied for commissions were from public schools. Of the 375 candidates at Sandhurst, only 23 came directly from their public schools.

independence; the sacrifice of selfish interests to the ideal of fellowship and the future of the race. In response we gave enthusiastically but we gave something rather different: we set up a 'good form', a standard of our own. 'To be in all things decent, orderly, self-mastering: in action to follow up the coolest common sense with the most unflinching endurance; in public affairs to be devoted as a matter of course, self-sacrificing without any appearance of enthusiasm: on all social occasions – except at the regular Saturnalia – to play the Horatian man of the world, the Gentleman after the high Roman fashion, making a fine art, almost a religion, of Stoicism'.

This Classical ideal was grafted onto a devout Christianity and pervaded the atmosphere of Clifton in the 1860s and 1870s: 'This doctrine was impressed upon us not only in Chapel, but on all suitable occasions – it communicated itself like "a latent fire" to everyone who came in contact with the man.' Although boys, being boys, set up some resistance to so high an ideal, Newbolt (and, one suspects, his contemporary, Douglas Haig) believed that 'the Percivalian doctrine [remained] true and effective in all the worthier activities of life, both for schools and for nations.' Amongst the worthier activities was working for Empire, a task to which Newbolt brought his slender but forceful literary talent. Percival was also fired by chivalric zeal, probably in order to shift the basis of his philosophy from the Classically pagan to the Christian. Imperialists thus became paladins, and were appropriately commemorated at Clifton.

The news that Percival was to leave Clifton to go to Trinity College, Oxford was more shocking to the sixteen-year-old Newbolt than the announcement of the death of the Queen: 'It would be hard to exaggerate the consternation with which we received the news,' he recalled. One is reminded of Stanley's shock upon hearing news of Arnold's death, and Newbolt's proselytising on behalf of Clifton and its first headmaster is similar, if more robust, than Stanley's efforts on behalf of Rugby and Arnold. Like a great many Old Boys, Newbolt recalled his schooldays 'like wealth that is spent, and would be good to spend again'. The first sight of the great school is remembered in Newbolt's novel *The Twymans* (1912). The hero, a heraldry-obsessed little boy called Percival (naturally), goes to 'Downton' to take his scholarship examination. Walking through the town, the first intimation of the school to reach him is the sound of 'the sweet crack of bat on ball'. Through the trees he sees the school, but it is not the stately buildings which take 'his breath away with an entirely new delight' but the sight of the cricket field: 'a wide green sward, level as a lawn, flooded with low sunlight, and covered in every direction with a multitude of white figures, standing, running, walking, bowling, throwing, batting – in every attitude that can express the energy or the expectancy of youth.' This fairly commonplace scene impresses the small boy, who is a keen sportsman, but it also moves him with a Wordsworthian sense of wonder:

> At the second glance something broke over his spirit like a wave; he took it for the tide of joyful anticipation, but I think it was more than that – the inrush of an idea, the sudden perception, however vague and distant, of the meaning of the scene: a glimpse, behind the mere beauty of the white young figures shining so coolly in the slant of evening sunlight, of the finely planned order and long descended discipline they symbolised.

Quite what this is Newbolt does not reveal, but in a later book he claimed that the public schools were in a direct line of descent from medieval court life. This is indeed a vision caused by a trick of the light, since there is no evidence whatsoever to support such a notion.[1]

This bold assertion is typical of Newbolt, whose entire output is swathed in similarly romantic misapprehensions. The liberal aspects of Clifton, such as its fine academic record, its science laboratories and its Jewish house,[2] pass Newbolt by. He is complacent in his acceptance of the supremacy of games in the school, and echoes *Tom Brown's Schooldays* when he writes: 'It is I believe a mere truth to say that there were very few members of the school who would not have bartered away all chance of intellectual distinction for a place in the Cricket Eleven or Football Fifteen.' It was Newbolt, of course, who immortalised the tendency to regard war as a glorified cricket match, exhorting boys to 'Play up! play up! and play the game!' It needs a considerable imaginative leap to take seriously the preposterous verse and prose of Newbolt. Like *Eric* and other deathless works, Newbolt's poems have survived largely

---

[1] Nonetheless, chivalric codes became part of the public-school ethos, and various other writers and schoolmasters convinced themselves that Newbolt's fantasy about public-school history was true. (*See* Chapter Two).

[2] Cheltenham also had a house for Jewish boys where they could follow their own faith. Other schools merely excused Jews chapel. According to Shane Leslie, Eton at the turn of the century had a house, known disparagingly as 'The Synagogue', in which a number of Jews boarded. This, however, was because few other houses would accept Jews, and the house in question was considered then, and in 1919 when Anthony Powell entered it, very infra dig.

because we find them funny. It now seems inconceivable that the fatuities of 'Vitaï Lampada' were ever read without a derisive smile, but when first published in 1879 they were, and they continued to exert a baleful influence on popular patriotic verse and thought to the Somme and beyond.

Not all Imperialists were as crude as Newbolt. Not all those who believed in the Empire agreed that training for its service should necessarily involve the annihilation of individuality for the common good and a rigorous deference to conformity. Whilst the standard picture of the imperialist ideal working within a school can be found in *The Hill*, a more subtle (and, some would argue, a more disturbing) version of training for Empire is seen in Kipling's *Stalky & Co*. Whereas *The Hill* is set at a typical public school, Harrow, Kipling's book is set at his anomalous old school, the United Services College. Just as USC was not a typical public school, Kipling's heroes are not typical public-school boys.

To the average parent USC would have seemed cheapskate. It was a school without traditions, without even history, founded only four years before Kipling was sent there in January 1878. The headmaster was not a public-school man,[1] nor in holy orders. There was no organised fagging, the games fields were of secondary importance to the classrooms, there was not even a chapel. (Services were held in the gymnasium.) USC was something between a traditional public school and an army crammer, and was less expensive than either. Although its foundation – to train boys to be army officers – was different from other public schools, its development was parallel and despite the anti-Imperialist views of its headmaster, old USC boys served the Empire as administrators and soldiers in large numbers. In a famous episode in *Stalky & Co*, which still surprises readers who imagine Kipling to be Jingoism incarnate, an MP is invited to address the pupils. The boys are outraged by the MP's speech, in which he urges them to defend their country and honour the flag. When he unfurls a Union Jack there is none of the expected applause, rather an appalled silence: 'It was a matter shut up, sacred and apart'. Dismissed by Stalky as a 'jelly-bellied Flag-flapper', this armchair patriot has insulted the boys, the majority of them the sons (and some the orphans) of soldiers. His vulgar display is almost a blasphemy: 'He profaned the most secret

[1] More important than one might think, Eton, with characteristic exclusiveness, insisted that its headmasters should not only be Old Etonians, but also Collegers. Warre was the first Oppidan headmaster. Poor Sanderson of Oundle, a physics teacher without either dog-collar, cricketing blue or public-school education to his credit, was looked down upon by his first pupils because he wore a made-up bow tie and detachable shirt cuffs.

places of their souls with his outcries and gesticulations.' For these boys patriotism was like religion, deeply felt but rarely expressed. Whilst they may share Newbolt's faith in essence, in practice they are non-conformist. Unlike the boys in most public schools and most school stories, Stalky, Beetle and M'Turk are heroes because they do *not* conform or rally round the flag with fabricated emotionalism. Above all they are heroes because of their individuality and their ingenuity.[1] These are the sort of people the Empire needs, according to Kipling, not 'The Islanders', 'the flannelled fools at the wicket or the muddied oafs at the goal'. Although men should serve the Empire selflessly, they would be of little use if they were self-effacing conformists. In many ways Kipling's schoolboys seem throwbacks to the golden age of the unreformed schools. Not everyone approved of Kipling's ideal; H.G. Wells thought them 'mucky little sadists' who exemplified the very worst aspects of British Imperialism. Other writers more favourable to the traditional public school were equally appalled and joined in a chorus of denunciation, often stressing that USC bore no relation to a 'real' public school. In spite of the inventive liveliness of *Stalky & Co* compared with most school stories (a liveliness, it must be said, that sometimes seems merely frenetic), the book does contain scenes which make uncomfortable reading. Whilst we may applaud the trio for spending an afternoon ridiculing the works of F.W. Farrar (a gift to Beetle from a maiden aunt) when they should be watching cricket, it is difficult to sympathise with some of their more riotous exploits. The underlying nastiness of the practical joke frequently surfaces in the stories, but even this seems acceptable compared with the scene in which some bullies are treated in kind. Revenge was never a wilder kind of justice than it is in 'The Moral Reformers'.

There is no doubt that the Boer War was seen by many apologists as a vindication of the entire public-school system. J.G.C. Minchin's *Our Public Schools*, published in 1901 in the wake of the Boer War, was confidently subtitled 'Their Influence on English History'. Whilst much is made of the achievements of generations of public-school men, Minchin's real business is to show how well more recent alumni have done in the service of the Empire. Although Byron, Shelley and Thackeray are given their due, Minchin's admiration is particularly focussed upon such people as the Marquis of Wellesley, the Governor-General of India who was educated at both Harrow and Eton ('an ideal public-school boy') and Baden-Powell, hero of Mafeking.

---

[1] 'Stalky' (presumably derived from the verb 'to stalk') was USC slang for native cunning.

The book contains an appendix listing public-school men who were killed in the South Africa War. Like Warre, Minchin's one criticism is that not enough attention is paid to military training, in particular rifle practice: 'It is to be hoped that one result of our present war in South Africa will be the sweeping away of many cobwebs, notably of that schoolboy prejudice which does not regard rifle shooting as equally manly as cricket and rowing.' What the other 'cobwebs' are Minchin does not reveal, but they are not traditions: 'You might just as profitably argue with a physical law of nature as set up your puny individuality against the wisdom of your ancestors as expressed in the unwritten laws of your public school', he writes with approval. Accusations that scholarship is languishing are airily dismissed. Whilst the Clarendon Commissioners felt that character-building was a justification of the system, Minchin sounds a more sinister note: 'In times of strain and stress England can rely upon her public schools . . . We have also learnt, through our school, to love and (if need be) die for our country. Long before the British Public at large had been fired with a faith in the British Empire, one and indivisible, that was the faith in which every English public-school boy was reared.'

5 Being Prepared

In the wake of the Boer War and Edmond Warre's campaigning for some form of compulsory military training within the schools, military issues were frequently debated at school societies and reports published in school magazines. Debates ranged over general, philosophical subjects as well as particular issues such as conscription. The Salopians of 1910 seem fairly belligerent. In March the motion before the house was 'that in the opinion of this house Warfare is essential to the welfare of the human race', a motion which was carried by a substantial majority. The views of those supporting the motion suggest a generation spoiling for a fight and not overblessed with analytical intelligence: 'War was an important factor in advancing the cause of such a science as that of medicine . . . war killed off unnecessary numbers. War brought us engineering works such as roads . . . war was no more cruel than the surgeon's knife and, in addition, made men of us . . . it certainly brought virtue and was a distinct encouragement to hospitals.'

There is little evidence in such arguments that war was 'a call to the highest qualities', an assertion made by the Proposer. In 1911 the wording of the motion suggests a slight change of heart: 'The abolition of War is both impossible and unnecessary.' This was defeated, but by only two votes. In March 1914 the wording changed once more: 'In the opinion of this House mankind has at last learnt the wicked folly of war.' Salopians decided resoundingly and prophetically that this was not the case.

Once war had been declared, attitudes hardened further. At Westminster in December 1914 a motion that 'it will be disastrous to the world when Arbitration takes the place of War' was carried by 11 votes to 7. The Proposer felt that without war 'decadent nations would come to the front, and war was needed to abolish them . . . absence of warfare was incompatible with human nature.'

Such remarks suggest the influence of W.E. Henley:

> Sifting the nations,
> The slag from the metal,
> The waste and the weak
> From the fit and the strong. . .

However, public-school boys were not all Bulldog Drummonds and Richard Hannays in the making, and when it came to practical issues rather than windy theorising the boys' attitudes changed with circumstances, as can be seen in debates about conscription. In 1900 boys at Marlborough decided by 20 votes to 6 that the safety of the Empire was assured without the necessity of resorting to conscription. Ten years later, in the shadow of the growing German aggression frequently condemned in the press, the motion that 'conscription is necessary to the welfare of this country' was carried in the house by 'a considerable majority'. In the earlier debate one speaker asserted that, 'citizens who would gird on their fathers' swords, supposing they possessed such relics, and rush out to strike for home and country, would go for very little. They would be quite destitute of all military knowledge.' The OTC was instituted by the government precisely to ensure that this enthusiasm should be matched by competence.

It was fear of invasion by France which led to the founding of what must count as the first public-school volunteer force, at Rugby in 1804. Boys paraded with wooden broadswords ready to repel any Frenchman who might make his way to Warwickshire. However, it was the later threat posed by

Napoleon III which resulted in the Volunteer Movement both within the schools and elsewhere in the early 1860s. In May 1859 the Secretary of State for War announced that arms for volunteer forces would be supplied by the Government, but that the public would have to bear the cost of any other equipment. By the spring of 1860 the Movement was flourishing, with more than 100,000 recruits. Various schools have claimed to have had the first rifle corps, and the matter was finally cleared up by 'A Rossallian' in the *Times Educational Supplement* during the first months of the Great War. Rossall's Rifle Corps was founded on 1 February 1860. Eton, Harrow, Rugby, Marlborough and Winchester all started rifle corps later that year. Despite Rossall's pioneering, it was the Eton Volunteers who were the most celebrated of corps, their proximity to Windsor enabling them to be exhibited on numerous state occasions. Though not as grand as Dr Warre's force, other corps drilled and paraded assiduously and took part in inter-school shooting competitions.

This enthusiasm was eventually harnessed in Haldane's Army reforms of 1906 onwards, in which he set up England's Territorial reserve force. The OTC was divided into senior (university) and junior (school) branches, supported by the War Office and governed by a set of regulations first issued in 1908. By this time the majority of schools had founded OTCs, or adapted their Rifle Corps. Officially there was no compulsion to join the OTC, but quite how voluntary these organisations were in practice is open to doubt. The pressure to conform and evidence of coercion suggests that some of the recruits were less eager than their COs would have us believe. Figures suggest a keenness which is absent from reminiscences. At Harrow the Rifle Corps, 'went through parlous days, received a large accession of strength from the South Africa War fever, and survived in considerable vigour the reaction following an enthusiastic period,' according to one historian, writing in 1911. Just over one half of the school were members of the corps in 1909, some 38 per cent of whom attended the annual camp at which various schools forgathered for several days during the long summer holiday in order to drill, parade and take part in mock battles. In 1910 the number of recruits had risen by a mere four, but the number of those attending camp had risen by 10 per cent. The anonymous Old Etonian contributing to the same series of books entitled *Public School Life*[1] noted that, 'The Corps has increased tremendously in popularity and prestige in recent years. It is now taken very seriously by

[1] Published by the Sport & General Press Agency in four volumes (1910–1911): *Eton, Winchester, Rugby, Harrow.*

members of the Corps and by the War Office . . . great keenness is shown by all ranks, at the summer camp. In the Rugby volume we read that, although voluntary, the camp has 'for seven years attracted over 100 of the Corps.' This burst of enthusiasm is, one suspects, not unconnected with a printed cirular sent to the parents of pupils of all three schools (and of Winchester) by their headmasters in March 1909: 'It will be within your knowledge that the Government, in the formation of the Territorial Army, have laid down as a strict condition of efficient training that members of the Rifle Corps should attend a Camp annually for not less than eight days.' These camps, parents were told, were 'essential to the training of young officers, without whom our Territorial Army must prove a failure.' The warning note had been sounded and instructions followed: 'May we ask of you, then, to make such arrangements as you can that the boys may feel their attendance at the Camp is a real engagement demanded of them, not a mere school matter, but as a duty to their country?'

Summer Camps took place during the first week or so of the summer holidays and it must have taken considerable keenness to enrol for them when one's school-fellows were driving off to their homes. S.P.B. Mais thought that the Camp was the only part of the Corps that boys enjoyed before the War. Boys at Westminster clearly thought otherwise. As late as June 1914 a letter of complaint appeared in *The Elizabethan*:

> The number of names on the 'certain list' for Camp is at present only 65. The number in the Corps is over 170. These figures tell their own tale. A contingent that does not send more than half its strength to Camp cannot be considered efficient or in any way satisfactory. A small attendance at Camp gives the School a bad reputation among other Schools, to many of which Westminster considers herself superior, although they send a larger proportion of their Corps to Camp. It is, therefore, the duty of every able-bodied cadet to consider seriously whether he cannot give up a small part of the holidays to maintaining the honour of the School, even at some slight personal inconvenience.

Such moral blackmail proved effective and in the next issue of the magazine it is reported that, 'The number of those going to Camp has shown a very gratifying increase during the past few weeks'. An increase of over fifty per cent in fact.

Such measures were necessary for the simple fact that drilling was extremely boring and boys would much rather have spent their time playing sports. At Shrewsbury the corps was small and 'regarded as rather a joke'. Before Field Days were arranged the Captain of Boats had to be consulted, and no drilling could take place without the permission of the Sports Committee. Mais admits that at Sherborne the OTC was regarded as 'a bally sweat' and 'a piffling waste of time', a view endorsed by one of his pupils, Alec Waugh. The only keen person at 'Fernhurst' is the odious chaplain, Rogers, 'amazingly arrogant and conceited. In the pulpit and on the parade ground he was in his element.' For everyone else, 'everything connected with the corps was "a hell upon earth".'

The public-school code of conformity was clearly in operation at Marlborough where, according to the official history of the school's OTC, 'by 1913 almost every able-bodied boy had joined'. A 'Marlburian' writing in the boys' magazine *The Captain* in 1914 (before the outbreak of the War) admitted: 'Of course, a few fellows do not join. They are not exactly looked down upon, but they inevitably come in for a certain amount of chaff as mere civilians. On the other hand, no one in his senses would dare to make fun of the Corps, even in a friendly way. Even the worst grumblers would turn on him if he did so, and teach him the error of his ways.'[1]

This is a rather different picture to that painted by Beverley Nichols in his autobiographical novel *Prelude*, set at Marlborough just before and during the War. Nichols refers to pre-War Field Days as 'all very idyllic and charmingly civilian – no one ever dreamt that there would be a war except the Colonel, and "he only does it because otherwise no one would join his old Corps".' The little aesthetes of *Prelude* lounge around amidst the gorse reading Yeats to each other and use their bayonets to perform Ballets Russes dagger dances. Safely in Germany Charles Sorley felt free to send a Marlburian a verse which dared to mock the OTC as well as several other Marlborough institutions:

> And is there still a Folly called the Corps
> Allowed out twice a week and thinking then
> It's learning how to kill its fellow-men?

Perhaps it was a suspicion that the OTC was not being taken seriously that led to coercion and attempts to instil the warrior spirit into schoolboys. The

[1] The July 1914 issue of *The Captain* contained a story entitled 'The Prisoner of War' which concerned the conversion of a reluctant OTC recruit.

headmaster of the Beacon School, a preparatory school near Sevenoaks which numbered Siegfried Sassoon amongst its Old Boys, spent the summer vacation of 1910 with some French professors who had predicted that there would be a war in 1914. When he returned to school he sat down to write to the headmasters of all the leading public schools urging them to prepare their pupils for this eventuality. Archibald Fox, who contributed the Harrow volume to *Public School Life* in 1911, had warned that:

> Giant armies, the nearer approach by foreign powers to our own naval strength, the ever doubtful complexion of foreign politics, make it desirable that every able-bodied boy should take steps to ensure his having definite genuine personal help to offer when old enough, if danger threaten. It may well be that of all School recreative institutions the future is with the Corps.

Visiting politicians and generals spoke equally gravely of foreign aggression. At Speech Day 1909 Lord Rosebery had told the pupils of Wellington that 'the stress that patriotism will have to bear in days not far distant, and perhaps imminent will be greater than has yet been known in the history of this country. There are encroaching opinions which threaten patriotism, menace our love of country, and imply the relaxation, if not the destruction, of the bonds which hold our Empire together.' Field Marshal Lord Roberts, schoolboy hero and saviour of the Boer War, returned home convinced that there should be some form of conscription and that the lead should come from the top. He wrote to public-school headmasters inviting 'their co-operation in bringing the deficiencies of the Volunteer force before their pupils'. A Volunteer writing in *The Captain* in 1907 reported that: 'This stirring appeal, it is remarkable to relate, had little appreciable effect, notwithstanding the urgency and, in many cases, eloquence, with which it was placed before their charges by the various heads of schools and colleges.' Captain Herbert Jones was at a loss to account for this, but put it to a school-master acquaintance that most recruits of school Rifle Corps at this time were those not needed on the games field and who played soldiers merely in order to escape from the classroom for the occasional Field Day. When they left their schools, the mainspring of their military enthusiasm was removed and so they did not bother to join an adult Volunteer force. This accusation gave the teacher – and, it is implied, the reader – something to think about. Meanwhile Roberts followed up his unsuccessful appeal by appearing in person at various schools in order to drum up enthusiasm. In 1913 he assured members of the OTC who had assembled for a combined schools camp on Salisbury Plain that 'war would come soon'. This note was frequently sounded. Edmund Blunden remembered the OTC at Christ's Hospital being 'paraded on the playing fields and inspected by a real general, who perhaps made a speech at the conclusion and might utter a view which I confess seemed to me a gloomy, even horrible view: We were not just playing soldiers; we should be "wanted".' Indeed they would.

The Commanding Officer of the Eton OTC sent parents of boys who were leaving at the end of the summer half 1912 a letter urging them not to let his work with their sons go to waste. He explained the necessity of training soldiers, and the formation and function of the British Expeditionary Force and the Special Reserve, and reminded parents that 'no European army in time of Peace has its full complement of officers'. If war did break out '600 additional officers would be needed to make up the immediate deficiencies and 1200 more to meet the wastage of the first few weeks of the war.' This sinister 'wastage' would presumably be the result of severe fighting, for 'the military authorities anticipate that in any European war in which we are likely to be involved a decisive battle will be fought within the first few weeks'. There would be no time for the leisurely training of officers which the Boer War had afforded.

> There is no doubt that the Public Schools can supply the type of officer that is needed.[1] They have a great opportunity now, and if Old Etonians will set a bold example the consequences will, I am convinced, be far-reaching. If your son is not already destined for some other branch of the Service, I would ask you therefore to consider carefully the possibility of his joining some Special Reserve Battalion.

Mais, writing during the War, was concerned that people might imagine that the outcome of OTC keenness would be:

> a love of militarism, which is just what we are striving with so great a sacrifice and cost of men and money to eradicate from the world. But from what I have seen as an officer in the OTC my impression is that bloodshed and war are absolutely repugnant to the boy-mind; he is keen, keener than he ever was, to join the Army and to do his bit, but he is no lover of war for its own sake. It is one thing to be an ardent signaller and bugler, and quite

---

[1] The War Office agreed, as can be seen by the list of 2,000 'young gentlemen' from the public schools and universities who were to be offered immediate commissions if war was declared.

another to want to kill a fellow-creature; it is one thing to play a sort of hide-and-seek in the dark on a wintry night in a blizzard, but quite another to want to kill your antagonist if he falls into your hands.

A Public School in War Time (1916) is a depressing example of a critical intelligence addled by circumstances. The spuriousness of Mais's argument is all the more disgraceful because published during a war, not in anticipation of one. Militarism, it is stressed time and again in the War, is something to do with the Prussian strain in the German character, and wholly alien to the British way of life. Military training in England is a measure of defence, not an index of aggression. Compare, for example, Mais's assertion with the entirely false analogy produced by 'The Old Fag' in answer to a suggestion made by one of *The Captain*'s correspondents that, 'If boys have military training they will grow up with the idea that war is a glorious thing, that soldiering is the one thing to live for.'[1] Such a notion is pooh-poohed: 'If you are taught fire drill at school you don't believe that fires are a glorious occurrence, do you?' Well, no.

Such blinkered and self-deceiving attitudes resulted in an absurd dislocation between war and killing, the facts of war smeared over with such euphemisms as 'to do one's bit'. The final paragraph outlining the duties of a Platoon Commander in the War Office booklet *Instructions for the Training of Platoons for Offensive Action* effectively dispels Mais's comforting notions about playing soldiers: 'Being blood-thirsty, and for ever thinking how to kill the enemy, and helping his men to do so'. Mais contributes an intolerably jocular account of the fun and games to be had in 'Night Operations', apparently unaware that at the Front some of the most dangerous exercises were night-time wiring parties and bombing raids, exercises in which casualties were the rule rather than the exception. War results in death and in injuries; this particular War resulted in casualties of an appalling nature in appalling numbers. However much of a lark or a bore the Corps may have seemed to its participants there can be no doubt of its intention. The OTC was founded at a time when a war in the near future was considered a probability; the standard of training, in theory at least, was considered sufficiently high for boys to be offered commissions immediately when war was declared; the OTC was administered by the War Office, which published its regulations and set its exams. It may very well be, as Blunden suggested, that the OTC was 'an influence directing the world, in its limited way, out of the paths of peace'.

[1] A motion debated at Shrewsbury 'That modern weapons have destroyed the Romance of War' was defeated by five votes in October 1914.

[2]

A Noble Tradition?

THE WAR MEMORIAL at Nottingham High School is a statue of a young officer who is beckoning to his men as he leads an attack. Part of the inscription reads:

> In lasting and grateful memory of those former members of this School who, by the sacrifice of their lives for the cause of their Country in the Great War, 1914–1918, ennobled the traditions which they had here received.

In this section of the book I will be examining these traditions, their sources and their development during the decades before the War. The public-school ethos was like a complex piece of music, a symphony in which the various elements overlap, combine and reinforce one another. What I have attempted to do is to extract five themes for closer investigation. It will be seen that each section draws upon the others: for example, the cult of athletics reinforced the cult of the schools themselves, looked back to classical idealism and promoted hero-worship. The 'organic' development of this system of education, so often praised, led to a synthesis of seemingly disparate components, an ethos which shaped the attitudes of those within the system and those who experienced it vicariously in fiction, memoirs, articles and other propaganda.

By way of illustration I will be referring to fiction in much the same way as factual evidence. In doing so, I am aware that many of the novels bathe the schools in a warm glow of reminiscence rather than in the more direct light of critical enquiry. However, most of the writers attempted to create an authentic atmosphere and to ensure that details were correct, for reasons which will become clear in Chapter Three. That certain aspects of public-school life were suppressed is no surprise; to a greater or lesser degree the school novel was propagandist and self-congratulatory. If they do not reflect some of the less attractive characteristics of schoolboys, they at least reflect the codes by which it was intended that the pupils should abide. A habit of conformity, encouraged by the schools, led most boys to accepting the public-school ethos. It is significant that it was the clever boy, such as Arnold Lunn, Alec Waugh and Charles Sorley, who rebelled. That the attitudes of the majority of their peers were formed within the schools and persisted thereafter may be seen in the correspondence columns of almost any school magazine of the period. It will be clear where evidence adduced from fiction appears to be flagrantly at odds with verifiable fact.

1 The Best House of the Best School in England

As soon as the first schools took in boys who were not local, it became necessary to provide accommodation of some sort. Since the earliest schools were monastic in structure, the scholars tended to live in, ready to rise at odd hours in order to safeguard the soul of their founder. At Eton the scholars were housed in the College (hence 'Collegers'), whilst the other pupils were boarded out in the town (hence 'Oppidans', from the Latin *oppidum*). At Winchester boys who did not live in the school were called 'Commoners', originally 'Street Commoners' because they received their 'commons', or board and lodging, in the streets outside the college precincts. As the number of pupils increased it seemed sensible that they should be gathered together rather than left dotted around the attics of the local town. At Eton organised boarding houses run by 'Dames' had developed by the mid-seventeenth century. Gradually these local entrepreneurs were replaced by assistant masters who needed the extra money in order to eke out sometimes pitiful salaries which had been fixed by the statutes several centuries before and had never been increased.

Arnold had recognised that a system of boarding houses could not only improve the finances of his assistant teachers, but could also improve the moral tone of the school by keeping boys under the watchful eyes of the staff for longer than was customary. His belief that schoolmastering was a serious, full-time occupation was thus emphasised, for the masters were expected to look after the boys' moral as well as their intellectual welfare. Discipline was not part of their brief; this was maintained by Arnold himself, assisted by his current Sixth Form.

Throughout the nineteenth century the system of houses developed as schools were expanded or newly founded. Many of the abuses and much of the violence of the schools in the eighteenth century clearly had been the result of herding together far too many pupils into one space. With increasing numbers this unwise practice was rendered impractical. By breaking down the schools into smaller units, and by delegating authority, headmasters were able to maintain discipline far more easily. Thus, like games which also became invested with spiritual qualities, houses were initially developed as a means of control. Indeed, the two elements of houses and team sports reinforced each other as the century progressed. A healthy rivalry was promoted between houses which could be tested on the games fields.

Within twenty four hours of arriving at Rugby, Tom Brown finds himself playing what passes for football in the School house match. This chaotic brawl involves the whole school and takes place on an unmarked pitch, with the fifty or so School house boys pitted against all the other pupils. The boys play in their ordinary clothes (although the School house pupils wear distinguishing white trousers) and no referee is involved. Even in a game as apparently disorganised as this one, the sense of house loyalty is strong, enshrined in a speech made at a celebratory supper by the captain of games, 'Pater' Brooke. Brooke ascribes the house's success against overwhelming odds not to the skill of individual players, as might be expected, but to what came to be known as 'House Spirit': 'It's because we've more reliance on one another, more of a house feeling, more fellowship than the school can have. Each of us knows and can depend on his next hand man better – that's why we beat 'em today. We've union, they've division – there's the secret.' This speech, like the following dismissal of the Balliol Scholarship, is greeted with cheers. But Brooke goes on to develop his theory into a sermon about how such prowess can be maintained. Bullying is cowardice in disguise, he says, and excess drinking (the pupils were allowed a ration of beer) 'isn't fine or manly' and 'won't make good drop kicks or chargers' of the boys. Following this 'the Doctor' is praised. He had been accused of curbing the boys' traditional 'liberties', including beagling, but Brooke insists that Arnold has not 'meddle[d] with any one that's worth keeping'. He asks the house to support the headmaster who is, after all, 'a strong true man, and a wise one too, and a public school man too'. Arnold's health is drunk amidst predictable loud cheers. Brooke finishes his speech with a few words of farewell to the house he is to leave at the end of term:

> If I hadn't been proud of the house and you – aye, no one knows how proud – I shouldn't be blowing you up . . . But before I sit down I must give you a

toast to be drunk with three-times-three and all the honours. It's a toast which I hope every one of us, wherever he may go hereafter, will never fail to drink when he thinks of the brave bright days of his boyhood. It's a toast which should bind us all together, and to those who've gone before, and who'll come after us here. It is the dear old School-house – the best house of the best school in England!

Although this sort of scene became the staple of public-school fiction, it is doubtful whether Arnold himself, however much he might have applauded the sentiment, would have approved of the accompanying rowdiness. Brooke's speech demonstrates not only the emotionalism that house loyalty could exact, but also how the house system was already being used as a means of coercion in matters of discipline. An appeal is made directly to 'house feeling'. Not only are drinking and bullying *morally* bad, they also reflect badly on the house. This is a theme that was to become dominant as the century progressed. Hughes writes of this speech:

> The last few words hit the audience in their weakest place; they had not been altogether enthusiastic at several parts of old Brooke's speech; but 'the best house of the best school in England' was too much for them all, and carried even the sporting and drinking interests off their legs into rapturous applause, and (it is to be hoped) resolving to lead a new life and remember old Brooke's words.

Hughes admits that, of course, not all of them do. There would hardly be a story without evil to combat and overcome. Indeed, later that same evening Flashman is terrorising small boys by tossing them in a blanket. There are clear reasons why Flashman should not be doing this, but it is the sense that he is a disgrace to the house and is letting the side down that is uppermost. By neglecting an appeal to house spirit Flashman is set on a course followed by the majority of juvenile villains in public-school fiction.

Despite the manifest Christian intent of *Tom Brown's Schooldays*, and its fulsome praise of 'the Doctor', Hughes undermines the Arnoldian doctrine with his secular enthusiasm. Hughes's boys are pious enough (rather too pious for modern taste, in fact) but the individual conscience is in danger of being overwhelmed by a corporate ethos. The pupils may revere God, but their enthusiasm is seen in their devotion to the house and the school. Hughes clearly felt that one form of worship reinforced the other, but to Arnold they would have seemed in conflict. A Christian Gentleman's fealty should be to Christ and his civic dues should be paid to the City of God. Any divergence from these primary allegiances, however well-intentioned, was to be discouraged. Arnold's fears were justified, for his ideals were gradually subverted.

Just as the prefect system did not develop along lines envisaged by Arnold, so a similar process took place in the development of the house system. Housemasters at other schools tended to become figureheads and the welfare of the house – including the moral welfare – was left in the hands of the prefects. The pious deputies who had formed Arnold's ideal were replaced by boys who were given more and more responsibility and who became more and more powerful and rather less pious. By the end of the century the opinion of a housemaster was often sought only as a final resort. In E.F. Benson's *David Blaize* (1916), for example, the housemaster reluctantly intervenes only when prefectorial authority is challenged. This novel is set as a fictionalised Marlborough, and that Benson was not exaggerating can be seen from the manuscript minutes book of the prefects' meetings which is in the College's archives. This book demonstrates that the prefects virtually ran the school as far as discipline was concerned, particularly in 'matters of public conduct, and when necessary on matters concerning the *moral* conduct of the school'. The Head Boy's assertion, in 1906, that the prefects constituted 'a *body* with unlimited power if they choose to use it' is no delusion of grandeur. The prefects took it upon themselves to discipline boys who had been ragging a teacher, to act upon rumours of immorality and 'filthy talk', even to arrange for hymns to be sung with different tunes in the chapel. A new headmaster in 1913 was thought to represent a threat to their power, since he failed to realise that the prefects were more competent than housemasters to address the school on ragging. In a meeting held in September of that year 'the Master's attitude was condemned'. This unfortunate man was finally outflanked by the prefects and when he left in 1915: 'He said he was not going to tell them what he really felt as he would only make a fool of himself. They all knew how sorry he was to leave the place and to say good-bye to them. It was the perfect understanding and friendship between him and them that had made life worth living.'[1] The arrival of Cyril Norwood restored the balance of power somewhat, but the War resulted in staff shortages, with inexperienced, unwell or pathetically doddering teachers filling the places of those who had enlisted. More

---

[1] This entry is dated 1 April, and it occurred to me that it might be a joke. However, if this is the case, it is completely out of keeping with the rest of the book which displays a thoroughly humourless high-mindedness throughout.

responsibility was loaded onto the prefects, but calls were being made upon them as well, and not even their 'unlimited power' could prevent indiscipline from 'reach[ing] a climax' by the end of 1918.

It should perhaps be said that Marlborough had something of a reputation for indiscipline. It was one of the first schools to have a house system, introduced by G.E.L. Cotton and based upon Arnold's model at Rugby. This was a disciplinary necessity, since Cotton had been imported from Rugby to replace the Revd Matthew Wilkinson, whose reign at Marlborough had ended in a humiliating defeat at the hands of his pupils after a violent, week-long rebellion in 1851.

Cotton, who had taught at Rugby after Arnold's death, decided that the Sixth Form should maintain discipline, remaining answerable to him. He recruited staff from amongst his former pupils and these young men were expected to take an Arnoldian interest in their charges and an unArnoldian interest in games, which were henceforth organised and institutionalised. By these methods, Cotton regained control of the school so that when he handed over to G.G. Bradley, his chosen successor, Marlborough was emerging as a model Victorian public school. Bradley consolidated Cotton's gains, improving the house system and expanding the school facilities.

Although some of the schools founded during the Victorian period of expansion were built in towns or installed in already existing buildings, the ideal was a school which was purpose-built, preferably in parkland. Just as in a village, the centre of the community would be a chapel; there would be a hall for secular assemblies; the boarding houses would be separate mansions. The schools became more self-contained and the social structure became more rigid, conforming to a standard throughout the entire system. After 1850 uniforms began to appear and, as part of these uniforms, various sartorial accessories which acted as badges of rank. Relicts from the statute-books of the older foundations, previously regarded as hindrances, were now polished up and revered as traditions. Newer foundations either borrowed the traditions of older schools or simply confected their own. Old Boys' Societies provided continuity whilst memoirs and histories enshrined the most trivial of past glories and events.

Solidarity was also demonstrated in the emergence of the School Song, anthems which celebrated individual institutions and which were sung on communal occasions. After Tom Brown's first match the School-house boys sing patriotic songs such as 'The British Grenadiers' and complete their celebrations with 'Auld Lang Syne'. This may be because Rugby had no school song of its own. None is included in Gavin Ewart's anthology of school songs, *Forty Years On* (1969).[1] Other schools, however, are amply represented. The oldest of these songs are in Latin, the earliest example being late-eighteenth century and from a grammar school. The majority date from the period of expansion and consolidation, 1870–1900, and the overwhelming impression they give is of a celebration of caste, of loyalty to the school and to one's fellows both at school and beyond. The most celebrated of these songs was written by William Johnson Cory for his beloved Eton, and played to Lord Rosebery upon his deathbed. Sport, solidarity, nostalgia for the carefree days of youth and a sense of the beauty of the school's surroundings are all elements of this most skilful of school songs:

> Jolly boating weather,
>   And a hay-harvest breeze,
> Blade on the feather,
>   Shade off the trees;
> Swing, swing together,
>   With your bodies between your knees.
>
> Rugby may be more clever,
>   Harrow may make more row;
> But we'll row for ever,
>   Steady from stroke to bow;
> And nothing in life shall sever
>   The chain that is round us now.
>
> Others will fill our places,
>   Dressed in the old light blue;
> We'll recollect our races,
>   We'll to the flag be true;
> And youth will be still in our faces
>   When we cheer for an Eton crew.
>
> Twenty years hence this weather
>   May tempt us from office stools:

---

[1] Rugby might have had several songs had it not dismissed James Robertson, a master who went to Harrow, where he wrote songs in praise of his new employer, presumably in genuine gratitude.

We may be slow on the feather,
And seem to the boys old fools:
But we'll still swing together,
And swear by the best of Schools.

Although Eton provides the best and most famous example, no school can match Harrow for quantity. A large percentage of the fifty songs included in the *Harrow School Song Book* were written by E.E. Bowen, the man responsible for creating the school's Moderns Side. He wrote 'Forty Years On', a song calculated to reduce the singers to tears, as it does in *The Hill*, where even an Old Etonian Field-Marshal with a VC weeps upon hearing it. Like many of the Harrow Songs, its application is general rather than particular:

Forty years on, when afar and asunder
Parted are those who are singing to-day,
When you look back, and forgetfully wonder
What you were like in your work and your play.
Then it may be, there will often come o'er you,
Glimpses of notes like the catch of a song –
Visions of boyhood shall float them before you,
Echoes of dreamland shall bear them along.

However, the tenor of the majority of songs is that Our School is the Best School; Look to the Past, Look to the Future, and Rejoice. They were the hymns of the new religion, that secular faith which Thomas Arnold feared would usurp the throne of true Christianity. In Desmond Coke's *The Bending of a Twig*, written in 1906 partly to provide a truer picture of school life than had been seen in novels previously (and illustrated with photographs of Shrewsbury to that end), the hero has a final interview with his housemaster before leaving the school. The parting advice is as follows:

. . . both at Oxford and afterwards, remember how much Shrewsbury has done for you, and all you can do for her. I want your School – and, of course, your 'Varsity – to be a kind of minor religion with you, ranked by the side of patriotism. Make it a sort of bond, a free-masonry, between you and all who have been here. Always help Old Salopians, wherever, whoever, they may be, when you are able, and never let any one of them be your enemy.

By 1906 this ideal was for a large number of those educated in the system a reality, and the Old School had become a *major* religion.

2 *The Great Game*

Until the mid-nineteenth century, sport in England had been fraught with bouts of official disapproval. Far from being an index of proper behaviour, in the fourteenth century cricket was categorised as one of the *ludi inhonestes* and was proscribed by Edward III. Games were frequently criticised because they occupied time that would have been better spent in military training. By the second decade of the twentieth century it was military training, in the shape of the Officers' Training Corps, that was resented in schools, because it interfered with games. The Victorian philathletes would have been bewildered by the sixteenth-century *Anatomy of Abuses* in which Philip Stubbes suggested that football was unholy and promoted undesirable emotions. This view seems to have been shared by Shakespeare. In *King Lear* one of the insults heaped on Oswald by Kent is that he is a 'base football player', an accusation which suggests not only lowness of rank, but also baseness of character, as a later tirade makes clear.

The educative value of games (though not of football) was put forward as early as 1531 in Thomas Elyot's *Boke named the Governour*, but schools did not force sport upon their pupils. Indeed, the first cricket match between Winchester and Eton, at the end of the eighteenth century, was played in contravention of school rules. Later, games were sensibly regarded as a recreation for those who enjoyed them and they seem to have been played without supervision. Even in *Tom Brown's Schooldays* games are not compulsory. However, it was this book, published two years after Cotton left Rugby to institute games as a means of control at Marlborough, that fixed the idea of the moral value of sport in the public consciousness. Tom's school career is framed by two matches. During his final cricket match at Rugby Tom discusses the benefits to be derived from the game with Arthur and a master, and this conversation acts as a reprise of Pater Brooke's speech about football and 'house feeling' after Tom's first match at the school. The master, who is ignorant of the rules of cricket, nonetheless understands its moral value and describes it as a 'noble game':

[77]

'Isn't it? But it's more than a game. It's an institution,' said Tom.

'Yes,' said Arthur, 'the birthright of British boys old and young, as *habeas corpus* and trial by jury are of British men.'

'The discipline and reliance upon one another which it teaches is so valuable, I think,' went on the master, 'it ought to be such an unselfish game. It merges the individual in the eleven; he doesn't play that he may win, but that his side may . . . And then the Captain of the eleven! . . . what a post his is in our School-world! almost as hard as the Doctor's; requiring skill and gentleness and firmness, and I know not what other qualities.'

Many of us may share the master's vagueness about these qualities, but they became an essential part of public-school education during the nineteenth century.

It would, of course, be foolish to deny that the majority of boys actually enjoyed playing games. It is significant that the Harrow Philathletic Club was founded in 1853 by the boys rather than by zealous staff. The cult of athleticism was self-generating; athletic public-school boys flooded the universities and strove there to attain further athletic honours, which in turn made them desirable as teachers in schools with an athletic reputation to maintain. The consequence of this was a further decline in academic standards within the schools, as unworldly scholars devoted to the Classics were ousted by bone-headed rugby players who conducted classes of endless repetition, thereby further alienating pupils from the classroom. It is small wonder that boys gazed longingly out of classroom windows onto the hallowed turf of the games fields when the quality of teaching was so poor and uninspiring. A rugger blue had replaced the first-class degree as a qualification for a career as a public-school master.

Furthermore, once it had been decided that prefects should be recruited from the First XI or XV rather than from the Sixth Form, there was little to be gained from being what at Eton was known disparagingly as a 'sap'. In Shane Leslie's *The Oppidan*, the protagonist, Peter Darley, is a studious boy and his friendship with the athlete, Scotson, nearly founders because of this. When Peter proclaims, in a deliberate reversal of Pater Brooke's assertion, that he 'would rather get the Newcastle [scholarship] than make a century at Lord's', Leslie writes:

> Scotson looked at him for a moment as a Mohammedan looks at a Hindoo. A faint indefinable disgust as of caste swam into his consciousness.

Their friendship trembled in the sudden balance. As a successful runner and a growing favourite, he knew he had every right to despise and relinquish this queer boy, who was not above confessing such odious tastes on Windsor Bridge.

Leslie's vocabulary is telling: disgust, despise, queer, odious. However 'pity' overcomes Scotson and their friendship continues.

The Oppidan is set at the Eton of Edmond Warre, an Eton dominated by the philistine, philathletic and militaristic values of its headmaster. Although headmasters, unlike some members of their staff, were not recruited upon their athletic prowess, many of them were keen sportsmen or encouraged games because of their supposed educative value. For example, Warre's successor in 1905 was Edward Lyttelton, who came from a famous Eton sporting family and, according to one of the few friendly commentators on his headmastership, 'was no scholar; indeed his mind turned like a needle to the pole, to whatever was the reverse of scholarship'. His reign at Eton was highly controversial, plagued by open criticism in the press and ending in his eventual resignation amidst undisguised jubilation in some quarters. Although eccentric, he seems positively sane compared with some of the philathletic headmasters. Oddest of the lot was H.H. Almond, a brilliant Scot whose own academic achievements had been gained, he felt, at the expense of his physical well-being. When he was appointed to Loretto in 1862 he brought to it a love of the Great Outdoors he had acquired at Oxford. Like Arnold, he set down in order his educational priorities: 'First – Character. Second – Physique. Third – Intelligence. Fourth – Manners. Fifth – Information.' In order to promote such things he made a 'scientific' study of health. One of the few benefits of this was an improvement in the school diet, something long overdue in all public schools. Alongside this, however, was the introduction of an absurd uniform, dubbed in the face of the obvious 'rational clothing'. A famous photograph taken in 1901 depicts Almond and his then headboy arm-in-arm on a doorstep in preposterous garb. It looks like a snapshot from Edward Carpenter's family album, and although Almond would have loathed Carpenter (whose influence at the progressive school, Abbotsholme, upon another eccentric headmaster, Cecil Reddie, was striking), there are certain cranky similarities between the two men. Almond's continual disparagement of the 'languid, lisping babbler about art and culture' (all too typical of the Victorian pedagogue) was such that when he died in harness in 1903, his successor's first task was to perform a rescue operation upon the school's academic standards.

[79]

It may be imagined that once games had been sanctified by the schools the enthusiasm of the pupils would be correspondingly dampened. This was not the case; it seems that by and large the appropriation of the games field by the authorities was welcomed. Some, it is true, resented the consequent curbing of other hobbies (chiefly confined to the devastation of local wildlife), and felt that traditional 'liberties' should be retained, but once organised, and once masters had become involved, games grew in importance and popularity. It was a short step to make them compulsory. Whatever Arnold's own feelings about sport, his successors realised that the less free time their pupils had, the less mischief they could pursue. The moral fervour of this new breed of headmasters led them to suppose that the Devil would find work for idle hands. More specifically they were concerned that boys' idle hands should be kept off each other. More and more of the boys' time was overseen by masters, although even this did not entirely eradicate 'vice' from the schools. It was further believed that running around after balls would release high spirits which might otherwise be directed towards rebellion or sex. Even so, some headmasters felt it necessary to take further precautions and the football players of Clifton were obliged to keep their provocative bare knees covered by breeches.

It is difficult to determine exactly when games became invested with spiritual qualities, but the influence of Muscular Christians such as Thomas Hughes clearly played a major part in the process which escalated throughout the century and reached a crescendo as the First World War provided the muddiest games pitch in history. The error was compounded by headmasters and soon became part of the fabric of school society. Quite apart from enjoying games, boys also admired their fellows who showed skill in sports, so that athletes began to be seen as heroes who upheld the honour of house and school. It became obvious that such boys would make natural leaders and soon prowess at cricket, rugger and rowing began to be rewarded with prefectship. Arnold's ideal of saintly, scholastic leaders remained just that, and was not widely imitated. Few boys respected a 'sap'; how much easier to have a ruling body composed of those already respected, whose authority would need little reinforcement from a headmaster. Once headmasters had decided to make their sportsmen community leaders they began to believe that this was not simply a matter of expediency – an almost democratic gesture of electing those most admired – but that there was a sound theory behind it. Prefects were awarded certain privileges in order to sweeten their duties, and discipline, especially that enforced by canings, became their province almost entirely.

A wholly spurious alliance was forged between physical and moral courage which led to an even less tenable proposition that moral worth was a concomitant of athletic prowess. That this was not the case may be judged from the emergence of one of the least admirable of public-school types: the blood. The swaggering, vain, imperious young athletes who held sway in the schools, strutting about in variegated waistcoats, mistreating their fags, caning indiscriminately, a law unto themselves, were monsters of the schools' own creating. They should not be confused with unlicensed bullies such as Flashman, but often there is very little to distinguish the behaviour of the two types. To outsiders they often seemed, and seem today, insufferable, but within the schools they commanded a sort of awed reverence, composed partly of admiration for schoolboy bravado and partly of fear. In Arnold Lunn's *The Harrovians*, which delivers a sacrilegious attack upon athleticism, even masters show deference to the bloods and seem delighted to be patronised by them. 'What is a Master compared with a Blood?' C.S. Lewis asked, recalling his time at Malvern College. Both Lewis and Alec Waugh claim that the bloods were quite open about their liaisons with younger boys. A boy in *The Loom of Youth*, expelled because his relationship with a junior had been discovered by the headmaster, rails bitterly at the values of his school:

> Fernhurst made me worship games, and think that they alone mattered, and everything else could go to the deuce. I heard men say about bloods whose lives were an open scandal, 'Oh, it's all right, they can play football.' I thought it was all right too. Fernhurst made me think it was. And now Fernhurst, that has made me what I am, turns round and says, 'You are not fit to be a member of this great school!' and I have to go.

Another reason why the educative value of games was stressed was that it became necessary to justify the inordinate amount of time and money that was soon being spent upon athletics in establishments which were supposed to be devoted to learning. Vast amounts of money were invested in purchasing land so that fields could be lovingly transformed into games pitches. Headmasters, their assistants, parents and Old Boys all dug deep to buy up huge tracts of land and build elaborate sports pavilions and gymnasiums. Uppingham under Thring, for example, underwent massive expansion, thus reflecting the headmaster's imperialist interests. This expenditure could only be justified if even more time was devoted to athletics, and so a spiral was created.

Games were taken seriously not only by the schools, but also by the public, with public-school matches reported in the press in the same depth as international fixtures. The classic public-school sporting event was the Eton *v.*

Harrow cricket match, held every July at Lord's and in its time as much a part of the social calendar as the Ascot Races and the Henley Regatta. Vachell's portrayal of such a match at the turn of the century is traditionally sentimental, emphasising the social importance of the match. The coaches of the aristocracy are lined up, overflowing with opulent late-Victorian hospitality, whilst the ground is packed to bursting point with 'the youth, the beauty, the rank and fashion of the kingdom'. The match is described by one character (with Vachell's unblushing approval) as 'England at its best', where the 'mighty prelate and humble country parson' can meet on equal terms as Old Harrovians, where a 'great Minister' can forget the 'troublous' affairs of state ('A war-cloud, as large as Kruger's hand, has just risen in the South, and is spreading itself over the whole world'), only to be reminded when Eton is batting too well: 'The Minister is frowning; things may look black in South Africa, but they're looking blacker in St John's Wood.'

Whilst *The Times* and other newspapers took note of major matches between public schools, the boys' magazines found in sport a rich and constant source of fiction, articles and comment. The first issue of the *Boys' Own Paper* (18 January 1879) included the story 'My First Football Match'. The 'Old Boy' credited with authorship was Talbot Baines Reed, later to become one of the most popular exponents of the full-length school story. This tale of football at 'Parkhurst' (not to be confused with H.M. Prison) was followed by other sporting stories set at this imaginary school. Such was the authenticity of Reed's narrative that a games captain at a real public school wrote in to the magazine, challenging 'Parkhurst' to a number of sporting fixtures. The *BOP* and its numerous imitators filled their columns with profiles of school teams (with photographs), articles by eminent sportsmen ('How I Swam the Channel' by Captain Webb), features explaining the rules of assorted sports, articles showing boys how to improve their game contributed by distinguished coaches (W.G. Grace amongst them), and stirring tales in which manliness and good sportsmanship were vigorously promoted. 'The Honour of a Boy: A Football Story' (*The Champion*, 1914) is a characteristic title.

The moral values attributed to the games-field gave rise to such notions as 'the Great Game, the Game of Life'. This idea is at its most preposterously explicit in *Baxter's Second Innings* (1892), a curious allegory in which 'life is simply a cricket match – with Temptation as the Bowler'. If this little-remembered book seems arcane, many of the ideas it embodied were commonplace. The legacy of the games cult is still with us, for people still talk jocularly of 'playing the game' and criticise behaviour as being 'not cricket' in contexts far removed from the world of sport. The British still pride themselves upon their amateurism in both games and business, that clinging to gentlemanly values, often in the face of massive defeat. Other countries continue to be expected to cheat or behave badly if losing. The notorious 'bodyline' series of test matches in the 1930s was considered outrageous because the bowling tactics involved (quite literally 'not cricket') were instigated not by foreigners, which would have been expected, but by the English captain, Douglas Jardine.[1]

Just how valuable games were as training for moral leadership is open to doubt. It could be (and was) argued that a communal activity which relies upon co-operation between team members and, in matches, a sense of rivalry and concomitant loyalty to the team, could be extended to a wider context. Rugby, for example, relies upon a certain selflessness: passing the ball to the person who stands the best chance of scoring a try and thus sacrificing personal glory for the greater glory of the team. The rivalry between teams chosen from different houses led to a loyalty to that division within a school. Loyalty to house could be extended to loyalty to the whole school in inter-school matches and this could be seen as a sort of patriotism in miniature. There was also a sense that people would abide by a set of rules which made the game fair, won by quality alone. The game would be played not for financial gain (professionalism of any sort being anathema) but for glory; the winning of the game would be its own reward, though perhaps accompanied by the presentation of some hideous trophy or battered shield. Team captains would acquire the skills of leadership, enabling them to make quick decisions, organise and inspire a group, and plan and execute complicated strategies. Furthermore — as the recent debate in medical journals concerning serious injuries sustained by schoolboys during games of rugger demonstrates — courage would be required as well as skill. Such qualities would, of course, be particularly useful in the event of war.

It could equally be argued, from the same set of facts, that this was nonsense. Some critics at the time felt that fanatical devotion to house and school was too narrow a 'patriotism', one that detracted from devotion to the country. It is also clear that whilst a captain of games might command respect in the small community of a school in which everyone knew and admired him, there is no reason to suppose that he could maintain that respect amongst strangers.

---

[1] As a schoolboy at Winchester, Jardine had once been seen to have played within the rules but 'unsportingly' during a match against Eton. The child was indeed father of the man.

[83]

Furthermore, the worship of the athlete often worked against the ideal of team spirit. Boys did indeed strive for individual glory, a glory rewarded with caps, colours, flannels, and their accompanying privileges.

The suggestion, which became common after 1900, that the games-field was valuable training for military leadership is even less tenable. The only thing that games promoted which was of the slightest use for military training was physical fitness. Strategy and the ability to take quick decisions during a game of football or cricket is a very different matter to planning military actions and making snap decisions that involve other people's lives. Apart from anything else, junior officers in the Great War rarely planned anything. They received their orders from above and frequently carried them out with as little idea as their men of what such manoeuvres were supposed to achieve. The discipline of a games-field is very different to that of a battlefield. Quite apart from the disruptive elements of fear and death, men needed to be self-reliant. The Germans were instructed to pick off the officers in any advance because it was known that once the leadership had been removed, the men (the majority of whom, unlike the German troops, were not professional soldiers) would be running around in confusion, unsure of what they were supposed to be doing. Amidst all this instinct rather than reason was liable to take over. Furthermore, there was little point in going to war just for the sake of taking part. Wars are fought to win; without this goal they lose their point altogether. Finally, the fact that war was not a game may be judged from the fact that rain did not stop play.

Nonetheless, the pre-eminence of games was only toppled in 1914, when the outbreak of war meant that hours previously spent on the games-field were now spent on the drill-square. Even after this, games were still felt to be of incalculable value not only as preparation for what was fatuously referred to as 'the Greatest Game of All', but also as a means of propaganda and recruiting.

3 Youth, Death and the Classics

The Classics have been at once the backbone and the bugbear of the public-school system from its earliest days. The intention of the first foundations was to educate a clerical class, a class which would transact the nation's business in Latin. The original schools taught Latin Grammar, in which the language was spoken; Rhetoric, which consisted of written work in Latin and acquiring the ability to argue cases persuasively in documents and letters; and Dialectic, which was a training in formal logic with its basis in Aristotle via Boethius. With the Renaissance the utilitarian value of Classics was weakened as English began to be accepted as a suitable language for writing as well as speaking. However, the broadening interest in the intellect meant that the Classics began to be studied as literature rather than merely grammar. Greek, which had hitherto lagged behind, was not taught alongside Latin since the literature of Greece was considered rather more edifying than that of Rome. Although other subjects were introduced sporadically, the Classics remained the foundation of an education for centuries. Interest in the Classics was boosted by advances in archaeological research which was unearthing evidence of the lost cultures studied in the classroom. Poetry and prose in the eighteenth century were based upon classical models, as were sculpture and architecture. A knowledge of Latin and Greek had become the mark of a cultured man. By this time such schools as Eton and Harrow had become enclaves for the upper and the wealthier middle classes for whom the Classics served no other purpose than that of a status symbol. The lower middle classes no longer required Latin to become clerks and so started going to schools which offered a broader curriculum. Just as the higher echelons of society had appropriated the schools from those they were founded to benefit, so they appropriated the Classics. Both the schools and the Latin and Greek taught in them had ceased to serve any useful educational function. Boys went to school in order to while away the period between childhood and maturity, and their boredom is reflected in the unruliness of public school life during this period. The Classics were learned by rote, frequently beaten into unwilling pupils.

Reforming headmasters of the nineteenth century, such as Arnold of Rugby and Butler of Shrewsbury, improved scholastic standards, but not the popularity of the subjects taught. One of the aspects of the schools investigated by the Clarendon Commission was the emphasis placed upon the Classics. Was it misguided? Clarendon himself thought that it was because it placed 'the upper classes in a state of inferiority to the middle and lower' (an observation which tells us much about the aims of the Commission). Whatever the emphasis placed upon Classical learning, attainments in this field were pitiful, and could not, reported the Commissioners, 'by any stretch of indulgence be deemed satisfactory'. Since the indulgence of the Commissioners was notably elastic, we may take it that standards were very low indeed. Even so, it was thought that the curricula of the schools should be enlarged without sacrificing the central position of the Classics 'because they were considered the best

[85]

mental training, and because they had moulded the English race politically'. What evidence there was for these assertions is unclear, and it may be thought that any race which was mentally trained and politically moulded by the witless repetition of Greek and Latin, indifferently taught and scarcely absorbed, ought to be concerned. But complacency ruled the day and and in this the Commissioners merely reflected their time and class. Consequently well over fifty per cent of classroom hours remained devoted to the Classics and divinity. In 1905 a corresponding percentage of masters at Eton were Classics teachers. Since the vast majority of public school headmasters were themselves Classicists (92 of the 114 listed in 1914), it was unlikely that the reform from within desired by the Commissioners would involve cuts in the teaching of Latin and Greek.

The controversy about the public-schools' curricula, prompted by the findings of the Clarendon Commission, continued down the century. Those who believed in England's industrial future demanded a more practical education with an emphasis upon modern subjects such as science, mathematics and modern languages. Occasionally concessions were made to critics whose hearts were clearly in the right places. E.E. Bowen, whose devotion to Harrow was evident from the innumerable songs he wrote in praise of the school, felt that the Classics taught there were wellnigh useless. He was allowed to start a Moderns side in 1869 by the extremely traditional headmaster, Montagu Butler, and within ten years it had been accepted on the same footing as the Classics side. Elsewhere modern subjects were introduced on top of the Classics with the result that boys became overburdened with work and learned even less than they had before. The division into 'sides' was an attempt to sort this out, but, as we have seen, not everywhere had the success of Harrow and boys frequently languished, as bored in Modern and Army as they had been in Classics. There was a conservative distrust of anything modern, including classroom subjects. Had not the schools grown to their pre-eminence by an adherence to old traditions and methods? Furthermore the schools were still in the business of educating gentlemen. Of what use were science, mathematics and the languages of England's enemies to a gentleman? Specialisation smacked of professionalism, a concept wholly alien to the schools.

At Eton, always the extreme model of attitudes prevailing elsewhere, masters who did not teach Classics were considered socially inferior and for a long time were not entrusted with houses. In *The Oppidan* Morley's is a bad house precisely because Mr Morley teaches mathematics. Even a teacher of French, provided he was himself English, was more acceptable than a mathematics tutor. Two masters discussing the unfortunate Morley claim that he has no authority:

'Mathematical masters don't seem to be able to keep better order in their Houses than, than –' 'Than a French master!' Mr Robertson [who teaches French] finished his sentence with a laugh. 'No, no, old fellow,' said Classics, 'you are a Briton, and one of us. I mean our French colleagues. They never could keep discipline since Crecy.'

At 'Fernhurst' even an English-born French master, an Oxford Blue with a Double First to his credit, is unable to keep order in the classroom, which is 'considered a sort of YMCA entertainment hall, where there was singing and dancing, and a mild check on excessive rioting'. The French option is 'filled with the most arrant collection of frauds that have ever sat together this side of the Inferno.'

Imperialists were divided between the mystical and the practical. The former believed that the Classics, by way of example, contributed to Imperialist sentiment, patriotism, honour and the like. Had not Lord Kitchener of Khartoum once claimed that Latin prose had taught him more than anything else? The latter group thought that by fixing their eyes upon the past and studying dead cultures and languages the public schools were failing to train men for the competitive commercial world in which expansionism played so prominent a part. Despite the stridency of the progressives, it was the idealists who usually prevailed.

Much was made by those defending the Classics of the ideals found in ancient literature. It was, of course, necessary to filter these ideals, some of which were not altogether suitable as models for the public-school boy. 'Homer metamorphosed into a Pre-Raphaelite poet, Plato seen as a great headmaster, Greek homosexuality merged into heroic comradeship', as Anthony Powell recalled of Eton in 1919. A flavour of this at a lower level is given in *David Blaize*, in which the headmaster is reported to have been giving lectures on Greek life and literature to members of the Sixth Form, who learn that 'Socrates was jolly to young fellows, and told them heavenly stories about the gods'.

Victorian and Edwardian schoolboys seem to have spent a considerable time writing Greek epigrams for their teachers or for prizes and publication in the school magazine. The elegiac couplet was suitable for imitation because it was used by the Greeks to celebrate many occasions and was 'equally suited to the epitaph of a hero or the verses accompanying a birthday present, a light jest

[87]

or a profound moral idea, the sigh of a lover or the lament over a perished empire.' Whilst for the majority of boys the composing (and indeed the construing) of Greek epigrams was a tiresome, empty exercise, usually hammered out with the aid of a crib, for the clever boy it became a graceful accomplishment, rather like his sister playing a piano sonata.[1] If boys were lucky enough to have a gifted or enthusiastic teacher their Classics classes were not entirely dull. Ronald Knox was a temporary and unorthodox teacher at Shrewsbury where he allowed the dullards to pursue their own devices at the back of the classroom whilst he livened up the lesson for clever boys with exercises of his own devising which involved countless strips of paper and coloured inks, and which were reproduced on a 'jellygraph' (a primitive duplicating device). *The Salopian* is studded with verses and jests in Latin and Greek contributed by this eccentric (and unsalaried) master. The verses of an earlier Classics master, William Johnson Cory of Eton, were praised as 'the best and most Horatian Sapphics and Alcaics . . . that have been written since Horace ceased to write'. Testimonies to his gifts as a teacher are numerous and although he was dismissed in 1872, his influence remained strong in the school.

Another influence, according to Cyril Connolly, who came to Eton just after the Great War, was J.W. Mackail's *Greek Anthology*, first published in 1890, and revised with a substantial Introduction in 1906. It became the standard selection from the *Palatine Anthology* and was described by Connolly as 'one of the sacred books of the inner culture' at Eton. The anthology:

> exhaled pessimism and despair, an over-ripe perfection in which it was always the late afternoon or the last stormy sunset of the ancient world, in which the authentic gloom of Palladas was outdone by that attributed to Simonides, Callimachus, or Plato . . . I knew all the sceptical epigrams by

---

[1] One of the first requirements for a boy returning to 'Fernhurst' for a new term, along with health certificates and tips for the porter, was a visit to the second-hand bookshop, 'out of bounds during term-time', to find 'an English version of Virgil and Xenophon'. According to L.S. Jones, Classics masters at Eton may have been socially superior to their colleagues but their teaching 'left me and most of my contemporaries unable to construe an inscription on a memorial tablet, let alone read with enjoyment an Ode of Horace or a Greek epigram. It was all right for the clever Collegers, the Selwyns and Macmillans, a Ronald Knox or a Patrick Shaw-Stewart. These were born scholars, with the enviable gift of seeing and apprehending whole sentences at a glance, not, as we did, single words, lonely and adrift, or rubbing shoulders with other unrelated waifs. Should not the use of cribs, so far from being a penal offence, have been made compulsory? Is it not more sensible to read Virgil knowing what he means than not knowing what he means?'

heart and most of those about love and death and the fate of youth and beauty.

The book's title-page bore a Pre-Raphaelite woodcut of a robed woman picking flowers in a wood. Mackail's own Pre-Raphaelite credentials included his father-in-law, Sir Edward Burne-Jones, who executed several commissions for public schools, mostly of a religious or chivalric nature (notably the panels in Marlborough's chapel and a tapestry in the chapel at Eton).

Mackail was faced with certain problems of editorship when he undertook his anthology. There were a large number of epigrams wholly unsuitable for publication, particularly those by Meleager and Strato in which the paederasty was rather too frank for a Victorian and Edwardian audience:

> Closely connected with the passion of love as conceived by Greek writers is a subject which continually meets us in Greek literature, and which fills so large a part of the Anthology that it can hardly be passed over without notice.

This warning note sounds very similar to those oblique and distressed sermons delivered by headmasters who had been alerted to outbreaks of 'immorality' amongst their pupils. Mackail continues:

> The few epigrams selected from the Anthology of Strato and included in this collection under the heading of Beauty are not of course a representative selection. Of the great mass of these epigrams no selection is possible or desirable. They belong to that side of Greek life which is akin to the Oriental World,[1] and remote and even revolting to the western mind. On this subject the common moral sense of civilised mankind has pronounced a judgement which requires no justification as it allows of no appeal.

One imagines that even the dullest boy might be inspired by this awful warning to scurry off, armed with a lexicon, to look up Strato in the index of the *Palatine Anthology*.

Whilst many teachers defended the Classics as noble and inspiring, others shared Mackail's concern about the example of Ancient Greece and Rome. F.W. Farrar, who took time off from writing his ludicrous fiction to collect

---

[1] cf. Desmond Coke's use of this term to describe morals at Shrewsbury pp 112.

and edit *Essays on Liberal Education* (1867), declared that parts of Classical literature were unwholesome fare for schoolboys. At the opening ceremony of Cheltenham College in July 1841, the Vice-President of the founding body thought it necessary to emphasise the Christian base of the school's curriculum in view of its Classical bias:

> Every pious parent must feel that there is great peril in putting into the hands of youth the abominable mythology of the ancients, tending as it did to warp their understandings, and destroy their better feelings. It is painful to think that a classical education could not be acquired without the use of such works; but how can this baleful tendency be so effectually neutralised as by a constant and pious inculcation of Christian truths?

The effective neutralisation of the Classics by the constant application of Christian principles (rather like spraying the roses for greenfly) was not as simple as the rector of Cheltenham imagined. In his patient explanation of Classical aberrations Mackail gets into considerable difficulties. The personification of love in the form of a winged boy, Eros, although alien to a modern audience is sanctified by tradition, he states. Tradition, as we have seen is a cornerstone of the public-school system, dragged out at every opportunity to justify absurd rules and customs and to preserve the *status quo*. Mackail explains that in Greece there was:

> a feeling, half conventional, and yet none the less of vital importance to thought and conduct, which elevated the mere physical charm of boyhood into an object of almost divine worship. Beauty was a special gift of the gods, perhaps the choicest one, and not only so, but it was a passport to their favour. Common life in the open air, and above all the importance of the gymnasia, developed great perfection of bodily form and kept it continually before all men's eyes. Art lavished all it knew on the reproduction of the forms of youthful beauty. Apart from the real feeling, the worship of this beauty became an overpowering fashion. To all this there must be added a fact of no less importance in historical Greece, the seclusion of women. Not that this ever existed in the Oriental sense; but . . . the share which women had in the public and external life of the city, at a time when the city meant so much, was comparatively slight.

It can not have escaped all Mackail's readers that this description of Greek life, with its celebration of boyhood, its worship of the athlete, and the exclusion of women, bore very close similarities with the public schools of the period.

The elevation of boyhood's charms 'into an object of almost divine worship' is also symptomatic of the Edwardian period. Perhaps the surfeit of publicity for the gilded youth of the public schools was responsible for this. Books, newspapers and magazines all extolled these young gods,[1] leaving one with the impression that for the Edwardians beauty was youth, youth beauty. The Victorians sentimentalised all children, but more particularly little girls, whom they also debauched casually in brothels run for this purpose. A similarly dark side to the glittering coin of youth is to be found in the Edwardian era, in which boys and young men were worshipped, but also sent off to die on battlefields. Two writers who celebrated children exemplify this shift of interest. Lewis Carroll once confessed: 'I like all children – except boys', a preference evident from his photographic studies of little girls. This oversight was more than made up for by J.M. Barrie, also a keen photographer, who took many photographs of small boys, notably the Llewelyn Davies brothers, whom he befriended and later adopted. Just as Carroll created the archetypal Victorian Dream Child, so Barrie created the archetypal Edwardian 'Boy Who Wouldn't Grow Up'. Barrie's *Peter Pan*, first performed in 1904 and part of the theatrical calendar thereafter, isolates a tendency in the Edwardian view of childhood, a view reflected in much of the literature of the period.[2] The cult of the public school

---

[1] J.E.C. Welldon, headmaster of Harrow from 1885 to 1899 and Bishop of Calcutta thereafter, was able to write unblushingly that, 'No being, perchance, is so distinct, none so beautiful or attractive, as a noble English boy.'

[2] Both *Peter Pan* and Barrie's prose version of the story, *Peter and Wendy* (1911) are examples of popular works which are a repository of the public school ethos, albeit ironic ones. Barrie's attitude to public schools was equivocal, to say the least: 'I never feel myself a foreigner in England except when trying to understand them. I have a great affection for one at least of them, but they will bewilder me to the end', he said. That one was Eton where four of the Llewelyn Davies boys were sent. References to the school gradually crept into his yearly revisions of the play, including Captain Hook's famous cry as he leaps to his crocodilian doom: '*Floreat Etona!*' In *Peter and Wendy* we learn that Hook has been better educated than his pirate crew, for 'he had been at a famous public school; and its traditions still clung to him like garments, with which indeed they are largely concerned . . . he still adhered in his walk to the school's distinguished slouch. But above all he retained the passion for good form'. And indeed for Eton slang, such as 'Pop' and 'scugs'. Good form also obsesses the Darlings. John and Michael are almost tempted to become pirates until they discover that this would involve crying 'Down with King George'. Wendy's speech to the Lost Boys as they are about to walk the plank is grimly prophetic: 'These are my last words. Dear boys, I feel that I have a message for you from your real mothers, and it is this, "We hope our sons will die like English gentlemen".' (Compare this with Billy Grenfell's last speech to his platoon in 1915 as they were about to go over the top: 'Remember you are Englishmen. Do nothing to dishonour that name.')

reached its zenith between 1900 and 1914, an orgy of celebration to which the Great War provided an ironic climax. So glorious was the youthful life that there seemed a feeling that, like the mythic summer of 1914, it could not, perhaps *should* not, last. A member of the Souls writing about the young Etonian Julian Grenfell, expressed this view: 'I used to think of that Greek epigram of the boy who was so beautiful he died'. Mackail's *Anthology* provides several instances of such sentiments, though it was probably the anonymous epitaph on Cleotes that was being recalled: 'Looking on the monument of a dead boy, Cleotes son of Menesaechmus, pity him who was so beautiful and died.' The Souls, a group of lugubrious, narcissistic and highly influential aristocrats, spent much time descanting on the beauty of death. Any decease in their circle was greeted with a chorus of rapturous keening, and even as public a death as that of Queen Victoria provided an opportunity for the exchange of quotations about 'the beauty and blessedness of death'. Death-beds were rushed to as eagerly as balls; gazing upon expiring members of the circle reassured the survivors of the beauty and radiance of death. The children of these people were the generation that was destroyed by the Great War, a cataclysm which provided further opportunities for choruses of transcendental grief.

Contemplating the post-war generation of privileged Etonians, Cyril Connolly posited his 'Theory of Permanent Adolescence': 'It is the theory that the experiences undergone by boys at the great public schools, their glories and disappointments, are so intense as to dominate their lives and to arrest their development.' This was equally true of the pre-war generation, an attitude encouraged by the interest in and approval of the activities and ideals of these schoolboys. Echoes of it are to be heard in letters, articles, memoirs, novels and stories of the period. Saki's 'Unbearable' Comus Bassington, for example, in a novel which is a prophetic (1912) anthem for doomed youth, is described by his housemaster as one of those young men 'who are Nature's highly finished product when they are in the schoolboy stage'. This description, incidentally, (and Bassington's distinctively pagan forename and nature) shows how far we have come since Dr Arnold's attempts at curtailing childhood and rushing his charges as quickly as possible to maturity. The schools had become so popular and so revered that it was generally felt that the golden afternoons of boyhood should be prolonged as much as possible. Rupert Brooke bitterly regretted the end of his schooldays:

> I had been happier at Rugby than I can find words to say. As I looked back at those five years I seemed to see almost every hour as golden and radiant,

and always increasing in beauty as I grew more conscious; and I could not and cannot hope for or even imagine such happiness elsewhere.

This sort of dwelling upon the glories of school was so commonplace that one sometimes feels that death was regarded as the only possible climax to such a 'career'.[1] For if these golden lads lived on, what would they find apart from disillusion? Brooke's life after Rugby was neurotic and aimless, clouded by disastrous love affairs and characterised by attempts at escape. His sojourn in the South Sea islands, for example, lived up to his storybook expectations (more H. de Vere Stacpoole than Gauguin) but was marred by the suspicion, as he confessed to Eddie Marsh, that 'I am just too old for Romance' (twenty-six). The outbreak of war one year later brought him a happiness similar to that which he had experienced at Rugby, a sense of purpose and, curiously, freedom. Brooke, needless to say, adored *Peter Pan*, and wandered around Cambridge quoting it to himself and imagining King's Chapel vanishing to be replaced by the tree-house which Wendy continues to visit until her burgeoning adulthood prevents her from flying.

Whilst Barrie's suggestion that 'Nothing that happens after we are twelve matters very much' would have seemed a little extreme – thirteen, after all, was the age when most boys embarked upon the great experience of their lives by entering a public school – Saki's observation that 'To have reached thirty is to have failed in life' is symptomatic of prevailing notions. Barrie, who gained inspiration for his play from the death of his thirteen-year-old brother (his mother found consolation in the idea that her dead son would remain a boy forever), was later to modify his view in a letter to Arthur Quiller-Couch, whose son was about to leave his public school:

To think he is leaving Winchester instead of putting on his pinafore. Tomorrow he will be leaving Oxford. *An English boy has almost too good a time*.[2] Who would grudge it him, and yet he knows too well that the best is past by the time he is three-and-twenty.

Closely related to Barrie's boy who wouldn't grow up (note, incidentally, the wilfulness of that 'wouldn't') were A.E. Housman's 'lads that will die in their glory and never be old'. It is no surprise to find that Barrie read *A*

---

[1] Recalling a serious attack of appendicitis whilst at Eton, Ronald Knox, according to his biographer, Evelyn Waugh, would remark in later life that if he had died then it would have been at the apogee of his earthly glory.

[2] Emphasis mine.

Shropshire Lad 'year in, year out – over and over again'. First published in 1869, *A Shropshire Lad* had not been an instant success. However, sales began to improve around the time that *The Hill*, Saki's first collection of 'Reginald' stories and *Peter Pan* first appeared. In 1905 the book sold 886 copies; by 1911 the average yearly sale was 13,500 copies. The popularity of the work was no doubt increased by the number of Housman's poems which were set to music. Although Housman disliked this practice, he never refused permission and, perhaps more significantly, never accepted any fee. Amongst the better-known settings of poems, either individually or as song cycles, were those by Somervell (1904), Gardiner (1906), Gurney (1908), Vaughan Williams (1909), Peel (1910), Butterworth (1911 and 1912) and Ireland (1917).[1] Housman had been educated at King Edward's School, Bromsgrove, whose headmaster, a fine Classicist, had reformed the school two years before the poet's arrival. Steeped in the Classics and, what is more important, good at them, Housman infused his poems with a pagan pessimism. Mackail knew Housman and was one of the people the poet asked to look over his volume of *Late Poems* (1922) at proof stage. Housman's pessimism was similar to the doomed, romantic melancholy seen by Mackail in the *Palatine Anthology*. 'For over all life there lay a shadow', Mackail wrote in the Introduction to his selection:

> Man, a weak and pitiable creature, lay exposed to a grim and ironic power that went its own way careless of him, or only interfered to avenge its own slighted majesty . . . And besides the bolts launched by fate, life was as surely if more slowly weighed down by the silent and ceaseless tide of change against which nothing stood fixed or permanent, and which swept the finest and most beautiful things away soonest.

This could be a critique of Housman's poetry. It was *A Shrophire Lad* that Connolly's fellow-pupil at Eton, George Orwell, knew by heart. He later wrote that Housman's themes 'were adolescent – murder, suicide, unhappy love, early death', which explained their appeal for schoolboys. 'To my generation,' wrote Auden (that generation being the one that was at school during the Great War), 'no other English poet seemed so perfectly to express the sensibility of the male adolescent.' Rupert Brooke, addressing Rugby's literary society, the *Eranos*, on modern poetry, recommended *A Shropshire Lad* for its simplicity, adding that the poem should be read 'on an autumn morning

---

[1] Both Gurney and Ireland produced further settings after the War.

when there is a brave nip of frost in the air and the year is sliding quietly towards death.' Another young public-school poet, Charles Sorley, felt in 1913 that Housman's book deserved an entire paper to itself. He suggested that the Greeks would have approved of such verses as 'When I watch the living meet'. At 'Fernhurst' a small boy, affronted that Carruthers should be surprised that he is able to quote Housman, remarks pertly: 'We are not all Philistines, you know.'

One way in which youth was doomed both in Houseman and in Classical literature was in battle. The public schools' view of military death, which was always understood to be swift, brave and clean, was only partially derived from a casual reading of *The Iliad*. Once again it was the *Greek Anthology* which provided a noble model. E.V. Rieu, the Classical scholar who founded the Penguin Classics Series, was at St Paul's at the beginning of the century. When he came to translate *The Iliad* in 1950 he found that the realism of Homer's character-drawing 'entirely banished from my mind . . . the idea that I had received in my schooldays that Homer was harking back to the so-called "heroic age", when "heroes" were apparently as common as blackberries.' Whilst it might be possible, particularly when translating isolated extracts in the classroom, to gain an impression of Classical heroism from *The Iliad*, it would be difficult to overlook entirely the bloody nature of battle. Homer's soldiers do not fall, they are hacked to the ground; their deaths are not swift and clean, but prolonged and messy. Rieu points out that whilst most of the gods are treated with respect, Homer 'persistently degrades and ridicules' Ares, god of war. This, Rieu suggests, is because *The Iliad* was written 'not to glorify war (though it admits its fascination) but to emphasise its tragic futility.'

The anodyne notion of death as swift, painless oblivion is to be found in many epitaphs in the *Greek Anthology*. In commemorating death, Mackail writes:

There, if anywhere, the Greek genius had its fullest scope and most decisive triumph; and here it is that we come upon the epigram in its inmost essence and utmost perfection . . . the Greek mind here as elsewhere came more directly than any other face to face with the truth of things, and the Greek genius kindled before the vision of life and death into a clearer flame. The sepulchral reliefs show us many aspects of death; in all of the best period there is a common note, mingled of a grave tenderness, simplicity, and reserve. There is none of the horror of darkness, none of the ugliness of dying; with calm faces and undisordered raiment they rise from their seats and take

[95]

the last farewell. But the sepulchral verses show us more clearly the grief that lay beneath the quiet lines of the marble and the smooth cadence of the couplets.

Simonides, author of the famous couplet on the Spartans at Thermopylae, is particularly commended. His epitaphs are:

among the most finished achievements of the greatest period of Greece; and in them the art touches not only its highest recorded point, but a point beyond which it seems inconceivable that art should go. They stand as the symbols of perfection in literature; not only from the faultlessness of their form, but from the greatness of spirit, the noble and simple thought that had then newly found itself so perfect a language to commemorate the great deeds which it inspired.

Mackail particularly draws the reader's attention to similar epitaphs:

On the Athenians, slain under the skirts of the Euboean hills, who lavished their young and beautiful lives for Athens; on the soldiers who fell, in the full tide of Greek glory, at the great victory on the Eurymedon. In all the epitaphs of this class *the thought of the city swallows up individual feeling;*[1] for the city's sake, that she may be free and great, men offer their death as freely as their life; and the noblest end for a life spent in her service is to die in the moment of her victory.

This was Imperialist sentiment, and the attitude to the city is similar to boys' attitudes to their schools. Literature such as this infused generations with notions such as *Dulce et decorum est pro patria mori* and 'Whom the Gods love die young'.

The combination of the Classical and the Romantic, seen in the poems of Housman and in Mackail's translations, was fatally attractive, as Connolly observed. His fellow-pupil Anthony Powell recalled that Eton,

historically and architecturally, was unusually well-placed to indoctrinate the romantic mystique; her antique towers, beside the still unpolluted

---

[1] Emphasis mine.

Thames, offering a dreamlike sanctuary for the antithetical deities presiding over that particular romantic vision: Honour and Discipline; Success and Failure; Death and Victory.

This was in 1919, but much the same atmosphere prevailed in the 1890s. The protagonist of *The Oppidan* is made to be half in love with easeful death by his Eton surroundings. Dwelling upon the hideous death in 1825 of thirteen-year-old Francis Ashley, beaten to a comatose pulp during a 'mill' with an older, larger boy, Peter Darley is misled to imagine Ashley 'lying like the lithe and graceful Sarpedon in Flaxman's illustrations to Homer, carried by Death and Sleep. How glorious it was to have attained fame as an Eton boy and to be remembered from generation to generation.' Deluded into the belief that Ashley's death was in some way 'heroic', Peter recalls 'the haunting phrase that those whom the gods love die young', with which his Classics teacher has made him familiar. 'He too began to wish to die at Eton. Could there be a sweeter fate than to die in battle under the Wall and be gathered into the bosom of a mourning Mother?' ('Mother' as in *Alma Mater*, as the capital initial makes clear). Later on, when he begins to read Plato's *Phaedo* in which Socrates talks of death, Peter wonders: 'Why should a man fear death, for either there is immortality or there is not. If there is not, then death is a timeless sleep. If there is immortality, how wonderful to meet all the famous and clever men of the past. Both Socratic alternatives seemed better than life. Peter had never thought of death as an absolute good before.' It is his fate to die, not in battle under the Wall, but in the Eton fire of 1903. Like Flaxman's Sarpedon,[1] there is no mark upon the dead boy. Two of his friends find an epitaph scribbled in Peter's 'burry', written in imitation of epigrams from the *Greek Anthology*, 'those exquisite little tear-bottles of pagan grief'.

The archetype of the serious school story of the period, *The Hill*, combines all the Classics-related themes in one unashamedly sentimental, snobbish and patriotic novel. It also contains a military death which follows the classical ideal. The book concerns the relationship between two boys, in the course of which Vachell descants upon the doomed beauty of youth, evanescence, self-sacrifice, imperial glory and honourable death. The besotted John Verney is shattered when his friend Henry 'Caesar' Desmond is killed in the Boer War. His lament, however, is not in keeping with the attitude taken by the school,

---

[1] But unlike Homer's Sarpedon who was struck in the diaphragm by a spear. When Patroclus pulled the spear from Sarpedon's body, 'the midriff came with it'.

which is stoic and celebratory.[1] The sermon preached by the headmaster is a perfect example of the public-school ethos rising to the occasion with a string of meretricious platitudes. The headmaster begins by quoting a poem which mentions the hill upon which Harrow stands, then says:

> Henry Desmond died on another hill, and died so gloriously that the shadow of our loss, dark as it seemed to us at first, is already melting in the radiance of his gain. To die young, clean, ardent; to die swiftly, in perfect health; to die saving others from death, or worse – disgrace – to die scaling heights; to die and to carry with you into the fuller ampler life beyond, untainted hopes and aspirations, unembittered memories, all the freshness and gladness of May – is that not a cause for joy rather than sorrow? I say – yes. Henry Desmond is one stage ahead of us upon a journey which we all must take, and I entreat you to consider that, if we have faith in a future life, we must believe also that we carry hence not only the record of our acts, whether good or evil, but the memory of them; and that memory, undimmed by falsehood or self-deception, will create for us Heaven or Hell. I do not say – God forbid! – that you should desire death because you are still young, and, comparatively speaking, unspotted from the world; but I say I would sooner see any of you struck down in the flower of his youth than living on to lose, long before death comes, all that makes life worth living. Better death, a thousand times, than gradual decay of mind and spirit; better death than faithlessness, indifference, and uncleanness. To you who are leaving Harrow, poised for flight into the great world of which this school is the microcosm, I commend the memory of Henry Desmond. It stands in our records for all we venerate and strive for: loyalty, honour, purity, strenuousness, faithfulness in friendship. When temptation assails you, think of that gallant boy running swiftly uphill, leaving craven fear behind, and drawing with him the others who, led by him to the heights, made victory possible.

Whatever the modern reader may make of this, there is no doubt that Vachell struck a responsive chord in the hearts of his Edwardian audience. Published in April, it was in its fifth edition by September, and had been

---

[1] This is echoed in Ernest Raymond's Great War novel, *Tell England*, in which the insufferable Padre Monty admonishes the grieving Rupert Ray: 'Rupert, Edgar is dead . . . And there's only one unbeautiful thing about his death, and that is the way his friend is taking it.'

[98]

reprinted twenty-one times by the outbreak of the Great War. The headmaster's wish to see his pupils cut down would be very thoroughly fulfilled, and amongst the names on the Harrow Roll of Honour is that of Vachell's only son, Richard, who was serving with the Royal Flying Corps. One wonders how far the novelist was comforted by the words he put into the mouth of his headmaster when commemorating another victim of war. This sermon is a mixture of the Christian and the Classical, of Newbolt and Simonides, and bears a marked resemblance to sermons delivered at the dedication ceremonies for the Great War memorials which were erected in the schools after the Armistice.

The Classics, as perceived by the schools, were a binding agent which held together the various particles of an ethos. Ancient Greece, in particular, was regarded as a model civilisation founded upon ideals suitable for emulation. As the long years of peace began to be threatened and as expansionism became a popular ideology, so the example of the Greeks as a warrior nation was held up for comparison. War became ennobled, Death lost its sting, Youth became an object of worship. Emasculated and prettified, the Classics provided a precedent, or an excuse, for the activities and ideals of these very English institutions.

4 Public-School Paladins

The notion of self-sacrifice is firmly embedded in the public-school ethos, which relied upon the individual being subordinate to and working for the community. Whether a boy was fagging for his seniors or passing the ball in a game of rugger and allowing the other fellow to score the try, he was seen to be striving for the common weal. Underlying this were the Christian precepts of Thomas Arnold and his followers, and behind every little sacrifice lay the greatest sacrifice of all, that of Christ. Although the early schools were religious foundations, and church services always formed an important part of life there, it had not been expected that pupils should be especially pious. A large number of boys would enter the Church after University, but this did not make them any less boisterous than their fellows. Indeed, some of the worst excesses of the unreformed schools cited by John Chandos in *Boys Together* (1984) were perpetrated by future churchmen. Despite evidence to the

[99]

contrary, it was tacitly accepted that boys were Christian Gentlemen. Arnold, convinced of boyhood's natural state of sin, could not accept the assumptions of his predecessors and determined that Rugbeians should be demonstrably Christian.

The ideal of the Christian Gentleman was one that combined a Tory respect for social order with a Radical desire for social justice. Properly structured and sensibly governed, the English class system was seen as a rational, workable basis for society in which everyone knew, acted according to, and kept his place. The working model of this utopia was the country estate, the seat of power in the land before the rising bourgeoisie made its presence felt. The lord of the manor ruled a little kingdom where the workers toiled for his and their own benefit. In exchange for their labour they would be paid out of the wealth they created for their employer. They would be housed and, when ill or bereaved, would be visited by the landowner's wife and daughters, who brought physical and spiritual sustenance. If they got into trouble they would go before the magistrate who, as likely as not, would be their employer, and they would receive a fair hearing. The conscientious squire took his duties to the community very seriously as a tithe paid to privilege. The entire social order would be celebrated in the local church as part of 'All things bright and beautiful, . . . wise and wonderful' which Mrs Alexander in the popular hymn saw as ordained by God:

> The rich man in his castle,
> The poor man at his gate,
> God made them, high or lowly,
> And ordered their estate.

The reality, of course, did not always conform to this pattern, which is as picturesque and anodyne as a painting by Helen Allingham. It represented the ideal, and it was upon such ideals that social philosophy and politics were based. It was the disparity between the ideal and real life that moved such people as Arnold with reforming zeal. A public-school education should prepare boys to be leaders of a truly Christian society. Whilst Arnold might have hoped that this purpose could be fulfilled by example, many of his Christian Socialist followers were rather more belligerent. George Arthur might be delicate and in need of Tom Brown's protection, but his father, a vicar possessed of 'a real wholesome Christian love for the poor, struggling, sinning men' of his parish, is remembered as 'a man who had fought the Lord's fight even unto death'. Muscular Christianity may involve laying down one's life, but not before a good set-to. Hughes mocked those who thought a bout of bloody fisticuffs between two small boys 'with the weapons which God has given us all, an uncivilised, unchristian or ungentlemanly affair'. The Revd Sabine Baring-Gould in his celebrated hymn urged Christian soldiers onward, as did John Monsell:

> Fight the good fight with all thy might,
> Christ is thy strength and Christ the right.

The notion of battling Christians is perhaps unsurprising in a nation whose patron saint is a soldier. In fact virtually nothing is known about the real St George, an obscure martyr who was probably killed in Palestine at the turn of the third and fourth centuries. The popular legend of knight, dragon, maiden in distress and mass conversion is a late-medieval concoction, possibly the result of a confusion between the saint and the crusaders who brought back his name from the Holy Land. George seems to have been adopted as the patron saint of England during the fourteenth century. His popularity was enhanced about 150 years later by such works as Edmund Spenser's *The Faerie Queene* in which the Red Cross Knight who represents the Anglican Church bears the same arms as St George and takes part in escapades similar to those of the legend. Shakespeare's *Henry V*, written at about the same time, represents the king as a valiant warrior who, in the famous rallying speech before Harfleur, aligns himself with the saint, instructing his troops to 'Cry, "God for Harry, England and Saint George!"'

George became the prototype of the chivalrous knight, forever pricking on the plain in defence of the realm. 'Chivalry', like 'cavalry' is derived from *cheval*, and the knight was a mounted soldier with an almost centaur-like affinity with his horse, a symbiosis reflected by the knight of the chessboard, usually represented by a horse's head. He was generally of noble birth and pious inclination, so that knightly virtue was connected not only with the Church but also with the state and the ruling caste. The medieval knight who rode into battle on a heavy horse was encased in some 250 lbs of protective, decorative and expensive armour. Only the wealthy could afford such trappings, and indeed afford to go off on crusades to Palestine to demonstrate their piety and military prowess against the Moslems. Although the armour-clad knight could be effective in warfare, the skills he had learned in the tiltyard were rarely shown to their best advantage in the chaotic mill of a battlefield. Knights could better show off their talents in mock battles and so tournaments were devised, upper-class occasions in which courage, skill and fair-play could be demonstrated in controlled circumstances. The advent of gunpowder made the armour-clad knight obsolete and the chivalric codes which inspired him died with him. The light cavalryman, although magnificently uniformed, was rather different from his predecessor, employed less as a skilled individual than as part of a combined force.

The revival of chivalry during the Victorian period was divorced from its warlike heritage and diluted with romance. It was a conscious anachronism in which art, literature and fancy dress played a large part. Tennyson and the Pre-Raphaelites celebrated a medieval past based on Arthurian legend and populated by languid maidens and somewhat effete but nonetheless honourable and brave knights. William Morris looked for a practical application for such ideals to nineteenth-century life and the Arts and Crafts movement attempted to imitate medieval guilds. More bellicose figures, such as Henry Newbolt, looked to the Empire for an arena in which to demonstrate more forcibly chivalric ideals. It can be seen how far these became divorced from their origins by their application to the Boer War.

Like several other aspects of the late-Victorian and Edwardian public schools, the cult of chivalry was not sanctioned by Thomas Arnold. However, the architecture of many of the schools – genuinely or pseudo-medieval – and the sense of tradition – ancient or acquired – were conducive to chivalric fantasies. Shields and their accompanying mottoes emblazoned upon uniforms and games clothes suggested an entirely fictitious chivalric heritage. Inspired by his old headmaster, Newbolt asserted:

> The old method of training young squires to knighthood produced our public-school system, which is not at all the same as the monastic system. The monastic kind of school aimed at making clerics and learned men, and it was as much like a juvenile monastery as possible. The public school, on the other hand, has derived the housemaster from the knight to whose castle boys were sent as pages; fagging, from the services of all kinds which they there performed; prefects, from the senior squires, or 'masters of the henchmen'; athletics, from the habit of out-of-door life; and the love of games, the 'sporting' or 'amateur' view of them, from tournaments and the chivalric rules of war.

In fact, the public schools were indeed derived from monastic foundations, however far they may have strayed, down the centuries, from the ideals of William of Wykeham, who founded Winchester in 1382.

Nonetheless, the schools lapped up chivalric ideals with the decorative figures of King Arthur and his knights held up as wholesome Christian alternatives to the heroes of Greece and Rome. For a start they wore more clothes. Although there were some problems with Lancelot and Guinevere, the legends were free of the taint of the Orient.[1] Sir Galahad, in particular, seemed an avatar of the public-school ideal, entirely unspotted and thus the winner of the Grail. Indeed, painted by Burne-Jones (exquisitely sexless) or Watts (ethereally blurred), Sir Galahad bore scarcely any relation to the flesh, let alone its accompanying sins.

Although conceivably there were tots like Percival Twyman who spent childhood hours doing watercolours of heraldic devices – and there was of course a considerable percentage of boys who came from families entitled to bear arms – the idea of Clifton and Eton overrun by young paladins resided in the imaginations of overwrought teachers and nostalgic alumni. A.C. Benson, revisiting Eton in 1916, recognised (without approving) the College's chivalric idealism:

> Drove down in soft sunshine along the old streets; the first sight of the boys in the ridiculous dress – yet looking so handsome and fine, many of them – moved me a great deal . . . But it isn't my native air at all. It represents an aristocratic life, a life pursuing knightly virtues – chivalry, agility, honour, something Spartan.

Boys were perhaps less impressed. The staff at Eton may have felt that Watts' picture of Sir Galahad was a relevant icon for the Chapel, but the protagonist of *The Oppidan* finds the knight 'remote from the hearty Eton ideal. . . . Perhaps it was only a Tennysonian poster. Peter studied it long, but failed to gather any religious impression from the masterpiece.'

Other schools pointed to particularly inspiring Old Boys. Sir Philip Sidney, who passed his water-bottle to a fellow soldier whilst lying wounded at the Battle of Zutphen with the words: 'Thy need is yet greater than mine', was deemed a splendid example of what was being striven for at Shrewsbury. He

---

[1] Or were they? 'All earnest schoolmasters' were urged by one reviewer to read the Revd E.E. Bradford's 'vigorous and refreshing' and frankly paederastic volume of poems entitled *The New Chivalry* (1918). It was the Greeks all over again. (cf. Alec Waugh's defence of Romantic Friendships in terms of courtly love, p 112).

was 'a character-sublime, and fearless unto death – very dear to the hearts of Englishmen'. Merchant Taylor's boys could be inspired by the author of *The Faerie Queene*. Unsurprisingly, both Spenser and Sidney were incorporated by their respective schools into Great War Memorials.[1]

More recent Old Boys, whose heroic deeds in the cause of Empire were celebrated by such men as Newbolt and Minchin, were seen to be behaving with exemplary, if bellicose, chivalry and were frequently held up before a new generation of schoolboys. But even militarists such as Warre could be inspired by gentler visions of knighthood. Tennyson was invited to read 'The Holy Grail' to the great man in the privacy of his garden at the college. His colleague F. Warre Cornish contributed a volume on *Chivalry* to an historical series entitled *Social England* in 1901. Percival of Clifton went so far as to christen his unfortunate sons Arthur and Lancelot. Warre's only other professed literary taste was for Sir Walter Scott, a taste he shared with his antipathetic colleague William Johnson Cory. Scott and Ruskin (another purveyor of medieval fantasy) were influences upon Warre's fellow Imperialist, Edward Thring. Thring's biographer, J.H. Skrine, a Warden of Glenalmond, concocted an entire educational 'theory' out of chivalric ideals, published in 1902 as *Pastor Agnorum*. This tract, which begins tentatively 'At A Ladder's Foot' and ends triumphantly 'In Avalon', is an example of the higher dottiness. Skrine's declared mission was to Christianise the public schools and to do this through the teachers. Those critics who felt, like Dr Arnold, that chivalry elevated personal honour above duty to God could be reassured by the Warden's assertion that 'Chivalry . . . is the Divine become flesh in the estate of gentleman'. Like Newbolt, Skrine makes a case for the public schools being modelled upon medieval court life, referring to the academies run for noble children where they acquired 'some tincture of the arts . . . [and spent] much time in training lungs and heart and muscle, in learning to run, vault, leap, climb and throw.' Whilst this vision may bear some resemblance to public-school life at the turn of the century, it has little to do with the long history of public school development. Fagging is seen to have a knightly precedent and the games field is quaintly described as 'The Tiltyard *de Nos Jours*'. Skrine's ideas, as inflated and as ludicrous as his prose style, are symptomatic of the delusions suffered by headmasters of the period. Even Dr Cyril Norwood, headmaster successively of Bristol Grammar School, Marlborough and Harrow, would claim in 1928 that:

[1] The Burgomaster of Zutphen attended the unveiling of Shrewsbury's statue of Sidney and laid a wreath.

What has happened in the course of the last hundred years is that the old ideals have been recaptured. The ideal of chivalry which inspired the knighthood of medieval days, the ideal of service to the community which inspired the greatest of men who founded schools for their day and for posterity, have been combined in the tradition of English education which holds the field today. It is based upon religion; it relies largely upon games and open-air prowess, where these involve corporate effort.

What any objective critic would see as a decline in education in the schools is here presented as some sort of renaissance; what should be causing disquiet is celebrated with complacent pride.

By the time the Great War was declared, notions of chivalry and patriotic duty combined with the various other elements of the public-school ethos to inspire a generation. The sacrifice of self-interest to the welfare of the community reached its apotheosis as young men marched straight out of the school gates into a commission and the trenches. George Orwell wrote that for the public schools, 'the duty of dying for your country, if necessary, is laid down as one of the first and greatest of the Commandments'. The Boer War had provided plenty of opportunities for this and memorials testified to the chivalric nature of death upon the battlefield. Clifton's armour-clad knight, unhelmeted and with a sword that has a crucifix upon the hilt, is an impressive, if irrelevant, memorial to the Old Boys who died in South Africa. If chivalric ideals could be brought to the Boer War, about which there was a great deal that was neither honourable nor noble, it is hardly surprising that the Great War should be regarded as a knightly quest.

5 Passing the Love of Women

One significant aspect of public-school life which was a result rather than a part of the ethos was what came to be known as the Romantic Friendship. Passionate but sexless liaisons between boys became a staple of public-school fiction and illuminate the memoirs of public-school men. As Leigh Hunt wrote in his autobiography:

If I had reaped no other benefit from Christ's Hospital, the school would be ever dear to me from the recollection of the friendships I formed in it, and of the first heavenly taste it gave me of that most spiritual of the affections. I use the word 'heavenly' advisedly . . . if ever I tasted a disembodied transport on earth, it was in those friendships which I entertained at school, before I dreamt of any maturer feeling.

Even someone who had not been to a public school could tune in to such emotions. Disraeli wrote of Millbank's attachment to Conningsby at Eton with considerable authority:

At school, friendship is a passion. It entrances the being; it tears the soul. All loves of after-life can never bring its rapture, or its wretchedness; no bliss so absorbing, no pangs of jealousy or despair so crushing and so keen! What tenderness and what devotion; what illimitable confidence; infinite revelations of inmost thoughts; what ecstatic present and romantic future; what bitter estrangements and what melting reconciliations; what scenes of wild recrimination, agitating explanations, passionate correspondence; what insane sensitiveness, and what frantic sensibility; what earthquakes of the heart and whirlwinds of the soul are confined in that simple phrase – a schoolboy's friendship!

What, it may be asked, did headmasters make of such relationships? The classic pronouncement on the subject was made by G.H. Rendall, Headmaster of Charterhouse from 1897 to 1911, who blithely informed fellow-members of the Headmasters' Conference that: 'My boys are amorous, but seldom erotic'. These immortal words can be looked upon as innocent, complacent or simply idiotic, but they are symptomatic of Victorian and Edwardian thought upon the matter. It is notable, for instance, that Harrow, which seems to have had an outstanding record in every variety of vice,[1] was also the school which inspired *Gerald Eversley's Friendship* and *The Hill*, two of the most romantically charged, but rigorously chaste, of all school stories. The former was actually written by a revered Harrow headmaster. Most headmasters of the period were clergymen and bachelors, cloistered and remote. Their sexual confusion was considerable and widespread, compounded of suspicion, ignorance and repression. Their assistant masters were often little better. It would be easy to make excuses for these men living in a pre-Freudian era, but sex existed for many centuries before Freud and if they remained in

[1] J.A. Symonds, a precocious Juvenal amidst the stews of mid-Victorian Harrow, gives the impression in his *Memoirs* of an education more reminiscent of Krafft-Ebbing than Socrates.

ignorance of what one of their more astute charges described as 'the inevitable emotional consequences of a monastic herding together for eight months of the year of thirteen-year-old children and eighteen-year-old adolescents', it was largely because they wanted to. When forcefully enlightened they acted as though betrayed. They insisted upon attempting to differentiate between what they saluted as the highest of all affections, which led to panegyrics in the chapel, and what they called 'beastliness', which generally led to expulsion. To anyone but the most blinkered pedagogue it would be clear that the two were closely entwined, as indeed all too often were the participants.

Amidst the suffocating conformity and repression of feelings within the schools, idealised relationships between boys flourished. In view of the social conditions and moral and intellectual training of the schools, this is unsurprising. The tendency of much Classical literature has already been noted; the rise of games produced sporting gods who were set up for hero-worship; the fagging system promoted associations verging upon the marital between boys of different ages. All these elements were encouraged. A lack of female company resulted in burgeoning romantic feelings being channelled towards other boys, particularly the younger ones who, with their fresh complexions, unbroken voices, and the vulnerability of their position in the school society, approximated to the status of women in the outside world. As long as these feelings remained merely romantic, such relationships were smiled upon if not actually encouraged. It was when sexual activity (even of the most rudimentary and harmless nature) was involved that confused boys found themselves not only out of favour, but often out of the school.

The model for the Romantic Friendship was not that of Achilles and Patroclus or Alexis and Corydon, but that love passing the love of women enjoyed by David and Jonathan. David's lament was frequently read as the lesson in chapel and the effect of this unarguably beautiful passage upon its young audience may be gauged from H.O. Sturgis's Eton novel, *Tim* (1891), in which the eponymous hero is in love with another boy confusingly called Carol. Tim, sitting in chapel,

> listening to the history of the two friends long ago, felt his love for his friend almost a religion to him . . . 'What woman could love him as I do?' thought Tim, as he looked to the seat where Carol sat. At that moment a sunbeam from some hole high in the roof fell on the golden curly head, which seemed transfigured; and as Tim's hungry eyes rested on the face of his friend, he turned towards him and smiled upon him in his place.

The Gospel according to St Matthew as much as the Second Book of Samuel seems to lie behind this scene of transfiguration, with the light from heaven shining upon Carol. Whether or not this is intentional or conscious, the relationship between the two boys, thus sanctified, continues, passionate yet chaste, until its fatal and lachrymose conclusion.

Not everyone invoked the Biblical pair with such innocent intent. At Abbotsholm, in a chapel adorned with, amongst other things, the statue of a naked boy, pupils followed a liturgy compiled for the school by its eccentric headmaster, Dr Cecil Reddie. This included David's lament, a feature apparently recalled by Lytton Strachey after he had transferred from Abbotsholm to Leamington. In a diary, in which the symbol '†' was used as a substitute for the word 'love' (with somewhat suggestive results), Strachey recorded his wooing of an athlete called Underwood:

> . . . three days ago, the confession was on my lips. He mentioned – the † of women. I said, thinking of the † greater than that of women, 'You know who Jonathan was, he –', then who should come in but Providence in the shape of Tommy Clarke to put an end to everything.

It was time to return to the Greeks. Strachey read the *Symposium*, so 'running parallel with my thoughts on [Underwood] have been my thoughts on Plato.'

References to David and Jonathan abound in public-school fiction (rather more so than references to Plato). In *The Hill*, which is subtitled 'A Romance of Friendship', the cynical Scaife dubs hero-worshipping John Verney 'Jonathan' and clearly intends Harry Desmond as 'David'. Desmond, who, like most heroes of public-school stories, is decent, upright, brave, honest, but rather slow, says:

> 'All the same, we can't call either the Duffer or Fluff – David, can we?'
> 'I was not thinking of Kinloch or Duff,' said Scaife, staring hard at John. And John alone knew that Scaife read him like a book, in which he was contemptuously amused – nothing more.

Unfortunately for symmetry it is 'David' who is killed in battle in this novel and 'Jonathan' who is left to lament.

In a later panegyric of public-school life and love the hero really is called David. When the Christian name of the protagonist of *David Blaize* is revealed, the boy is highly embarrassed. However, an adoring junior, 'Bags' Crabtree, feels that he would 'have rather liked it if someone had proclaimed that his own name was Jonathan'. (It is in fact George.) When David goes on to his public school he captivates an older boy called Maddox. An indulgent housemaster meets the two boys just after they have partnered each other in an important cricket match. He refers to them as 'you blest pair of sirens',[1] and says to Maddox: 'And take care of David, Jonathan . . .' (Maddox is in fact called Frank.) Benson is too sophisticated (and not sufficiently disinterested, one suspects) to overlook the sexual element that is an inevitable part of such relationships. Maddox undergoes a severe test when he discovers David playing squash in the rain. Hitherto attracted by David's 'hopelessly seraphic face', Maddox's attention become focused upon other charms. David presented:

> a completely dishevelled and yet a very jolly object, and he was altogether wet, his knickerbockers clinging like tights to his thighs, the skin of which showed pink through them, whilst water trickled steadily down his bare calves into the dejected socks that lay limply round the tops of his shoes. They and his legs were stained with splashes of watery gravel, his shirt, open at the neck and slightly torn across the shoulder, lay like a wet bag glued to his back, and his hair was a mere yellow plaster from which the water could have been wrung in pints. Bags was in a similar plight, except that he wore a thick woollen jersey over his shirt, which gave him a slightly less drowned aspect.

And a considerably less erotic one. After this vision Maddox contrives unsuccessfully to get David to come to his study. He discovers the boy in a further state of undress, towel-draped after a shower, and becomes aware of the nature of his feelings. Back in his study he stares into a mirror, expecting to see some Hyde-like transformation, and passes a suitable sentence upon himself: '"You damned beast," he said. "You deserve to be shot."'

During a shared holiday Maddox reveals to David that it was the latter's 'innocence' which had made him 'suddenly see what a beast I was':

> 'I tried, instead of corrupting you, to uncorrupt myself. But you did it; it was all your doing. You made me ashamed.'
> David gave a shy little wriggle towards him.

[1] This tag is from Milton's 'At a Solemn Music', and refers to 'Voice and Verse'; but it looks back to the Platonic Sirens of *Arcades*.

'I have never heard of anything so ripping', he said. 'Though it sounds rather cheek.'

Maddox sat up.

'That's what you've done,' he said. 'And if it was cheek, the other name of that is salvation.'

The tension here between tone and intent is characteristic of the novel and of the confusion which reigned within the schools.

Although David and Jonathan may have seemed a chaste, biblical alternative to Classical couples, it cannot have passed unnoticed that their relationship was cited by the notorious Oscar Wilde during a much-publicised contemporaneous trial:

'The love that dare not speak its name' in this century is such a great affection of an elder for a younger man as there was between David and Jonathan, such as Plato made the very basis of his philosophy, and such as you will find in the sonnets of Michelangelo and Shakespeare. It is that deep, spiritual affection that is as pure as it is perfect.

This pronouncement was apparently greeted with an outburst of spontaneous applause at the Old Bailey in 1895, Wilde's eloquence deflecting any suspicion that what he was saying had little relevance to the matter in hand. It was, of course, nonsense to drag in David and Jonathan, since they were *both* young men. Similarly, there was very little that was spiritual, pure or perfect about Wilde's liaisons with male prostitutes and blackmailers, as the evidence had already made clear.

The same might be said about much of what was happening at the schools. Wilde's morals and prose style had their effect upon a sophisticated Sixth Former at Rugby in 1906, Rupert Brooke. Flattered to discover that a school-fellow had purchased a photograph of him from the school photographers, Brooke began an epistolary romance with his admirer, full of Wildean phrases:

The Greek gods lived that you might be likened to them: the world was created that you might be made of gold and ivory: the fragrance of your face is myrrh and incense before the pale altar of Beauty.

And so on. Brooke addressed the boy as 'Antinous', and the two went for walks where cricket was the chief topic of conversation and: 'Only a rare tinge of poetry flickered & faded through the mundane words'. Unfortunately, the romance flickered and faded in its turn, although the cause of its decline remains a mystery. Perhaps 'Antinous' became bored with being told how Greek and gracious he was. Even his identity remains a mystery. There was a youth whom Brooke seduced in the autumn of 1909 and with whom he had carried on some sort of affair whilst at Rugby. He has been identified by John Lehmann as Denham Russell-Smith. If this surmise is correct, it seems unlikely that 'Antinous' is the same person, since after the disintegration of the romance, Brooke went to stay with the Russell-Smiths in order to recuperate from a bout of ophthalmia and to 'be ordinary and, I hope, merry'. What is clear is that Brooke's poem 'The Beginning', published in *Poems, 1911*, is addressed to 'Antinous', since it was written at this time and contains verbal echoes of letters written about the boy.

Further poems which seem to be addressed to fellow-pupils were also appearing in *The New Field*, a Winchester magazine edited by the future translator of Proust and friend of Wilfred Owen, C.K. Scott-Moncrieff. The magazine also contained reviews of such recherché items as 'The Priest and the Acolyte,' a sacrilegious and paederastic story which had been used against Wilde in his trial, and carried advertisements for Stuart Mason's books on Wilde. No one seems to have raised any objections to this magazine until the editor decided to publish his own school story in it. 'Evensong and Morwesong' opens:

> . . . 'And if we're found out?' asked Maurice. He was still on his knees in the thicket, and, as he looked up to where his companion stood in an awkward fumbling attitude, his face seemed even more than usually pale and meagre in the grey broken light. It was with rather forced nonchalance that Carruthers answered: 'O, the sack, I suppose' – and he stopped aghast at the other's expression.

Carruthers becomes a headmaster and expels a boy for a similar offence, only to discover that the pupil is the son of Maurice. The magazine was hastily suppressed.

That such activities were directly connected with romantic friendships was a circumstance strenuously denied by public-school headmasters. The standard response to concerned enquiries about the incidence of homosexuality within the schools was 'a grudging admission "Perhaps in a bad house, in a bad school, in a bad time".' When another Carruthers, the hero of *The Loom of*

Youth, becomes involved with a younger boy, this occurs in a chapter entitled 'Romance', and is very discreet. Waugh was later to write in lofty terms of 'an idealistic, un-self-seeking, Platonic love; a love that is based on service and devotion, that has a kinship with the love practised by the troubadours in the medieval courts of love.' However, the correspondence on *The Loom* which Waugh donated to Sherborne after he had been forgiven his 'treason' suggests a rather less idealistic view of things. Arthur Waugh realised that if his elder son's book was published there would be no possibility of sending Evelyn to Sherborne. Alec suggested Uppingham: 'it is rather immoral, but I imagine no more so than any other school'. Fellow-publisher Humphrey Milford wrote to Arthur Waugh after the novel's publication to say that his son 'tells me — and I gather from what he does not tell me — that the general tone in [Rugby's] houses is lower than we expected — to put it mildly!' Desmond Coke thought the language in the novel rather strong, but admitted that 'we sank pretty low at Shrewsbury, towards the end of Ross's too long reign: — our morals were quite Oriental.' Arnold Lunn suggested that although he had not made much of it in *The Harrovians*, sexual licence was one of the Harrow traditions which had not died.

Elsewhere there are testimonies to the sexual mores of assorted schools. C.S. Lewis wrote extensively about the activities of School Tarts at 'Wyvern' (i.e. Malvern) in *Surprised by Joy*. Robert Graves, although amorously inclined himself, revealed that eroticism was not unknown at Charterhouse. The prefects at Marlborough met in 1913 to discuss the problem of 'cases'. Scott-Moncrieff's story was presumably based upon experience at Winchester. An old gentleman who had been at Haileybury at the time of the Great War informed Jonathan Gathorne-Hardy that he had enjoyed 'an enormous amount' of sex there. Indeed 'the usual thing' became the current euphemism for 'immorality' when explaining why a boy's school career had been suddenly terminated. Distraught parents could apply to Alex Devine, the headmaster of Claysmore, who accepted these pariahs, even offering one of them, the adult Alec Waugh (so much for courtly love), a job on the staff.

The same blinkered attitude which proclaimed that the OTC had nothing to do with killing prevailed in moral matters, so that it could be claimed that the Romantic Friendship had nothing to do with mutual masturbation. Just as not every boy who had trained with the OTC ended up bayonetting a real enemy, so not every passionate friendship ended in consummation. Both activities had become swathed in the romance which swirled and eddied around the schools at this period. Chivalry, patriotism and self-sacrifice draped the less acceptable facts of warfare; Disraeli's catalogue of special effects from *Coningsby* blurred images of boys on their knees in thickets. It is significant that what can only be described as love stories provide an identifiable sub-genre of the school story. In such books it is noticeable that the glamorous sporting heroes are invariably cricketers rather than football-players. The summer term at a traditional public school, with age-gilded buildings and immemorial elms forming a backdrop to the smooth expanse of green where white-clad figures played cricket, provided an atmosphere conducive to romance in all senses of the word. It would have been rather difficult to bring the same charge to a bare rugby-pitch in mid-November, with bawling, mud-streaked boys hurtling around in the drizzle. Cricket was aesthetically superior to rugby football and also provided an opportunity for two boys to play as partners, clocking up runs between them, as in *David Blaize*. Meanwhile, admiring juniors could loll under the trees with bags of cherries watching their heroes at the wicket.

It is also noticeable that few heroes of public-school fiction are unprepossessing. 'I'm the best-looking person in this room,' Archibald Pennybet claims at the beginning of Rupert Ray's narrative in *Tell England*. (Book I is called, alas, 'Five Gay Years at School'.) Ray concedes that Pennybet is the 'handsomest', but adds that Edgar Doe is the 'prettiest'. So pretty, indeed, that Ray dreams of him transformed into a girl:

> As I produced this strange figure, I began to feel, somewhere in the region of my waist, motions of calf-love for the girl Doe that I had created.

At this point in Ray's fantasy: 'Doe's prowess at cricket asserted itself upon my mind, his gender became conclusively established, and – ah well. I was half asleep.' It is not altogether clear whether the confusion here is Ray's or Raymond's (the chapter closes in a riot of Freudian *double-entendre*), but Pennybet's inevitable references to David and Jonathan seem more than ever glib. Poor Ray, who is rather more modest than Pennybet, spends much time wondering whether or not he is attractive, an insecurity which also dogs Verney in *The Hill*. Even Scaife, the villain of Vachell's novel, is no ugly cur. Indeed, nicknamed 'the Demon', he is like Milton's Satan, a fallen angel outshining myriads of fellow-Harrovians with a dangerous, sexy glamour. Verney, who is hopelessly jealous of Scaife's hold upon Desmond, is nonetheless 'captivated by his amazing grace, good looks, and audacity.' When Scaife walks on to the pitch at Lord's 'thousands of men and as many women are staring at his splendid face and figure'; the reversal in the expected order of the sexes here is indicative of the atmosphere of such novels, and the cult of youth and beauty in the Edwardian era.

Raymond confessed that when he re-read *Tell England* in the late nineteen-sixties he was astonished by its latent homosexuality. This astonishment would almost certainly be shared by other writers such as Vachell and Welldon had they lived into an age more sexually aware than their own. Their very innocence, and that of their audience, is what makes these overwrought books acceptable. In an age where good-fellowship was the limit of relationships between heterosexual men, the lush unfolding of a chaste romance between two boys was clearly considered charming. The Romantic Friendship had all the agreeable elements of a clandestine yet carefree affair, without the complication of sex. Desmond and Verney realise the depth of their feeling for each other during a concert in which the latter sings a solo. Vachell's description of Verney's performance might also serve as a representation of the Romantic Friendship in its purest form: 'Higher and higher rose the clear, sexless notes, till two of them met and mingled in a triumphant trill.' No wonder that Desmond feels 'quite weepsy'. When it comes to a declaration, however, the boys are as reticent as they are about religion:

'You like me, old Jonathan, don't you?'
'Awfully,' said John.
'Why did you look at me when you sang that last verse? Did you know that you were looking at me?'
'Yes.'
'You looked at me because – well, because – bar chaff – you – like – me?'
'Yes.'
'You – you like me better than any other fellow in the school?'
'Yes; better than any other fellow in the world.'
'Is it possible?'
'I have always felt that way since – yes – since the very first minute I saw you.'
'How rum!'

Rum, indeed, but immensely popular, as the publishing history of Vachell's novel demonstrates.[1] The breathless punctuation is worthy of Barbara Cartland at her most climactic and the atmosphere of this and other novels

[1] See pp 98–9.

discussed is little different to the 'bold' novels of the 1940s and 1950s on homosexual themes, those coy weepies which frequently end in death or despair, but never in bed. Stories such as these paved the way for the reams of elegiac verse produced during the Great War, in which the love between men, in all its shadings, was celebrated, and its destruction in battle was richly mourned.

[3]

Spreading the Word

1 The School Story

THE acceptance of an ethos within a closed society was relatively simple to achieve. Acting *in loco parentis*, schools were able to impose moral values upon their charges not only by example but also by force. School rules were usually a mixture of common sense and fanciful tradition maintained by the frequent use of the rod, wielded not by the men supposedly in charge of the pupils (except in extreme and rare cases) but by other boys to whom they had delegated authority. In the latter decades of the nineteenth century and the early ones of the twentieth the sounds of swishing, whopping, flogging, bumming, whacking and thrashing echoed around the corridors of most of the schools. Amongst the boys there was also a self-regulating system by which codes of behaviour were maintained, one also accompanied by physical violence. '"Conform or be kicked" is the command written over the portals of every school,' asserted Arnold Lunn, and he meant this order to be taken literally. His hero is forced to wear an overcoat in all weathers in order to protect the base of his spine from the well-aimed boots of a boy who regards a knowledge of English literature as bad form. One chapter of the novel is entitled 'More Lessons in Bushido' and the reference to a feudal code of self-discipline, courage and loyalty is apt.

Beyond the school gates, however, was a large world which by 1914 seems to have absorbed much of the public-school spirit. 'Eton, Harrow and Winchester are three schools of which all Englishmen are proud,' claimed a writer in *The Sphere* at the beginning of that year. 'One need not have been educated at one of them to feel the thrill which these names recall.' Whilst it may be doubted whether *all* Englishmen responded in so Pavlovian a manner,[1] it is clear that the schools had come to represent a revered ideal in the popular imagination. We have already seen how the ideas of Dr Arnold were spread within public schools other than Rugby, but as well as serving as propaganda for interested bodies, *Tom Brown's Schooldays* also founded a genre peculiar to this country: the public/school story. The developing interest in education during the nineteenth century was fuelled by tales of public/school life, which augmented – and for the most part acted as a corrective to – the articles in journals about the education of the upper classes. Almost without exception, certainly up until the second decade of the twentieth century, these stories were celebratory, whether they took the form of serious novels for adults or comic romps in boys' magazines. Like Thomas Hughes, many of the writers of these stories were 'Old Boys' who recreated the snakeless Edens of their schooldays with minute attention to detail and unabashed nostalgia. Sometimes the dividing line between memoir and fiction was so thin that it was simply a matter of changing a few names.

Tom Brown's Schooldays was almost as much a memoir as fiction and in this it was not the first of its kind. A public/school education was something that men seemed to relish and which they recalled with affection. That the schools were largely a closed world meant that any books about them were likely to enjoy sales not only amongst the authors' fellow/alumni but also amongst curious outsiders. At least three memoirs of Rugby were published before Hughes wrote his book. Eton, naturally enough, was an even greater spur to memoirists since they were likely to have shared their schooldays with future statesmen. Who would not be tempted by *The Confessions of an Etonian* by 'I.E.M.' (1846) or *Memories of Eminent Etonians* by Sir Edward Creasey (1850)? Those whose interest did not extend to three volumes of *Confessions of an Etonian* (these by Charles Rowcroft, 1852) might be tempted by H.S. Cookesley's *Brief Memoirs of an Eton Boy* (1851). Those interested in *The Ups and Downs of a Public School* could read the memoirs of an anonymous 'Wykehamist' published in 1856, and the portals of Harrow, Westminster and other schools were also opened by an assortment of Old Boys. Apart from these reminiscences there were official histories following on from J.L. Paston's *The English Public Schools* (1805); numerous articles on public/school education which appeared in a variety of journals; collections of letters; and inspiring

---

[1] Although denizens of 'the Windsor slums' apparently shouted 'Three cheers for Florit Etona! Look at the rising generation, young 'eroes all o'them. Gawd bless them!' at a parade of disdainful Etonians on Mafeking Day.

sermons in which headmasters could display the moral lessons which had been preached within the schools. After the success of *Tom Brown's Schooldays* and with the increase of interest in school and Empire, the memoirs and histories continued to flood the booksellers alongside a rapidly increasing output of school fiction as the century drew to a close. Such was the deluge of Etoniana that *An Eton Bibliography* was deemed necessary in 1898.

How much of all this was read by the general public is impossible to gauge. Compared with public-school fiction the readership of such memoirs and histories was probably narrow. No doubt parents looking for a school for their offspring might have read these unsolicited prospectuses, and presumably the books enjoyed good sales amongst present and former pupils of the schools described. But as the schools grew in size, number and popularity, and as their activities became the cause of debate in newspapers and parliament, the audience for what once might have seemed publications intended for limited circulation widened. The earlier memoirists had good stories to tell and nostalgia to indulge and that was that. Proselytism started with Hughes and soon became the motivating force behind his followers.

Like many publishing successes, *Tom Brown's Schooldays* is of slight literary merit. It begins well and its first half has pace, exuberance and charm. But as the book progresses and as Arnold becomes more dominant, the spirit seems to go out of the story and it ends in a slurry of soggy moralising. One cannot help feeling that Tom Brown is a good deal duller at the end of his Rugby career than he was at the beginning. The book is clearly intended, however, as a paean to the school and its headmaster. At times Hughes is aware that he may be overdoing it:

> My dear boys, old and young, you who have belonged or do belong to other schools and other houses, don't begin throwing my poor little book around the room and abusing me and it, and vowing you'll read no more when you get to this point. ['Pater' Brooke's speech after the School-house match.] I allow you've provocation for it. But, come now – would you, any of you, give a fig for a fellow who didn't believe in, and stand up for his own house and his own school? You know you wouldn't. Then don't object to my cracking up the old School-house, Rugby. Haven't I a right to do it, when I'm taking the trouble of writing this true history for all of your benefits?

Hughes sets out his scheme very clearly here. At this early stage of the story readers might be lulled into the pleasant illusion that his aim is simply entertainment. However, the benefit written about here is a moral one as becomes all too apparent in later chapters. We also note Hughes's assertion that the story is *true*. It would be fairer to say that the novel is true in spirit rather than in actual incident.

Certain episodes were altered to the advantage of Arnold, but a visitor to the school in the 1850s would recognise most of the features and some of the characters he found there.[1] Hughes ends his address: 'If you ain't satisfied, go and write the history of your own houses in your own time and say all you know for your own schools and houses, provided it's true, and I'll read it without abusing you.' The number of Old Boys who took up Hughes's challenge is extraordinary.

Hughes set the pattern for novels about public schools, so much so that by the twentieth century a boy in a story by P.G. Wodehouse is asked: 'Are you the Bully, the Pride of the School, or the Boy who is led astray and takes to Drink in Chapter Sixteen?' The boy is Mike, the questioner Psmith, and this conversation first took place when *Mike* appeared in serial form in *The Captain* in 1908. By 1913 Arnold Lunn could write of 'the tyranny of fiction' which dominated the lives of boys at school and *The Harrovians* (like Coke's *The Bending of the Twig*) set out explicitly to demolish the myths of the school story and to show what public-school life was really like. The expectations of school life brought about by fiction were frequently confounded both in novels and in life. Lunn's hero arrives at his preparatory school knowing 'exactly what to expect', but his attempts at following codes of honour gleaned from books are completely farcical. Any illusions left to Peter are rapidly dispelled upon his arrival at Harrow, where every cliché of the school story is set up and knocked down. Similarly young Siegfried Sassoon arrived at Marlborough ready to play his part:

> I merely saw myself against a vague background of the public-school stories I had read, and went rapidly on to the moment when the headmaster was bidding good-bye to me at the end of my career. 'Well, Sassoon,' he would say, 'superlative scholastic ability isn't everything in the battle of life. Your sterling qualities of character have been an influence for good which I shall not readily forget. Thank you, my boy. I am proud of you.'

'Try to be more sensible', was in fact the parting advice of his housemaster. Even boys entered for schools without the illustrious heritage of Marlbor-

[1] cf. *The Oppidan* which is less a novel than a *vade mecum* of Eton life and love.

ough had expectations gained from literature. Borne by a scholarship from his barbaric elementary school to Kettering Grammar School in 1916, H.E. Bates recalled:

> I had not read the school-stories of popular writers for nothing. I knew very well that the masters would wear black gowns and possibly mortar-boards too. The prefects would have studies in which they fried sausages and drank beer on the quiet . . . I should have to learn Latin and French and a new kind of English in which words like cads and rotters, and expressions like bally bounders and beastly fellows, played a large part. Life was going to be on a higher plane altogether. I was prepared for that.

Alas, such notions were instantly demolished. The young Bates was twice assaulted by fellow-pupils on the train, but this was as nothing compared to the shock of his first sight of his destination:

> The school was newly-built, of fresh red brick, not at all beautiful, and stood in a large asphalt playground. It was a little grander, but not much, than the school I had left. There were no quadrangles and no vast playing-fields of lovely grass with avenues of quiet elms.

If the plot of the school story had been set by Hughes and become familiar through constant repetition in the works of his imitators, so too did the hero of such tales. Although Tom Brown is generally considered the Arnold ideal, it is rather doubtful whether 'the Doctor', had he lived to read the novel, would have wholly approved of the boy. His ideal was rather nearer to the grotesque mannikins of F.W. Farrar who bear little resemblance to boys at all. Hughes's ideal boy combined pluck with piety, a boy unafraid of fighting for his principles ('the natural and English way for English boys to settle their quarrels'), a boy who was loyal, honest, forthright, high-spirited and yet solemn when the occasion demanded. Down the centuries they march: Tom Brown and Ned East, Stephen and Oliver Greenfield, Carol Darley, Harry Venniker, John Verney and Harry Desmond, Godfrey Marten, Lycidas Marsh, Percy Twyman, David Blaize and Frank Maddox, Jeremy Cole, Rupert Ray, Edgar Doe and Archie Pennybet, not to mention Harry Wharton, Bob Cherry, Frank Nugent, George Wingate and the other denizens of Greyfriars and lesser establishments created by lesser pens than Charles Hamilton's.

As the school story developed, the firmly Christian base was weakened. The stories had attempted to instruct through pleasure (to appropriate one Old Salopian's defence of poetry); gradually pleasure overtook instruction, a circumstance which added considerably to the readability of the stories. By 1905 the frankly-expressed piety of Tom Brown and his fellow Rugbeians was too much for the Harrovians of *The Hill*. Religious discussion was pared to a minimum:

> 'Religion means a lot to you, Jonathan, doesn't it?'
> 'Yes.'
> 'But you never talk about it.'
> 'No.'
> 'Why not?'
> 'I don't know how to begin.'

This is in marked and pleasant contrast to the characters of Farrar, who don't know when to stop. What happened was that a code of honour, in which religion played its part, was evolved and began to dominate the lives of public-school boys. It was what Arnold had always feared, and intimations of which he had seen when his Sixth Form failed to identify the poachers in 1833: the secular had ousted the spiritual. Honour, personal and communal, had become the religion of the public-school system, a concept which, although difficult to define, guided the actions of pupils, a god to whom they turned in times of trouble, a moral arbiter.

Perhaps this development was partly a reaction against the religious zeal of Arnold's elect, a realisation that excessive piety is neither a natural nor an attractive state for schoolboys. In fiction it may well be a reaction against the novels of Farrar, disliked by Talbot Baines Reed and burned by the heroes of Kipling's *Stalky & Co.*. Farrar was an aberration, a writer whose stories of school life harked back to the tract-publications inflicted upon children earlier in the century. His intentions were lugubriously Christian and his concern was more with individuals than with schools, with personal morality rather than a corporate ethos. In this his novels are closer to the German rather than the English model.

In an exhaustive study of *The School in English and German Fiction* published in 1933, W.R. Hicks noted that the difference between the English and German systems of education was reflected in the difference between English and German novels set in schools. Despite claims in Victorian and Edwardian journals that all Europe looked to the public-school system with awe and admiration, it is also noticeable that critics of the British system looked to Germany as a model for change and improvement. The Germans were more concerned with intellectual than moral training, their education theorists being leading philosophers rather than senior churchmen, as in England. Indeed, although a great deal of debate about public-school education took place during the nineteenth century, it would be difficult to claim that England produced any coherent theories about education. We have already noted the Clarendon Commission's approval of the 'organic' development of the public-school system and it would be fair to say that most headmasters followed Arnold in their religiously motivated efforts at running schools. The schools relied upon mystique and prestige and the support (and worship) of their alumni. Such theorists as were produced were usually lone men like Sanderson of Oundle (so known because, despite the encomiums of H.G. Wells, his sphere of influence was limited to his own school), autocratic empire-builders like Thring of Uppingham, or eccentrics like Reddie of Abbotsholm.

In German literature there are novels set in schools, but the emphasis is upon the individual rather than the community.[1] Consequently most of the books are attacks upon boarding schools in which the individual is oppressed, defeated and even destroyed by the system. Hermann Hesse's *Unterm Rad* (1905; translated as *The Prodigy*) is a characteristic and popular example.[2] The death of Hans Giebenrath, the prodigy of the title, is ambiguous – did he slip into the river or deliberately drown himself? – but the tendency of the novel is not. It is suggested that Hans has been driven to his death by the circumstances of his education, a notion unthinkable in an English school story before the Great War. However, suicides were not infrequent in the German equivalent, and the celebratory tone of Hughes and his followers is in marked contrast to the German tradition of attack, which, according to Hicks, is marked by 'a vindictiveness verging at times upon the pathological'. Hesse's book was vilified by adherents to the system and by men who had been at the same school, but, unlike *The Loom of Youth*, which provoked a similar response in England twelve years later, *Unterm Rad* was representative of the German school novel.

This is not to say that the heroes of English school stories never rebel against the system; however, the system usually emerges triumphant and the rebel

---

[1] The French tradition of novels set in schools is largely confined to paederasty and anti-clericalism.

[2] Within two years it was in its fifteenth edition in Germany.

emerges full of gratitude. In E.W. Hornung's *Fathers of Men* (1912), for example, the hero is a working-class boy who is sent to a public school where he eventually conforms. Even Peter O'Neil, who burns articles on the Public School Spirit, loathes games and exposes the clichés of the genre, leaves Harrow with a certain amount of traditional regret. Nor is it to be inferred that German fiction is devoid of celebratory books in which traditions very like those found in English school stories are applauded (H.A. Krüger's *Gottfried Kämpfer*, published in the same year as *Unterm Rad*, for example). Novels about cadet schools approximate those set in English schools, concerned with codes of honour and a corporate ethos, but they are rather more brutal than would have been acceptable in England. A boy might refuse to sneak on his peers and thus endure a beating, but when bullying is fatal, one would have thought that it would take more than British pluck to prevent the victim from divulging the names of his persecutors. However, in a novel by Paul von Szczepanski published in 1901 under the evocative title *Spartanerjünglinge*, a boy's lips remain sealed unto death. Beating and bullying might mar some of the fictional schools of England, but one would hardly expect to discover a pair of boys systematically torturing one of their sexually submissive fellows in an attic room as in Musil's *Die Verwirrungen des Zölings Törless* (1906; translated merely as *Young Törless* – 'perplexities' (*Verwirrungen*) clearly regarded as hardly adequate for the case).

The most apparent and important difference between school novels published in England and those published in other countries is that the former constitute a separate, identifiable genre, whilst the latter belong to the mainstream of literature. There is still no Great Public School Novel,[1] although there are several good ones. No 'major' novelist has set a work entirely within the walls of a public school. It may be that the formula which attracted so many writers is too restricting to appeal to novelists of the first rank. The advantages of the closed community of a boarding school for less adventurous writers are obvious. A society with its rules, rivalries and hierachies ready-made, with its inward-looking self-containment and its distinct set of characters, is ideal material for fiction. There is also plenty of opportunity for light moralising and for the demonstration of certain virtues – honesty, courage, loyalty – in action. That the formula comes ready-made explains why so many of these stories are extremely dull indeed, following the set pattern with

---

[1] Claims have been made for *Stalky & Co.*, but the book's origins as a series of individual stories is quite apparent and the episodes, some of which are markedly better than others, never add up to a satisfactory whole.

scarcely a deviation, tracing the passage through adolescence of the hero from tremulously apprehensive new boy to swaggering star of the final cricket match. Although the novels are ostensibly about the fortunes of an individual boy, the ivy-clad school, the traditions it enshrines and the corporate body of its inhabitants tend to dominate the proceedings.

What might be called the mainstream popular school story was developed by Talbot Baines Reed, whose tales were first published in the *Boy's Own Paper*, founded in 1879 by the Religious Tract Society, of which his father was a prominent member. Clearly there was a moral purpose here, though it was rather better disguised than in the works of Farrar and Hughes. Although *The Fifth Form at St Dominic's* might appear to be an enjoyable romp, its publishers claimed that it 'forcefully illustrates how rapidly they may sink who once tamper, for seeming present advantage, with truth, and how surely, sooner or later, a noble character comes to vindication and honour, and in all such respects it is eminently true to life.' This was more likely to appeal to the adults who purchased the books than the boys who read them, one imagines. Reed's heroes had 'that moral grit and downright honesty of purpose that are still, we believe, the distinguishing mark of the true public-school boy'. The mark, perhaps, but not the preserve. Reed believed that: 'The strong should look after the weak, the active must look after the lazy, the merry must cheer up the dull, the sharp must lend a helping hand to the duffer', and that the public schools should give the lead to the lower classes. He told members of a Manchester Boys' Club to: 'Pull together in all your learning, playing and praying.' He also believed that such aims should not be uninvitingly preached, a view shared by the first editor of the *BOP*, G.A. Hutchinson, who insisted that the magazine should appeal to 'boys and not their grandmothers'. Reed signed his first story in the very first issue of the *BOP* 'An Old Boy'. He had been a day-boy at the untypical City of London School and his notions of traditional public-school life were based upon the recollections of his Old Radleian Cambridge friends. The signatory alliance with Hughes was appropriate since the *BOP*'s editorial policy was guided by Muscular Christianity ('a truly Christian paper – helpful in the very highest and best and manliest sense of the word'), and Reed's stories are direct descendants of the first half of *Tom Brown's Schooldays*. All the elements which were to become familiar in school stories are to be found in Reed's work: games, inter-House rivalries, fagging, cribbing, mild rebellion, mild bullying and mild romantic friendships.

As well as promoting the public-school ideal, Reed was concerned that his stories should be authentic. If boys could be persuaded to believe in the schools and their inhabitants, they would be more forcibly struck by the moral message. 'Does someone tell me he never heard of Fellsgarth?' Reed asked on the second page of his novel *The Cock-House at Fellsgarth*. 'I am surprised. Where can you have been brought up that you have never heard of the venerable ivy-clad pile with its watch-tower and two wings, planted there, where the rivers Shale and Shargle mingle their waters a mile or more above Hawkswater?' Before long it could be replied that wherever a boy had been brought up he was likely to have heard of Fellsgarth or schools very similar. The popularity of Reed led to many lesser hands attempting the school story and the popularity of the *BOP* resulted in other magazines for boys in which the antics of boys similar to those of St Dominic's were endlessly recounted. In the 1914 volume of *The Champion*, to take an example at random, three of the four serials are set in schools, a large percentage of the short stories bear titles such as *Noblesse Oblige: A School Tale* or *Dixon's Choice: A Public School story*. A similarly high proportion of the articles are concerned with public schools: 'A Letter to a Boy at School' (concerning games), '*Tom Brown's Schooldays* and Rugby School', 'A Schoolboy's Diary of 34 Years Ago', 'The Schooldays of Two Great Prime Ministers', 'School Songs of Shrewsbury', 'Arnold of Rugby', 'Privileges of Christ's College Boys', and so on.

Charles Hamilton, the creator of Greyfriars and Billy Bunter, and the man behind a phalanx of *noms de plume* in numerous magazines, is supposedly the most prolific author in the history of literature. Such was the insatiable demand for school stories that Hamilton managed to sell some 72,000,000 words' worth of fiction during his working life.

2 Boys' Magazines

Boys' magazines evolved from mid-Victorian family journals suitable for Sunday reading to become repositories of such public-school ideals as patriotism, chivalry, honour, fair play, discipline and, latterly, militarism. However, it was not until 1940 that questions were raised about the contents of such publications. In his celebrated essay, *Boys' Weeklies*, George Orwell discerned a sinister establishment plot behind *Gem*, *Magnet* and other seemingly innocuous magazines. The fact that then, as in the Edwardian period, the Amalgamated Press owned a large proportion of the weeklies as well as several right-wing newspapers, suggested to Orwell that there was a deliberate plan to infect the working classes with upper-class values and to 'Catch Them Young'. 'All fiction from the novels in the mushroom libraries downwards is censored in the interests of the ruling class', he claimed. 'And boys' fiction above all, the blood-and-thunder stuff which nearly every boy devours at some time or other, is sodden in the worst illusions of 1910. The fact is only important if one believes that what is read in childhood leaves no impression behind. Lord Camrose[1] and his colleagues evidently believe nothing of the kind, and, after all, Lord Camrose ought to know.'

Orwell's concern would have been even more valid if applied to Victorian and Edwardian boys' fiction. *Tom Brown's Schooldays* had its roots not only in Old Boy piety but also in the Christian Socialist movement, of which Hughes was a prominent member. This movement also founded missions amongst the poor in which the gentlemanly ideals, and some of the gentlemanly pursuits, of the upper classes were introduced to the working classes. The *Boy's Own Paper* was published by the Religious Tract Society and, despite Hutchinson's view of the readership, there is no doubt as to the tendency that underlay its ripping yarns. The RTS also published the stories of Reed and his imitators in book form, not to mention *The Empire Annual for Boys* and other patriotic volumes. Whilst the *BOP* and its rivals spread the gospel of the public schools, the magazines of the Amalgamated Press spread the gospel of Lord Northcliffe. Northcliffe's magazines maintained the popular mixture of public-school, detective and historical fiction, but they also addressed themselves to the concerns of their proprietor, notably the need for a stronger army to repel invaders. As 1914 approached, this theme was to be found in most boys' magazines, but in Northcliffe's publications the propagandist intention was most blatant. That the establishment was involved can be seen in William Le Quex's *The Invasion of 1910*, which first appeared as a serial in the *Daily Mail* in 1906. Lord Roberts, busy president of the National Service League for the promotion of conscription, and frequent visitor to the public schools, took time off to collaborate with Le Quex and the *Mail*'s naval correspondent in order to lend authenticity to this warning tale.[2]

---

[1] Lord Camrose (1879–1954) was the newspaper proprietor who took over the Amalgamated Press in 1926. By 1928 he controlled 'two national, one specialised, and six provincial morning papers; 8 provincial weeklies; and about 70 periodicals.'

[2] Roberts's meticulous strategy was somewhat compromised by Northcliffe's insistence that the invading force should march through every town in which *Daily Mail* sales needed boosting.

The distribution and readership of these magazines was wide. There was a newly-literate population, a result of the Elementary Education Act of 1870, and both commercial and philanthropic motives guided publishers towards this previously untapped market. Low prices brought the magazines within the reach of the working classes and the *BOP* was often distributed free, or awarded as a prize, in Elementary and Sunday Schools. The later Education Act of 1902, which helped to establish a wider system of secondary education gave rise to schools which sometimes aped the public schools of fact and fiction. Malcolm Muggeridge's state secondary school may have been peopled by South London Cockneys, but:

> Its organisation was vaguely derived from that of public schools. There were four 'houses' – Alpha, Beta, Gamma and Delta – which, in practice, had little more than a nominal existence, as well as prefects, colours, and other trappings reminiscent of *Tom Brown's Schooldays*, not to mention the *Magnet* and the *Gem*. We had a Latin motto '*Ludum Ludite*', or 'Play the Game', invented, I suppose, by one of the masters.

Muggeridge was there during the War, when the school ran with a skeleton staff as eccentric as anything found in the public-school system of the period. There was even a compulsory cadet corps.

The incongruity of Board School children devouring tales, and thus the codes, of public schools was not acknowledged. However, in order to thoroughly involve working-class readers in the magazine stories, the public-school and Oxbridge-educated heroes were sometimes given young assistants whose backgrounds were less impeccable than their own. The two most famous boy sidekicks were Sexton Blake's Tinker and Nelson Lee's Nipper.[1] What they lacked in social status they made up in ingenuity and bravery. Colourful and street-wise, they played their own heroic parts, looking up to their partners with the sort of admiration a favoured fag might feel for a glamorous prefect. Indeed, at one point Lee became a schoolmaster and the ageless Nipper mingled with the pupils, a circumstance which proved so popular that the pair remained at St Frank's, solving the sort of mysteries in which fictional schools of the period were constantly embroiled.[2] Another way

---

[1] Nipper's origins were somewhat mysterious. He was able to recite Latin and, unlike poor Scaife in *The Hill*, his hands were 'perfectly modelled'.

[2] The (other) Baker Street detective, Ferrers Locke, also had a boy assistant, called Jack Duck, who was required to upgrade his forename to 'James' when he posed as a pupil at Greyfriars or St Jim's.

of infiltrating working-class boys into public schools was by a scholarship. Greyfriars boasted several such pupils, including Mark Linley and Tom Redwing, whilst at St Jim's Dick Brooke's disadvantages were compounded by an alcoholic father. Only cads treated these boys with disdain; Hamilton and the decent pupils treated them seriously and unpatronisingly. By deliberately overplaying the snobbishness of some of his schoolboys, Hamilton ensured that the working-class pupils had to fight to survive and to prove themselves 'natural gentlemen'. This device worked both ways: public-school readers could see the pitfalls of snobbery and learn about *noblesse oblige*, whilst working-class readers could see that birth was no obstacle as long as one behaved nobly. Robert Roberts, writing about Salford during the early years of this century, remembered how the boys of what he called *The Classic Slum* imitated the language and behaviour of the boys created by Charles Hamilton:

> Over the years these simple tales conditioned the thought of a whole generation of boys. The public-school ethos, distorted into myth and sold among in weekly penny numbers, for good or ill, set ideals and standards. This our own tutors, religious and secular, had signally failed to do. In the final estimate it may well be found that Frank Richards during the first quarter of the twentieth century had more influence on the mind and outlook of young working-class England than any other single person, not excluding Baden-Powell.

Occasionally this vicarious hob-nobbing with the upper classes gave boys ideas above their station, but these were soon slapped down. Correspondence columns in the *BOP* were always to the point, particularly during the cold tub era of Dr Gordon Stables:

> The fact of your being a tradesman's son would not, of itself, be a bar to your becoming an officer in the army; but a far higher standard of education would be required than, to judge from your letter, you possess. 'Rigiment', 'standered', 'standerd' and 'tradman' are dreadful! . . . The Engineers, as you are fond of 'making *skeetches*', might suit you.

Another correspondent was told: 'We are afraid that, under the circumstances, you have no chance of entering the army as an officer. You certainly would not be allowed to keep your parentage and place of birth a secret.' Stories such as *A Narrow Escape*, which appeared in 1880, also helped to keep things in proportion. An officer in difficulties in India gallantly tells a soldier to ride away and save himself, but the soldier, equally gallantly, replies: 'Take off your stirrup, sir, and let's give 'em something. If you be killed I'm killed too, but I bain't agoing to leave you to be killed alone.' Public-school readers were thus encouraged to identify with the noble and self-sacrificing officer, whilst working-class readers could identify with the dutiful and loyal private. The proper relationship between officer and man, and the correct behaviour of each in such circumstances, are neatly demonstrated.

Although the *Boy's Own Paper* was the most famous and widely-read[1] of boys' magazines, it was not the first of them. In 1855 the similarly-named *Boy's Own Magazine* had been founded by Samuel Beeton, husband of the cookery writer. His intention was to provide boys with stories rather more edifying than those found in the 'penny dreadfuls' of the day. Perhaps the idea came to him whilst he was contemplating the success of Harriet Beecher Stowe's *Uncle Tom's Cabin*, an eminently moral read, which his publishing company had pirated from the original American edition. Sales of the *Boy's Own Magazine* were encouraging, but it was not for another eleven years that a spate of rivals appeared. E.J. Brett and four brothers called Emmett left Beeton behind in their unseemly battle for sales, which bears a marked resemblance to that currently waged by the tabloid press. Brett founded the *Boy's Own Reader* in 1866, but it only survived six months. He then founded *Boys of England* and this ran for thirty-three years. The Emmetts chose the *Young Gentleman's Journal* to launch their empire of wholesome juvenile fiction. After this the two companies produced a seemingly endless set of variations: *Young Men of Great Britain, Young Gentlemen of Britain, The Young Briton, The Young Englishman, Sons of Britannia, Boys of Our Empire*. Further confusion ensued when another publisher, Charles Fox, produced the *Boy's Standard, Boy's Champion* and *Boy's Leisure Hour*. If these magazines seem indistinguishable from one another, they were also very little different to the penny dreadfuls they were supposed to be supplanting. Since Brett, the Emmetts and Fox had all started their careers publishing penny dreadfuls this is scarcely surprising; it would seem that sound Victorian commercial sense played as large a part in their move to 'higher standards' as sound Victorian moral values. The chief difference between the two types of magazine seems to have been that formerly criminals were the perpetrators of unspeakable barbarities; now they were the victims.

Fox's *Boy's Standard* was advertised as 'A Healthy Paper for Manly Boys',

---

[1] The readership in 1884 was estimated at around 250,000.

but it was the *BOP* that is best remembered and became part of England's cultural heritage, its title used as shorthand to describe a type of adventure story and a breezy outlook on life. Perhaps its incredible longevity was responsible for this, for it continued to appear until 1967, although by then it had become monthly. Although it was not the first magazine to contain school stories, the quality of those contributed by Reed helped to establish the genre very firmly. The paper attracted other good writers, including some of the best-known names in juvenile fiction: Conan Doyle, Verne, Ballantyne and Henty. Furthermore, unlike the products of Fox, Brett and the Emmetts, the *BOP* had no murky antecedents; the Religious Tract Society imprint was a more reassuring guarantee than any number of claims about healthiness and manliness. Its 'improving' tone led to its being urged upon youths of all classes by fond parents and its action-packed stories and stirring illustrations ensured that it was read. Its chauvinism appealed to a country involved in expansionism; empire-building could be presented as individual endeavour, the adventurous, pioneering spirit labouring for the common weal.

Quite apart from merely fulfilling editorial policy and providing the reader with what was expected, writers became aware of the influence they were exerting upon the young. Poor Conan Doyle felt obliged to volunteer for military service in the Boer War at the age of forty because, as he told his mother: 'I have perhaps the strongest influence over young men, especially young athletic sporting men, of anyone in England (bar Kipling). That being so, it is really important that I should give them the lead.'[1] Giving boys the lead was a major pre-occupation of the *BOP*, a fact reflected in the large number of contributors who held military rank. Such was the proliferation of these old soldiers that it is unsurprising that one of the magazine's chief rivals, founded in 1899, was called *The Captain*. Although the name was primarily referring to school rank (captain of games, captain (i.e. head boy) of school), as the blazered figure on the covers of the annuals suggests, it seems likely that the military connotations were also intentional.[2] Captain was a popular rank amongst these writers; *The Captain*'s athletics editor was a captain, as was F.S. Brereton,[3] whose Great War sagas (*With Haig in Flanders*, *With Allenby in Palestine* and so on) were extremely popular.

[1] Conan Doyle applied to the Middlesex Yeomanry, but fortunately a friend intervened and persuaded him to join a non-combatant medical unit instead.

[2] In army hierarchy a captain was in charge of a company and often acted as adjutant to the CO of the battalion. His position was roughly equivalent to that of Senior Prefect in school hierarchy, the subalterns being his deputy prefects.

[3] Brereton was raised to the rank of Lt. Colonel during the War.

Captains also figured largely amongst the contributors to *Chums*, founded in 1892.[1] The first issue of this magazine included 'A Chat About Harrow School', which dealt in some detail with public-school life, and 'How to Train for the Football Season'. The magazine's title-page depicted two boys, one in an Eton collar, holding a book, the other in sports-clothes leaning nonchalantly against the 'C' of 'Chums'. Above them a Union Jack unfurls, whilst at their feet lies a clutter of sporting equipment. By the Great War this had changed. On one side of the title was a bugler on a prancing horse with a military ship behind him; on the other a games-player is reading a book, sitting next to another boy who is smartly-dressed, in front of a large building, presumably a school. These titles show the preoccupations of *Chums* and how the emphasis became more military. Amongst their distinguished contributors – Henty, Fenimore Cooper, Sax Rohmer – were a number of writers who specialised in the school story: Gunby Hadath, Richard Bird and Hylton Cleaver. Amongst its regular columns were 'Our Olla Podrida', a miscellany of useless information, and 'Five Minutes with the Famous'. In the former readers could learn, along with such snippets as 'It is estimated [by whom, one wonders] that Ireland contains 14,000,000 fowls', that 'Till 1840 Eton Collegers were fed upon mutton chops every day of the year'. The latter column informed boys that 'The Czar of Russia is a very energetic monarch'; that the late Lord Blachford left 'an interesting account' of the production of *The Eton Miscellany* amongst his papers; and that a Harrow schoolboy was punished for attempting to empty a pan of water onto the head of Gladstone when he visited the school. Such intriguing items about the public schools, almost subliminally introduced, naturally prompted readers' questions about education. It is no surprise to find that the Editor in 1905 was 'all in favour of the public school'. Under the headline 'Makes Britons of Them', the Editor elaborates:

A public school teaches a boy, first of all, to be self-dependent; it develops his finer qualities; gives him a code of honour than which there is no sounder in the world. In short it makes a Briton of him. And that, surely, is the finest task that any school can accomplish. However poorly a boy may do at a public school, its influence will remain to his life's end. A schoolmaster who has a private school may be the best and cleverest fellow in the world;

[1] Philip Warner, who edited *The Best of 'Chums'* in 1978, appears to follow in the tradition. Ex-army, a Senior Lecturer at Sandhurst, he 'is interested in all forms of sport – fishing, Rugby football, athletics, squash, clay-pigeon shooting – and castles. He is author of twenty-two other books.'

but how can he compete with an institution which has written its story upon the centuries and can point to attainments which the whole world has recognised? The thing is impossible. Europe envies our greater schools; America tries to imitate them. But they are a heritage of which nothing can rob us. And I can conceive no greater happiness for my British lad than that which must come to him as a public-school boy.

Nothing, it will be noted, is said about academic standards; this is propaganda for an ethos, not an education.

Chums also ran a series of stirring essays contributed by a sinister figure known as 'Sandy'. Homilies about 'The Braggart', 'The Boy Who Doesn't Fit' and 'A Boy Who Is Bound To Get On' clutter the pages of the 1914 volume. Occasionally there are flashes of pure Christopher Robin, but the advice is invariably stern and manly. For example, in 'The Boy Who Can't Play Games', 'Our "Chum" Sandy has a Chat about Doing Things Thoroughly'. This consists of making sure that boys play games properly and do not merely 'fool': 'Depend upon it, if you start fooling in your games, you'll do the same thing with your lessons, and continue it when you start your life in earnest.' A friend in the City has told Sandy that he only employs rugby players, since 'during a "boom" on the exchange, if a fellow couldn't stand his ground with a lot of fellows pushing and elbowing through a crowd, he would be of no use to him. The chap who could pile up a scrum at Rugger was just the man he wanted.' Boys must have looked at their stockbroker fathers with renewed respect after reading this.

In a piece which appeared in April 1914 Sandy addresses himself to 'The Funk':

> Watch the boy who funks at sports; watch him as he sneaks on his pals; then follow him when he gets into the Army. Is there such a thing as a hell on earth? Ask the funk what he feels like when his company is ordered to attack. Look at his half-hearted rushes, his furtive glances about him . . . How solicitous he is for a wounded chum – in a sheltered spot! Is he always such a Good Samaritan?
>
> You funk! You are ordered *to advance, to attack*. Others behind will attend to the wounded.

Sandy portrays the funk attempting to creep past his own company's sentry in the hope of getting out of this imaginary war by being taken prisoner by the enemy. The funk is careless, is challenged, runs and is shot:

Poor funk! You've done it this time. You funked that catch in the long field, you let your pals in for a swishing rather than risk one for yourself, you were afraid to face the music of the guns in open fight. You've been shot in the *back*.

This is exactly the sort of specious argument boys were to face when they returned to their schools for the autumn term that year. Slackers would not be wanted in the trenches. The idea that if a boy was such a funk it was unlikely that he would choose the army as a career seems not to have occurred to Sandy. Or had he foreseen, in April, the events of August?

The Captain was aimed specifically at public-school boys, whilst *Chums* and the *BOP* were addressed to boys of all classes. The magazines of the Amalgamated Press were aimed at office boys. Alfred Harmsworth was the founder of the popular press who had started his career with magazines entirely devoted to trivia, made up of page after page of *olla podrida*. He then graduated to boys' magazines which were intended to undercut those of his rivals. In order to emphasise their cheapness, and to set them in contrast to 'penny dreadfuls', he incorporated their price in their titles: *Halfpenny Wonder* (1892) and *Halfpenny Marvel* (1893). Office boys were not the only people who read these new magazines. The father of a Harrovian testified that 'at all the public schools there is a great rush for the *Halfpenny Marvel* and boys read it with evident enjoyment.' In 1894 Harmsworth acquired the *Evening News* which, he assured its readers, 'will preach the gospel of loyalty to the Empire and faith in the combined efforts of the peoples united under the British flag.' That same year saw the launch of two further boys' magazines, *Union Jack* and *Pluck*, which, as can be judged from their titles, were in line with the editorial policy of the *Evening News*. Despite expansion, Harmsworth had not progressed much in outlook from his early years in the business. He described the *Daily Mail*, founded in 1896, as 'The Busy Man's Daily Journal'. The sort of qualities one might look for in a newspaper – balance, depth, analysis – were time-consuming for both the journalist and the reader; what Harmsworth wanted was a digest of news, entertaining and easy to read. The *Mail* was aimed squarely at the lower-middle-class and pandered to the snobbery, chauvinism and prejudice of the man in the street. Just as this newspaper gave its readers a sense of familiarity with high society by reporting the junketings of the aristocracy and royalty at length, so Harmsworth's boys' magazines – notably *The Boy's Friend* (1895), *Gem* and *Magnet* – provided tales of public-school life for a large proportion of readers who would never be able to attend such

[133]

establishments. The coarseness of Harmsworth's politics, as peddled in his newspapers, also had its counterpart in the crude public-school ethos to be found in his boys' magazines. His influence, as malign as it was extensive, must have been difficult to avoid. Whilst parents read the *Mail*, the *Daily Mirror* (founded 1903), the *Observer* (bought in 1905) or *The Times* (acquired in 1908), their offspring had an even wider choice of reading matter produced by the Amalgamated Press.[1]

Whilst boys in the schools joined the OTC in preparation to repel any foreigners foolish enough to threaten England, so in the magazines of Lord Northcliffe (as Harmsworth had become in 1905) a warning note was sounded. We have already noted Northcliffe's obsession with what he saw as an unprepared Britain vulnerable to invasion. This was directly linked with another of Northcliffe's obsessions: powered flight. With the fantasies of Jules Verne apparently about to be realised, the possibilities of aerial bombardment were endless, and endlessly repeated in boys' stories. Rather tempting providence, Northcliffe offered a prize for the first man to cross the Channel by air. To his chagrin a Frenchman performed this feat and after Blériot's success an aerial invasion of Britain left the realms of fantasy and became (at least in the fervid mind of Northcliffe and his boys' writers) a genuine threat. Few people doubted the supremacy of Britain's naval power and this, as Northcliffe saw it, meant that the country had become complacent in other areas. A year after Blériot's flight, by which time the French had spent £47,000 on aircraft for military use and the Germans had invested £400,000 in research, the British Committee of Imperial Defence baulked at the cost of aeroplanes (about £1,000 each), and proposed that the money would be better spent on airship research. The War Office considered that £2,500 was too much to spend on experiments with aeroplanes. Sir Douglas Haig, addressing a meeting of the military in the summer of 1914, said: 'I hope none of you gentlemen is so foolish as to think that aeroplanes will be able to be usefully employed for reconnaissance in the air.' As at the Somme, he put his faith in the cavalry.

Northcliffe's fears were constantly aired in his boys' magazines and in case the readers became too caught up in the sweep and excitement of the stories, direct addresses were made to ensure that the message got through. 'Will my readers believe that there are at the present time but a few hundred trained soldiers in this country to resist any attack an antagonistic foreign nation might

---

[1] Apart from the magazines already mentioned, there were the *Boys' Realm* (1902), the *Boys' Herald* (1903) and the *Dreadnought*, the *Penny Popular* and the *Penny Wonder* (all 1912).

choose to make on our little island home?'[1] asked the editor of the *Boys' Friend*. The 'antagonistic foreign nation', hitherto France, Russia or, on one picturesque occasion, the Dowager Empress of China, was more and more frequently identified as Germany. ' "The Invasion of England" – it is no wild dream of the imaginative novelist, this threat of an invasion of our beloved shore. It is stolidly discussed in French, Russian – ay, and in German – newspapers'. The emergence of Germany as the baddies was in line with the editorial policy of Northcliffe's newspapers, and his journalistic persecution of that country was thought by some to have started the Great War. Whilst this is clearly nonsense, his campaign against the Hun made it a great deal easier to foist atrocity stories on the public once war had been declared. Of his boys' papers it was said in 1912 that they 'aimed from the first at the encouragement of physical strength, of patriotism, of interest in travel and exploration, and of pride in our empire.' There is no doubt where such a tendency was to lead: 'It has been said that the boys' papers of the Amalgamated Press have done more to provide recruits for our Navy and Army and to keep up the esteem of the sister services than anything else.' Presumably, had these eager volunteers been able to have foiled invasions in the suave manner of Sexton Blake they would have done so.

The invasion theme was also to be found in the works of writers more eminent than the Harmsworth Hacks. Invariably it was public-school types who thwarted any attempts made by foreign powers jealous of 'our huge possessions and colonies . . . our enterprise and grit' to invade Britain. Amongst popular works of this theme were Erskine Childers' *The Riddle of the Sands* (1903) and Saki's *When William Came* (1913). P.G. Wodehouse made a mocking contribution with *The Swoop* in 1909. Meanwhile, on the London stage, there were two plays by C.M. Doughty about a war with Germany, performed in 1909 and 1912, and *An Englishman's Home* by 'A Patriot' (in fact, Guy du Maurier and J.M. Barrie) which was first performed in 1909 and ran for eighteen months.

A characteristic example of an invasion story (not in fact from the Amalgamated Press, but from *Chums*) is *Lion's Teeth and Eagle's Claw*, 'A Thrilling New War Story by Captain Frank Shaw' (the military title no doubt bolstering illusions of authenticity). War breaks out between England and Germany: 'It's a boundary dispute, you know, down there in the Balkans.

---

[1] This (wholly inaccurate) assessment of the army's lack of strength may be compared with the letters to Etonian parents mentioned in Chapter I (p 67). No doubt such advice led to enlistments in the Territorial as well as the Regular Army.

We say one thing, Germany says another, and our way has to go. Unless Germany backs down, which I don't think likely, for she's been waiting for this ever since '71, it's war.' This news is greeted with glee by Roy Carrington, a typical *Chums* schoolboy-hero: 'War, war, war – giddy, joyful war! . . . Pater, get me an appointment aboard the *Empire*. She'll be first in the fighting and in the thick of everything.' Roy's brother Gerald has a club foot but nonetheless contrives to get into the Royal Flying Corps Reserve. This air of unreality is also seen in the escape of Tom Blaydon, a young Territorial officer who defends Crummock Hall against the invading forces until he is the last of his unit left alive. He escapes by clambering onto the roof from which he is hauled to safety by a lassooist in an aeroplane. A fleet of airships is defeated and the boys get honoured by George V, with whom they appear to be on easy terms. An indemnity of £250,000,000 is exacted from Germany, which puts paid to any further war aims of that notoriously belligerent nation. The final scene is a royal procession through London: 'George and Roy Carrington were receiving their reward in the acclamations of the throng. Honours would be showered upon them later, but it was enough for them to know they had done their best for England. Boys, it is for you to follow in their path.' These closing sentences appeared in the issue of 25 April 1914; the message could hardly be clearer, the scenario could hardly be less accurate.[1]

An aspect of the Great War which has constantly baffled later generations is its popularity when it was declared. Was it simply a matter of absurd optimism that drew the crowds to the recruiting station or was it the result of a concentrated barrage of disinformation? The two are closely connected. Few people can look any longer at the faded photographs of the waving, hatted figures without murmuring with Larkin: 'Never such innocence again'. To many the War seemed an opportunity to escape from the drudgery of everyday life. What Graham Greenwell wrote in retrospect might stand for the expectations of the young volunteer:

That [the War] contained moments of boredom and depression, of sorrow for the loss of friends and of alarm for my personal safety is indeed true enough. But to be perfectly fit, to live among pleasant companions, to have responsibility and a clearly defined job – these are great compensations when one is very young

[1] Invasion stories continued throughout the War, but British pluck needed a helping hand by 1918, to judge from the *Chums* saga *The Phantom of the Sands* which concerned 'The Exploits of Two Patriotic British Boys who, Aided somewhat by a Weird Old Legend, Upset Some of the Kaiser's Fiendish Designs on Our Coast'.

People have always run away to wars as a means of avoiding personal problems, uncongenial jobs, boredom and loneliness, or simply out of a sense of adventure. That the boys' magazines of the period encouraged a sense of adventure is in little doubt. That they presented abroad as somewhere an English chap went to sort out other nations, either the savage or the treacherous, is also true. That the Amalgamated Press in particular promoted belligerence, especially towards Germany, is indisputable. One little boy, an avid reader of *Chum* and the *Boys' Friend*, set up fortifications in Hampstead Garden Suburb in 1909. He and some friends, whose father worked in the War Office, converted a building site into a redoubt, above which a Union Jack fluttered. The children styled themselves 'The Pistol Troop' and repelled other groups who came to investigate. However, their real purpose was all that Lord Northcliffe could have wished: 'We were reserving our strength for the Prussian Guard', Evelyn Waugh recalled. 'We were rather priggishly high-minded. "Honour" was a word often on our lips. Dishonesty, impurity or cruelty would have been inconceivable to us.'

3 Sounding Bugles

Before the Great War there was no War Poetry as we now conceive the term; instead there was martial verse. Most of this was written by civilians who, far from playing up and playing the game themselves, were generally cheering from the stands. Victorian Britain had enjoyed a long period of peace; such wars as interrupted this took place far away and were conducted by professionals. A civilian's view of war in 1914 might be gained from what little history he had learned at school and from popular and serious fiction. A curriculum based upon classical texts tended to emphasise the noble aspects of warfare, particularly when taught by imperialists. The patriotic certainties of *Henry V* were much better known than the subversive depiction of war in *Troilus and Cressida*.[1] Until Owen it was the Classical rather than the Romantic heritage which influenced poetry written about warfare. Indeed,

[1] *Henry V* has always been held as an inspiration in time of trouble. It combines a rousing patriotism with a sense of Britain's great literary heritage. In the Second War there was Laurence Olivier's triumphant film. During the First War Frank Benson's production of the play, which opened on Boxing Day 1914, apparently inspired 300 members of its audiences to enlist.

when Victorian and Edwardian poetry addressed itself to this subject, it tended to look to a Classical or distant national past and to extol the virtues of heroism and chivalry and patriotism. When Victorian battles were commemorated it was in terms far removed from the actuality of the front line. Tennyson's 'The Charge of the Light Brigade', perhaps the most celebrated of war poems, admits that 'Some one had blunder'd', but regards the blunder as a perfect opportunity for a display of reckless heroism. An undeservedly popular piece, its vision of the Battle of Balaclava is lofty and vague, with references to 'the valley of Death' and 'the mouth of Hell'. It is worth imagining briefly the sort of mess that would result from a light cavalry charge against large, well-defended field-guns. The chaos and carnage are not vividly rendered:

> Cannon to right of them,
> Cannon to left of them,
> Cannon behind them
>   Volleyed and thundered;
> Stormed at with shot and shell,
> While horse and hero fell . . .

Tennyson's epitaph to the victims of a pointless military action is lamentably anodyne:

> When can their glory fade?
> O the wild charge they made!
>   All the world wondered.
> Honour the charge they made!
> Honour the Light Brigade,
>   Noble six hundred!

The stirring rhythms disguise a slackness of thought and expression, whilst the tone is that of a hectoring schoolmaster of limited vocabulary.[1] Compare this with Thackeray's Crimean War verses, 'The Due of the Dead', in which the writer admits the consequences of warfare and makes a practical suggestion as to how its victims might be commemorated. It is not by any means a great poem, but it is at least an intelligent one.

The rise of imperialism at the end of the nineteenth century produced its

---

[1] A Salopian in 1910, who no doubt gained his knowledge of the Charge from Tennyson, thought it 'a healthy incentive to bravery'.

quota of military verse, mostly from the pens of W.E. Henley and Henry Newbolt. Of both these men it might be said that all a poet could do in their day was to encourage. Henley's anthology of verse for boys, *Lyra Heroica* (1892), left the reader in no doubt of his intentions:

> To set forth, as only art can, the beauty and joy of living, the beauty and blessedness of death, the glory of battle and adventure, the nobility of devotion – to a cause, an ideal, a passion even – the dignity of resistance, the sacred quality of patriotism, that is my ambition here.

The critics felt that Henley had succeeded. The *Illustrated London News* thought the anthology 'admirably adapted to stimulate courage and patriotism in the young'. The *Irish Daily Independent* thought it 'like the blast of a trumpet . . . it would be hard indeed to make a milksop of a lad nourished on these noble numbers.' This view of literature as some sort of tonic pill was reflected in other journals: 'A manly book', 'the kind of reading which will help to make them men', 'enough . . . to stir all the boys' hearts in the kingdom as by a trumpet', and so on. More trumpet-blasts sounded from Worthing in 1900 when Henley greeted the Boer War with *For England's Sake: Verses and Songs in Time of War*, which was dedicated to the memory of a young lieutenant with a VC and 'many valiant souls whose passing for England's sake has thrilled the ends of the world with pain and pride'. Another volume, Henley asserted, was 'nothing if not a fighting book. It is designed to bring out such old, elementary virtues as the dignity of patriotism, the beauty of battle, the heroic quality of death.' Such old elementary virtues as inspiration, inventiveness and diction were usually subordinate to the message of mindless jingoism.

Newbolt sounded a similar note in his stirring verses of England's seafaring heritage and her imperial triumphs, in which he broadcast his fatal confusions between the playing-field and the battleground. His facility for rhyme and rhythm made his poems easily accessible to schoolboys, and his small collection celebrating his old school, *Clifton Chapel and Other School Poems* (1908), was published at the request of the then headmaster. Love of the old school and patriotism were intertwined and both could be proved in battle. Both these men sacrificed poetic imagination to a formula, and managed to forestall analysis of what (little) they were saying by taking refuge in lofty rhetoric. At the heart of their work was a patriotism ossified by blind reverence, unchallenged and therefore uninspired. Rather than analysing the patriotic impulse, they simply elevated it to a mystical religion which brooked no criticism. There was a great deal of nonsense in their verse about eternal fires, sacred flames, sweeping swords and bright honour, much arising and awaking, rolling of drums and sounding of trumpets. Life and Youth and Spirit were rarely printed without a capital initial. It was the *Boy's Own Paper* in verse, part of what Bertrand Russell called the 'whole foul literature of "glory" . . . with which the minds of children are polluted'.

4 Missionaries

As well as producing the most popular and effective piece of public-school propaganda, Thomas Hughes was also instrumental in spreading the public-school ethos amongst the illiterate working classes. The two great influences on Hughes's life were Thomas Arnold, whilst he was at Rugby, and Thomas Carlyle, whilst he was at Oxford. The combination of these two mentors resulted in an alliance with Christian Socialism, in which Carlyle's radicalism was tempered by Arnold's piety. A group of ardent young men decided to act upon their principles and attempt to do something to alleviate the lot of the East London working classes. They helped to set up workers' co-operatives, a scheme which eventually led to such utopian organisations as C.R. Ashbee's Guild of Handicrafts. In the early stages, however, there was a concentration upon education; not the teaching of trades, but a broad, liberal, 'improving' education of the sort to be found in public schools and at Oxbridge. Not that the labourers were taught Latin and Greek, of course; but they were to be made into gentlemen. The educational programme began with evening classes and then, in 1854, the Working Men's College was founded in Red Lion Square. The teachers would also benefit by this programme in the sense that they were performing their gentlemanly duties of service to the community. Graduates from Oxford and Cambridge could visit the College to hear the likes of Ruskin and Rossetti, and be fired with ideals of romantic socialism.

Meanwhile, Hughes, not by any stretch of the imagination an academic, looked to the physical well-being of the pupils. Whilst his friends addressed themselves to *mens sana*, Hughes aimed to develop the *corpus sanum*. Grinding poverty and a bad diet had produced men in need of some beefing-up and Hughes performed the task with relish. A favourite form of exercise, and one calculated to appeal to the men, was boxing 'with the weapons which God has given us all'. The men were also encouraged to row and to play cricket, two favoured Etonian pursuits.

Hughes's lofty view of games was shared by the first priest at Eton College Mission, W.M. Carter: 'It must be the duty of the Christian Church to care for men's bodies as well as for their souls', he wrote; 'the one has so much to do with the other.' The Eton Mission at Hackney Wick was one of the earliest of the public-school settlements, founded in 1880. Christian Socialism was fed back into the universities by people like Ruskin and Kingsley, who lectured there. Eager undergraduates who had experienced the Working Men's College and other such foundations of a less educational and more basically philanthropic nature, went on to teach in public schools and to spread the word there. The Eton Mission was founded after Walsham How, Suffragan Bishop of London, visited the school to address pupils and staff upon conditions in the poorer areas of his diocese. It was decided that there was an opportunity for the cream of society to do something positive to help the dregs, and Eton undertook to support a priest in any area the Bishop chose to nominate. How took the school at its word and suggested Hackney Wick, an area wretched even by the standards of the day. Commonly known as 'The Sink', it was separated from the rest of Hackney by a viaduct, and bound by the lines of the Great Eastern and North London Railways. A population of some 6,000 was crammed into an area 'about the size of the Eton Playing Fields'. The inhabitants were railwaymen, dockers and factory-workers, employed in the manufacture of jam, dyes and india-rubber. Many people worked at home in sweated labour, making clothes for the wealthy, shoes for the colonies, or matchboxes for the Bryant and May works at Bow.[1]

Hornby approached Carter, an Old Etonian, who agreed to take the job on the condition that he was not employed as a curate to the vicar of the local church, as was customary, but was 'licensed as an East End Missionary responsible to the Bishop of the Diocese alone'. Some idea of the living conditions in Hackney Wick can be gained from the fact that Carter's house, which was two up, two down and a kitchen, was intended to house two entire families. His chosen centre of operations was a disused undertaker's shop, the downstairs room of which could hold thirty to forty people. The first celebration of the Holy Eucharist was attended by one elderly man, whose piety was rewarded with an appointment as verger when the Mission's first church

---

[1] Bryant & May paid 2¼d per gross of matchboxes, for the construction of which the workers had to provide their own paste or string. This gives some idea of the level of poverty.

was built. Carter was pelted with flour and eggs during his investigative walks around the area, but he capitalised upon the natural curiosity of local children and gradually won the community's respect and support. Services, meetings, Sunday School and a boys' club were all run from the undertaker's shop until a tin tabernacle was built on a rubbish dump at the back of the street. By the end of the first year Carter could report that there were 300 Sunday School pupils, 20 volunteer teachers and 50 to 60 members of the boys' club. 25 confirmations had taken place.

Old Etonians came to work at the Mission, or to visit it and help out on a temporary basis, organising cricket and football pitches and arranging for rowing to take place on the River Lea or the Cut in a boat called 'The Bounder' which an OE had donated. Chaps' Sisters were roped in to teach in the Sunday School and to organise women's meetings, whilst 'the Ladies at Eton made provision for a district nurse'. Dr Warre, the Mission's first treasurer, came for a weekend to preach and was no doubt cheered by the sight of a Cadet Corps drilling under the instruction of an OE. However, he 'could not sleep owing to the whistling and shunting of the Great Eastern Railway at Stratford', and thereafter confined his visits to day-trips. Another future headmaster, George Lyttelton, visited the Mission and sang Plantation Songs.

Apart from subscriptions from Etonians past and present, subscriptions which raised some £30,000 between 1892 and 1912, money and gifts flowed in from a variety of sources. When Carter wanted to start a parish library, all OEs in publishing were asked to donate books. The usefulness of other gifts was not always immediately apparent. Half a dozen 'jockey suits made of beautiful silk' were eventually sold, the proceeds going to the poor fund. On another occasion several containers of turtle soup left over from a banquet at Mansion House arrived and this exotic fare was ladled out to 'the sick and aged'.

In spite of the evident success of the enterprise, some people were critical of what C.R. Ashbee called 'top-hatty philanthropy'. A notable critic was the *Church Reformer*:

A mission to Eton from Hackney Wick, which, with all its ugliness and misery, is probably an infinitely more moral place than Eton,[1] would be a

[1] Carter was pleased to recall very little 'sexual immorality' in Hackney. Perhaps recalling conditions at Victorian Eton, he added: 'and this was wonderful considering the hugger-mugger conditions in which so many of them had to live.'

[142]

great deal more reasonable. If the 'classes' who get false views of life and education at Eton think they can spiritualise the 'masses' by such kid-glove enterprises as that now set on foot, they are mistaken. They want spiritualising themselves a vast deal more than the people of whose miseries they are, in a very large degree, the cause. If they want to do any missioning in the East End let them take to heart the case of the rich young man in the Gospel and divest themselves of their great possessions beforehand.

There is much to criticise in the University and Public Schools missions (their cultural colonialism, for example), but this jibe is hardly fair. Not many people took much notice of such carping, and the success of Eton's Mission can be seen from the number of its imitators. Winchester and Uppingham had already founded missions by 1880, but in the wake of Eton's pioneering other schools began a programme of social work. By 1887 there were sixteen London missions as well as others in cities such as Liverpool (Shrewsbury) and Manchester (Rossall).

The pupils' attitude to their schools' missions is difficult to gauge. W.F. Bushell, who taught at Rossall, thought that the mission 'meant little to the boys except a terminal subscription'. However, after pupils had been allowed to spend weekends in Manchester with the Old Rossallian vicar, their involvement became more real and they 'got to know some of the things that were being done in the name of Rossall'. He thought that the boys' clubs were much the most useful element of school missions. Lunn's Harrovians are subjected to an appalling sermon delivered by the Bishop of the Diocese, full of cricketing analogies which even the fags recognise as bogus, in which an appeal is made to the school's honour. The boys are urged to make the Harrow Mission superior to the Eton one and to ensure that older brothers who have left the school continue to pay their subscriptions. If Lunn's account is accurate (and he claimed that his novel was based upon diaries he kept whilst a pupil), it would be hardly surprising if boys took little interest in the activities at Notting Hill. Lunn's cynical interpretation of the Bishop's concept of mission subscriptions is that 'sentimental doles were perhaps a necessary insurance against Socialism'. Peter O'Neil is horrified to find his fellow-Harrovians jeering at a meeting of the unemployed and writes to the school magazine complaining that they are not 'playing the game':

> The ideal of a Harrovian should be the ideal of a gentleman . . . the ideal of chivalry, and I ask you is it chivalrous to heckle those who are down even though we disagree with them? Do we learn at Harrow to treat with chivalry

those of less fortunate birth, or do we merely learn to consider them as 'cads',
'chaws' and 'the great unwashed'?

The editor refuses to publish the letter and Peter gains the reputation for being
'a beastly Socialist'.

Against Lunn's cynicism we should perhaps place the views of one of his
novel's sternest critics, Charles Sorley. He wrote to his parents about the visit of
a party from the Marlborough Mission in Tottenham in 1912. He gave them a
guided tour of the school and found that 'most were exceptionally lively and
interesting and oh! their intelligence! I took a couple of them up to the
Museum, and they turned out to be disappointed Darwins. The amount I
learned from them was simply stupendous.' At the same time Sorley was
discovering the poetry of Masefield, whom he found to 'express the spirit of the
age', which he defined as 'the upheaval of the masses of the population'. These
experiences led to his decision to abandon his planned career in the Indian
Civil Service ('always a bit of a bogey to me') and 'become an instructor in a
Working Men's College or something of that sort'. He had also been inspired
by a lecture given at Marlborough by Alexander Patterson, author of *Across the
Bridges* (1911), a book about social work in Bermondsey: 'I have never heard a
better: he was humorous and practical and had no nonsense or cant or
missionary canvassing about him.' One cannot help feeling that it is this sort of
influence, intelligently received, rather than proficiency on the games field, that
made young men like Sorley good officer material.

In 1951, when Eton still maintained its links with Hackney, someone
wrote: 'The Mission is a queer mixture of religion, sport and social service. But
the aim is never in doubt. It is to help the people of Hackney Wick to Heaven;
and if they are not interested in Heaven, to help them to make the best of this life,
anyway.' The same could be said of the Eton Mission, and all other missions,
during their heyday. The Christian Socialist Movement believed in 'the
natural gentleman', a state to which everyone should aspire regardless of birth
and circumstances. The working classes were eligible, but needed assistance,
and although religion was the medium, the message was that of the public-
school ethos, particularly in boys' clubs. Newbolt worked in a club in Notting
Hill and recalled that the boys 'enlarged my sense of patriotism'. There is no
doubt that the boys' own sense of patriotism was enlarged at Notting Hill and
elsewhere. Their new lives revolved around the church, sports and cadet corps,
just as did those of their social superiors at Eton, Harrow, Sherborne and
elsewhere. The Federation of Boys' Clubs which grew out of the Eton Mission

promoted inter-club competitions and sporting events which were 'a great help, as . . . an "esprit de corps" was established'. One inter-Mission sporting event was 'always of special interest': the cricket match between the Hackney Wick (Eton) and Notting Hill (Harrow) Missions. On at least one occasion this mimic match was played on the hallowed turf of Lord's.

The establishment of an *esprit de corps* was also a principal aim of the large number of Youth Movements which were founded at the same time as the missions. The first of these was the Boys' Brigade founded in Glasgow by William Alexander Smith in 1883. Although Smith was a keen Volunteer, his aim was not militarist, but religious. The Brigade drilled, but this was for pacific reasons of discipline rather than as preparation for war. Indeed Smith resisted the blandishments of Haldane who wanted to incorporate the Brigade into a national cadet force administered by the Territorials and financially supported by the War Office. Haldane was not a man to be crossed and Smith's intransigence lost the Brigade a government grant and the right to hire army camping equipment. As a wartime measure, and after Smith's death, the Brigade allowed its individual companies to decide whether they wanted to apply for W.O. recognition. It is a tribute to Smith's influence that only 291 of the 6,368 companies did apply.

Smith's mistake was to allow his boys to parade with dummy rifles, thus suggesting militarist intent. The Church Lads' Brigade, despite its name, was quite openly militaristic. Founded in 1891 by another Volunteer, its national executive was composed of members of the National Service League, its governors were of high military rank and its officers were largely public-school men. Like the missions, the CLB was intended to bring the benefits of a public-school education to the working classes. 'Remember that the CLB aims at all its members being gentlemen', officers were instructed. One of the objects of the Brigade was to give its members 'something of the free discipline, the manly games, the opportunities of wholesome society which a Public School gives'. One result of such a programme was that the CLB was able to boast that more than 250,000 of its members enlisted during the Great War.

Similar results were reported by the school missions, where, as at the schools of their sponsors, the cadet corps had increased in importance over the years. The First London Cadet Battalion was formed of young men from missions run by Oxford, Eton and Sherborne. These boys were later joined by those from the Westminster Mission in Vincent Square. During the Great War the officer commanding 'E' Company was able to report that he and his second lieutenant:

made a special point of instilling in NCOs a sense of responsibility and control of their sections and of developing something of the Public-school spirit in the whole Company, and it has both surprised and encouraged us to find in what good measure this sense exists amongst these lads who have so few advantages.

At Hackney Wick by February 1914 there were enough cadets to form an entire company: 'D' (St Mary of Eton) Company, 11th Battalion, 11th City of London Cadets. When war was declared the Company had more applications than it could handle due to a lack of funds and officers. The Men's Club provided so many recruits that, like the Public Schools Club in Albemarle Street, it was closed during the War. In October 1914 the *Salopian* reported that 73 Liverpudlians from the Shrewsbury Mission had joined the colours.

Although generally regarded as a force working towards international co-operation and unification, the most famous of all youth movements, the Boy Scouts, was founded during a period of national unease in the wake of the Boer War. The Scout Movement grew out of the experiences in Africa of Robert Baden-Powell, a devoted Old Carthusian and the hero of Mafeking. Baden-Powell was one of the young officers who contributed articles to the *Boy's Own Paper* in the 1890s. He had formed his ideas about scouting as an activity adaptable for boys whilst bear-hunting in Kashmir (a suitably *BOP* occupation), and these 'Aids to Scouting' were serialised in *Boys of Our Empire* magazine whilst the siege of Mafeking was taking place. A cadet corps was formed in the besieged town and provided with uniforms. The cadets acted as orderlies, messengers and look-outs, and the likeness of one thirteen-year-old sergeant major was used on a stamp devised by Baden-Powell. One of the first deliveries of mail to be received after the relief of the town was twenty copies of each issue of the *BOP* which had been published during the siege.

A curious mixture of Malory, Fenimore Cooper and F.W. Farrar, the Scout Movement proved extremely popular and influential. Although appealing to all classes, the Scouts were intended to be of particular benefit to working-class boys, and the first camp, held on Brownsea Island at the same time as the annual OTC camps in 1907, consisted of a judicious mix of East End and public-school lads. The movement's bible, *Scouting for Boys* (1908) stressed ideals that were recognisably those of the Edwardian public school: honour, courtesy, loyalty, obedience, discipline, chastity and fair play. 'Play-up!' Baden-Powell commanded in this book. 'Each man in his place, and play the game!' Indeed, several prep schools whose pupils were a little young to form a corps formed Scout troops instead.

The Movement spread rapidly, particularly after the appearance of *The Scout*, a weekly magazine which was soon selling more than 100,000 copies of each issue. A famous cartoon which appeared in *Punch* in 1909, entitled 'Our Youngest Line of Defence' depicted a tiny scout taking a bombazine-clad 'Mrs Britannia' by the arm and declaring: 'Fear not, Gran'ma; no danger can befall you now. Remember, *I* am with you!' This sentimental notion was treated with some seriousness by Saki in his surprisingly mawkish *When William Came*, where the Boy Scouts defy the occupying Germans by not turning up for a grand march-past. The novel, published a year before the War, ends with the optimistic declaration: 'The younger generation had barred the door.' As with most invasion fiction, the book's message was clear; it was the Scouts' own motto: Be Prepared. Prepared or not, when War was declared the Toynbee Hall troop of Scouts was marched to the recruiting office by its scoutmaster and enlisted *en bloc*. As the New Army formed, the lack of officers particularly in the industrial north, led to some *ad hoc* arrangements. Martin Middlebrook records that when the 1st Manchester Pals were settling into camp, it was often a former Boy Scout who was detailed to be in charge of a tent. Baden-Powell would have been delighted.

PART TWO

[4]

Now, God Be Thanked

Honour has come back, as a king, to earth,
And paid his subjects with a royal wage;
And Nobleness walks in our ways again;
And we have come into our heritage.

Rupert Brooke

W HEN war was finally declared many people felt a sense of relief after the
mounting tension of that bank holiday weekend. The Government's
decision to enter the War was a popular one and there is a feeling that for some it
seemed that the holiday was to be extended indefinitely. Rather than return to
factory or office for the drudgery of another week, men could queue at the
recruiting office and look forward to several weeks of training in the open air.

Men who had been at public school and had thus been prepared for their
role as officers for a New Army must have felt with Brooke that they had come
into their heritage, though it is doubtful whether they would have expressed it
quite like that. Poets too felt that they had a role to perform and a subject worthy
of their verse. However, not everyone was unequivocally enchanted at the
prospect of war. Rupert Brooke and Charles Sorley display the different stances
taken by two public-school poets, whilst the men of the University and Public
Schools Brigade represent the public-school ranker who preferred to serve with
his fellow Old Boys than to officer the masses.

1 Anglo-Saxon Attitudes

He's an Anglo-Saxon Messenger – and those are Anglo-Saxon attitudes.
He only does them when he's happy.

The White King

[151]

Contemplating the efflorescence of patriotic verse which greeted the outbreak of war, Charles Sorley wrote: 'I'm thankful to see that Kipling hasn't written a poem yet.' He felt that his own sonnet 'Whom We Therefore Ignorantly Worship', written in September 1914 'should get a prize for being the first poem written since 4 August that isn't patriotic'. Most of the establishment poets churned out the rhetoric and anthologies such as *Poems of the Great War* were rushed out and gobbled up by the public who apparently had an insatiable appetite for the profundities of Robert Bridges, William Watson, Owen Seaman and others.

> There is not anything more wonderful
> Than a great people moving towards the deep
> Of an unguessed and unfeared future,

proclaimed John Freeman, prevented from moving towards the recruiting office by a weak heart (physiologically speaking). In a poem entitled 'Duty' which prefaced an anthology produced for the National Relief Fund, Watson demanded:

> Give gladly, you rich — 'tis no more than you owe —
> For the weal of your Country, your wealth's overflow!
> Even I that am poor am performing my part;
> I am giving my brain, I am giving my heart.

On the evidence, this contribution is negligible. Even poets from whom admirers might have expected better capitulated to the general mood. Reading Hardy's *Satires of Circumstance* in November 1914, Sorley complained:

> I think that 'Men who march away' is the most arid poem in the book, besides being untrue of the sentiments of the rankerman going to war. 'Victory crowns the just' is the worst line he ever wrote — filched from a leading article in *The Morning Post* and unworthy of him who had always previously disdained to insult Justice by offering it a material crown like Victory.

Earlier he had written to a friend:

> For the joke of seeing an obviously just cause defeated, I hope Germany will win. It would do the world good and show that real faith is not that which

says 'we *must* win for our cause is just', but that which says 'our cause is just: therefore we can disregard defeat'.

Sorley saw through the posturings of his contemporaries as devastatingly as he saw through those of his elders. A lone voice, he considered Brooke's sequence of war sonnets:

> overpraised. He is far too obsessed with his own sacrifice, regarding the going to war of himself (and others) as a highly intense, remarkable and sacrificial exploit, whereas it is merely the conduct demanded of him (and others) by the turn of circumstances, where non-compliance with this demand would have made life intolerable. It was not that 'they' gave up anything of that list he gives in one sonnet: but that the essence of these things had been endangered by circumstances over which he had no control, and he must fight to recapture them. He has clothed his attitude in fine words: but he has taken the sentimental attitude.

Indeed, one might have expected something less like the contents of a public-school hymnal from the rebellious Fabian who once kept his sentiment in check.

A comparison between Brooke and Sorley is instructive, partly because in many ways they were not dissimilar. Both came from academic, Scottish families and received traditional public-school educations. Both enjoyed their time at school, but felt free to criticise and mock the system. Both had socialist leanings and both had visited and liked Germany before the War. 'It hurts me, this war,' Brooke wrote to a friend, 'because I was fond of Germany. There are such good things in her, and I'd always hoped she'd get away from Prussia and the oligarchy in time. If it had been a mere war between us and them I'd have hated fighting. But I'm glad to be doing it for Belgium . . . But it's a bloody thing, half the youth of Europe blown through pain to nothingness, in the incessant mechanical slaughter of these modern battles.' This is a rather different Brooke to the ecstatic patriot of the sonnet sequence. Brooke's personal life was somewhat tangled and it seems likely that he saw the War as a way out of his difficulties. But Brooke, unlike Sorley, was a romantic and, it has to be said, something of a poseur. Part of his charm was that he was aware of this. At Rugby he had posed as a Wildean decadent; when his father died he enjoyed his brief role as a public-school housemaster; his relationships with women seem to have been highly-charged but rather insubstantial; his South Seas trip was pure *Blue Lagoon*; his espousal of the War was the final gesture of someone in search of a cause and a role. Once he had decided upon this course – and there was considerable indecision at first – he stuck to it. As he admitted in another context (that of charming Henry James): 'I did the fresh, boyish stunt, and it was a great success.'

What, indeed, could be more boyish than the persona presented in the war sonnets? Unlike Sorley's poems, these are unclouded by irony; they are the clear-eyed, frank expressions of some school-story Sixth Former. Indeed, the first of the sequence echoes Catherine Winkworth's words of thanksgiving in a hymn frequently sung at the end of a school year: 'Now thank we all our God, / With heart, and hands and voices'. The similarity is surely intended:

> Now, God be thanked Who has matched us with his Hour,
> And caught our youth, and wakened us from sleeping . . .

The next lines of the poem are pure *Boy's Own Paper* posturing as Brooke adopts the stance of Reginald Rupert, hero of P.C. Wren's *The Wages of Virtue*, who:

> hoped to continue to turn up in any part of the world where there was a war. What Reginald, like his father, loathed and feared was Modern Society life, and in fact all civilised life as it had presented itself to his eyes – with its incredibly false standards, values and ideals, its shoddy shams and vulgar pretences, its fat indulgence, slothfulness and folly.

> To turn, as swimmers into cleanness leaping,
> Glad from a world grown old and cold and weary,
> Leave the sick hearts that honour could not move,
> And half-men, and their dirty songs and dreary,
> And all the little emptiness of love!

In the third sonnet, the bugles which blow out over the rich Dead show Brooke drifting perilously close to Henley. In the final and most celebrated sonnet, 'The Soldier', Brooke infuses a countryside he has previously depicted with affectionate irony with the sort of mystical apprehensions of England to be found in such anthologies as the *Poems of To-Day* series. The repetition of 'England' (four times) and 'English' (twice), similar to the exhortations of the king in *Henry V*, is responsible for its incantatory power. So well known is it that it is difficult to sweep aside the clutter that surrounds it and recognise it as not very far removed from the sort of poem that Bridges might have written. The entire sequence recalls the ethos of *The Hill* and is both uncharacteristic and unworthy of Brooke. However, the country in the dark days of 1915 needed an icon, and Brooke offered himself up, thus partaking in a rather different sort of self-sacrifice than perhaps he intended.

A writer in the *Star* claimed of Brooke: 'He is the youth of our race in symbol.' A similar misappropriation of Sorley was attempted in various quarters, perhaps prompted by the title given by his father to his posthumously published volume of poetry. *Marlborough and Other Poems* is in fact far removed from *Clifton Chapel and Other School Poems*, but it led some people to see Sorley as the model public-school subaltern. E.B. Osborn, who included Sorley amongst his company of *New Elizabethans*, assumed that he 'loved Marl-borough as well as any boy loved his old school'. In fact Sorley assured a friend who was just about to leave the school:

> I am not a patriotic OM; neither, I imagine, will you be. But if I must have an appellation to go through life with – and I suppose one must be labelled something – it is Marlburian: for Marlborough to me means the 'little red-capped town' (sorry for quoting from myself!) and the land that shelters it: not the school which has given it so much and so transient notoriety.

Osborn also asserted that Sorley was 'undying proof of the validity of a true classical training'. After a foiled attempt to give up the subject altogether, Sorley had complained: 'I find Classics more and more boring every day.' Even worse than Osborn's attempt to gather the poet into his fold is St John Adcock's *For Remembrance*. The first chapter is prefaced with the couplet:

> Compare this England of to-day
> With England as she once has been.

The context from which these lines have been wrenched is a long poem entitled 'A Call to Action', as Adcock acknowledges. However, the poem has nothing to do with the War; it is a critique of the indolence of a public school in 1912. Adcock at least quotes Sorley's 'All the Hills and Vales Along' in full, but then completely misinterprets it. Perhaps he was rather puzzled by it, for he describes it as a 'bizarre metaphysical fantasy', but he nonetheless discerns 'the rapt sense of mystical joy in dying for a great end that shines through Grenfell's

'Into Battle' and Rupert Brooke's ['The Soldier']'. The comparison would no doubt have amused Sorley.

Sorley was simply too intelligent to swallow the public-school ethos whole:

> O come and see, it's such a sight,
> So many boys all doing right:
> To see them underneath the yoke,
> Blindfolded by the older folk,
> Move at a most impressive rate
> Along the way that is called straight.

He grew increasingly irritated by the conventional emphasis upon success and by the 'artificial positions of responsibility [which] are a poison to the characters of those who hold them'. He felt that 'as public schools are run on the worn-out fallacy that there can't be progress without competition, games as well as everything degenerate into a means of giving free play to the lower instincts of man'. This is a widely different view to the schools' own idea of games as a moral force which brought out the best in people. He was in fact Head of House, but felt that this position was a threat to his integrity and his intelligence. Unlike Brooke, he was chary of talking 'public-school-story rot', and had had 'a dreadful warning' when he took some misdemeanour very seriously, instead of laughing it off. It is significant that although Sorley took part in games and the OTC, his favourite occupation was the solitary one of running, particularly on the beautiful downs above the school.

His reaction to the outbreak of war was savage: 'I am full of mute and burning rage and annoyance and sulkiness about it. I could wager that out of twelve million eventual combatants there aren't twelve who really want it. And "serving one's country" is so unpicturesque and unheroic when it comes to the point.' This is in marked contrast to the reaction within the schools, where he imagined that papers given to literary societies would be 'confined to Lyra Heroica, William Watson, the Oxford Pamphleteers,[1] and the wickedness of George Bernard Shaw.'

The handful of poems he produced in response to the War were more equivocal in tone than his letters, but reflected his rejection of any glorification of war: 'I do wish that all journalists etc., who say that war is an ennobling purge etc., etc., could be muzzled,' he wrote to his brother. 'All illusions about

[1] The 'Oxford Pamphlets' were propagandist tracts concerning the justice of the War, commissioned from academics who should have known better.

the splendour of war will, I hope, be gone after the war.' It is perhaps fortunate he did not live to see Adcock's volume. He saw death as simple annihilation:

> Such, such is Death: no triumph: no defeat:
> Only an empty pail, a slate rubbed clean,
> A merciful putting away of what has been.

Dead before Owen even enlisted, he also wrote poems which were in no sense consolatory. His best poem is a bleak sonnet which undermines the cult of the Glorious Dead, a cult into which he was eventually subsumed:

> When you see millions of the mouthless dead
> Across your dreams in pale battalions go,
> Say not soft things as other men have said,
> That you'll remember.

That last line neatly exposes the self-regard which was so often an element of those poets who wrote verses which supposedly commemorated the dead. The dead, he states, are beyond caring, annihilated and anonymous, and do not require honouring: 'It is easy to be dead'. It is characteristic that the one Classical line which Sorley remembers is Achilles's remark to Lycaeon, whom he is about to kill: 'Even Patroclus died, who was a better man than you by far', words which he felt 'should be read at the grave of every corpse in addition to the burial service', as he told his former headmaster; 'no saner and splendider comment on death has been made.'

It is unsurprising that Sorley should have been so admired by poets who came later and saw more of the waste of warfare, notably Sassoon and Graves. Outside the literary establishment, outside the restricting groove of his traditional education, Sorley stands alone.

> It has always seemed to me that, magnificent as the prospect of a nation in arms may be, the old system of hiring your Wellington and a handful of hundred thousand criminals to bleed for you, that your scholars and students might not let out the torch of learning in its passage from hand to hand, was, from the point of view of civilization and culture, more beneficial to the country.

It would be difficult to find a clearer rejection of 'Vitaï Lampada' (which means 'The Torch of Life') and of the ethos which embraced it.

[157]

2 *The University & Public Schools Brigade*

We were keen! And we were earnest!
(Brimming are our bitter cups!)
'Mud thou art, to mud returnest,'
Is the motto of the UPS.

A battalion of 1,000 men required about 35 officers, so that Kitchener's First
100,000 men needed some three-and-a-half thousand officers. This left a great
many young men of the officer class without an opportunity to demonstrate
their keenness. Kitchener had also caused offence amidst athletic types by
placing the upper age-limit at thirty. A letter to *The Times*, dated 26 August
1914, put forward the proposal for an élite contingent composed entirely of
university and public-school educated men. The letter came from 'Eight
Unattached' who described themselves as 'between thirty and thirty-five,
absolutely fit and game for active service.' The Eight insisted that:

> there must be hundreds of men in the same position as we are, who, between
> the years 1898 and 1903, were marksmen, and attended the Bisley musketry
> camps and Aldershot training camps with school or university corps. We
> have applied for commissions in the new Regulars, but find we are too old.
> We have offered our services as musketry instructors, and are informed that
> we are too young, and that none under thirty-five are selected.

There was only one thing for it: 'joining the ranks'. But not any old ranks:

> Many advantages would result if we all joined the same regiment, and all
> public-school men of similar age and qualifications are invited to attend a
> formal meeting . . . with a view to discuss the formation of a 'Legion of
> Marksmen' with a view to offering its services en bloc to one of the new
> battalions.

The meeting was so well attended that Claridge's had to be commandeered
to accommodate everyone. The idea of a mere 'Legion' was abandoned in
favour of an entire regiment. An invitation was extended to all frustrated

public-school men aged between 19 and 35, 'Height 5ft. 3in. and upwards; Chest 34in. at least', to enlist, 'thus upholding the glorious traditions of their Public Schools and Universities'. The anonymous historian of the UPS is at pains to stress that no snobbery was involved in this enterprise, and quotes a writer in *The Spectator*: 'There is no suggestion that public-school men are better than others, but it is natural to wish to spend possibly many weary months or years with people of one's own upbringing.' The UPS might be compared with the Pals Battalions which were forming in the North of England, in which men of one town, or of one civilian occupation in a large city, came together to form an entire battalion. However, despite the protestations of the UPS historian, the tendency of the battalion had a great deal to do with class. The very first point in the organisers' proposed submission to the War Office was that 'there are a great number of old public-school boys who are anxious to serve their country, but at the same time are somewhat chary of joining the regular army with the ordinary run of recruits'. Not content with isolating themselves from the rude soldiery, the Brigade also intended to screen applicants very thoroughly to prevent men like Sherriff slipping in: 'For the purposes of deciding what schools are public schools, all past members of those schools the names of which appear in the current number of *The Public Schools Year-book* shall be eligible.' It was even hoped that the battalion could be broken down into companies of Old Harrovians, Old Carthusians, Old Etonians and so on.[1] Not since the Spartans had sent an army of lovers to war had a group of soldiers been proposed whose loyalty to each other would be so assured.

Given the go-ahead by Kitchener ('And if you can raise 10,000 men I shall be all the better pleased'), the organisers recruited in over fifty towns all over England. The schools' headmasters were asked to raise funds to support the recruitment programme. The response was encouraging: 'Old Boys of all our big Public Schools and Universities – Eton, Harrow, Rugby, Oxford, and Cambridge – all have rolled up as keen as mustard. We are out to make history. "For King and Country and School" is our motto. There is no trace of snobbishness. Every one accepts that he is merely a "Tommy Atkins" and is proud to be one. The reason for our forming battalions of ourselves is *esprit de corps*. Every man will remember his old school, and do his utmost to keep it level with the others in this undertaking.'

---

[1] This feat was in fact achieved by a grammar school. The Grimsby Chums were formed around the nucleus of a company of 250 Old Boys of the Grammar School, who had been recruited by the headmaster.

Three hundred applicants turned up on the first day of recruiting in London and within eleven days more than 5,000 men had attested in the country, and a waiting list had to be created. Drilling began almost immediately in Hyde Park, and route marches wound through the streets of London. Onlookers remarked on 'the soldierly appearance, splendid marching, and general physique' of these fine public-school specimens. No officers were appointed at first, since all the men recruited were of the officer class and had had OTC experience. Training therefore took place 'under men who held no commissions, but who nevertheless had absolute command'. It was noted that most of the men were 'above average height', 'many of them over 6 feet, and all of them born athletes'.[1] Indeed, so splendid were the recruits that the War Office was worried as to how officers would be appointed to the Brigade. The Committee, which had already undertaken to meet the enormous expense and bureaucracy involved (15cwt. of paper was apparently used within the first two weeks), agreed to find officers from amongst the recruits whose names would be put forward for W.O. approval. The War Office, under considerable strain at this chaotic period of the War, gratefully and unprecedentedly agreed to this.

Four battalions were formed and attached to the Royal Fusiliers. The Brigade was to be trained at Epsom, billeted upon the local inhabitants (who were very obliging since their new lodgers showed 'consideration and all the other true instincts of gentlemen') until a vast camp was built in Woodcote Park. The men travelled there in the third week of September and required ten London omnibuses to carry their valises. Although without uniform (most wore riding or shooting clothes, enlivened with school scarves or university pullovers), the men drilled very efficiently. They did not get their first rifles until October, and then only one between five men. There were frequent lectures, some ('Military Hygiene' and 'Explanations as to the Belligerents and any Peculiarities regarding their Methods of Warfare') useful, others ('The Japanese Soldier' and 'The Kaiser as I knew him') less so. Unfortunately, as building work on the camp progressed, more and more recruits left for commissions in other regiments. By the time the camp was complete, some 3,000 men had left. There was considerable controversy about this. The founders of the Brigade wanted it to remain true to its original intentions, but the growth of the New Army and heavy casualties at the Front meant that the

[1] Several well-bred officers were astonished at the small stature and the pallor of their working-class men. On average, boys from public schools were five inches taller than their working-class contemporaries.

F. E. Robeson's House XI at Eton, 1913. Of the ten boys who fought, six were killed in action. Lionel Sotheby (foreground left) wrote: 'Eton will be to the last, the same as my Parents and dear Friends are to me now ... To die for one's school is an honour.'

'A Perfect Day for the Festival of Youth':
Society gathers at Eton for the Glorious
Fourth, 1914.

Programme for the Fourth of June
celebrations at Eton, 1914. 'A Pageant of
Youth, Beauty and Tradition'.

Inspection of the Eton College Officers' Training Corps, 1914.

Etonian Generals at Eton.

A royal recruit. Prince Henry on an OTC exercise.

A gowned master talks to a
young recruit at
Westminster.

Standard bearers of the Eton College OTC.

The Boy's Own Paper ran a series on Public-School Missions, showing 'What "Old Boys" have Done, and are still Doing for their Less Fortunate Brothers in Poor Districts.' (*Above*) The Charterhouse Mission Footballers, Southwark 1916. (*Below*) The Haileybury Mission Cadets, Stepney 1916.

'At school, friendship is a passion'

'What illimitable confidence . . . what bitter estrange/
ments and melting reconciliations . . . what earthquakes
· of the heart, and whirlwinds of the soul . . .'

The Hill : 'A Romance of Friendship',
which is nonetheless fine, wholesome, and thoroughly manly.

From playing-field to
battlefield: illustration for
the song 'An Average Bit
of a Briton', published in
the *Boy's Own Paper* 1918.

'England at its best': Spectators at the Eton
v Harrow Match at Lord's. The 1914 match
was the last one to be played until after the
war and was attended by 38,000 people.

'A bumping pitch and a blinding light . . .': Cricket at the Front, 1915.

'If [a commander] induces his platoon to be determined to produce the best football team in the battalion, he will have done a great deal to make it the best platoon in every way.' (War Office booklet).

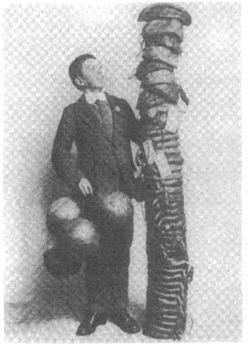

Footballs for the Front, December 1914. Before footballs became official Army issue, volunteers collected them to send to the troops.

Baptism of mud: the Eton Wall Game and Eton casualties.

UNIVERSITY & PUBLIC SCHOOLS BRIGADE
5000 MEN AT ONCE

The Old Public School and University Men's Committee makes an urgent appeal to their fellow Public School and University men

to at once enlist in these battalions, thus upholding the glorious traditions of their Public Schools & Universities.

TERMS OF SERVICE.

Age on enlistment 19 to 35, ex-soldiers up to 45, and certain ex-non-commissioned officers up to 50. Height 5 ft. 3 in. and upwards. Chest 34 in. at least. Must be medically fit.

General Service for the War.

Men enlisting for the duration of the War will be discharged with all convenient speed at the conclusion of the War.

PAY AT ARMY RATES.

and all married men or widowers with children will be accepted, and will draw separation allowance under Army Conditions.

HOW TO JOIN.

Men wishing to join should apply at once, personally, to the Public Schools & Universities Force, 66, Victoria Street, Westminster, London, S.W., or the nearest Recruiting Office of this Force.

GOD SAVE THE KING!

The Call. 'We are out to make history', the UPS boasted.

The immaculate luggage of 'University and Public School Men' being loaded into London omnibuses in Hyde Park for the journey to Woodcote Park training camp.

Playing the game and rallying round the flag. A selection of covers of *The Boy's Own Paper* during the War.

'Catching them young'. Gamages help to 'make a strapping soldier of a kid' with diminutive uniforms advertised in *Chums*.

The evolution of a type:
The slacker at school, from the *Young England Annual*.
The slacker in War: 'He, She and It', a popular postcard.

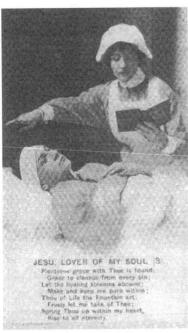

JESU, LOVER OF MY SOUL [3]

A VAD
demonstrates 'the
beauty and grace of
womanhood',
whilst giving
spiritual comfort to
the wounded.

'The White
Comrade'. A
characteristic
example of War-
time religiosity.

'Our menus would rival those at the Ritz,' one officer wrote. This Christmas
dinner at the Front in 1915 seems relatively modest.

'And is there still a Folly called the Corps?'
An unsoldierly Sorley (front row, second from
the right) at Camp with the Marlborough
College OTC, 1913.

Rupert Brooke doing 'the
fresh, boyish stunt . . . it was
a great success'.

Alec Waugh,
controversial pupil of Sherborne.

Edward Lyttelton,
controversial Headmaster of Eton.

'*C'est magnifique, mais ce n'est pas la guerre.*' A fantasy of cavalry action from the *Young England Annual.*

'They might as well be mounted on bloody rocking-horses for all the good they are going to do,' remarked one soldier of the cavalry at Arras. Cavalry training in 1915.

Prince Henry helps his schoolfellows to unload supplies at Didcot, 1915.

From playing-field to potato-patch. Digging the hallowed turf of 'Mesopotamia', 1917.

Epitaph for a generation. Simonides' lines
upon the Spartan dead, 480 BC, adapted for
the English dead, 1915 AD.

'Of gallant St Georges to-day we've a legion', 226 of whom were
recorded upon the War Memorial at Westminster School (destroyed
by bombing during the Second World War).

demand for new officers was continually increasing.[1] It began to be rumoured that the Commanding Officers of the UPS were holding back men who could be usefully employed elsewhere. 'Is it to the general good of the Army that, at a time when officers are urgently needed, men who should be officers should be kept in the ranks of privates, who should fill the vacant places?' asked one irate and sarcastic correspondent in the Tory *Morning Post*. 'Men of university and public school training; men who have been for years in the OTC; men who have handled men, men who have made great sacrifice, to serve? Certainly not. They are in the ranks, and in the ranks they must remain. Their COs must be considered first. Neither War Office orders, nor men, nor the highest interests of the nation in peril count.' Undoubtedly the Committee of the UPS was worried that the Brigade was in danger of becoming a glorified OTC, merely preparing men for service in other regiments. But the War Office assured them of the Brigade's status.

The 18th, 19th, 20th and 21st Battalions of the Royal Fusiliers did not get to the Front until November 1915. Their months of training failed to impress an old regular like Frank Richards: 'They were very decent chaps but hopeless as soldiers. The only thing they ever became proficient in was swearing.' Like other battalions, their identity was gradually eroded as men were drafted in from other regiments to fill the places left by casualties. Just as the Pals Battalions became diluted with 'foreigners' (particularly after the devastation caused by the Battle of the Somme), so the UPS ranks were filled with men who could not have declined *mensa*. Eric Hiscock, an impressionable young librarian at the Bodleian, had been dazzled by 'the spurious glamour' of the UPS when they were stationed in Oxford. Although only just fifteen, Hiscock joined them, and was to recall that 'University and Public School Battalion of the Royal Fusiliers was already becoming a misnomer in 1916'. In July of that year the 20th Battalion was virtually wiped out at High Wood. Further depredations were made by the authorities and by 1917 the Brigade had supplied over 7,000 officers for other regiments and had been reduced to a single battalion.

Other battalions, equally exclusive, were raised by patriotic gentlemen, and were listed in *All Can Help: A Handbook for War-Time* issued by the Duty and Discipline Movement. The Old Boys Corps invited people to enrol at Lord's

[1] Other regiments of 'superior' recruits experienced similar difficulties. The Artists' Rifles were intercepted at Ballieul on their way to the Front in November 1914, inspected and deprived of fifty NCOs and privates who were granted 'probationary' commissions then and there and posted to other regiments.

for an officers' training course; the entrance fee was three guineas and it was claimed that 'over 350 members have obtained commissions'. The Honourable Artillery Corps charged two guineas entrance and recruits had to be personally vetted. As well as the UPS, the Royal Fusiliers also boasted two 'Sportsmen's Battalions' for the 'upper and middle classes only'. Other specifically public-school contingents included the Public School Corps ('Men who have been at public schools are eligible up to 40. Each provides his own kit.') and the 16th (Public Schools) Battalion of the Middlesex Regiment, which like the UPS was plundered for officers. Some 1,400 obtained commissions and their places were filled by men who had no connections with either Middlesex or private education.

[5]

Officers and Men

1 Gentlemen and Players

PERHAPS the decision to recruit officers from men of public-school background made sense after all, for the New Army merely reflected the society which had given birth to it. At a period when anyone who could afford it had servants there was an obvious division as to who was to lead and who was to follow in an army of civilians. Captain Arthur Gibbs, a young officer in the Welsh Guards who had been educated at Eton and Brasenose, reported to his parents from the trenches that his new servant was 'a very nice boy who promises well. An ex-footman, he has quite the correct manner.'

The distinction between an officer and a private was one both marked and carefully maintained. We have already noted that working-class recruits were, on average, five inches shorter than the men of the officer class, and this was emphasised by the uniform each wore. Officers' uniforms were made to measure by a tailor and purchased at the recruit's own expense. The smart tunic jacket, open at the collar to reveal a shirt and tie, was crossed by a polished leather field-service belt called a Sam Browne. They wore high leather riding-boots into which neatly-pressed jodhpurs were tucked. Compare this with the ill-fitting army issue uniform of a private, its baggy tunic held together by a webbing belt, the trousers stuffed into puttees (often difficult to roll on, particularly in the finger-numbing depths of winter), and clod-hopping boots. The service cap was a great deal less flattering than the immaculately peaked cap of an officer. Robert Graves thought that an officer's uniform turned a young man into 'a sort of military queen bee', about which the admiring drones swarmed with devotion. This uniform had its drawbacks. It was distinctive enough to separate the officers from their men as they advanced across No-Man's Land in any attack, and thus made them easy targets for the enemy. The lumbering ranker, weighed down by some 70lbs of equipment and carrying a rifle was a very different figure to the unencumbered officer urging his men on with a revolver. The rewards for those who did well in such attacks were also differentiated: a Military Cross for the officer; a Military Medal for the ranksman.

As in peacetime cricket there was a nice distinction between gentlemen and players: second lieutenants were addressed and referred to as Mr So-and-so, whilst privates were simply called by their surnames. The personal letters home of NCOs and men were left unsealed in order to be censored by their officers. Some officers were embarrassed by this duty, but others found that by reading the letters of their men they began to understand their characters and so find them easier to command. Although a junior officer's mail was liable to censorship in the line, few COs felt comfortable about reading the personal correspondence of their social equals. Stanhope's decision to read Raleigh's letter in *Journey's End* violates an unwritten code, and is proposed for unjust personal motives, but would have been quite in order. Perhaps in order to avoid such unease, the War Office issued special envelopes for its officers and gentlemen which bore the following declaration which the writer had to sign: 'I certify on my honour that the contents of this envelope refer to nothing but private and family matters.' This stationery was not available to everyone, it seems, and Captain Gibbs was 'very annoyed' to find that one of his letters had been opened by the censor at the Base: 'I think it awful cheek.' In the line officers had dug-outs, often crudely constructed and certainly nothing like those of the Germans (some of which had wallpaper, floor-boards and even electric lighting) but certainly a great deal better than the holes scooped out in the trench walls by the men, in which they huddled, singly or in pairs, muffled in great-coats. This disparity in accommodation extended to periods 'in rest' behind the lines, when officers would take the houses and the men, if lucky, the farm buildings.

Officers each had a soldier-servant who acted as a sort of military valet-cum-cook. They spent much time attending to their officers' elaborate uniforms and maintaining a proper menu. In this second duty they were considerably aided by the tradition by which officers' servants were given the pick of the rations when they arrived. Whilst the men's diet was largely restricted to the sort of food now recommended by top breeders for their pedigree dogs, officers frequently ate very well. Captain Gibbs told his parents that the food at

Battalion Mess was 'mostly stews or roast beef and milk puddings and stewed fruit: bacon and eggs for breakfast and tea to drink at every meal.'

Once in the line, however, the menu stopped resembling school food: 'We feed much better up in the trenches than we do in the Battn. Mess, as we supply our own food in the trenches.' Personal servants cooking for a few officers were reckoned rather better than army cooks. This is scarcely surprising, if we are to believe Major Vivian Gilbert, who claimed that cooks were selected not because of any culinary skills they might possess, but because their general appearance and behaviour let the company down on parade.

Apart from this, ingredients tended to be better because many of them came from England, parcelled-up by fond parents. Gibbs wrote that breakfast in the trenches usually included porridge with cream, sausages, bacon, eggs and, occasionally, kippers. At the beginning of 1916 he records a luncheon of oxtail soup, sausage and mashed potato, pork pie, fruit, chocolate, cake and champagne.

It was not only the Guards who ate well. Second Lieutenant R.B. Talbot Kelly, serving at Vimy Ridge with the Royal Field Artillery in September 1916 wrote to his father giving a description of the sort of dinners he enjoyed: 'Soup, fish (if possible), meat (or fowl when poss.) asparagus, vegetables (always fresh); savoury (always), pudding (always), Whisky, Perrier, Port (every night), Vermouth, Sherry, biscuits, cigarettes and cigars, coffee, tea or cocoa, fruit (if desired).' Greenwell's officers' mess in the trenches was extremely comfortable, well-stocked with fresh food, potted meats, preserved fruits, sweets, pickles, cigarettes and magazines. It was, in fact, rather as he had imagined his rooms in Oxford would be like had he gone to university instead of the Front.

Food might be supplemented in several ways, especially if there were field-sportsmen in the battalion. In Mesopotamia officers fished for their dinner; an Etonian recorded someone landing an unspecified creature weighing 80lbs. In Salonika Desmond Allhusen shot duck amongst the reeds of Lake Beshik. The officers also shot and ate snipe, woodcock and hares, and it was rumoured that someone bagged an entire flight of seventeen geese with a machine-gun.

Back in France fresh game was less easy to come by, although Anthony Eden recalls chasing partridge on horseback and clubbing the weaker ones. However, it could be imported, usually from Fortnum & Mason who retailed hampers suitable for officers at the Front. Occasionally there were festive celebrations, such as the Fourth of June dinners attended by serving Etonians. The one in 1917 cost fifty francs a head and was extravagant enough to cause a twinge of guilt in one young officer when he recalled rationing back in England. However, the Fourth was a special occasion, he reasoned. As was a New Year's Eve dinner in 1915 at which Captain Gibbs and his fellow-officers consumed turtle soup, sardines on toast, pheasant, Christmas pudding and cream, all washed down with Krug 1904 and thirty-five-year-old brandy. This did not exhaust supplies, since on 1 January 1916 luncheon consisted of caviare (with hot toast and butter), *foie gras*, consommé, pheasant, chips, onions, and stewed pears with custard. 'Our menus would rival those at the Ritz', Leslie Woodroffe, the Shrewsbury schoolmaster, boasted to the *Salopian* in 1915. Just as fond mothers had packed their sons off to boarding school with tuck-boxes, so parcels and hampers made their way to the Front, usually taking about two days. Even Billy Bunter might have been sated by the profusion of food. A Guards officer assured his parents that there was no need to send anything other than Carlsbad plums or other sweetmeats since Fortnum & Mason were the mess caterers and thus the supply of food was assured.

Other officers asked their parents to send parcels to the men, and the bounty of Captain W.P. Nevill's mother towards his orderly was such that Private Miller addressed his letter of thanks to 'Lady Neville'[1]: 'It is with great pleasure I have to acknowledge your lovely parcel. It came as a great surprize to me and I cannot express my thanks enough to you for your generosity because what I have done by Capt Neville your son. Any man in C Company would have done the same.' Mrs Nevill had not despached a Fortnum's hamper, but, at her son's suggestion, 'A decent parsel [sic] . . . Lots & lots of *cheap* cigarettes, cakes, a pair of khaki mittens, a little chocolate & some Bull's eyes, etc.' Spirits were strictly forbidden the ranks.

Both officers and men shared whatever they received from home and a great deal of 'brewing' went on whenever possible. Of course the men did not have the same facilities as their officers and frequently had difficulty cooking anything, having to rely upon crude 'Tommy's stoves', which were often simply lumps of solid fuel which could just about heat water. Compare this with the worries of one Etonian officer who claimed in his diary that the first order he gave upon becoming temporary OC of his company was for proper port glasses since the greatest hardship of the War was having to drink port from chipped enamel mugs.

---

[1] Perhaps Mrs Nevill was grand enough to deserve such a title. She appears to have been well enough known for letters from the Front addressed merely to 'Mrs Nevill, Twickenham' to reach her within a couple of days.

Both officers and men when actually in battle sometimes went without food for several days. Transport was often bogged down and unable to get supplies through to the front line, so that what we have just seen represents the good times. Food and drink were undoubtedly a major comfort, particularly at times of great strain. Captain Gibbs told his parents about his exhausted men sitting down in the mud in December 1916 and weeping: 'I should like another bottle of champagne very much. It is splendid to have on these occasions, when you are feeling rather run down.' The men were sometimes denied such restoratives, according to Frederic Manning, who remembered shops behind the lines 'with bottles of Cliquot and Perrier Jouet in the window, and a label on them, *Reservée pour les officiers.*'

In spite of such disparities (which reached caricature proportions in the widely-held belief that brothels *réservés pour les officiers* had blue rather than red lights hanging outside them), relations between junior officers and their men seem to have been largely amicable. The correct manner was not only expected of soldier-servants by their officers, but also of officers by their men: 'What it was [they] could never have defined in words. But if an officer had it, then the soldiers instinctively recognised it, and that indefinable something was what was instilled into a boy at the public schools.' This was the opinion of R.C. Sherriff, the grammar-school boy who immortalised young public-school officers in *Journey's End*. Sherriff writes of this mystique that it had 'nothing to do with wealth or privilege. Very few of the public-school boys came from the landed gentry or distinguished families. For the most part they came from modest homes, the sons of local lawyers, doctors, or schoolmasters.' In spite of their comparatively humble origins, these boys had taken on the mantle of the gentleman at their schools, where 'they gained self-confidence, the beginnings of responsibility through being prefects over younger boys. Pride in their schools would easily translate into pride for a regiment. Above all, without conceit or snobbery, they were conscious of a personal superiority that placed on their shoulders an obligation towards those less privileged than themselves.' This is precisely what we have seen happening as the schools developed during the last part of the nineteenth century. Sherriff concludes that the other ranks appreciated this: 'The common soldier liked them because they were "young swells", and with a few exceptions the young swells delivered the goods.' Indeed, Sherriff claims that 'by keeping the men good-humoured and obedient in the face of their interminable ill treatment and well-nigh insufferable ordeals' the young officers averted the sort of mutinies suffered by the French army, and that 'through their patience and courage and endurance, [they] carried the

[167]

Army to victory after the generals had brought it within a hairsbreadth of defeat.'

2 *A Body and a Soul, Entire*

It was partly this common enemy of 'the generals' (rather than the common enemy of the Germans) which bound officers and men together. The Infantry officer was also the human face of that vast, incomprehensible mass called the Army in which the recruit found himself. Amidst the massed ranks of an army, which would be about 200,000 strong, the soldier whose individuality had already been eroded by training, was little more than a number when alive and well and a statistic when wounded or dead. It was not until battalion level that the trees began to emerge shadowily from the wood. A company of some 250 men would probably be known individually, at least by name, by the senior officer, a captain. However, it was the platoon which provided the working unit for a junior officer fresh from England. This numbered about sixty men whose characters and background would be known to a certain extent by the second lieutenant who commanded them. As a training manual put it:

> The Platoon Commander should be the proudest man in the Army. He is the Commander of *the* unit in the attack. He is the only Commander who can know intimately the character and capabilities of each man under him. He can, if he is so disposed, establish an esprit de platoon which will be hard to equal in any other formation.

It seems to have been recognised that once men had been trained and were at war, some of the old army methods could be abandoned by the subaltern. In order to gain the confidence of his men, the platoon commander is warned against 'incessant fault-finding', since 'a word of praise when deserved produces better results'. At this stage it is example and altruism which count, being 'well turned out, punctual, and cheery, even under adverse circum-stances', and 'looking after his men's comfort before his own and never sparing himself.' Apart from 'Being blood-thirsty, and for ever thinking how to kill the enemy, and helping his men to do so', the qualities expected of a platoon commander were very similar to those demanded of a model school prefect.

School prefects – especially sporting school prefects – would be accustomed to the admiration of striving junior boys. The attitude of the ranker towards his officer was similar. A character in Robert Graves's peculiar melodrama, *But It Still Goes On* (written at the request of Maurice Browne who had produced *Journey's End* and wanted a similar piece) discusses the relationship between an officer and his men in the trenches in the terms of a Romantic Friendship at a public school:

> Do you know how a platoon of men will absolutely worship a good-looking gallant young officer? If he's a bit shy of them and decent to them they get a crush on him. He's a being apart . . . Of course, they don't realise exactly what's happening, neither does he; but it's a very very strong romantic link. That's why I had the best platoon and then the best company in the battalion. My men adored me and were showing off all the time before the other companies. They didn't bring me flowers. They killed Germans for me instead and drilled like angels. It was an intoxication for them; and for me.

Although highly-coloured, since the officer in question (partially based upon Sassoon) is homosexual, Graves's analysis is broadly true.

It was not necessary for the officer to be a gilded youth. A characteristic example of a school prefect at war was Captain W.P. Nevill of the 8th Battalion of the East Surrey Regiment. At Dover College, which he had left for Cambridge one year before the War, he had been both head boy and captain of cricket. J.R. Ackerley left a rather unkind portrait of Nevill in *My Father and Myself* in which he is described as 'the battalion buffoon' whose loose-dentured smile was the East Surrey's secret weapon. However, when Nevill was killed on the first day of the Somme, his parents received a large number of letters which suggest that their son was held in a great deal more esteem than Ackerley remembered.[1] The standard letter from a senior officer would usually state that the deceased had been a brave and inspiring officer,

---

[1] Ackerley's reminiscences are rather suspect here. In fact, as Nevill's papers at the Imperial War Museum show, Ackerley and Nevill were quite close, billeted together and spending nights out in a haystack with loaded revolvers awaiting zeppelins. They were on first-name terms and their parents got to know each other. Nevill received a letter from Ackerley's sister whilst he was in France, just before his death. Ackerley's letter of condolence suggests that it was only in retrospect that he found Nevill, and his famous advance upon the German lines dribbling a football, idiotic.

adored by his men, valued by the battalion, and killed cleanly in the manner he would have liked. Thousands of such letters were sent from the Front, the sheer number producing a formula. However, amongst the letters received by the Nevills were two from non-commissioned officers in which the formula is fleshed out by a painful sincerity. 'It is seldom even in the army that a man gains the *love* of his fellow men,' wrote Sgt. H.L. Cunnington, 'but our feelings towards Capt. Nevill were deeper than mere admiration, & there wasn't a man in the Battn. who would not have followed him anywhere.' Sgt. H. Cutting wrote: 'I do trust you will not think this a liberty; but – though I was only a Sergeant and your son a Captain – I can safely say he was my friend . . . I was never good at saying to others those things which affect me very nearly so perhaps you will read between these few stammering lines thus perceiving what a MAN he was and how we all loved & respected him.'

The following Christmas Cutting sent the Nevills the official East Surreys's card, which recalled in verse Nevill's ill-fated kick-off into the German lines. The card is inscribed in elaborate calligraphy: 'My Officer & – My Friend'. Cutting has decorated the reverse of the card with a border of holly and written: 'May the Season be made brighter by the knowledge that the memory of your son will live forever.'[1]

That men did rise in waves to go over the top on 1 July 1916 owes something to the leadership of young men like Nevill who led the attacks. The ranks recognised that although young Mr So-and-so 'talked posh', wore a different uniform and enjoyed rather better food and accommodation than they did, when it came to battle, his circumstances were very much the same as their own. The fact that subalterns were obeying orders just as much as their men, and were often left in the same state of ignorance as to the purpose of various missions, earned them a respect and affection more genuine than anything that could have been produced by centuries of the class-system and hours of army training. Even old professional sweats like Frank Richards could be impressed by a good temporary officer, such as Siegfried Sassoon. One of his fellow-regulars who had witnessed Sassoon on a bombing-raid said to Richards:

God strike me pink, Dick, it would have done your eyes good to have seen young Sassoon in that bombing stunt. He put me in mind of Mr Fletcher. It

[1] It was not merely his untimely death (aged just short of 22) that brought out the devotion of Nevill's men. When he was forcibly transferred from 'C' to 'D' Company ('It's rotten, & I loathe it') Pte. Miller and 'quite a little retinue' asked whether they could transfer with him. He was only allowed to take his personal servant.

was a bloody treat to see the way he took the lead. He was the best officer I have seen in the line or out since Mr Fletcher, and it's wicked how the good officers get killed or wounded and the rotten ones are still left crawling about. If he don't get the Victoria Cross for this stunt I'm a bloody Dutchman; he thoroughly earned it this morning.

Richards recalls that: 'This was the universal opinion of everyone who had taken part in the stunt . . . He hadn't been long with the Battalion, but long enough to win the respect of every man that knew him.' Although Sassoon was clearly exceptional ('it was only once in a blue moon that we had an officer like Mr Sassoon,' Richards admitted), there are many records of young, unprofessional officers who fulfilled Sherriff's ideal.

In their turn, the officers could be devoted to their men in a manner that echoed their schooldays. For Nevill and other young officers like him there was continuity in the exchange of one all-male environment for another at the Front. Former prefects found themselves once again responsible for a group of subordinates and the protective ties between an officer and his men could be very strong. For E.A. Mackintosh, a lieutenant in the Seaforth Highlanders, the ties between an officer and his men seemed stronger than any ties of blood. Educated at Brighton College, he was a classical scholar at Oxford when war was declared. His most celebrated poem, 'In Memoriam', is addressed to the father of Private David Sutherland and contains the following comparison between the love of a father and the love of an officer:

> You were only David's father,
> But I had fifty sons
> When we went up in the evening
> Under the arch of the guns,
> And we came back at twilight –
> O God! I heard them call
> To me for help and pity
> That could not help at all.
> Oh, never will I forget you,
> My men that trusted me,
> More my sons than your fathers',
> For they could only see
> The little helpless babies
> And the young men in their pride.

[171]

They could not see you dying,
And hold you while you died . . .
For they were only your fathers
But I was your officer.

Herbert Read addresses his men more as a lover than as a father:

A man of mine
                    lies on the wire;
And he will rot
And first his lips
The worms will eat.

It is not thus I would have him kiss'd,
But with the warm passionate lips
Of his comrade here.

The poem from which this (and the title of this section) is taken is 'My Company' which Read prefaces with a quotation by Jules Romains: '*Foule! Ton âme entière est debout dans mon corps.*' This gives a platonic slant to what otherwise might seem a morbidly erotic, even Baudelairean, imagery. The poem describes Read's burgeoning relationship with the men and then imagines his life without them:

In many acts and quiet observances
You absorbed me:
Until one day I stood eminent
And I saw you gathered round me,
Uplooking,
And about you a radiance that seemed to beat
With variant glow and to give
Grace to our unity.

But, God! I know that I'll stand
Someday in the loneliest wilderness,
Someday my heart will cry
For the soul that has been, but that now
Is scattere'd with the winds,
Deceased and devoid.

[172]

I know that I'll wander with a cry:
'O beautiful men, O men I loved,
O whither are you gone, my company?'

Such desolation was frequently felt by officers on leave, particularly after they had spent time with uncomprehending civilians. When Sassoon was sent to England with trench fever in August 1916, he wrote in his diary: 'Think I deserve a holiday, but feel rotten at forsaking the Battalion, when I could have been fit for work in three or four weeks.' After his 'Soldier's Declaration' he realised that he needed to be back with his old battalion at the Front. Instead he was sent to Egypt and wired a frantic telegram to a senior officer in his old battalion: 'Am ordered to Egypt can you do something to get me back to France. Signed, Sassoon'. Frank Richards, who received the message, hoped as much as Sassoon that this could be arranged, but the major was unable to help. When he was finally posted to France in April 1918 he asked himself: 'I wonder if I can stand another dose of France', then added, once he was there: 'Yes; the men made me able to stand it.' It seems that this was mutual. A soldier left behind in Egypt wrote to Sassoon: 'You may think me a queer sort of being, but I am really awfully bucked at having met someone who had a little sympathy for me, the only particle I ever had the whole twelve months of my perfectly wretched existence with the 25th Battalion.'

Sassoon felt that his purpose in France was no longer to kill Germans: 'I am only here to *look after* some men'. And when he is unable to do this, because he has been sent back to the Base having been shot in the head, he feels 'amputated from the Battalion. When I was hit it seemed an unspeakable thing to leave my men in the lurch, to go away into safety'. Writing to fellow-officer Vivian de Sola Pinto from hospital, Sassoon confesses: 'I lie and sweat in bed at night and wonder what you're all up to, my dears. I wish to God I could lend you some of the empty luscious comfort that is heaped around me . . . Do look after Law [Sassoon's servant], please, and keep him safe, if you can'. That same week Sassoon wrote a poem which echoes Sgt. Cutting's Christmas card sent to his own captain's family:

Can I forget the voice of one who cried
For me to save him, save him, as he died? . . .

Can I forget the face of one whose eyes
Could trust me in his utmost agonies? . . .

I will remember you; and from your wrongs
Shall rise the power and poignance of my songs:
And this shall comfort me until the end,
That I have been your captain and your friend.

The power and poignance of Wilfred Owen's songs arose from a similar devotion to the men in his command. Writing to his mother after he had returned to the Front in the autumn of 1918, Owen explained: 'I came out in order to help these boys – directly by leading them as well as an officer can; indirectly by watching their sufferings that I may speak of them as well as a pleader can.' Owen's destiny as a soldier and as a poet were inextricably entwined. He saw himself as both protector and spokesman. On the last day of 1917 he had written:

I go out of this year a Poet, my dear Mother, as which I did not enter it . . . I am started. The tugs have left me; I feel the great swelling of the open sea taking my galleon . . . last year I lay awake in a windy tent in the middle of a vast, dreadful encampment . . . I thought of the very strange look on all faces in that camp; an incomprehensible look, which a man will never see in England; nor can it be seen in any battle. But only in Etaples.[1]

It was not despair, nor terror, it was more terrible than terror, for it was a blindfold look, and without expression like a dead rabbit's.

It will never be painted, and no actor will ever seize it. And to describe it, I think I must go back and be with them.

Owen was aware that his position was ambivalent: not only was he their Captain and their friend, but he was also a 'cattle-driver'. To Sassoon he wrote: 'And now I among the herds again, a Herdsman; and a Shepherd of sheep that do not know my voice.' This is a puzzling statement; like many of Owen's letters it is obfuscated by self-dramatisation. Owen seems to see himself as a shepherd who looks after sheep, but also leads his beasts to the slaughter. The capital letter, though, suggests the Good Shepherd Himself, perhaps taking the suffering of (his) men upon himself. And why should the sheep not know his voice? Because prophets are not recognised in their own countries? Because the men do not have it in themselves to raise the voice of protest? There is perhaps less the sense here of the school prefect than of the lay assistant at Dunsden Church.

[1] Etaples was the largest and most desolate base camp in France, notorious for the 'Bull Ring' training ground.

3 Comrades in Arms

The relationship between officer and men, like that of the prefect and a junior boy, was compounded of protective paternalism and possessive hero-worship. It was a power relationship, however affectionately expressed. The relationship between men of equal rank was if anything even more intense, because without barriers. Some combatants found such relationships outside their previous experience and therefore difficult to define. 'We did not call it love; we did not acknowledge its existence; it was sacramental and therefore secret', wrote Herbert Read. This was written in retrospect, in the nineteen-sixties and for a more cynical and prurient age.

In fact, men *did* speak of love when describing the passion that both surprised and sustained them. Gurney, mourning the assumed death of his friend, the poet F.W. Harvey, called his memorial poem 'To His Love'. More sophisticated men realised that this might be open to misinterpretation: 'Friendships between soldiers during the war were a real and beautiful and unique relationship which has now entirely vanished, at least from Western Europe,' wrote Richard Aldington in *Death of a Hero* (1929). 'Let me at once disabuse the eager-eyed Sodomites among my readers by stating emphatically once and for all that there was nothing sodomitical in these friendships . . . It was just a human relation, a comradeship, an undemonstrative exchange of sympathies between ordinary men racked to extremity under a great common strain in a great common danger. There was nothing dramatic about it.' Like much of Aldington's unpleasant novel, this won't quite do. The virulent misogyny of *Death of a Hero*, in which the only pleasant female is virtually a child, Aldington's marriage to a bisexual woman and his intemperate assault upon T.E. Lawrence in another abrasive book, all suggest that he felt considerable unease about sexual matters. He rests his case upon the fact that 'no vaguest proposal was ever made to me; I never saw any signs of sodomy, and never heard anything to make me suppose it existed'.

Eric Hiscock, an altogether more attractive prospect that Aldington, received proposals about which there was nothing at all vague: 'I awoke from an uneasy sleep to find him pressed up close to me and that his hand was undoing my fly-buttons . . . I groaned inwardly. Another bugger. Was I ever to be free of them?' Hiscock introduces such characters partly in order to set

[175]

against his relationship with his two pals Brook and Jackson, which although not 'Sodomitical', was certainly demonstrative: 'Blimey, you blokes,' Jackson exclaims when Brook kisses Hiscock before going out on a trench raid. 'I can't think why you don't get married.' Hiscock writes that the three friends 'were as close as Martin Clifford's Terrible Three at *St Jim's*: Tom Merry, Monty Lowther, and Manners.' Although the school story parallel is significant, the emotions Hiscock describes are more reminiscent of *The Hill* than of the world of Charles Hamilton. They were an oddly-assorted trio: Hiscock was a small, dark seventeen-year-old ex-chorister; Jackson was a libidinous Cockney who had worked in the infant British film industry; and Brook was a blond, public-school Galahad. Just as there are 'beastly' boys in school stories devoted to romantic friendships, whose unspoken (because unspeakable) desires are set against the central relationship, so Hiscock has the fumbling unfortunate referred to earlier and the pimply, cowardly Lt. Clarke, forever leering at Brook and jealously persecuting Hiscock. Against this rogues' gallery we have tender and moving scenes such as this:

> [Brook] took my hand in his, and looked into my eyes. There was no laughing light in his as he said softly: 'Love's a wonderful thing. I think we've experienced it at times, haven't we?' Then he laughed and mentioned one of my favourite passages from Rupert Brooke's work, about 'the rough male kiss of blankets'. 'We haven't often kissed, have we? But we're none the less close to each other for all that. There are three people in this wicked world I love. My mother, my father, and you.'

Hiscock comments:

> There was nothing embarrassing in what he was saying. I had known long before [then] we were in love with each other and such a feeling left us both immune from the need or urge for sex. What else is it but love that makes one wonder where someone is, and how he is, and when he will appear at one's side after waking in the morning. To wish to stand at his side when, those days, we formed fours on the parade-ground. To strive with the Orderly Sergeant and make him promise to put us on guard together . . . Ours was a pure love, where neither refused the other anything if it was wanted. Selfless, flame-like, it burned in me long after that day I heard he was dead, and even now [in 1976, over fifty years later] I can conjure up his face, serene, beautiful, pure. Ours was a love that is difficult to write about, impossible to forget . . .

It is what we have seen in many school stories.

One of the old men interviewed by Ronald Blythe for *The View in Winter* asserted that 'there was no question about comradeship. It was made all the more intense because of the fact that so much of it was brief. The whole atmosphere was conducive to deep and intense friendships. And to mourning. Comradeship was a very powerful emotion in all sorts of ways.' Another recalled:

Conditions were so bad in 1916 that it was a vital thing, if you could be a friend. You got huddled up sometimes in a dug-out, or you would cuddle up somewhere else in the deep mess to try and dodge shells, and you became emotionally warm towards the man you were with – very. I think of one fellow in particular named Bishop who came from the East End of London and he was always laughing and joking. A fellow with a ruddy complexion who was the picture of strength and happiness, and he shared everything with me, and I know he loved me. Soon killed, of course, this fellow, this comrade.

The effect of the death of a soldier upon his best friend could be devastating. In Frederic Manning's *The Middle Parts of Fortune* Bourne goes beserk when his friend Martlow is killed. Three of the enemy run towards him attempting to surrender, but Bourne shoots them: 'the ache in him became a consuming hate that filled him with exultant cruelty, and he fired again, and again . . . "Kill the buggers! Kill the bloody fucking swine. Kill them!" All the filth and ordure he had ever heard came from between his clenched teeth . . .'

Frank Richards recalls a soldier who blew up six prisoners with grenades after his best friend had been killed. Richards says that he had heard similar stories and remarks laconically: 'No doubt the loss of his pal upset him very much.' Both scenes recall the reaction of George Sherston to the death of Kendle in *Memoirs of an Infantry Officer*. He captures an entire German trench.

Mourning need not be always as vengeful. After Nevill was killed on the Somme, a fellow-officer, 2nd Lt. Alan Jacobs wrote several letters to Nevill's mother in which he gives full rein to his grief:

With his brilliance as a soldier he was always my ideal hero as an officer and a gentleman while as a personal friend it is now that I fully realise that I loved him as boys rarely love one another . . . I feel his loss personally more than

[177]

any other . . . my God, how I wish I could have led the platoon myself; N. would not have needed to run up to the front wave then.

Both Sassoon and Graves were similarly devastated by the death of their fellow-officer in the Royal Welch Fusiliers, David Thomas: 'I felt David's death worse than any other since I had been in France,' Graves recalled, 'but it did not anger me as it did Siegfried. He was acting transport-officer and every evening now, when he came up with the rations, went out on patrol looking for Germans to kill. I just felt empty and lost . . . My breaking-point was near now . . .' Sassoon rode into the woods to grieve in private, writing his friend's name on a beech tree and hanging a garland of ivy and primroses there as a wreath: 'Now he comes back to me in memories, like an angel, with the light in his yellow hair, and I think of him at Cambridge last August when we lived together for four weeks in Pembroke College in rooms where the previous occupant's name, Paradise, was written above the door.'

4 Another Kingdom

The feeling of camaraderie was strengthened by the absence of women at the Front. The only women men were likely to encounter, apart from the occasional prostitute, or French or Belgian peasant (with whom they might not be able to converse)[1] were VAD nurses. Basil Liddell Hart recalled that these women satisfied the 'aesthetic desire for the beauty and grace of womanhood'. However, a soldier was unlikely to meet a VAD unless seriously wounded and probably in no state to appreciate her, or worse, feel that his wounds were more likely to repel a woman, or at best stimulate professional sympathy. Although many women served with distinction, and indeed were killed in action, the soldiers associated them with home, a place which seemed further away and more alien as the War progressed. Whilst individual women were cherished and the idea of Womanhood was idolised, there is little doubt that women received a fairly bad press in the War. The literature of the War is marred with a strong and unattractive streak of misogyny.

[1] Guy Chapman recalls billets unappetisingly 'presided over by grim slatterns of repellant aspect but of amorous intent'. However, R.H. Mottram's The Spanish Farm describes a touching relationship between an English officer and a Flemish peasant-girl.

It is also true to say that even before the War women had received a bad press. The activities of the suffragettes, although advancing the cause of women amongst the more sensitive and intelligent sections of society, were nonetheless persistently ridiculed. Although there were more attractive representatives of the sex during the War, it is the Little Mother, Jessie Pope, the recruiting chorus girls and the women handing out white feathers who endure. It is also significant that women were used in the most cynical way by the propagandists.

Whatever Mrs Pankhurst may have thought, for most people the War merely provided an opportunity for women to perform their traditional role. Although women moved into industry and filled the gaps left by the men who marched away, particularly after the introduction of conscription,[1] their role as far as the propagandists were concerned was to stand on the sidelines and encourage recruitment. Britannia pointed the way with her sword, whilst mothers, wives and sweethearts stood bravely by. The most famous image was E.V. Kealey's poster of the stoical women gazing out of the window at a column of soldiers: 'Women of Britain say – GO!' At first glance, the onlooking group seems to be a family: wife, daughter and young son. However, they are more symbolic and representative than they first appear, for on closer inspection, one notices that the older woman, comb in golden chignon, fur on collar and cuff of her buttercup dress, is of a very different class to the younger one, with her untidy, dark hair, her black dress, white apron and dowdy shawl. One figure is from the big house; the other is from the mill cottage.

Another poster addressed 'TO THE WOMEN OF BRITAIN' asked four questions:

1) You have read what the Germans have done in Belgium. Have you thought what they would do if they invaded this Country?

2) Do you realise that the safety of your home and children depends on our getting more men NOW?

3) Do you realise that the one word 'GO' from you may send another man to fight for our King and Country?

4) When the War is over and someone asks your husband or your son what he did in the great War, is he to hang his head because you would not let him go?

[1] Even this was sometimes misinterpreted as 'stealing' men's jobs.

[179]

The women's expected contribution to the war effort was plain: 'Won't You Help And Send A Man To Join The Army To-day?' The attitude of women, as seen by the propagandists, was one of brave selflessness; in the words of the famous recruiting song: 'Oh we don't want to lose you, but we think you ought to go'. The cheery stoicism of this song suggests a complete ignorance of, or disregard for, the circumstances of war:

> But now your Country calls you
> To play your part in war
> And no matter what befalls you
> We shall love you all the more.
> So come and join the forces
> As your fathers did before.
>
> Oh we don't want to lose you,
> But we think you ought to go,
> For your King and your Country
> Both need you so.
> We shall love you and miss you,
> But with all our might and main
> We shall cheer you, thank you, kiss you,
> When you come back again.'

Infuriated by this, the soldiers answered back in kind:

> For we don't want your loving,
> And we think you're awfully slow
> To see that we don't want you
> So, please, wont you go.
> We don't like your sing-songs,
> And we loathe your refrain,
> So don't you dare sing it
> Near us again.

Some women, it seems, were prepared to offer more than a kiss, notably Gwendoline Brogden who made famous the appalling 'I'll Make a Man of You' in *The Passing Show*. This is a skilful song in which a sexually suggestive 'perfect dream of a new recruiting scheme' is put forward with considerable wit. The singer explains that she only goes out with members of the forces and is thus occupied every night except Saturday, when she is 'willing, if you'll only take the shilling, to make a man of any one of you':

> I teach the tenderfoot to face the powder
> That adds an added lustre to my skin,
> And I'll show the raw recruit
> How to give a chaste salute,
> So when he's presenting arms, I'm falling in.
> It makes you almost proud to be a woman
> When you make a strapping soldier of a kid,
> And he says, 'You put me through it
> And I didn't want to do it,
> But you went and made me love you, so I did'.

That '*almost* proud' says something about the view of women at the time. For men who had to deal with under/age recruits and saw 'kids' posing as strapping soldiers and being blown to pieces for their pains, this song was scarcely likely to endear women. Unsurprisingly, it provoked one of the most bitterly obscene parodies of all songs:

> I don't want to be a soldier,
> I don't want to go to war.
> I'd rather stay at home,
> Around the streets to roam,
> And live off the earnings of a well/paid whore.
> I don't want a bayonet up my arsehole,
> I don't want my bollocks shot away;
> I'd rather stay in England,
> In merry, merry England
> And fornicate my fucking life away.

Rather more elegant, but nonetheless savage was the response of E.A. Mackintosh:

> 'Lads, you're wanted, go and help,'
> On the railway carriage wall
> Stuck the poster, and I thought
> Of the hands that penned the call.

Fat civilians wishing they
'Could go and fight the Hun'.
Can't you see them thanking God
That they're over forty-one?

Girls with feathers, vulgar songs –
Washy verse on England's need –
God – and don't we damned well know
How the message ought to read.

'Lads, you're wanted! over there,'
Shiver in the morning dew,
More poor devils like yourselves
Waiting to be killed by you.

Go and help to swell the names
In the casualty lists.
Help to make a column's stuff
For the blasted journalists.

Leave the harlots still to sing
Comic songs about the Hun
Leave the fat old men to say
'Now *we've* got them on the run' . . .

Mackintosh contrasts the honest, masculine world at the Front with the meretricious patriotism of those at home: the chorus girls, the war profiteers, the propagandists and the self-appointed 'girls with feathers' who accused any man not in uniform (often wounded and decorated veterans in mufti) of cowardice.

The ideal of 'the beauty and grace of womanhood' was kept alive in sentimental poems and songs: 'When the Fields are White with Daisies', 'Farewell, Isabelle', 'How Can I Bear to Leave Thee?', 'The Soldier's Good-bye' and so on. Songs from earlier wars such as 'Just Before the Battle, Mother' (American Civil War) and 'Good-bye, Dolly Grey' (Boer War) were revived, and T.W. Bamforth produced a series of postcards on which these and other songs were illustrated with photographs of dreaming Tommies in the trenches and tearful farewells in England. Most of these songs were parodied, usually facetiously or obscenely, by the men at the Front, as were hymns (also illustrated by Bamforth; notably 'Fight the Good Fight' in which church parade, a gunner's prayers and a see-through Christ administering to a theatrically-dying officer are ludicrously depicted).[1]

Images such as those found on Bamforth's postcards and in popular songs like 'Keep the Home Fires Burning' were at once attractive to soldiers, but also so out of touch with reality as to seem alien:

> Keep the home fires burning,
> Though your hearts are yearning,
> Though your lads are far away
> They dream of home.
> There's a silver lining
> Through the dark clouds shining;
> Turn the dark clouds inside out
> Till the boys come home.

Whilst 'the boys' dreamed of home, when and if they got there they might have reflected that the only silver lining was the silver lining the pockets of the profiteers. Dreams of home were often shattered when men got leave, for they found an England cut off from the War. With newspapers exaggerating gains and minimising losses, and dwelling on heroics without counting the individual cost, the public had been stranded in a state of ignorant complacency which shocked war-weary troops. Vivian de Sola Pinto recalls arriving wounded at Victoria Station, where 'a lady in black offered me some cake, which I accepted, and a religious tract, which I refused'. Once patched up, his wound-stripe stitched on to his second lieutenant's uniform, his arm in a sling, he found himself 'the perfect exhibit for an English middle-class family in the winter of 1917 . . . As I gulped down their champagne with a fatuous smile on my face, I felt horribly unreal, a sort of ghost from another world, the real world of the brotherhood of the front line.' In order to prevent the real world from slipping away he bought a copy of *The Old Huntsman*, a collection of poems written by a fellow-officer in the RWF, Siegfried Sassoon.

Much of Sassoon's war poetry exemplifies how wide, psychologically speaking, the Channel had become. The alienation felt by the combatants whilst on leave further strengthened the camaraderie of the trenches, just as the

---

[1] The first stanza of Sassoon's 'How To Die' recalls this card.

exclusively male world at the Front, where men were dependent upon each other for physical and emotional survival, drove a further wedge between the soldiers and the society they had left behind them. Someone who had attended one of Sassoon's poetry readings in America after the War remarked: 'I wonder whether he would have cared so much if it were a thousand virgins who had been slaughtered.' This is pertinent, if ungallant, since for the homosexual Sassoon there was little compensation when he found women behaving unthinkingly. 'Apropos the improvement of the world, [Ralph Hodgson] said "Look at the legs of the girls you see in the street, and think what they were twenty-five years ago!"', Sassoon recorded in his diary in 1921. 'Not a very convincing argument as far as I'm concerned'. He was repelled by what he saw as 'the pride of women with child by a warrior. O their gluttonous eyes: I think they love war, for all their lamenting over the sons and lovers'. Speaking to Lady Brassey, with whom he was convalescing in 1917, he was astounded by such declarations as: 'But death is nothing . . . Life, after all, is only the beginning. And those who are killed in the war – they help us from "up there", *they are all helping us to win.*' Such sentiments make him aware of the gap between soldier and civilian: 'For a moment he was struck dumb: he had forgotten that he spoke to an alien intelligence, that would not suffer the rebellious creed that was his. She was a good woman as well as a Great Lady. But her mind dwelt in another kingdom from his.'

Even less palatable was 'a fashionable young woman whose . . . manner implied that she was ready to take me into her confidence, intellectually.' Needless to say, intellect is not much in evidence, rather 'a good deal of trumped-up intensity'. In a poem written largely to vent his spleen, and never published, Sassoon portrayed this woman as 'A War Widow'. Sherston merely observes that 'her dark eyes goggled emptily while she informed me that she was taking lessons in Italian'. In the poem, scribbled in his diary, Sassoon emphasises the meretricious nature of her beauty by making references to jewels:

'Life is so wonderful, so vast! – and yet
We waste it in this senseless war', she said,
Staring at me with goggling eye-balls set
Like large star-sapphires in her empty head.
I watched the pearls that dangled from her ears,
Wondering how much was left for *her* to buy
From time but chattering, comfortable years,
And lust that dwindles to a jewelled sigh.

[184]

Sassoon makes the woman a widow, but withholds sympathy entirely. As Sherston reflects: 'Unsusceptible to her outward attractions, I came to the conclusion that she wasn't the stamp of woman for whom I was willing to make the supreme sacrifice . . .'

Graves asserted that: 'In English preparatory and public schools romance is necessarily homosexual. The opposite sex is despised and treated as something obscene. Many boys never recover from this perversion.' Many boys, it might be added, had little chance. At a period when the sexes were segregated to an extent unimaginable today, it was possible for a boy to have virtually no social (let alone sexual) experience of women who were not members of his own family. The chaperonage system was still flourishing and even in the relatively liberal and adult atmosphere of a university young women were securely corralled within the precincts of their own colleges. Harold Macmillan, comparing the Oxford of his time ('before the Deluge') and that of the 1970s wrote that:

in one respect there was a profound and vital difference – difficult today wholly to realise. There were no women. Ours was an entirely masculine, almost monastic, society. We knew, of course, that there were women's colleges with women students. But we were not conscious of either. Their colleges were situated on the suburban periphery. Their students never came into our college rooms. Curiously, I believe the proportion of women to men was almost the same as now. But they played no role at all in our lives. They were not, I think, full members of the University. They were not members of the Union. They joined no political societies. If they came to lectures they were escorted by a chaperone or duenna. For practical purposes they did not exist.

Macmillan compares boys and girls of eighteen and writes that girls were far more mature and already seeking husbands, not undergraduates of their own age, but older men already entered in their chosen career. Thus, a young man going to the Front straight from university might be in as woeful a state of ignorance as a boy just out of school. The schools managed to reduce all women to Matron, Mothers and Other Chaps' Sisters. That there were women who did not fit those roles was not something which the schools encouraged boys to think about. Inexperienced boys often confused Other Chaps' Sisters with the Other Chaps themselves. In *Journey's End*, Stanhope's relationship with Raleigh's sister is a more shadowy affair than his relationship with

[185]

Raleigh, an emphasis which is even stronger in the novel than in the play. Stanhope is worried that if Raleigh writes to his sister describing the toll that the war is taking (Stanhope drinks heavily in order to survive), she will become disillusioned. However, hero-worship, continually praised by Osborne, a kindly old schoolmaster, is much stronger than mere romance, and Raleigh's admiration for Stanhope is undimmed:

> He looks tired, [Raleigh admits in a letter to his sister] but that's because he works so frightfully hard, and because of the responsibility. Then I went on duty in the front line, and a sergeant told me all about Dennis [Stanhope]. He said that Dennis is the finest officer in the battalion, and the men simply love him. He hardly ever sleeps in the dug-out; he's always up in the front line with the men, cheering them on with jokes, and making them keen about things, like he did the kids at school. I'm awfully proud to think he's my friend.

Sassoon was also vaguely involved with the sister of a friend, Bobbie Hanmer. His experience of the War made him realise that this was unreal, and that his real affections lay with other men. He vowed in his diary, during the Battle of the Somme, that if he survived his life would change and that there would be 'No fat settling down; the Hanmer engagement was a ghastly blunder – it wouldn't work at all. That charming girl who writes to me so often would never be happy with me. It was my love for Bobbie that led me to that mistake.'

5 Greater Love

> *batty*: Interchangeable with 'china' but more definitely used of a most intimate companion. Jonathan was certainly David's batty.
>
> *David Jones (Note to* In Parenthesis*)*

Given this background, it is unsurprising that much of the literature of the Great War celebrates relationships between men at the Front. Whilst the song-writers at home produced sentimental ballads about sweethearts and wives, the combatants wrote about their fellow-soldiers and a love passing the love of women.[1] Paul Fussell has suggested that the poetry of the War follows in what he calls 'The British Homoerotic Tradition', which he sees arising from the Aesthetic Movement via the 'Uranian' poets who celebrated paederasty in Wilde-and-water verses. Fussell admits: 'It is impossible to say how widely known the work of the Uranians was. Although some of it circulated "privately", most was quite public. If it could not be said that their performances created an atmosphere favourable to a wider homoerotic concept of soldiering, they are at least an indication of what was in the air.' The works of the Revd E.E. Bradford may indeed have been read by a proportion of 'earnest schoolmasters', but the audience for the works of such authors as Edward Cracroft Lefroy, John Gambril Nicholson, C.E. Sayle and J.M. Stuart-Young must have been severely limited. The existence of such works as *Erotidia*, *A Garland of Ladslove*, *Cytisus and Galingale* and *The Antinomian: An Elegiac Poem* is perhaps of less significance than the tradition to be found in widely-read public-school stories, such as *Tim*, *Gerald Eversley's Friendship*, *The Hill* and *David Blaize*. It is the celebrated genre of the Romantic Friendship rather than the frustrated scribblings of these obscure aesthetes which created an atmosphere in which Robert Nichols's *Ardours and Endurances* became a best-seller.

Nichols dedicated the war poems in this volume to the memory of two friends killed at the Front. His poetry aims at an emotional pitch which his slender talent is unable to sustain, but which clearly had its audience. Nichols had been invalided out of the army after three weeks' service and so was in England and thus able to promote his work for most of the War. Graves left some wicked accounts of Nichols's career: 'It was the usual story – shellshock, friends all killed, too much champagne, sex, desperate fornication, syphilis.' He was later to embellish this in a letter to Liddell Hart written in 1943: '. . . he went to the war, spent 3 weeks with the Gunners in a quiet part of the line, fell off a roof, went home as shellshocked, slept with 17 prostitutes in 3 weeks and got a bad dose. As his mother was in the looney-bin and he himself was always pretty unsettled, this did him no good; he recovered, was a terrific comet of success in poetry in 1917, went to the USA to lecture, told frightful lies about his war service and involved me in them . . .' and so on.

Whatever the truth, Nichols's success was undeniable and such poems as 'Plaint of Friendship by Death Broken', 'The Burial in Flanders' ('He has fallen in battle/(O Boy! Boy!)') and 'Boy' ('In a far field, away from England,

[1] Murray McClymont made the mistake of sending Owen some 'VAD love poems'; as a result of which 'he will remain a private in my section of poets' Owen told Sasoon.

lies/A Boy I friended with a care like love') were received with enthusiasm in the salon of Sybil Colefax and elsewhere. Sassoon described Nichols's histrionic delivery of his verse in *Siegfried's Journey*, and very embarrassing it sounds too. Sassoon felt that neither he nor Owen 'were designed for fashionable exploitation in a Kensington drawing-room', but there is no doubt that Nichols connived at such 'exploitation', with the result that *Ardours and Endurances* outsold Sassoon's infinitely superior volume *The Old Huntsman*. This popularity was an index of the acceptance by an audience in 1917 of poetry which seems today both overwrought and curiously unselfconscious. Part of the reason that school stories seem a more likely influence upon poetry of the Great War than Uranian verse is the question of tone. There is something at once arch and furtive about Uranian poetry which is not noticeable in school novels and is entirely absent in the frank, open poetry of the War.

It is also significant that a number of poems of the Great War, like public-school novels, make reference, directly or implicitly, to David and Jonathan. The young shepherd, an amateur soldier who marched out against the Philistine army, was an obvious icon with similarities to the young public-school subaltern. Harold Monro's 'Youth in Arms' is a direct descendant of the son of Jesse:

> Happy boy, happy boy,
> David the immortal willed,
> Youth a thousand thousand times
> Slain, but not once killed,
> Swaggering again to-day
> In the old contemptuous way;
>
> Leaning backward from your thigh
> Up against the tinselled bar –
> Dust and ashes! is it you?
> Laughing, boasting, there you are!
> First we hardly recognised you
> In your modern avatar.
>
> Soldier, rifle, brown khaki –
> Is your blood as happy so?
> Where's your sling, or painted shield,
> Helmet, pike, or bow?

Well, you're going to the wars —
That is all you need to know.

For other poets the association is more personal and far less cheerful. Robert Graves's 'Goliath and David' was published with the dedication: 'For D.C.T., killed at Fricourt, March 1916'. David Thomas is also seen as a modern avatar, and Graves's poem plays upon the fact that Saul and his army were in trenches when they faced the Philistines:

Once an earlier David took
Smooth pebbles from the brook:
Out between the lines[1] he went
To that one-sided tournament . . .

The reversal of the expected order of names in the title is intended to prepare the reader for the outcome of this battle. Goliath parries the stone from David's sling and advances upon the shepherd-boy:

. . . but David, calm and brave,
Holds his ground, for God will save.
Steel crosses wood, a flash, and oh!
Shame for Beauty's overthrow!
(God's eyes are dim, His ears are shut.)
One cruel backhand sabre cut —
'I'm hit! I'm killed!' young David cries,
Throws blindly forward, chokes . . . and dies.
And look, spike-helmeted, grey, grim,
Goliath straddles over him.

This is an extremely effective poem, both on a personal and a public level. The grief and horror Graves feels is compressed into the appalled final couplet. The imperative 'look' draws the reader in so that he too can be shocked by God's failure to order events. David puts his faith in God, for 'God will save', but in a war such as this one 'God's eyes are dim, His ears are shut'. This looks forward to Wilfred Owen's 'The Parable of the Old Man and the Young', in which

[1] Emphasis mine.

[189]

another Old Testament story is overturned.[1] Graves instructs us not to believe those who report battles, for in this case

> . . . the historian of that fight
> Had not the heart to tell it right.

Graves has the heart, and this poem provided the title of his second volume of poems, which Sassoon, David Thomas's other friend, helped to edit.[2]

Graves's war-time letters show that the emotional focus of his life for much of the War was his romantic friendship with a boy at Charterhouse whom he calls 'Dick' in his autobiography but whom he always referred to as 'Peter'. This friendship lasted beyond Charterhouse and the two corresponded regularly, the boy sending fifteen-page letters to Graves in France. On sick-leave Graves visited his friend, who was still at school. Unfortunately, in May 1916, Graves reported to Sassoon:

> A great, a hardly bearable disaster has overtaken R.G. His Peter has been taken from him by the terrible old mother who has been nosing around and reading all his letters. So terribly has she been shocked at finding quotations from Samuel Butler and [Edward] Carpenter and people in them and at such signatures as 'ever yours affectionately, Robert' and 'best love, R' that she has extracted a promise from the poor lad that he will have nothing to do with me till he leaves Ch'house. Complications too long to enumerate leave no loophopes of evasion for either of us, so I am now widowed, laid waste and desolate.

Worse was to come, for in July 1917, 'Peter' was arrested for soliciting outside a barracks. Graves, who had described himself as 'honourably chaste and sentimental' and had lectured his headmaster upon Platonic friendships, was appalled, perhaps because the incident revealed the sexual possibilities of such

---

[1] Owen's indebtedness to Graves's poem has not, I think, been appreciated. Like Graves, Owen emphasises the parallel between the biblical and the contemporary theme by references to 'parapets and trenches'. For Owen, more devout than Graves, it is not God's ears which are shut, but Abram's.

[2] This volume, which appeared in February 1917, contained only nine poems and was privately printed in an edition of 200. The title poem, however, received a wider circulation, appearing in Osborn's *The Muse in Arms*, Marsh's *Georgian Poetry 1916–1917* (along with Graves's other poem about Thomas, 'Not Dead') and in his own later volume, *Fairies and Fusiliers*.

a relationship (an element Graves denied in his autobiography but admitted to his biographer). Graves was left with a there-but-for-the-grace-of-God fear of homosexuality, a neurosis which caused him to undervalue the work of Owen and Auden. It seems that he associated the Great War with homosexuality, producing a homosexual melodrama when asked for a play about the War, and excising his war poetry from later selections of his work.

As well as providing an avatar for young subalterns, the biblical David also provided the model for a relationship between men that was chaste, but passionate, 'passing the love of women'. The fact that David's Lament, familiar from school chapels, was one soldier's threnody for another led to this passage suggesting itself to the combatant poet of the Great War writing elegies for friends killed in action. Nichols contrasts conventional romance with the love of soldiers for each other in a poem entitled 'Fulfilment':

> Was there love once? I have forgotten her.
> Was their grief once? grief yet is mine.
> Other loves I have, men rough, but men who stir
> More grief, more joy, than love of thee and thine.
> . . .
> Oh loved, living, dying, heroic soldier,
> All, all, my joy, my grief, my love, are thine!

Owen's poem 'Greater Love' clearly refers to the New Testament: 'Greater love hath no man than this, that a man lay down his life for a friend'. However, there also seems to be a suggestion of the bond between soldiers modelled upon David and Jonathan. One draft of the poem is given the title 'To any Beautiful Woman', and Jon Stallworthy has traced the poem's origins to Swinburne's 'Before the Mirror', written about a painting by Whistler which depicts a woman gazing at herself.[1] Owen contrasts qualities conventionally attributed to lovers with the stronger bonds between soldiers who are fighting and dying together:

[1] In another poem Owen contrasts beauty as perceived by men and women, and incidentally snipes at female vanity. Owen depicts men looking at a sunset and seeing beauty in a horse, and, finally, in a 'Blighty' wound:

> Men seldom speak of beauty, beauty as such,
> Not even lovers think about it much.
> Women of course consider it for hours
> In mirrors . . .

Red lips are not so red
  As the stained stones kissed by the English dead.
Kindness of wooed and wooer
Seems shame to their love pure.[1]
O Love, your eyes lose lure
  When I behold eyes blinded in my stead!

Each comparison is between some feminine aspect – 'Your voice sings not so soft', 'Heart, you were never hot / Nor large', 'And though your hands be pale . . .' – and the images of love applied to the dead men of Owen's company. Most shocking of all is the comparison between the sexually-aroused female body and the last twitchings of a bayoneted corpse:

Your slender attitude
  Trembles not exquisite like limbs knife-skewed . . .

It is no wonder that in 'Apologia Pro Poemate Meo' Owen can claim:

I have made fellowships –
  Untold of happy lovers in old song.
For love is not the binding of fair lips
With the soft silk of eyes that look and long,

By Joy, whose ribbon slips, –
  But wound with war's hard wire whose stakes are strong;

[1] Paul Fussell's case for the influence of the Uranians upon the poetry of Owen might rest with this poem. Is it possible to detect an echo here of the most notorious of all Uranian poems? Lord Alfred Douglas's 'Two Loves' personifies heterosexual and homosexual love as two youths in a garden, one called Love, the other called Shame. Love says:

'I am true Love, I fill
The hearts of boy and girl with mutual flame.'
Then, sighing, said the other, 'Have thy will,
I am the Love that dare not speak its name.'

If Owen had this poem in mind, he turned its conclusion inside out, as he did with other poems he echoed. Douglas's poem was used against Wilde during his first trial, after his libel action against Lord Queensberry had collapsed. Owen would have been acquainted with Wilde's life since he owned a copy of Robert Sherard's unreliable biography of the writer.

Bound with the bandage of the arm that drips;
Knit in the webbing of the rifle-thong.

The conflation of Old Testament and New Testament ideals in such poems is characteristic of Owen's response to the War.

6 All About Heroes

Oh! world you are making for me, Sassoon!
Wilfred Owen

When Paul Fussell analysed the 'homoerotic' impulse in the poetry of Owen and others, he caused some offence,[1] perhaps prompted by the over-cute chapter title: 'Soldier Boys'. However, far from being 'cheap', Fussell's identification of Owen's relationship to Sassoon as 'a poetic crush' seems to me entirely apposite. Sassoon was ripe for hero-worship: a published poet, a decorated soldier, tall, handsome and aristocratic. Compare this with Owen: an unpublished poet, a soldier worried by (unfounded) accusations of cowardice, 'a quiet, round-faced little man' of humble origins.[2] 'I think if I had the chance of making friends with Tennyson or with Sassoon I should go to Sassoon', Owen wrote to his mother after reading *The Old Huntsman*. Eventually the chance arose and he plucked up courage to introduce himself to the older poet, who was a fellow-patient at Craiglockhart Hospital. He was not disappointed: 'He is tall and stately, with a fine firm chisel'd (how's that?) head, ordinary short brown hair. The general expression of his face is one of boredom', he told his cousin, the poet Leslie Gunston, adding: 'He himself is 30! Looks under 25!' Their friendship flourished and Owen wrote to various members of his family spreading the Sassoon gospel. Like many a small boy at school he took great pride and pleasure in this friendship with his senior. (Owen was twenty-four when they met.) When feeling downcast, he told his

[1] See, for example, Jon Glover, 'Owen and Barbusse and Fitzwater Wray' in *Stand* Vol 21, No 2.

[2] Stephen Spender, taken to meet Sassoon for the first time, was tactless enough to show no interest in his host, asking instead what Owen was like. Infuriated, Sassoon snapped: 'He was embarrassing. He had a Grammar School accent.'

[193]

sister, 'one word from Sassoon, though he is not a cheery dog himself, makes me cut capers of pleasure.' When the two men parted, Sassoon gave Owen a photograph,[1] a ten-pound note, and Robert Ross's address. Owen wrote an extravagant letter, which, like the first draft of a poem, he discarded. Scarcely less effusive was the letter which he *did* send, in which he explained his admiration for his friend:

> Know that since mid-September, when you still regarded me as a tiresome little knocker on your door, I hold you as Keats + Christ + Elijah + my Colonel + my father-confessor + Amenophis IV in profile.
>
> What's that mathematically?
>
> In effect it is this: that I love you, dispassionately, so much, so *very* much, dear Fellow, that the blasting little smile you wear on reading this can't hurt me in the least.
>
> If you consider what the above Names have severally done for me, you will know what you are doing. And you have *fixed* my life – however short. You did not light me: I was always a mad comet; but you have fixed me. I spun round you a satellite for a month, but I shall swing out soon, a dark star in the orbit where you will blaze. It is some consolation to know that Jupiter himself sometimes swims out of Ken!

This letter is signed: 'Your proud friend, Owen'.

Sassoon himself was not above playing school prefect to this admiring junior. He felt that Owen had handed his manuscript poems to him 'like school exercises to be blue-pencilled', and that this, and their difference in age and experience and fame, set the pattern of their relationship. All this is delineated by Sassoon, with retrospective irony and unnecessary modesty in *Siegfried's Journey*.

It is unsurprising that someone as prone to hero-worship as Owen should enjoy *The Hill*. Since it appears that he did not own a copy of the novel, I surmise that it was loaned to him by Philip Bainbrigge, the Shrewsbury schoolmaster with whom the poet spent some time in Scarborough. It is certainly the sort of novel that Bainbrigge is likely to have owned and admired.

---

[1] Presenting friends with a 'phiz' (i.e. portrait photograph) was a widespread custom in public schools, notably Eton, where they were collected and displayed like superior cigarette cards. Boys who were leaving gave them to selected friends who proudly placed them on study mantelpieces.

Owen read the book whilst acting as Camp Commandant to the remnants of his Battalion in Scarborough in February 1918, and it gave him an insight (albeit a lushly sentimental one) into the enclosed world of the public school. He described it to his mother as: 'a tale of Harrow, and the hills on which I never lay, nor shall lie: heights of thought, heights of friendship, heights of riches, heights of jinks. Lovely and melancholy reading it is for me.' The end of the novel, with Desmond going off to war and being killed, whilst Verney stays behind anxiously awaiting a letter that only arrives after his friend's death, must have had a particular poignancy for Owen. He told Sassoon: 'I wish you were less undemonstrative', and his surviving letters nearly all contain requests that Sassoon should write to him.

On his last day in England, Owen went down to the beach at Folkestone, where, as if by magic, 'there issued from the sea distraction, in the shape, Shape I say, but lay no stress on that, of a Harrow boy, of superb intellect & refinement; intellect because he hates War more than Germans; refinement because of the way he spoke of my Going, and of the Sun, and of the Sea there; and the way he spoke of Everything. In fact, the way he spoke –' To his mother, Owen described the boy as 'the best piece of the Nation left in England.' One senses that for Owen the Harrovian is the equivalent of Edward Thomas's handful of soil. When asked what he was fighting for, Thomas scooped up a handful of soil and said: 'literally, for this'. The boy emerging from the sea, form out of chaos, like the birth of Venus, was an individual representative of all the young men, that anonymous mass, dying in France.

[6]

The View from the Front

1 A Distant Prospect

I tried hard to convince myself that the moment I had lived for had arrived
and that I was now a real Service man. But this was difficult: there was no
band playing, no regiment bearing the old colours into the fray, only little
me, sitting behind an unwashed, unshaven driver, finding my way alone
because I had been told to.

Edwin Campion Vaughan

SASSOON wrote of the prospect of Marlborough that, apart from the vague
notions he had gained from school stories, he had 'no idea what it would be
like'. The same could be said of most young officers' prospect of the War.
'Charles Edmonds' (i.e. C.E. Carrington) has written snappishly that:

Young soldiers who enlisted without expecting hardships and danger must
have been foolish indeed; and any who misjudged the nature of army life
were quickly introduced to the realities of the situation by the old soldiers. It
can only have been a very stupid, insensitive, young man who did not
concentrate his mind sometimes, during the long months of military
training, on blood and wounds. We were pretty well prepared for the
horrors of war by the time we came face to face with them, and though, for
my part, I have never been able to work the Battle of the Somme out of my
mental system, nothing happened to me there which could be described as
'disenchantment' or 'disillusion'. It was what I had bargained for.

[196]

This seems to me to miss the point rather. Of course men who enlisted were aware that warfare would involve hardship and danger, but the nature of this was suppressed. Not only did the government continually stress the more ennobling aspects of war in the abstract, it also withheld news of defeats and did its best to underestimate casualties, so that 'massive losses' were something that only happened to the enemy. Poetry published in newspapers and magazines painted a similarly stirring picture of battle. Soldiers did not discuss the nature of warfare when on leave, allowing the civilian population to remain in a partially self-imposed ignorance of conditions at the Front. Concern about increasing the anxiety of relatives led to a formula of decent vagueness in letters home, seasoned by a reassuring jauntiness. Greenwell explained to his parents:

> If only you could realise how quickly and more or less happily the time slips by out here and how immersed we all are in the petty details of daily routine rather than in the Great War, you wouldn't be so anxious for me. It is so much easier for us out here knowing the dangers, such as they are, and they really are not great.

Greenwell's youthful buoyancy is not even dampened by his first encounter with bully-beef ('excellent') or trench duty at Hébuterne ('mudlarking'). Nevill sent his schoolboy brother a postcard from the Front depicting a child gazing at a recruiting poster: 'Hurry up & get old enough, not that you'll be in time for the sport then'. Major Sidney H. Baker may write to his brothers about the wounded in 1917, but advises: 'This is hardly a letter to show mother'. Indeed, such was the element of self-censorship that civilians, denied the truth about warfare and fed endless propaganda and censored press reports, became complacent. Major F. Sainthill Anderson, a professional soldier, wrote to his mother at the end of 1916: 'If people would cease to be stupidly casual and untruthful when on leave, and let people know the truth – you for one would very soon alter your opinion – Europe is mad and no one realises it.' Sassoon's protest in July 1917 was partly made because he felt it might 'destroy the callous complacency with which the majority of those at home regard the continuance of agonies which they do not share, and which they have not sufficient imagination to realise'.

Whether or not 'telling the truth' would have made any difference is open to question. Robert Nichols pointed out that there is a great deal of difference in being told that someone has been blown to bits and actually collecting up those bits for burial. He also thought that civilians, stuffed full of the euphemisms of war-reporting, felt that any attempt by a soldier to tell them the truth was simply a combatant's act of revenge upon a non-combatant. However, one can imagine the angry frustration of a soldier when civilians, quite happy to swallow whole any number of atrocity stories, suggested by their response that his description of conditions at the Front were an exaggeration.

Letters from Old Boys which found their way into school magazines tended to suggest that life at the Front was rather like school, tough but surprisingly enjoyable. A personal appearance in the immaculate uniform of a second lieutenant was also an act of unintentional propaganda. In the novel of *Journey's End*, Stanhope visits his old school where the boys are suitably impressed by the purple and white ribbon of an MC and want to hear about the excitement of a soldier's life. Stanhope reflects that there is no point in describing the horrors to Raleigh since he 'would never understand. The cursed war had built a barrier between them, a barrier which he could never cross however often he came down to Barford to play in cricket matches.' All he can say is: 'It's pretty beastly at times . . . But we have an awful lot of ragging when we're out of the line.' The next chapter opens with Raleigh ready to join the regiment at the Front. In the dug-out at St Quentin, Raleigh recalls Stanhope's visit: '"He'd just got his MC and been made a captain. He looked splendid! It sort of – made me feel –" "Keen?" Osborne suggests. "Yes, that's it. Keen to get out here."' Nevill was often at Dover College when on leave, visiting his brother and other boys and masters, no doubt peddling his own brand of 'cheer-oh!' jauntiness. Evelyn Southwell and Malcolm White visited their former pupils at Shrewsbury whenever possible and spoke of the nobility of death.

Even soldiers in training were sometimes denied a real insight into the nature of war. Whilst there was a great deal of bayonet practice upon bags of straw, not everyone was as imaginative as little Beverley Nichols, who 'could almost see the blood spurting from the straw sacks'. Blunden recalled that he enjoyed his training so much that he almost forgot about the Western Front. Far from being enlightened by veterans, he spent his time training with convalescent soldiers who would not speak of the War. Robert Nichols recalled that officers he had met who had returned from the Front were 'remarkably taciturn. At the time I attributed this taciturnity partly to tradition and partly to a very natural desire to forget the past in the present.' He later believed that 'Authority' had advised soldiers not to discuss conditions, but there seems little proof of this. When soldiers did arrive at the Front, they sometimes realised why the men they had met at home had said nothing. Vivian Gilbert, an extremely idealistic actor, wrote:

It was so unlike all my preconceived notions of warfare. I could understand at last why it was that officers returning from the front to the machine gun training centre at Grantham had had so little to say. There was so little one could say: it was all unutterably beastly – it wasn't fighting, it wasn't fair play, it was just slaughter!

The real point is that whatever the prospect of war, it was generally believed that there would be compensating factors. Wounds and even death might await a recruit, but it is in human nature to suppress fear, and such pessimistic notions would be subsumed by images of valour and glory:

> Horror of wounds and anger at the foe,
> And loss of things desired; all these must pass.
> We are the happy legion, for we know
> Time's but a golden wind that shakes the grass.

'People used to feel like this when they "joined up" in 1914 and 1915', Sassoon wrote in mitigation of these lines. 'Feel' is the essence here; there is, after all, little thought behind such notions. The use of archaisms such as 'foe' and a 'legion' which is glibly described as 'happy' suggests images of warfare imposed in the classroom, and the final line is pretty but meaningless. The poem from which this stanza is taken is called 'Absolution',[1] a title which gives a commonplace religious aura to the prospect of fighting, very similar to Brooke's 'Peace'. Sassoon noted of this poem: 'No one feels like it when they "go out again".' However, by that time it was too late to do much about it, since men had enlisted for 'three years or the duration' ('Roll on, Duration' was a popular saying in the trenches). It was simply a matter of carrying on. Once ensnared there was little a soldier could do to escape.

2 An Awfully Big Aventure

Living through war is living deep. It's crowded, glorious living. If I'd never had a shell rush at me I'd never have known the swift thrill of approaching death – which is a wonderful sensation not to be missed.

Ernest Raymond

[1] Sassoon makes what I take to be a mocking reference to this title in a later poem in which he rejects his earlier Brookean stance, 'The Poet as Hero'. (See p 238)

Not everyone who enlisted did so for exalted reasons of patriotism. For some the War offered an opportunity for the adventurous spirit, a chance to make *Boy's Own Paper* dreams come true. This was particularly true of those drawn to the Royal Flying Corps. Cecil Lewis's *Sagittarius Rising* opens with a scene that parodies the school story:

> I stood with Maynard Greville on the stone terrace outside the School House studies at Oundle in the spring of 1915.
> 'I vote we chuck all this at the end of term and join up,' said he.
> 'Wouldn't it be fine! – but they won't let us.'
> 'Why not? We're almost seventeen.'
> 'But the old King says you can't get a commission in anything until you're eighteen.'
> 'Rot! What about the Flying Corps? They'll take you at seventeen. They want young chaps.'
> 'Shall we speak to Beans?'
> 'No, he might stop us. I vote we write to the War Office and see what happens.'
> 'All right! Oh, Maynard, wouldn't it be ripping!'

And it is ripping. Lewis is too keyed up to take any notice of his anxious mother, thrilled both by the exhilaration of flying and the prospect of war. When he returns on leave she is overcome, but Lewis is too caught up in the War to appreciate this: 'Of course I was full of news. It was all so exciting for me. I had no sense of tragedy. It was a marvellous life, a sport, a game!' The youthfulness of the pilots leads to a great deal of Greyfriars-style ragging, although now the fun is fuelled by alcohol. Amongst other pranks is a 'gorgeous binge' in which there is 'a pitched battle with fire-extinguishers'. Walter Briscoe's boys' biography of Albert Ball, the flying ace, is entitled *The Boy Hero of the Air: From Schoolboy to VC* (1921) and is 'a school story, an adventure tale, and an air story all rolled into one'. Unlike Lewis's account, there is no dark side to this relentlessly cheerful story.[1]

However, it was not only the RFC that provided thrills. Two Old Etonians who had a splendid time were the Bortons, whose father kept a journal throughout the War. 'Since my last letter was written, THE WAR HAS ROLLED ON, LEAVING US BEHIND,' wrote Amyas 'Biffy' Borton to his father in

---

[1] Lewis was in the same squadron as Ball and was on the scouting mission in which Ball was shot down.

October 1918. 'I am now daily expecting THE BAD NEWS OF THE TURK DECIDING TO PUT UP HIS HANDS AND END THE BEST WAR I AM EVER LIKELY TO GET MIXED UP IN!!' Biffy was in fact in the RFC, but his brother Arthur ('Bosky') had an equally ripping time in the army. 'They really are the ONLY TWO MEN I know who seem to be really sorry that it looks like coming to an end,' wrote Bosky's wife. Indeed, disillusion only set in for Bosky after the War, when he found it impossible to settle down to civilian life; he died disinherited, drunk and in debt at the age of forty-nine. For such men the War was one long boys' adventure-story. Even Gallipoli was turned into a huge jape: 'AM HAVING A TOP HOLE TIME', Biffy reported. The evacuation of Sulva and Anzac was an opportunity for all sorts of pranks:

> Everyone let his imagination run riot in preparing surprises – my own contribution being to load the base of an oil stove full of AMENOL and run a few threads of fuse up the wick. It's about the most valuable piece of loot left behind and I trust will be collared by a German officer. Much good may it do him. Our old mess DUG-OUT at Jephson's Post had nearly 1,000 LB OF GUN COTTON in it, which will GO OFF AS SOON AS THE DOOR OPENS!

The Bortons may strike us as grotesques, but beneath all the schoolboy bravado was considerable courage. Both were wounded, mentioned in despatches nine times between them, and clocked up sundry foreign decorations, two CMGs, two DSOs, an AFC and a VC.

Danger and excitement became a highly flammable mixture in the War. Whilst our received notions of trench warfare are of discomfort, fear and misery, there is no doubt that many soldiers were stirred by the excitement of taking part in a battle. Nichols thought that the prospect of battle often rekindled that feeling of exultation the troops had felt when they enlisted. Fear and excitement are not always divisible, as can be seen by the large number of people who take part in dangerous sports. E.C. Vaughan, coming upon a party of Germans whilst on a night patrol 'lay frozen with fear and excitement', whilst his fellow-officer was overcome by a fit of laughter.

A Guardsman, waiting to go over the top, heard machine-guns opening fire, a signal that the first wave of his battalion had left their trenches. He recorded in his diary that he was trembling with excitement, and that he wanted to stand up and cheer for England. Paul Jones concurred: 'I have never in all my life experienced such a wild exhilaration as on the commencement of a big stunt, like the last April one for example. The excitement for the half-hour or so before it is like nothing on earth'. White, the Shrewsbury schoolmaster compared the tension of waiting for the Big Push on the Somme (in which he was instantly annihilated) with that of waiting for a rowing match to begin.

Raiding parties were perhaps the most stimulating experiences a soldier might take part in, because they involved individual stealth and courage. In a war characterised by random shell-blasts and futile advances against overwhelming odds, the chance of using initiative and skill was welcome. A patrol which had surprised a digging-party of Germans had an invigorating effect upon its participants. Vaughan recorded: 'This little jaunt left us with our tails well up, and I, for one, am very keen on No Man's Land. I fully appreciate the truth of the maxim that was dinned into us during training – "Fighting patrols are the finest stiffeners of morale".' Writing of the prospect of bombing a German working-party, Sassoon felt that it was: 'Better to get a sling at them in the open – even if on one's belly – than to sit here and have a great thing drop on one's head.' Crawling near the German trenches with a corporal who took 'delight in any excitement of Hun-chasing', Sassoon found the experience 'great fun . . . most exhilarating – just like starting a [point-to-point] race'. Recalling the atmosphere before the bombing-raid which earned him the MC, Sassoon felt that there were no signs of terror amongst his men: 'I think there was more delight than dread in the prospect of the dangers'. It was medal-winning 'stunts' such as these which captured the imagination of those at home, so that the War was often presented as a series of vignettes familiar to readers of boys' adventure strories. Lance-Corporal Kendle in *Memoirs of an Infantry Officer* is straight out of boys' fiction with his 'jaunty fag-smoking demeanour and freckled boyish face . . . his cheerfulness and courage, and his cheeky jokes'. Kendle joins Sherston on a wire-cutting escapade, 'unwilling to be left out of the adventure', and thereafter frequently accompanies his senior officer, Tinker to Sherston's Sexton Blake, fag to his prefect: 'I felt adventurous and it seemed as if Kendle and I were having great fun together. Kendle thought so too.' But, unlike a story-book hero, Kendle did not have nine lives, and Sherston's 'somewhat protective' feelings were no safeguard against a sniper's bullet.

The image of the great adventure persisted after the War. Bartimeus, the boys' writer, produced a book of naval stories in 1919 called *An Awfully Big Adventure*. This quotation from *Peter Pan* is used without any awareness of its irony. It comes from the end of Act III of Barrie's play, in which Peter is marooned upon a rock in the lagoon:

PETER (*with a drum beating in his breast as if he were a real boy at last*): To die will be an awfully big adventure.

In deference to the mounting number of boys who would never grow up, including Barrie's adopted son Second Lieutenant George Llewelyn Davies, this line and the scene which preceded it was cut from the Christmas revival of the play in 1915.

Remarque thought it necessary to stress that *All Quiet on the Western Front* (1929) was: 'neither an accusation nor a confession, and least of all an adventure, for death is not an adventure to those who stand face to face with it.' Publishers, however, must have the final word. When Penguin came to issue *Undertones of War* in 1937, Blunden's quietly devastating account of the horrors of warfare was published in the cerise wrapper of their 'Travel and Adventure' series.

3 For School, King and Country

In the day of battle they forgot not God, Who created them to do His Will, nor their Country, the stronghold of freedom, nor their School, the mother of godliness and discipline. Strong in this threefold faith they went forth from home and kindred to the battlefields of the world and, treading the path of duty and sacrifice, laid down their lives for mankind.

Inscription on the Memorial Cloisters at Winchester

When Paul Jones, a nineteen-year-old lieutenant in the ASC, went to the Front in 1915 he took with him two photographs. One was of Dulwich College, the other of the Founder's Day cricket match played there. A scholar and an athlete, he had left Dulwich laden with honours, and his gratitude towards his old school:

became a passion, sustained, coloured and glorified by happy memories. Everybody and everything connected with it shared in his glowing affection. Its welfare and reputation were infinitely precious to him. Like a *leitmotif* in a musical composition, his love of Dulwich College recurs again and again in his War Letters.

[203]

These were published in 1918 as *War Letters of a Public-School Boy*.

Love of the Old School is a *leitmotif* that frequently recurs in letters, diaries, poems and memoirs of the Great War. Malcolm Muggeridge wrote that when 'at Cambridge, and elsewhere, I got to know the products of public schools, the thing that struck me about them was their passionate entanglement in their schooldays.' Sifting through the relics of young men killed in action one is often aware that it is their School, as much as their Country, for which they are fighting and dying. Many had enlisted partly to uphold the honour of the school, as the boasts of figures in school magazines indicate. Their bravery brought added lustre to the school shield. Evelyn Southwell, the Shrewsbury schoolmaster, wrote of an Old Salopian who had been very badly wounded by a shell:

He seems, like all these wonderful people, to have been quite marvellous over it all. At least I don't suppose it *is* so wonderful really, considering where he came from: but somehow I am apt to feel more and not less surprise as time goes on and proof upon proof comes along of what good Salopians really are.

Southwell and his friend and colleague, Malcolm White, were extreme examples of men devoted to a school and all it stood for. Southwell was an Old Etonian and White an Old Marlburian, but their real love was for the school in which they taught. There was a group of young masters at Shrewsbury, some of whom had been brought there from Eton by C.A. Alington who became headmaster in 1908. They lived in a *garçonnière* called the New House on the edge of the school grounds and addressed each other as 'Man', White and Southwell commonly referred to as 'the Two Men'. White had been involved with the OTC before the War and imagined that he would be called up as a Territorial officer immediately, but, rather to his relief, the War Office had insisted that he should stay with the school corps. The encouragement and subsequent death of a former New House Man, George Fletcher, led both White and Southwell (who had only joined the OTC when war was declared) to enlist in the Rifle Brigade, but not, as they had hoped, in the same battalion. They were both killed in the Battle of the Somme; White blown to irrecoverable pieces on 1 July, and Southwell killed by a sniper in Delville Wood on 15 September.

Their attitude to Shrewsbury is most neatly encapsulated in a telegram which White sent to the New House after he had visited the school whilst on leave in July 1915: 'Have left bats, autostrop-strop and soul at Shrewsbury please send all if possible'.

One historian attributes the love of Shrewsbury shown by combatant Old Boys to Alington's brilliant sermons: 'The thoughts of many an Old Salopian in the mud of Flanders would turn on a Sunday morning towards the School Chapel.' Like the Turks, whom some of his pupils were fighting, Southwell had his Mecca; on his last night in England, before his division sailed to France, he went out onto a Wiltshire hill and turned to face Shrewsbury. 'I suppose it is needless to repeat to you what I said in a letter to Shrewsbury not so long ago,' he wrote to Alington, whilst he was in training, 'that I have for all these months seen *everything* in terms of Shrewsbury.' For him Shrewsbury was 'the centre of the universe'; his diary has headings such as 'The Last Sunday of Term', and his letters are shot through with 'homesickness'. He would stand in the trenches and indulge in 'End-of-Term Thinking', often with disastrous results: 'Oh Man, Man, shall I throw my pencil away and bury my poor, bewildered head in my arms? It came all so suddenly, and I have had, between ourselves, a pretty bad week, and I thought of Shrewsbury and nearly began to weep: never, I think, did I feel quite so much longing.' Two days before he was killed he was making 'a list of good things' in his diary, which included the beginning of the Autumn Term at Shrewsbury and 'Eton's fields under midsummer floods in boiling June, with the Winchester match to follow.'

If anything, White's devotion to Shrewsbury was even more intense. He visited the school at every possible opportunity and was as attuned as Southwell to the School calendar. From his camp in England he wrote to Alington:

It is strange, but I don't think I ever felt the end of a term so keenly before; perhaps because I have no nightmare of exam. papers and marks to put away from me, but chiefly because Shrewsbury alive and 'carryng on', has been such a comforting and solid fact to an exile, and it has been pleasant to picture the place at various routine times. And holidays mean the breaking up of all that, and the central fact of my life partially collapses for a time.

His posting overseas was repeatedly delayed, a fact which made the lure of Shrewsbury very powerful, but one that had to be resisted until he had 'faced things at the front'. Once in France his 'homesickness' increased: the sound of military bands and guns reminded him of Sports Day and the chalk-dust of a lecture-room made him 'sorrowfully reminiscent'. He asked Ronald Knox to send him the School roll, but this only made things worse: 'The hunger for

Shrewsbury this June is almost intolerable.' As the bombardment of the German lines was going on White anticipated his own death: 'Do you think that we all continue to have our part in the place after death, even when not remembered?' he asked Alington in a letter dated 27 June 1916. 'I am very jealous of mine; and though I know such an article of faith is called animism or some such horrible name, yet I cling to the idea of becoming, after death, more completely a part of Shrewsbury than when I was an unworthy, active member of the community; not by what I've done there, but by how much I have loved it.'

His last letter was written to Southwell on the same day:

> Oh Man, I can't write now. I am too like a coach before the Bumping Races or Challenge Oars.
> So, Man, good luck.
> Our NEW HOUSE and Shrewsbury are immortal, which is a great comfort.

The Two Men were extreme examples of devotion to a school, but others were entangled almost as passionately. One Etonian achieved White's final wish in a more concrete form. Geoffrey Madan, the anthologist, left Eton in 1913 after an outstanding career there. The entire School had once been given a day's holiday in recognition of his brilliant depiction of Eton in Herodotean Greek. He enlisted early in the War and served in many theatres of war: 'Letters from [A.C.] Benson (they wrote to each other once a week), visits to him on leave, and the remembered vision of Eton, all sustained his spirit.' His widow later said that: 'The elms of Eton, and the sunlight and shadow of that temperate valley, are recalled constantly and with longing in Geoffrey's letters from Gallipoli, Mesopotamia, an Indian hospital.' He was introduced to his future wife on an Eton lawn by Mrs Cornish after the War, and Eton dominated his conversation with people like Shane Leslie with whom he could share 'a phantasy world stretching between Luxmoore's Eton and Monty James's Kings and Arthur Benson's Magdalene.' (Not, it must be admitted, a wide canvas, since Benson went to Magdalene from Eton and James came to Eton from King's). When he died in 1947 his ashes were scattered in Luxmoore's Garden at Eton, becoming part of the School which, as his widow wrote, was 'part of his life to his last day.' Robert Sterling, who died the same day as Brooke, left countless poems in praise of Sedbergh, whilst it was said of Douglas Gillespie, one of Osborn's *New Elizabethans*, that

'Winchester was always with him'. The profits of a posthumously published collection of his *Letters from Flanders* were 'added to a fund provided (in accordance with his will) by the refunding of his Winchester and New College Scholarships for the benefit of boys that are not to well off'.

Reading such accounts, it comes as no surprise to hear loyalty to the Old School described at memorial services as 'a very beautiful thing'. At Marlborough, the Bishop of Salisbury, dedicating the bleakly unattractive memorial hall, said that: 'This passionate loyalty to our old schools is a mighty moral force in the land. It stands at the back of all those best things which our Public Schools have given.' To keep this moral force alive, Old Boys were frequently sent letters giving news of their schools, as well as copies of the school magazine. Along with the Fortnum & Mason hampers, J.M. Barrie sent George Llewelyn Davies copies of the *Eton College Chronicle*, a publication which seems to have been widely read in the trenches. Captain Gibbs was able to check up on his old school's sporting fixtures whilst the Battle of the Somme raged around him, whilst another Old Etonian, imprisoned in Germany, passed his copies round the camp so that the OE inmates could keep up with the news of the Beagle Pack. An Old Westminster with the 48th Division Cyclists' Company received the *Elizabethan* 'at rare intervals', whilst copies of the *Salopian* found their way to the Red Cross hospital at Rouen.

Boys were also kept in contact with their schools by letters from their former tutors or housemasters. At Sherborne A.H. Trelawney-Ross started House Letters in 1916. The same thing was done at Eton, and the results published later on, bound in distinctive pale blue: *Eton Letters 1915–1918* by 'A House Master'[1] and *Twenty Years After: The Letters of an Eton Housemaster* by A.C. Rayner-Wood, which were assembled and published as the Second World War approached in 1939. In 1915 Rayner-Wood posted a notice on the house board: 'WAR WORK FOR ALL. 40 Scribes Wanted! A Letter to the OLD BOYS will be dictated in Pupil Room from 7.00 to 8.00 tonight (Sunday). Volunteers bring Pens!' Rayner-Wood dictated Eton gossip and news about other Old Boys to an array of diminutive scribes who often used 'Trials' (examination) papers to write on. At the end of the hour, the boy signed his own name, and occasionally added a message of his own: 'To Nigel Anson. I fagged for you last summer half. Good luck. Signed Logan'. Rayner-Wood thought that a letter hand-written on Trials paper would 'provide more local colour and arouse more sentiments than a typewritten letter', but felt it necessary

---

[1] i.e. Hugh Macnaghten, (1920).

to add: 'I am not responsible for the spelling mistakes . . . the signature under mine at the end is that of the person who accepts full responsibility'. This was a wise precaution, since not all of the scribes were (as one of them put it) 'interlectual expurts'. To judge from the replies Rayner-Wood received, the scheme was very successful and 'some letters were passed round as long as they would hold together and even after they had dissolved in tatters. Others, more carefully guarded, were found on the wounded and the dead.' One Etonian in Mesopotamia wrote to say that he would 'much like a Pupil Room epistle, intact if possible. You don't know how we value them and the censor being an Old Etonian pinched half the last one and kept it himself.' Rayner-Wood, and other masters, also wrote individual letters to their former charges and there is no doubt that these were received with immense gratitude by soldiers who were wounded, imprisoned, or simply lonely and miserable in the trenches.

Another comfort was the presence of soldiers from the same school at the Front. One way to be sure of this, if an Old Etonian, was to join a Guards Regiment. Anthony Eden recalled that there was much talk at the school about which regiment to apply for. Although the most adventurous spoke of the RFC, the Coldstream Guards (whose barracks were at Windsor) and the Grenadier Guards were considered the crack regiments. The Welsh Guards were also respectable, but not the Irish: 'for goodness sake, don't let him go into the Irish,' Gibbs implored his parents when he heard of his younger brother's plans. 'They are a very bad regiment even in England . . . Far better get him into the Coldstream, which is a fine regiment, or the Life Guards.' A good regiment might well be judged by the number of OEs in it: 'The place is swarming with Etonians who are my contemporaries, and I run against them everywhere. Thank goodness I didn't go to any other school than Eton.' Even the interpreter turned out to be a man who had taught Gibbs French at school. Allhusen found in the 60th Rifle Brigade that 'most of those who are not rankers are OEs', and that the 7th Battalion was 'a very good one – quite a number of OEs'. One of their number, Nigel Anson, wrote to his old Tutor from the trenches: 'I hope the Bosh [sic] does not put one of his really fat shells amongst us here. If so he would get a first-class bag of OEs.' One officer who served with the Coldstream Guards, was advised by his publisher, John Murray, to give his memoirs 'a title such as "With the Guards in France" by "An Old Etonian". A title such as this would make an appeal to a large class who would not be attracted by the word "Anonymous" given as author.' Such was the concentration of Etonians in the Guards that on the Fourth of June 1915 the Provost of Eton received a telegram from Lord Cavan and 56 fellow-Guardsmen. Upon the same occasion in 1917 Cavan's greetings were accompanied by those of 206 Etonian Guards.

No war was going to stop so important a celebration as the Glorious Fourth and in almost every theatre of war festivities were held and the health of *Alma Mater* was drunk. These gatherings ranged from elaborate dinners in France, attended by several hundred, to the handful of Etonians at Basra who drank *Floreat Etona* 'in rather doubtful water', after which 'Bunny sang the Boating Song, accompanying himself on another man's banjo (of all unsuitable instruments!)'. In Salonika, Hazebrouck, Alexandria and aboard *HMS Caliope* Etonians foregathered in 1915 in order to celebrate the Fourth and send telegrams to the Provost. In 1916 telegrams came from the Sinai Peninsula, Mesopotamia, assorted towns on the continent and, of course, 'Somewhere in France'. Nine '*Etonenses internati*' sent a postcard from Ruhleben, where they had been interned as civilians at the outbreak of the War. In 1917 28 OEs sent greetings 'from the Gates of Gaza', whilst a dinner in France was so rowdy that one wag remarked: 'It shows that the "offensive" spirit is not yet dead.' Eton, patriotically tightening her belt, was proud that her sons had not forgotten her: 'The Fourth of June was spent quietly at Eton this year,' the *Chronicle* reported, 'but neither supper nor fireworks were forgotten by our representatives at the front, where the celebration seems to have been held in a manner thoroughly worthy of the occasion.' Members of the Rifle Brigade in the front line reported: 'We are sending up anti-German fireworks to celebrate the occasion.'

Other schools also celebrated their Founder's Days in similar fashion. At an Old Marlburian dinner £163 10s., was raised for the War Memorial Fund. As with a more widespread religion, it was frequently a case of when two or three are gathered together in the school's name. Five Old Salopians had dinner at Gibraltar in February 1915 and toasted their school and headmaster. However, no schools seem to have celebrated quite as elaborately as Eton, with the local *Mairie* decked out in flags and pale blue ribbons, the band of the Coldstream Guards playing and commemorative menus designed by an Old Etonian architect. Whilst there is something faintly ludicrous about Baden-Powell scouring Mafeking for a fellow Old Carthusian with whom to celebrate Founder's Day, the idea of soldiers, many of them only recently out of school, gathering to forget for an evening the filth of the battlefield and to meet once again their old school-fellows, is understandable. Anson, writing in June 1917, was aware of the poignancy of the occasion: 'It is so seldom one gets a chance of meeting one's old friends nowadays and there are less and less of them. It will be the last chance of meeting one's friends before we are engulfed in the heavy fighting this summer.' It was, in fact, to be the last chance ever, for Anson was killed in a German attack in which bombs and flame-throwers devastated his battalion on 10 July.

Boys who had gone straight from school into the army had had no time to widen their social circle much beyond their school-friends. For many, the school had become their world and there was not the same gap between them and boys who would soon be enlisting as there was between them and their parents and other civilians. Public-school soldiers frequently spent part of their precious leave visiting their old schools. Nevill's visits to Dover College were not merely to see his younger brother. Perhaps fearing that aunts and uncles would be offended if they knew he had visited his old school rather than them, he instructed his parents: 'Don't let too many relations know! I shall try to work in a night at Dover.' Southwell cut short a visit to his parents on what was to be his last leave in order to visit a boy who was ill at Shrewsbury, and Fletcher spent his final leave largely with Eton friends. So many boys were leaving prematurely in order to train for commissions that Old Boys sometimes found few familiar faces. Allhusen, on a weekend's leave in London in 1915, went to Eton 'and saw what remains of the lads'.[1] The *Chronicle* suggested that there were more deep-seated reasons for visiting the school than seeing old friends:

> Old Etonians too think much more than they have been accustomed to about Eton and all that it has done for them, remembering that it was there that they learnt the lessons which are to enable them to stand the ordeal which must now be undergone, and more than ever they take any opportunity which they may find of coming down here again before they have to go out to the front, to play their games for once more, to walk in the playing-fields, or on Sundays to sit again in Chapel.

Rayner-Wood was glad that this was the case. In a letter to a former pupil he quoted this editorial and recalled a sermon possibly given by Hornby, before the War, in which the speaker said: 'Your schooldays at Eton will, when you have left this place, crystallise into a jewel of remembrance which will stay bright for the rest of your lives and perhaps even longer.' 'In death as in life Dulwich was close to his heart,' Paul Jones's father wrote of his son. 'The very last letter he wrote is irradiated with love of the old school.'

Whilst it was reported that some boys died with the motto of their regiment

[1] In the back of a diary which Allhusen kept whilst in the trenches in 1917, he sketched out the first few pages of a novel set at Eton.

on their lips – an Old Salopian serving with the 9th Welsh Regiment muttered 'Better death than dishonour' when he was mortally wounded – others' thoughts, like those of Captain Hook and the Old Cliftonian of Newbolt's 'He Fell Among Thieves', turned to their schools. Another Old Salopian, although mortally wounded 'had time to send his last greeting "to the other Shrewsbury fellows" in the Battalion'. A few hours before he died, the anonymous boy commemorated in *Letters of an OE* (1919) wrote to the Old Etonian friend who edited the letters: 'I think my last thoughts in this world, whenever I die, will be of Mother, Eton and you. Such a Mother and such a friend are more than most people could hope for, and as for Eton – the love of Eton is like one's love of England, always . . .'. According to a fellow-officer who witnessed his death, 'George' was true to his word: 'He tried to say something after he was hit [in the throat], but couldn't get it out properly, and it was very hard to understand; the only words we could make out were "mother", and then something unintelligible, and then "Eton". The end was very peaceful.'

4 Our Team in Khaki

Where are those hefty sporting lads
Who donned the flannels, gloves and pads?
They play a new and deadly game
Where thunder bursts in crash and flame.
Our cricketers have gone 'on tour',
To make their country's triumph sure.
They'll take the Kaiser's middle wicket
And smash it by clean British cricket.

Jessie Pope

Denis Winter writes that: 'Up to mid-1915 the course for prospective officers lasted just one month with the final selection made in games of rugby or soccer according to the respectability of the violence displayed and quickness of reaction generally.' The importance of games was continually stressed during training and every War Office manual issued to help new officers included a paragraph upon the value of sport.

It was not only the games of officers that were watched carefully in England. Football stadiums proved useful recruiting grounds, where pressure could be brought to bear upon young men demonstrably A1 but not yet in khaki. Indeed, it was estimated that some 500,000 men had been recruited at football matches by the end of 1914. Sport was used in two ways: by way of example, and as a form of reproach.

> We've watched you playing cricket
> And every kind of game,
> At football, golf and polo
> You men have made your name.
> But now your Country calls you
> To play your part in war . . .

So sang the chorus-girls in a popular recruiting song. Boys at school were told that slackers would not be wanted in the trenches, but there was no point in being good at games *unless* this led to the trenches. Professional footballers were urged by Mr Punch and others to enlist, partially to set an example, but also because the sport had become so popular that it was felt that the continuance of public matches would deter people from going to enlist. Men of Millwall were encouraged to 'Let the Enemy hear the "LION'S ROAR". Join and be in at THE FINAL and give them a KICK OFF THE EARTH'. A killjoy named Charrington finally succeeded in getting professional football officially banned in the spring of 1915, an event celebrated by a final match between Chelsea and Sheffield United at which Lord Derby presented the trophy and urged the players to be reconciled on the field of battle.

The enthusiasm for sport continued at the Front, where games were deemed a suitable recreation for the troops. Although there was the occasional idyllic cricket match (very much a game for officers), football and rugger were the most popular sports, often played very hard indeed. Allhusen remembered an inter-battalion match in Salonika for officers in which 'two of the opposing side were carried away on stretchers . . . The rest of the match was never played, as the Brigadier objected.' As well he might. The 13th Battalion of the Rifle Brigade lost their commanding officer on the eve of battle on the Somme in November 1916; he had broken his collar-bone during a game of rugger in which the officers were pitched against the other ranks. Other sports were equally dangerous. Vaughan's diary records 'a fierce game of ice hockey' in which blackthorns served as sticks. One officer 'came an awful cropper, sailing through the air and landing on the back of his head. He was carried away, and the game continued . . .'

Despite such injuries soccer actually became compulsory at the end of 1917, played with army-issue footballs. One wonders how many casualties were sustained during these games, since they resembled Tom Brown's first match with as many as one hundred players on each side. Apart from providing healthy exercise for soldiers who had been bogged down in trenches, sport was also considered to be good for morale. Gibbs reported that the regimental sports 'made a tremendous difference to the men . . . Now, the whole spirit of the battalion has brightened up and the men haven't been so fit since they came out here.' Cricket could hardly be said to be of much practical value (although a practised bowler might prove useful in a bombing raid), but was nonetheless inflicted upon the troops. Perhaps it was meant to demonstrate the value of fair play, or was simply a distraction. However, as cricket balls hurtled towards players they might very well be unpleasantly reminded of the pieces of shrapnel they spent so much time trying to avoid in the front line.[1] Indeed, cricket could be quite as hazardous as the more energetic games. Gibbs told his parents that he was thankful that he had not taken part in an inter-company cricket match:

The pitch was rough, and there were several fast bowlers, who did terrible executions. I think every man on each side was hit at least once. One man in my platoon was hit in the middle of the forehead, but the ball bounced off all right and he didn't seem to mind in the least. He went on batting and there was soon a pretty big lump on the spot.

Perhaps he was hoping for a 'blighty'.

More important than such recreations was the metaphor they inspired. The most famous example of 'playing the game' took place on 1 July 1916, the first day on the Somme. The first sign of the British advance against the German front line before Montauban was a football sailing through the air, kicked by Captain W.P. Nevill of the 8th East Surreys. In an attempt to give the men of his company encouragement, Nevill had bought some footballs whilst on leave in May. Accounts differ as to how many balls there were; logically there should have been four, one for each platoon. However, according to the company's only surviving officer, Second Lieutenant C.W. Alcock, writing to Nevill's sister in order to correct newspaper reports: 'There were two footballs, & on one

---

[1] Douglas Gillespie recalled Winchester cricket matches as he watched bombs come hurtling out of the sky towards his trench.

was printed: "The Great European Cup-Tie Finals. East Surreys v. Bavarians. Kick off at zero." On the other in large letters was this: "NO REFEREE", which was W's way of telling the men they needn't treat the Hun too gently.' Nevill also offered a prize for the first platoon to dribble a ball as far as the German trenches. Apparently the 8th East Surreys went over the top with a 'wild cheer' which could be heard above the bombardment. Nevill was killed almost instantly, as were the majority of his men. Second Lieutenant C.C. Carver, whose nineteenth birthday it was, claimed that of the entire Battalion only four officers and 200 men emerged unscathed.[1] Two footballs survived and Major Unwin wrote to the Nevills to ask whether the East Surreys might keep one of them as a regimental trophy.

Meanwhile, news of this extraordinary event had become the basis of much ill-informed journalism back in England. 'GLORIOUS EAST SURREYS. A Football Match with Death in Picardy', the *Evening News* announced on 11 July, promising its readers 'delightful stories of a battalion of the East Surreys, which took part, with heavy loss but great glory' in the Big Push.[2] Further reports were published in *The Times*, the *Mirror*, the *Bystander*, and the *Illustrated London News*, which contained a grotesque double-page artist's impression of the advance. The apotheosis of this myth-making was a poem by the appositely-named 'Touchstone' in (where else?) the *Daily Mail*:

> On through the hail of slaughter,
>   Where gallant comrades fall,
> Where blood is poured like water,
>   They drive the trickling ball.
> The fear of death before them,
>   Is but an empty name;
> True to the land that bore them,
>   The SURREYS played the game.

And so on, through three verses. The malign influence of Newbolt is all too apparent, but the poem was dignified by being printed upon the East Surrey's official Christmas Card for 1916.

[1] Carver's estimate was made at the time and does not tally with the final estimate. The 8th East Surreys do not figure in Middlebrook's chart of battalions which suffered more than 500 casualties (i.e. 50 per cent).

[2] The standard of response to the action of 1 July may be gathered from the other sub-headings of this report: 'The Champagne Bottle' and 'A Bosche Who was Too Thin to Bayonet'.

Nevill's bravado was not unique. Similar incidents took place at Loos and Beersheba, whilst Denis Winter's father recalled his captain driving a golf ball towards the enemy line in the attack in which he was killed. Reginald Pound quotes the letter of a sapper, describing an attack at Aisne: 'You would have thought they were at a football match . . . A party of the King's Own went into battle shouting: "Early doors this way! Early doors, ninepence!"' Those who did not actually take the metaphor to its logical, but mad, conclusion frequently drew upon sporting imagery in their depiction of warfare. E.B. Osborn's popular war-time anthology *The Muse in Arms* has an entire section devoted to 'The Chivalry of Sport', demonstrating 'the insular conception of fighting as the greatest of all great games, that which is the most shrewdly spiced with deadly danger'. Osborn confesses that: 'The Germans, and even our Allies, cannot understand why this stout old nation persists in thinking of war as a sport.' Lieutenant Eric Wilkinson's 'Rugby Football' '(Written on receiving the football match list from Ilkley Grammar School)' fervently embraces the Newbolt ethic:

> They've met the foeman with a cheer,
>   And face to face have smiled on death.
> They are fighting still to the grand old rule,
>   That heart and courage must never fail –
> If they fall, there are more where the grey stone school
>   Looks out on the broad green vale.
>   Can you hear the call? Can you hear the call
>   That drowns the roar of Krupp?
> There are many who fight and many who fall
> Where the big guns play at the Kaiser's ball,
> But hark! – can you hear it? Over all –
>   Now, School! Now, School! Play up!

The proper showcase for this sort of verse was the school magazines, and indeed similar poems are to be found there. An elegy for 'Dick' in the *Eton Chronicle* is characteristic:

> So short a time ago you came,
>   So swift the years with work and play,
> And then you left. The Greater Game
>   Had called you, and you could not stay . . .

Inheriting a tradition of schoolmaster versifying from people like Bowen of
Harrow, John Bain filled the columns of the *Marlburian* with sporting elegies
for his former pupils. For some reason Bain was admired by the usually more
circumspect Charles Sorley. The undoubted sincerity of Bain's commemorative stanzas is vitiated by an egregious banality of imagery and expression. J.W.
Mangan in his study of *Athleticism in the Victorian and Edwardian Public Schools*
generously refers to Bain's 'poetic obituaries of gentle, unsophisticated sorrow',
but those he reprints in an appendix (cautiously labelled "Poets" of
Athleticism') are little better than Touchstone's epitaph upon Nevill's East
Surreys:

> Aye, Marlborough knows you played the game,
> Dying, you set the gem upon her,
> Giving her yet another name
> To sparkle on her Roll of Honour.
> *In Memory of Lt. E.S. Phillips*

> And now you've played a grimmer game
> Old England called – you heard and came
> To shot and shell, to fire and flame,
> To death or glory,
> To fight and fall, and link your name
> With England's story
> *In Memory of Lt. H.J.O. Leather*

> Falling they leave behind them as they fall
> A nobler fame than that of bat and ball.
> *In Memory of Capt. E.A. and Lts. B.H.G. & A.G. Shaw*

The recycling of these stale and meretricious images of sporting soldiers
meeting their match is reminiscent of the work of a monumental mason during
an epidemic. One cannot help feeling that these young men deserved better. To
be fair to Bain, Sorley himself *got* better, and the individual emerges from the
mass in this one elegy:

> Sweet, singing Voice from overseas,
> Lover of Marlborough and her Downs,
> Sure now thy Spirit, wandering free,

Is hovering near the Town of Towns,
There where the bents and grasses wave,
And winds roar round the Hoary Post –
No wormy earth, no gloomy grave
Shall hold thy homing, eager ghost.

Here, Bain makes a neat comparison between Sorley, the keen cross-country runner forever up on the Downs, and his now roaming ghost, which is both apt and touching. However, even this elegy descends to irrelevant bathos:

More than the most was thine to spend
For Mother, England, Freedom, Truth;
Gladly thou gav'st, dear poet friend,
The splendid promise of thy youth.

This is a deplorable betrayal of Sorley's character and a travesty of his attitude to war and death.

Given these attitudes, what could be more appropriate than the Senior Master's gift to King's Worcester in memory of pupils killed in the War:

This Pavilion, the gift of T.E. Rammell, was erected in memory of those who, having learnt in this place to play the game for their School, played it also for their Country during the years 1914–1918. *Haec olim meminisse juvabit.*

5 *Dying in Their Glory*

These men having set a crown of imperishable glory on their own land were folded in the dark cloud of death; yet being dead they have not died, since from on high their excellence raises them gloriously out of the house of Hades.

Simonides

'It's too wonderful,' Rupert Brooke exclaimed when he heard that his battalion was to sail for the Dardanelles. 'We're going in four days. And the

[217]

best expedition of the war.' For romantic young men like Brooke, the prospect of a naval expedition to the Aegean in order to fight the Infidel and capture Byzantium could hardly be more evocative. It was imbued with a sense of history, looking back to the past glories of the British Navy, beyond them to the Crusades, and beyond them to the Trojan Wars. Brooke told Violet Asquith:

> I've been looking at maps. Do you think that *perhaps* the fort on the Asiatic corner will want quelling, and we'll land and come at it from behind and they'll make a sortie and meet us on the plains of Troy? It seems to me strategically so possible. Shall we have a Hospital Base (and won't you manage it?) at Lesbos? Will Hero's Tower crumble under the 15 in. guns? Will the sea be polyphloisbic[1] and wine dark and unvintageable . . .?

Off Africa Brooke reported to Jacques Raverat that:

> We've been gliding though a sapphire sea, swept by the ghosts of triremes and quinqueremes, Hannibal on poop, or Hanno . . . And now we've left Tinacria behind (you would call it Sicily) and soon – after Malta – we'll be among the Cyclades. There I shall recite Sappho and Homer. And the winds of history will follow me all the way.

These visions are unsurprising for someone who had been a classical scholar at the King's of Sills, Wedd, Sheppard, Lowes Dickinson and Headlam, an environment where:

> . . . clever modern men have seen
> A Faun a-peeping through the green,
> And felt the Classics were not dead,
> To glimpse a Naiad's reedy head,
> Or hear the Goat-foot piping low: . . .

Brooke was not the only Classically-educated young officer on board *SS Grantully Castle*. There was Patrick Shaw-Stewart, using an edition of Herodotus, the Greek historian known as 'the father of history', as a guide-book; there was that other sprig of the Souls, Charles Lister, one of a set of

---

[1] This word, deriving from the Homeric Greek 'polyphloisboiothalasse' (a descriptive word for the roaring sea), is indicative of the way the Classics (in this case *The Iliad*) were entertainingly ransacked by the romantic and scholarly.

brilliant Etonian Classicists which included Ronald Knox; there was F.S. Kelly, another Old Etonian, and his fellow-musician Denis Browne, who had known Brooke since Rugby; and there was Violet Asquith's brother, Arthur. Together these men formed the 'Latin Club' and amused themselves by describing their location in terms of Classical history and myth, thus evading the watchful eye of the censor. Brooke was so enchanted by his surroundings that he remarked that he would like to be buried on a Greek island. In due course he was, 'in an olive grove on a noted Greek island of incredible beauty and appositeness', as Shaw-Stewart reported to Diana Manners. That island was Scyros, where Achilles hid in the court of Lycomedes disguised as a girl, 'Pyrrha' (because of his Brooke-like red-gold hair), and where Theseus was buried. 'One was transported back a couple of thousand years,' Kelly wrote of the funeral, 'and one felt the old Greek divinities stirring from their long sleep'. Amongst the last fragments of poems Brooke wrote were two verses about the expedition which recall Achilles, Hector, Sarpedon and Priam:

> And Priam and his fifty sons
> Wake all amazed, and hear the guns,
>   And shake for Troy again.

For the families and friends of Lister and Shaw-Stewart the Great War had all the inevitability of Greek tragedy. We have already noted that the Souls were romantically obsessed by death, and during the War they entered upon their inheritance. Julian Grenfell's mother, Ettie Desborough, had identified herself with the women of Greek tragedy long before the War, particularly those women whose sons, husbands or lovers had been killed. When the War came she took to her role with relish: 'Yes, you are a really great War Mother,' Julian wrote to her. Equally, he conformed to her idea of a really great War Child, something of a Coriolanus to her Volumnia. When it was realised that a fragment of shell had penetrated Julian's skull, not just bounced off it as he had boasted, the privileged Desboroughs got permission from the Admiralty to sail to Boulogne and his bedside. Ettie wrote an account of her son's gradual surrender to death, an account suffused with the same sense of resolution she had brought to other deathbeds before the War. Julian liked to recite a speech from Euripedes's *Hippolytus* in which Phaedra longs for the consolation of being at one with nature like her beloved stepson. It is a speech which seems to lie behind 'Into Battle', Julian's classically-inspired poem, the last line of which is a paraphrase of a line from *The Aeneid*. 'The thought that he was dying seemed to go and come,' Ettie recorded, 'but he always seemed radiantly happy and he never saw any of the people he loved look sad.' The scene seems to have been like the sepulchral reliefs described by Mackail in the Introduction to the *Greek Anthology*.[1] When the end came, it could hardly have been more perfect: Julian murmured 'Phoebus Apollo' as a shaft of sunlight fell across the bed and then said nothing more, apart from, once, his father's name, until he died: 'At the moment that he died, he opened his eyes a little with the most radiant smile that they had ever seen on his face.' Such was the beauty and blessedness of death that no mourning was worn at his funeral.

The letters that Lady Desborough received reinforced the idea that her son had fulfilled the ideal of some epigram from the *Greek Anthology* ('One does not offer consolation to heroines of Greek Tragedy,' Raymond Asquith observed). 'Like Castor and Pollux they are together now, shining in some other place', wrote Maurice Baring when Julian's brother Billy was killed two months later. 'How different the most terrible sorrow is to the blight of misery, isn't it? . . . To make up the harmony of the world, to make the inheritance glorious and worth having, the youthful death of the very bright and the very brave is, I have always felt, not only a necessary but a precious element. Glorious sorrow is as necessary, is as priceless, as the nightingale or the evening star.' It is as Castor and Pollux that the Grenfells appear in Osborn's *The New Elizabethans*, illustrated with a photograph of Billy dressed up as a Roman centurion. Their mother found consolation in compiling *Pages from a Family Journal*, 'a memorial of perpetual beauty'. Osborn thought that:

> It will survive as a living part of the Grammata whereby, as Gilbert Murray said in a beautiful discourse on the necessity of Greek and Latin books, we find our escape into that calm world of theirs, where stridency and clamour are forgotten in the former stillness, where the strong iron is long since rusted and the rocks of granite broken into dust, but the great things of the human spirit still shine like stars pointing man's way onward to the great triumph or the great tragedy, and even the little things, the beloved and tender and funny and familiar things, beckon across gulphs of death and charge with a magic poignancy, the old things that our dead leaders and forefathers loved, *viva adhuc et desiderio pulchriora*.

The Souls needed some sort of consolation for the swathe that was cut through their ranks by the War: Julian and Billy Grenfell, Ego and Ivo Charteris, John

[1] See above pp 95–6.

Manners, Charles Lister, Patrick Shaw-Stewart, Edward Horner, Raymond Asquith, Auberon Lucas, George Vernon. Osborn's epitaph upon the Grenfells might stand for the attitude of the bereaved to the deaths of all these young men: 'They lived unvanquished by any littleness, and they died as they lived – none doubted that no more complete victory over death than theirs had ever yet been won.'

All these young men had received a Classical education, and letters, diaries and memoirs of the War are studded with Classical allusions and Greek and Latin phrases used with an ease and naturalness which seems as much as anything to divide their era from our own. Robert Graves composed Latin epigrams to while away the time on parades and in the trenches at quiet periods. Cyril Falls, 'not being given to prayer', would repeat a mnemonic for Latin adverbs he remembered from the classroom. Bourne, the educated private in *The Middle Parts of Fortune*, is detailed to do some typing and practises speed by tapping out stray phrases of Latin. It was quite natural for men to take Classical texts into the trenches with them. 'No Parade in the afternoon,' wrote A.G. West, serving as a private with the Public Schools Battalion. 'Read the "Odyssey" and enjoyed it for itself and for the really novel exercise of making out the meaning of the lines and the new interest it gave to war.' Arthur Innes Adam, a Wykehamist and Balliol captain, was to be found wandering near Etaples 'with Homer, a novel, a pair of bathing-drawers and a small amount of paper.' T.E. Lawrence was another soldier who carried the *Odyssey* with him, and Harold Macmillan took Aeschylus, which he read whilst lying wounded in a shell-hole, waiting for stretcher-bearers at Loos. Just before his death Second Lieutenant Ivar Campbell asked for Xenophon's *Anabasis* to be sent to him in Mesopotamia. Robert Bridges's anthology of uplifting poetry for serving men, *The Spirit of Man* had a heavily Classical bias, containing many pages of extracts from the works of Homer, Plato and Aristotle.

Another popular volume was Housman's Classically-inspired *A Shropshire Lad*. Already widely-read by the well-educated – 'in every pocket' according to Robert Nichols – it became accessible to all when some of the poems were printed as a broadsheet for the troops by *The Times*. Soldiers were clearly tempted by this sample, since sales of the book soared; in 1918 some 16,000 copies were sold. This was in spite of the fact that Grant Richards had doubled the price (from 6d. to 1s.) in 1916. Housman hoped that a copy of the book, carried in a breast pocket like a Bible, would one day deflect one of the many bullets which, as Owen put it in a Housmanesque phrase, 'long to nuzzle in the hearts of lads'. After the War Housman received a letter, which he always kept, from an American who had offered his copy of the volume to a wounded British soldier, but the Tommy had his own, battle-scarred copy still with him. Paul Fussell has noted how Housman's 'theme of beautiful suffering lads' was particularly appropriate to the circumstances of the trenches; so was the theme of classical pessimism.

The cult of youth, death and the Classics, of which Housman's poems were representative, flourished in the trenches. When Robert Graves was badly wounded in 1916 and mistakenly reported dead, he was amused to reflect that 'it takes a lot to kill Youth and Ugliness however easily Youth and Beauty fade and die'. He told Sassoon: 'By the way, I died on my 21st birthday. I can never grow up now.' Those who did not recover could never grow up either and it appears that there was considerable consolation to be drawn from the idea of Youth and Beauty being in some way preserved by death, just as Margaret Barrie had been comforted by the notion that her dead son would always be thirteen.[1] What finer tribute to the cult of young men could be paid than that an entire generation of them would, like Henry Desmond in *The Hill*, be permanently suspended in their pristine condition? The traditional regret that boys grew up, and away, to be sullied by the world was countered by thousand upon thousand of Peter Pans.[2] Like fruit from which the bloom had not yet been rubbed off, these stars of the games-field and the classroom would be preserved at the peak of perfection. Laurence Binyon's poem 'For the Fallen, 1914' was published in *The Times* on 21 September 1915, the day that the preliminary bombardment for the attack at Loos took place. The poem, used ever since to commemorate the dead, seems almost a premonition of the casualties which were to result from that battle. 106 officers were killed in the first week; of these all but 22 were under twenty-six years old. Binyon had written:

> They shall not grow old, as we that are left grow old:
> Age shall not weary them, nor the years condemn.
> At the going down of the sun and in the morning
> We will remember them.

These lines are very similar to Housman's observations of the young men at Ludlow Fair in *A Shropshire Lad* XXIII. Of 'the lads that will never be old' Housman writes:

[1] See p 93.

[2] One of the more hideous ironies of the War was that the man chosen to design the Cenotaph and various other memorials, both in England and upon the battlefields, was Edwin Lutyens, who, before the war, had designed the nursery setting for *Peter Pan*.

I wish one could know them, I wish there were tokens to tell
　　The fortunate fellows that now you can never discern;
And then one could talk with them friendly and wish them farewell
　　And watch them depart on the way that they will not return.

But now you may stare as you like and there's nothing to scan;
　　And brushing your elbow unguessed⁄at and not to be told
They carry back bright to the coiner the mintage of man,
　　The lads that will die in their glory and never be old.

How evocative these lines must have been for families anxiously gathered at
railway stations watching the leave train depart for France once more.

Patrick Shaw⁄Stewart's final leave was blighted by the news that Edward
Horner had been killed; it seemed like a premonition of his own death:

　　　　I saw a man this morning
　　　　　　Who did not wish to die:
　　　　I asked, and cannot answer,
　　　　　　If otherwise wish I.

This poem was written on the flyleaf of his copy of *A Shropshire Lad*, which he
had carried with him along with Herodotus and the *Iliad*. It ends with Shaw⁄
Stewart comparing his own prospects with those of Achilles:

　　　　Achilles came to Troyland
　　　　　　And I to Chersonese:
　　　　He turned from wrath to battle,
　　　　　　And I from three days' peace.

　　　　Was it so hard, Achilles,
　　　　　　So very hard to die?
　　　　Thou knowest and I know not –
　　　　　　So much the happier I.

　　　　I will go back this morning
　　　　　　From Imbros over the sea;
　　　　Stand in the trench, Achilles,
　　　　　　Flame⁄capped, and shout for me.

The example of Achilles, who 'turned from wrath to battle' after the death of Patroclus, lies behind some of the reactions to the death of a friend mentioned earlier. Bourne's savagery upon realising that Martlow had been killed and Sassoon's reaction to the death of David Thomas are notable examples. But the most self-conscious example is that of George Sherston when Kendle is killed in *Memoirs of an Infantry Officer*:

> After blank awareness that he was killed, all feelings tightened and contracted to a single intention – to 'settle that sniper' on the other side of the valley. If I had stopped to think, I shouldn't have gone at all . . . I had lost my temper with the man who had shot Kendle.

In an act of lunatic bravery, Sherston captures an entire trench single-handed. Returning from this exploit he comes across Kendle's body: 'In my excitement I had forgotten about Kendle.' The allusion to Achilles is surely intentional. When Achilles hears of the death of Patroclus, he is similarly roused and sets out on a suicidal mission, suicidal because Thetis has told him that if he kills Hector, he too is doomed to die. In the elation of killing Hector, Achilles addresses the Achaeans and suggests marching upon Troy, then pauses: 'But what am I saying? How can I think of anything but the dead man who is lying by my ships unburied and unwept – Patroclus, whom I shall never forget as long as I am still among the living . . .' The parallel is explicit and owes rather more to art than life. Kendle is a portrait of a man called Gibson (who came from Cumberland, hence the pseudonym: Kendal/Kendle) who was not in fact killed until ten days *after* Sassoon's assault upon the German trench. Sassoon did not forget; looking back to the Somme five years later he felt that: 'Gibson is a ghost, but he is more real tonight than the pianist who played Scriabine with such delicate adroitness. I wish I could "find a moral equivalent for war". To-night I feel as if I were only half-alive. Part of me died with all the Gibsons I used to know.'

Like chivalry, the Classics elevated warfare and made some sense of death. Aubrey Herbert's poem in memory of Brooke combines the images of Greek hero and crusader:

> He who sang of dawns and evening, English glades and light of Greece,
> Changed his dreaming into sleeping, left his sword to rest in peace.
> Left his visions of the springtime, Holy Grail and Golden Fleece,
> Took the leave that has no ending, till the waves of Lemnos cease.

[224]

Similarly, Maurice Baring's poem commemorating 'Bron' Lucas conjures up images of both Achilles and Lancelot, and T.E. Lawrence took Malory as well as Homer to war with him.

Back in England the correspondence columns of the *Spectator* were clogged for some twelve weeks with clerics and academics attempting to combine elements of the public-school ethos by translating the phrase 'Play the Game' into Latin, as if to dignify it with a history more noble than that of Newboltian imperialism. No one seems to have hit upon a solution to this taxing problem: 'Doubtless the Romans knew not cricket or its spirit,' one correspondent ventured, 'and had they been more fortunate who shall say what Virgil might not have made of a conceivable addition to the Aeneid?'

If the Classics could not provide a satisfactory tag for the spirit in which the War was being fought, they could at least be relied upon to provide models for the spirit in which its victims were to be commemorated. The *Greek Anthology* had already been ransacked by Kipling, whose 'Epitaphs of War', written whilst attempting to come to terms with the death of his son John whom he had encouraged along the path to Loos, amounted, as he admitted, to 'naked cribs' (although the tone was very different). An even more naked crib was Raymond's epitaph for all the dead of the public schools:

> Tell England, ye who pass this monument
> We died for her, and here we rest content.

A version of this had in fact already been used in the Boer War in the cemetery on Waggon Hill, above Ladysmith. It is adapted from Simonides's epitaph upon the Spartan dead at Thermopylae: 'O Stranger, tell the Lacedaemonians that we lie here obeying their orders'. One of the now-forgotten poets thrown up by the War, Lieutenant Joseph Lee, had made a less happy adaptation of this epitaph, which appeared as a premature obituary in the *Spectator* (Lee was taken prisoner, but had been reported as missing):

> Here do we lie, dead but not discontent,
> That which we found to do has had accomplishment.

A peculiar poignancy attaches to the epitaph to the dead of the 8th and 9th Battalions of the Devonshire Regiment at Mansel Copse on the Somme. Captain D.L. Martin of the 9th Devons had worked out from models and sketches that he and his men were almost certain to be caught in machine-gun fire in the attack of 1 July. Nonetheless, obeying orders, he led the attack. Amongst those killed with him was William Noel Hodgson, son of the Bishop of St Edmondsbury and Ipswich, a distinguished classicist and a devout Christian. He lad left Durham School to go to Christ Church, Oxford as a Classical scholar and was renowned for 'his love of Homer and understanding of the *Iliad* especially'. His most famous poem, the much-anthologised 'Before Action' suggests his commanding officer's apprehension. It was written two days before the attack:

> By all delights that I shall miss,
> Help me to die, O Lord.

A trench was used as a mass grave for the 160 men of the 8th and 9th Devons, who were mown down, exactly as Martin had predicted. Above it someone, perhaps realising that a Classical scholar was amongst the dead, placed an epitaph of Classical simplicity:

> The Devonshires held this trench.
> The Devonshires hold it still.

6 Good-bye to Galahad

> Of gallant St Georges to-day we've a legion,
>   As sturdy and game as the knights of Romance;
> They are fighting their fight in that shell-battered region
>   That bears the vague pseudonym – 'Somewhere in France'.
>
> Though glittering armour has changed into khaki,
>   Though the dragon spits bullets and shrapnel and flame,
> Once more it's a fight to the finish, and harkee,
>   The glorious sequel will be just the same.
>   *Jessie Pope*

Chivalric notions about the War were those which were most difficult to relinquish, for they gave some sense of higher purpose to the squalor and slaughter. Indeed, they were not even relinquished after the end of the War, for knights and saints are a frequent device upon memorials, particularly those to the dead of the public schools. Propaganda aimed at the prosecution of the War and the recruiting of soldiers frequently took refuge in pretty pictures of armour-clad knights decoratively slaying dragons. Men were urged to 'Take up the Sword of Justice: Join Now', and to avenge 'Brave Little Belgium'. The Germans, forever barbarised by the name 'Hun', were depicted murdering Belgian women, and worse. According to propagandists there were hundreds of Flemish damsels in distress awaiting khaki-clad young knights. The melodramatic and archaic images used in propaganda carefully diverted attention away from the real business of war, and in retrospect it was clearly more pleasant for grieving relatives to imagine young men as shining knights laying down their lives than as all too mortal flesh blown to messy bits by shells.

Even disasters as unequivocal as the Gallipoli campaign could be dignified by references to chivalry. John Masefield's *Gallipoli*, published during the War (1916) and therefore not unnaturally making the best of a bad job, does not underestimate the suffering of the troops. However, after a harrowing description of the ways in which soldiers might be expected to fare during the landings, Masefield writes: 'But as they moved out [of Mudros harbour] these things were but the end they asked, the reward they had come for, *the unseen cross upon the breast.*[1] All they felt was a gladness of exultation that their young courage was to be used. They went like kings in a pageant to the imminent death.' The book was written as propaganda after Masefield had been heckled about the Dardanelles campaign during a lecture-tour of America in 1916. Masefield had worked with the Red Cross at Gallipoli and might perhaps have taken note of a directive from his hero, Sir Ian Hamilton (Commander-in-Chief to the expedition), who had learned that medical workers had:

> . . . allowed themselves to become too seriously impressed by the stories of young officers and men who have come on board sick or wounded. It is natural under the circumstances that these tales should be over-coloured; it is natural also that contact with so much suffering should incline the listeners to sympathy; but it is certain also that, whether from the standpoint of the individual sick or of the military operations as a whole, such ennervating influences should be resisted. All grades and degrees of medical staff must make it a point of professional honour to maintain a hearty tone of optimism

[1] Emphasis mine.

[227]

calculated to raise rather than lower the confidence and courage of the fighting men who have been temporarily committed to their charge.

A hearty tone of optimism certainly informs *Gallipoli*, combined with romantic notions of a chivalric quest, unflagging patriotism, self-sacrifice and glory. Although propaganda, it is the book of a poet. It is also the book of a hero-worshipper, dedicated to Hamilton, whom Masefield compares to 'Roland at Roncevaux, defending Christendom from Islam'. Indeed, each section of the book is prefaced with a quotation from the *Chanson de Roland*. Masefield's book bears out his opinion of the campaign 'not as a tragedy, nor as a mistake, but as a great human effort, which came, more than once, very near to triumph.' These vague sentiments seem so much chaff in the cold winds of fact: total military failure and some 252,000 Allied casualties. Later, and privately, Masefield was to refer to 'that insane move on Gallipoli'.

Whatever the strategic motives, any assault upon the Turks naturally encouraged fantasies about crusading, none more so than the Allied assault upon the Holy City itself. An example of how chivalric compensation could emerge from considerable misery and bloodshed is an extraordinary book by the actor Vivian Gilbert published in 1923. *The Romance of the Last Crusade* was issued in blue boards, stamped in gold with a shield, upon which a cross is emblazoned, mounted by a plumed casque. Whilst the main narrative of the book concerns Gilbert's wartime experiences, it is prefaced by a chapter entitled 'Once Upon a Time'. This opens with the following passage, printed in Gothic script:

'Sire, only come hither and I will show you Jerusalem!' Thus spake the valiant knight, Sir Brian de Gurnay.

'Nay,' replied King Richard of England, and he buried his face in his armour, tears were in his eyes, and with hands uplift to Heaven he exclaimed: 'Lord God, I pray Thee that I may never see Thy Holy City, if so be that I may not rescue it from the hands of Thine enemies!'

It transpires that this extract is from a book which is being read one summer's afternoon by one of the knight's descendants, who shares his name. Brian Gurnay, 'just down from his first year at Oxford, a typical product of the English public school', is stirred by this tale: 'What wonderful times to live in, those days of chivalry and romance, when gallant knights of old adventured forth to free the Holy Land with great swords by their sides and great faith in

[228]

their hearts!' Gilbert comments that: 'There were a great many boys like Brian in England in 1914, drifting into manhood with no settled purpose in life but a vague resentment at the apparent futility of existence.' The Last Crusade, that which would recapture Jerusalem for Christendom, had never taken place, a fact which galls this romantic youth: 'To fight in thy cause, to take part in that Last Crusade I would willingly leave my bones in the Holy Land! Oh, for the chance to do as one of those knight of old, to accomplish one thing in life really worth while!' Gilbert, with a heavy irony which post-War writers found irresistible, remarks that Brian 'realised how ridiculous it all was to think that such a prayer could be granted in these prosaic days – July 1914 – when all the world was at peace and nothing could be further off than a clash of arms, the call to battle.' At which point Brian's frail old mother totters out onto the lawn waving the *Daily Telegraph*, haloed by light as befits a participant in an annunciation scene. Brian is at once awed and thrilled by the prospect of war: 'he almost fancied the blood that had come down to him from Sir Brian de Gurnay was mounting to his head: his eyes shone and he held his mother to him. Her hand trembled still, but Brian felt somehow his prayer was going to be answered, and he was glad.' Indeed, one can almost hear Parry's anthem crashing in at this point.[1] However, this scene is merely a prelude, and no further reference is made to Brian.

The narrative now switches abruptly to Gilbert's own experience. Perhaps that quintessentially English scene was intended to counterpoint Gilbert's circumstances in 1914, an actor in *Peg o' My Heart* on the New York stage. Gilbert's patriotism is less atavistic than Brian's but nonetheless heartfelt: 'What is it, this deep-down love of country, this patriotism, that makes us all, even the least likely, burn with impatience to be soldiers to defend our native land when it is menaced?' he asks. 'What matters it if wars are made by financial profiteers and lying statesmen, if soldiers are deluded with false battle cries to fight for a country "fit for heroes to live in", only to return to it, those that are left, to die of starvation and want, forgotten by the people they went forth to save?' Something is wrong here; one feels that the tone should be ironic, in the vein of Sassoon's 'Does it matter?', written six years previously. However, Gilbert's answer is that patriotism absolves all horror, even the horror of losing one brother 'in that disastrous landing at Gallipoli', another 'during our useless advance in Macedonia', and yet another on the Western Front, a pilot shot

---

[1] A setting of Psalm CXXII for Edward VII's coronation in 1901: 'I was glad when they said unto me / We will walk into the house of the Lord / And we shall stand in thy gates, O Jerusalem!'

down in flames. A fourth brother also fought at Gallipoli where he received wounds that crippled him for life. Somewhat subdued by this catalogue of disaster, Gilbert's attitude begins to change: 'I had been so tremendously keen in those early days: war had seemed a wonderful thing then, ennobling, uplifting. Were all the books I had read of past wars untrue, lies strung together to deceive the credulous?' The expected answer is once again rejected: 'The spirit that was in those early Crusaders was just as much alive today as it was centuries ago. It was only that we had a different way of doing things. The men were just as fine as they had ever been; it was a great leader we lacked; or was it that there seemed no definite goal before us, no great prize to fight for?' This crisis of faith is interrupted by the news that both leader and cause have revealed themselves: Allenby and the capture of Jerusalem. Gilbert strides through the camp, which is buzzing with excitement: 'From the transport lines came the clang of hammers upon iron — horse and mule shoes were being fashioned for the march; but to me it sounded like the noise of riveting armour.'

Gilbert's progress through Palestine is illuminated by similar delusions. Every step of the way and every place-name recalls the crusade of Richard Coeur de Lion; not only were the soldiers 'descendants' of the early crusaders, but the horses too came 'from the English stock that had furnished chargers for King Richard and his knights and warriors'. Even the camel-men ('ignorant heathens') who realise that death is approaching bid farewell to their beasts in a manner 'which, in its way, was just as full of chivalry and romance as the impassioned speech to his steed of some medieval knight stricken on the field of battle'.

'In all the ten crusades organised and equipped to free the Holy City, only two were really successful', Gilbert writes, '— the first led by Godfrey de Bouillon, and the last under Edmund Allenby'. Glad to have taken part in the gruelling campaign, Gilbert concludes his book, romance undimmed, with the (now ironic) boast: 'We had finished our crusade, peace and freedom were in the Holy Land for the first time for five hundred years — and it all seemed worth while.' One wonders whether the widow of Gilbert's servant, whose legs were blown off by a random shell, felt the same when she received the news of her husband's death in her butcher's shop in Lancashire.

And what of Brian Gurnay? Could he be the young officer whom Gilbert saw as he wandered through the camp on the eve of the assault upon Jerusalem? The scene is reminiscent of the king's mingling with the troops on the eve of Agincourt in Shakespeare's *Henry V*. Gilbert sees the officer lighting a cigarette: 'It may have been the effect of the shadows caused by the lighted match, or some trick of my over-excited imagination – but the peak of his khaki helmet looked exactly like a raised visor,[1] whilst the face was the face of some armoured knight of old which I could not help thinking I had seen years before, perhaps in some painting in a gallery or book in the library at home. Somewhere in the past, that bold forehead, aquiline nose, firm chin, and those steadfast, unfathomable eyes, had impressed themselves on my memory.'

Over-excited imaginations everywhere prompted atavistic visions, and memoirs of the period are studded with descriptions of young men apparently more at home at Camelot than at Cambrai. The Souls, of course, were particularly susceptible to such visions. Billy Grenfell, glimpsed at Edward VII's funeral in 1910, provided (in retrospect) a premonition for one of his admirers: 'He was standing against the Dryden monument, and a shaft of sunlight came down on his head, and I thought what a beautiful picture of manly youth. He looked like a young knight who would ride into battle with joy.' His brother Julian, discovered asleep in some straw behind the lines in France, his greyhounds (characteristically named Hammer and Tongs) beside him, was 'like a freshly woven Gobelin subject'. The Hon. Hugh Danway also provoked anachronistic visions. A friend glimpsing him in St Paul's wrote of 'a sudden vision in my imagination of Danway striding down the choir in full armour like St Michael – with his head thrown back, and that extraordinary expression of *resolution* which he always seemed to me to possess more than anyone I have ever seen. His wide-apart eyes had more of the spirit of truth in them than almost any – also an intolerance of falsehood – or rather perhaps the disbelief in its existence.' Even bullet-headed, purblind Aubrey Herbert prompted memories of Malory; his biographer comments: 'In almost every published description of Aubrey the word "chivalrous" appears with tedious regularity.' When he died – not in the war, but of bad dentistry in 1923 – a memorial brass was erected to his memory in which he was depicted in full armour. This was something of a family tradition. When his uncle, Auberon, Lord Lucas, was killed whilst serving with the RFC, his friend Maurice Baring commemorated him in a long poem, 'To A.H.', in which Lancelot

---

[1] There were several attempts to produce helmets for the troops modelled upon the traditional casque. One, designed in response to the Queen of Belgium's concern for the welfare of her soldiers, incorporated a pierced-steel visor. Some 40,000 of these were produced for the Ministry of Munitions by a Wolverhampton manufacturer. Another design came with a chain-mail curtain for the face and was also produced in large quantities. It impaired the vision and caused dizziness and was consequently discarded in the trenches. A similar fate befell other archaic devices such as an impractically heavy breastplate known as a 'body shield'.

and Tristram are depicted welcoming 'Bron' to their company. The whole poem is a repository of chivalric imagery.

The very concept of the Soldier Poet recalls literary warriors such as Sir Philip Sidney, whose name was frequently invoked, and such figures as Chaucer's Knight. E.B. Osborn suggests that the men he dubs *The New Elizabethans* in fact outstrip their sixteenth-century predecessors because they are without the 'unpleasant shortcomings' of men involved in Court intrigues. A. St John Adcock claims that the soldier poet of the Great War is in a direct line of descent from an earlier age: 'their courage, chivalry, love of justice, are theirs by inheritance, the ideals that led them are the common ideals that have led the best of our race through the past.' Of Captain G.O. Roos, killed on the first day of the Somme, it was written in the *Elizabethan* that 'Chaucer might have had him for his "verray parfit gentil knight" . . .'. Another Old Westminster's death prompted an essay in genealogy:

> Since the days of the Crusades, when Sir Jasper Croft was created a Knight of the Holy Sepulchre by Godfrey de Boulogne at the taking of Jerusalem, A.D. 1100, the Crofts have continually served their King and Country as soldiers. Members of the family have fought in most of the English wars, notably at the Battle of Agincourt, in the Wars of the Roses . . .

John Masefield was not the only person to make references to the *Chanson de Roland*. Robert Nichols described himself as 'an exceedingly guileless, highly emotional and inordinately romantic youth, steeped in the *Chanson de Roland* and Vigny's *Servitudes et Grandeurs Militaires*'. He prefaced the anthology of Great War poetry he made during the Second World War with the closing lines of the *Chanson*. The translation he used was that made by C.K. Scott-Moncrieff, who had served as a captain in the War and been invalided back to England and a staff job. His verse translation of *The Song of Roland* was published in 1919 and dedicated to the memory of Philip Bainbrigge, Wilfred Owen and Ian Mackenzie: 'To Three Men, Scholars, Poets, Soldiers, who came to their Rencesvals in September, October, and November Nineteen Hundred and Eighteen, I dedicate my part in a book of which their friendship quickened the beginning, their example has justified the continuing.'

Of all soldier poets none was more likened to (and less like) a knight than Rupert Brooke. In a verse letter to Robert Graves Sassoon had written:

> I'd timed my death in action to the minute
> (The *Nation* with my deathly verses in it).

The same might be said about Brooke, who helped to create his own legend by expiring (like Aubrey Herbert, of septicaemia) on 23 April 1915, St George's Day. His deathless verses, 'The Soldier', had been printed in *The Times* on 5 April in the course of a report of the Easter Sunday sermon given in St Paul's in which Dean Inge quoted the poem and prematurely canonised its author. Whilst some people regarded it as apposite that Brooke should have died on the same day as Shakespeare, others were more impressed by the connection with St George. Had not Brooke been a crusader, sailing off to fight the heathen Turk? 'I suddenly realise that the ambition of my life has been – since I was two – to go on a military expedition against Constantinople,' he confessed with characteristic enthusiasm to Violet Asquith. 'And when I *thought* I was hungry, or sleepy, or falling in love, or aching to write a poem – that was what I really, blindly, wanted.' How seriously Violet Asquith, or posterity, was to take this is open to question. Brooke was very fond of the rhetorical flourish, and the 'since I was two' from this particular Peter Pan is telling. To others he wrote in even more mocking vein: 'This is probably the first letter you ever got from a Crusader,' he wrote to Jacques Raverat from the *SS Grantully Castle* as it steamed south west:

> You expect to hear that we saw the sea-serpent off Algiers, that the Patriarch of Alexandria has blessed us, and that an outbreak of scurvy was healed by a prompt application of the thigh-bones and pelvis of SS John the Divine, Mary Magdalene, and Chrysostom. Not a bit. But the early Crusaders were very jolly people. I've been reading about them. They set out to slay the Turks – and very finely they did it when they met them. But when they got East, to the Levant and Constantinople, were they kind to their brother Christians they found there? No. They very properly thwacked and trounced them, and took their money, and cut their throats, and ravished their daughters and so left them: for that they were Greeks, Jews, Slavs, Vlachs, Magyars, Czechs, and Levantines, and not gentlemen.
> So shall we do, I hope.

He told Dudley Ward that a gift of handkerchiefs would be useful to bind 'my scimitar-lopped stumps'. The *Grantully Castle* even docked briefly at the crusaders' island of Malta. However, it was the Classical world that really caught Brooke's imagination as he cruised towards war, and it was upon the island of Theseus and Achilles that Brooke was finally buried; but his epitaph, although in Greek, was that of a crusader: 'Here lies the servant of God, a sub-lieutenant in the British Navy, who died for the deliverance of Constantinople from the Turks.' As a final touch, the ground where he was buried, the plot that became forever England, was consecrated by a monk from the island monastery, which was dedicated to St George.

Obituaries elevated Brooke to mythic status almost immediately, following the Dean of St Paul's example. *The Sphere* compared him to Sir Philip Sidney, whilst everywhere the poet's apparent joy in laying down his life was recorded without much biographical authority. Churchill's famous obituary was more astute as recruiting rhetoric than as biographical insight: 'The thoughts to which he gave expression in the very few incomparable sonnets which he has left behind will be shared by many thousands of young men moving resolutely and blithely forward into this, the hardest, the cruellest, and the least-rewarded of all wars that men have fought.' Harold Monro was rightly appalled by the way the man was being blotted out by the icon: 'One fears his memory being brought to the poster-grade. "He did his duty. Will You do yours?" is hardly the moral to be drawn,' he wrote in the *Cambridge Magazine* in May. 'Few people trouble to know much about poetry – but everyone takes an intelligent interest in death.' Sorley saw the *Morning Post*'s sudden espousal of Brooke as similarly motivated. But the myth remained, fuelled by Brooke's Galahad looks which were immortalised in the famous photograph by Sherril Schell which adorned all editions of his poems. This photograph was used as the basis for Brooke's memorial in Rugby Chapel in which Harvard Thomas tidied the poet's hair and straightened the tip-tilted nose. Sir Ian Hamilton, Brooke's Commander-in-Chief, who gave the address at the unveiling of this anodyne plaque, was later to portray Brooke as a crusader to the boys of Rugby: 'I went into his tent, where he was lying stretched out on the desert sand, looking extraordinarily handsome, a very knightly presence.' Hamilton recorded that when he offered Brooke a staff post he behaved as 'a *preux chevalier* would' and refused.

Other knightly presences amongst the poets included the Prime Minister's barrister son, Herbert Asquith, whose 'The Volunteer' is the most famous of all poems on the chivalric theme:

> Here lies a clerk who half his life had spent
> Toiling at ledgers in a city grey,
> Thinking that so his days would drift away
> With no lance broken in life's tournament.
> Yet even 'twixt the books and his bright eyes

The gleaming eagles of the legions came,
The horsemen, charging under phantom skies,
Went thundering past beneath the oriflamme.

And now those waiting dreams are satisfied;
From twilight to the halls of dawn he went;
His lance is broken; but he lies content
With that high hour in which he lived and died.
And falling thus he wants no recompense,
Who found his battle in the last resort;
Nor needs he any hearse to bear him hence,
Who goes to join the men of Agincourt.

The combination of the classical and the chivalric is not only reminiscent of Brooke, but also of the period as a whole. The Roman legion with its eagle, and the echo of Simonides in line 11, is set against the medieval lance and oriflamme. The continuity of noble death and superb patriotism is suggested both by the echo of Simonides and the reference to Agincourt, a reference which sprang readily to those members of the British Expeditionary Force who sailed to the base camp fortuitously situated at Harfleur. It was here, of course that Henry V had made his rallying cry in Shakespeare's play: 'Once more unto the breach, dear friends, once more.'

The clerk's 'waiting dreams' might well have been derived from Sir Henry Newbolt, whose contribution to the war effort included two deplorable books of propagandist intent aimed at schoolboys: *Tales of the Great War* (1916) and *The Book of the Happy Warrior* (1917). The latter is the book already noted in which Newbolt suggests that the public-school system sprang from medieval court life. In the preface he outlines the principles of chivalry, which include Service, Brotherhood and Equality, a Right Pride, Order and 'Help and Defence of the Weak, the Suffering and the Oppressed'. The relevance of all this to the current situation is clear: 'While men continue to fight, these rules, and these alone, can save the weaker from slavery and the stronger from universal hatred and moral ruin. Our ancestors knew this, and took care to hand on the truth to us.' The book is concerned with the continuity of chivalry and contains the inevitable chapter about Agincourt. The earlier book is a catalogue of heroism from accounts of genuine, but largely unidentified combatants, in which chivalry is stressed, notably in the section to do with the RFC. An officer who describes a dog-fight concludes that the pilot 'was really a true knight-errant', a remark which gets Newbolt's support: 'That is well said; our airmen are singularly like the knights of the old romances'. One sometimes wonders if there is anything that does *not* remind Newbolt of knights. 'They go out day by day, singly or in twos and threes, to hold the field against all comers, and to do battle in defence of those who cannot defend themselves.' In fact, as Cecil Lewis noted, the correlation between jousting and aerial fighting is evident:

> To be alone, to have your life in your own hands, to use your own skill, single-handed, against the enemy. It was like the lists of the Middle Ages, the only sphere in modern warfare where a man saw his adversary and faced him in mortal combat, the only sphere where there was still chivalry and honour. If you won, it was your own bravery and skill; if you lost, it was because you had met a better man.

Newbolt was forced to concede that 'even the Huns, whose military principles are against chivalry, have shown themselves affected by it' in the air. Much was made of the custom of giving enemies who had been shot down a decent burial and getting news back to their squadrons, a practice that faltered later in the War. 'The German Flying Corps still retained some chivalry,' wrote Briscoe, 'for one of their pilots risked crossing our lines in order that he might drop a message to the effect that Captain Ball had been "Killed in an air-fight by an honourable opponent".' Briscoe also quotes Lloyd George's assertion that: 'The pilots are the Knighthood of the Air, without fear and without reproach.[1] Every aeroplane flight is a romance, every record an epic.'

Before the War took to the air, the main repository of chivalric aspirations lay, unsurprisingly, with the cavalry. The evidence of the unsuitability of the horse in modern warfare was overwhelming, and familiar to all from Tennyson's commemorative poem about 'The Charge of the Light Brigade', which took place at Balaclava in 1854. '*C'est magnifique, mais ce n'est pas la guerre*', commented Maréchal Bosquet, contemplating the futile assault by 600 horsemen against the big guns of the Russians, at a cost of over 65 per cent fatal casualties. Although horses were swift, it was necessary for them to remain ten miles behind the front line, out of range of the enemy's artillery, so that in the event of a breakthrough in the line by the infantry, cavalry support would be far

[1] The description originally applied to the French knight, Seigneur de Bayard ('*Le chevalier sans peur et sans reproche*') was frequently invoked during the nineteenth-century chivalric revival.

too long in arriving. It was planned to use the cavalry on the Somme: bombardment, infantry breakthrough, advance and consolidation. Three divisions were kept behind the line, each man armed with lance and sabre, but they were never used, a fact that contributed to the failure of 1 July. Martin Middlebrook believes that the cavalry could have been used effectively, but that Rawlinson failed to make provision for it. Old soldiers were less sanguine about the usefulness of cavalry in the War. Frank Richards at Arras, eight months after the failure at the Somme, recalled passing cavalry on the road and quickly disabusing inexperienced young soldiers who imagined that the cavalry would break through the Hindenberg Line. As another old soldier remarked: 'They couldn't break through my granny's apron strings. And they might as well be mounted on bloody rocking-horses for all the good they are going to do.' Richards recalls a troop of Bengal Lancers being wiped out by machine-guns on the Somme, and even a rifleman could fell an advancing horseman in poor light. In this particular instance the cavalry were British, shot by their own side who had mistaken them for the enemy.

Cavalry battalions were gradually converted to infantry, even a battalion of Household Cavalry who, unused to trench conditions, suffered 50 per cent casualties within 48 hours from 'trench feet'. After the War most cavalry regiments simply bowed to technology and although retaining their old names became tank regiments, an irony neatly exploited by the Second World War poet Keith Douglas. Nonetheless, the image of the gallant horseman persisted throughout the Great War. As late as 1918 the *Young England* annual ('An Illustrated Annual for Boys throughout the English-speaking World') had a title-page upon which lancers were depicted successfully charging enemy field-guns.

It was in the cavalry, of course, that the Fox-Hunting Man himself, Siegfried Sassoon, enlisted, as a trooper in the Sussex Yeomanry. He later wrote that:

> . . . once I sought the Grail,
> Riding in armour bright, serene and strong.

However, after spending the summer of 1914 in camp, grooming horses and taking part in 'unconvincing operations' on the Weald, Sassoon began to grow bored. A fortuitous broken arm released him temporarily, during which time he connived at gaining a commission in an infantry regiment, the Royal Welch Fusiliers. In camp he met a young officer called David Thomas ('Dick

Tiltwood' to Sassoon's 'George Sherston')[1] whose 'radiant integrity' impressed him: 'His was the bright countenance of truth; ignorant and undoubting; incapable of concealment but strong in reticence and modesty. In fact, he was as good as gold, and everyone knew it as soon as they knew him.' No wonder then that in Amiens cathedral Sassoon looks at his friend and thinks 'what a young Galahad he looked (a Galahad who had got his school colours for cricket).' This Galahad, however, does not attain the Grail, but is shot in the throat and unceremoniously lowered into a hole, wrapped in a sack. 'I knew death then,' Sassoon wrote. The poem just quoted, written in the wake of this catastrophe, continues:

> But now I've said good-bye to Galahad,
>   And am no more the knight of dreams and show:
> For lust and senseless hatred make me glad,
>   And my killed friends are with me where I go.
> Wound for red wound I burn to smite their wrongs;
>   And there is absolution in my songs.

This little-known poem, published in the *Cambridge Magazine* in December 1916 and never collected in Sassoon's lifetime, is perhaps the nearest the poet came to an artistic credo for his war poetry, in which his 'old, silly sweetness' is rejected in favour of poetry which is 'scornful, harsh, and discontented, / Mocking and loathing War'. It is called, equivocally, 'The Poet as Hero'. The reference to Galahad is particular (David Thomas) and topical, personal and public. All notions of chivalry are dispelled by that sack, lowered into a makeshift grave. 'I used to say I couldn't kill anyone in this war,' Sassoon wrote in his diary; 'but since they shot Tommy [i.e. Thomas] I would gladly stick a bayonet into a German by daylight.' In a poem written a fortnight after Thomas's death, Sassoon recalled that he used to think:

> . . . how England used me for her need . . .

> I was the Giant-Killer in a story,
>   Armed to the teeth and out for blood and glory.

---

[1] Although *The Memoirs of George Sherston* are carefully-wrought fiction as well as autobiography, and there are discrepancies of fact and chronology to be found when comparing them with Sassoon's diaries, I refer to 'Sassoon' even when quoting 'Sherston'. This is simply for convenience, and each quotation and paraphrase is properly ascribed in the notes, for those who are interested.

But such notions have vanished and the valiant knight is no longer recognisable, nor relevant:

> What Paladin is this who bleakly peers
> Across the parapets while dawn comes grey,
> Hungry for music, and the living years,
> And songs that sleep until their destined day?
> This is the Giant-Killer who is learning
> That heroes walk the road of no returning.[1]

Sassoon's reactions to his war experience are complex, but the destruction of chivalric ideals was clearly of significance to this particular horseman.

Perhaps the most moving, and far and away the most literary attempt to equate the Great War with a chivalric heritage is David Jones's *In Parenthesis*. After an unconventional education – he was a gifted draughtsman who learned to draw some time before he learned to read, and entered art school aged fourteen – Jones enlisted as a private in the Royal Welch Fusiliers. Of his service on the Western Front he wrote:

> I suppose at no time did one so much live with a consciousness of the past, the very remote, and the more immediate and trivial past, both superficially and more subtly. No one, I suppose, however much not given to association, could see infantry in tin-hats, with ground-sheets over their shoulders, with sharpened pine-stakes in their hands, and not recall
> > '. . . or may we cram
> > Within this wooden O . . .'

Of all the writers of the Great War, none was more given to association than Jones, whose remarkable book – part-novel, part-memoir, part-epic poem – portrays his fellow-soldiers as representatives of a type whose long line of descent stretches back through Shakespeare, Malory, *The Mabinogion* and the *Chanson de Roland* to *Y Gododdin*, a Welsh epic poem of the 6th Century. An enormous range of reference to these works and others in between, as well as to Catholic rites and the primitive myths and rituals of Frazer's *The Golden Bough*, necessitated some thirty-five pages of notes. This impressive array of

---

[1] Although 'Giant-Killer' immediately suggests Jack, the 'Paladin' looks back to the knights who had to slay giants as well as dragons; giants such as Orgoglio, killed by Prince Arthur in Spenser's *The Faerie Queene*.

scholarship, which occasionally threatens to engulf Jones's depiction of men at war, sets *In Parenthesis* well outside the mainstream of the literature of the Great War. One need only compare it with the works of three men who served in the same regiment – Sassoon, Graves and Richards – to recognise that it is *sui generis*. Although Jones is as attuned as Vivian Gilbert to images suggesting past wars and causes (as the extract just quoted shows), he is able to substantiate such observations with considerable erudition. His synthesis of all these elements is a great deal more sophisticated than the common process of refraction by which many combatants absorbed and gave out images of chivalry. Nonetheless, it could be argued that the effect of *In Parenthesis* is similar to other works discussed in this chapter, that of ennobling the experience of war. It is for this reason that Paul Fussell describes the book as an 'honourable miscarriage'. In order to emphasise the kinship of *In Parenthesis* with 'overtly patriotic and even propagandist' accounts of the War, Fussell complains that 'the meddling intellect, taking the form this time of a sentimental Victorian literary Arthurianism after Tennyson and Morris, has romanticised the war'. Whilst it is possible to sympathise with Fussell's objections, it is also necessary to point out that what *separates* Jones from other writers who place the War in a chivalric context is the complexity of his assimilation of a literary heritage. He remains, in fact, the only writer whose understanding of the chivalric tradition goes deeper than 'a sentimental Victorian literary Arthurianism'.

Chivalry was an extreme stylisation of a more general patriotic impulse. Whilst it would be foolish to suggest that the main reason for volunteering in 1914 was patriotism, plain and simple, there is no doubt that it was a significant factor. Guy Chapman claimed that he 'was not eager, or even resigned to self-sacrifice, and my heart gave back no answering throb to the thought of England.' That 'answering throb' was the one depicted in 'The Soldier':

> A pulse in the eternal mind, no less
> Gives somewhere back the thoughts by England given.

It was a throb to which people who had volunteered for all sorts of reasons less exalted than Brooke's tuned in by way of explaining their action. Once soldiers had reached the Front and learned something of the nature of trench warfare, a psychological defence was to believe in something to redeem the experience. Knee-deep in freezing mud, harassed by gunfire and shells, tired, hungry and lousy, it clearly made some difference to believe that the ends justified the means. The very name by which the War was known, the Great War, encouraged notions of a titanic struggle rather than a squalid war of attrition. Medals awarded to every surviving participant commemorated 'The Great War for Civilisation', a concept emphasised by the characterisation of the enemy as 'the Hun', a sobriquet coined by a newspaper comparing the German invasion of Belgium and France with Attila's hordes sweeping into the Roman Empire. A subsidiary (and historically vague) meaning of 'Hun' is 'vandal', and much was made in the press of German 'Kultur'. A peculiarly nasty cartoon by Bernard Partridge, which appeared in *Punch* during the first month of the War, depicted a German officer straddling the corpses of a Belgian woman and child, his revolver still smoking. Its caption was 'The Triumph of "Culture"'.

The historical and political reasons for England's entry into the War were less likely to gather recruits than sheer jingoism. The Boer War had demonstrated the popularity of crude patriotism and public reaction to the outbreak of war represented a heritage of nationalistic pride rather than any genuine insight into the reasons for England's involvement. In order to prosecute the War it was necessary for the government to continue to depict it as a clean fight in a just cause; in order for the troops to participate in it after they had found that the fight was anything but clean, it was still necessary to believe that the cause was just. Allhusen, reflecting upon the misery of Passchendaele which gave rise to 'a sense of personal injustice', felt that men survived psychologically because of 'the deep conviction that we were right: that there was no other path: that the cost was not too great.' At its crudest this belief could be reduced to a mantra. Martin Middlebrook interviewed a private in the Liverpool Pals who recalled going over the top on the first day of the Somme repeating the phrase 'For England' as a sort of talisman.

Those whose lovers, husbands, brothers and sons had been killed also found consolation in the thought that their personal tragedy had not been in vain but had been 'For England'. Indeed, the disaster on the Somme stiffened the resolve to continue the War until the bitter end; there had to be something to show for the massive, and mounting, casualties. The notorious letter from 'A Little Mother' to the *Morning Post*, made famous by its reproduction in *Goodbye to All That*, is a disturbing document, but it bears out this point. The writer is clear about the necessity of continuing the fight in order 'to uphold the honour and traditions not only of our Empire but of the whole civilised world'. She rejects calls for peace: 'The blood of the dead and the dying, the blood of the "common soldier" from his "slight wounds" will not cry to us in vain'. The rhetoric of justification, seen in this letter from a woman who was evidently of the middle classes (her dead son seems to have been to school and university), also spread to those less privileged. An extreme example is to be found amongst the papers of Captain Gibbs at the Imperial War Museum. It is a letter from the mother of one of Gibbs's men, a Welsh private who has been wounded:

> Of course, we are exceedingly glad of the fact that he had the grit to do his duty to the satisfaction of his chiefs . . . Hoping that this stupendous and tragic affair ends in speedy and glorious victory for British arms and triumph of the sacred principles fought for in the redemption of Europe from brute force.

It was the suspicion that such aims were no longer in view which prompted the most famous protest of the War. For Siegfried Sassoon the ideals of a generation were being cynically exploited. The cause forgotten, he was no longer prepared to fight:

> I believe that this War, upon which I entered as a war of defence and liberation, has now become a war of aggression and conquest. I believe that the purposes for which I and my fellow-soldiers entered upon this War should have been so clearly stated as to have made it impossible for them to be changed without our knowledge, and that, had this been done, the objects which actuated us would now be attainable by negotiation.

7 The Old Lie Exposed

> I want so much to get at children about it. We've been wrong in the past. We have *taught* schoolboys 'war' as a romantic subject . . . And everyone has grown up soaked in the poetry of war – which exists, because there is poetry in everything, but which is only a tiny part of the great dirty tragedy. All those picturesque phrases of war writers . . . are dangerous because they show nothing of the individual horror.
>
> *T.P. Cameron Wilson*

By the time Wilfred Owen came to enlist, the army was less fussy than it had been when Sherriff had been rejected. In April 1915, whilst in London, he had seen a notice which proclaimed that 'any gentleman (fit, etc.) returning to England from abroad will be given a Commission – in the "Artists' Rifles". Such officers will be sent to the front in 3 months.' Owen had been in France when war was declared and so had missed out on England's initial euphoria. He nonetheless received the *Daily Mail* regularly and also read *War Poems from The Times* with interest, particularly approving of poems by Newbolt, Dudley Clark, Watson and Binyon. There is little doubt that another poet, whose works were a regular feature of the *Mail*, must have caught his attention: Jessie Pope. Some of these clearly stayed in his memory, along with the works of *The Times* poets and contributors to *Poems of To-Day*, as examples of verse against which to set his own.

Owen was well-educated, well-read and an officer, but his background was not that of the public schools. The son of a railway clerk, he was educated at the Birkenhead Institute and encouraged to read widely by his ambitious and possessive mother. When he was fourteen the family moved to Shrewsbury and Wilfred became a pupil at the Technical School, where his absorption in literature was encouraged by the English mistress. Shakespeare and the Romantic poets, particularly Keats, seem to have been his favourite, and most influential, reading. This is in marked contrast to the sort of education and influences a boy at a public school would have received, and it undoubtedly played an important part in the development of his poetry and the way his poetry recorded warfare.

Owen's view of war was Romantic rather than romantic. It rejected all received notions about the glory and honour of war and dwelt rather upon the consequences of battle for the sentient participants. But Owen's poetry is also a reaction against the heritage of martial verse, and is didactic. In the first weeks of the War he had visited a French hospital and sent an illustrated account of the battle injuries which were being treated there to his younger brother, Harold: 'I deliberately tell you all this to educate you in the actualities of war.' Owen frequently sounds like a teacher in his letters, and the education of the young was something which passionately interested him. The dissemination of information, whether within schools or in newspapers, concerned him and helped to shape his poetry. In a draft preface to a projected volume of his poems Owen set forth the aims of his poetry:

This book is not about heroes. English poetry is not yet fit to speak of them.

Nor is it about deeds, or lands, nor anything about glory, honour, might, majesty, dominion, or power, except War.

> Above all I am not concerned with Poetry.
> My subject is War, and the pity of War.
> The Poetry is in the pity.
> Yet these elegies are to this generation in no sense consolatory.

Much attention has been paid to Owen's choice of subject – 'the pity of War' – but what is equally significant – what the book is '*not* about' – has been largely ignored. Critics looking for a stick with which to beat Owen have picked upon the declaration, 'Above all I am not concerned with Poetry', but it would be possible to argue that the capital initial suggests the concept of poetry as a public art. Owen's concern with the mechanics of poetry is, after all, quite apparent. It has been observed that a great many of Owen's poems contain echoes of the work of other poets, notably Gray, Keats and Shelley. Equally intriguing are echoes which seem to act as refutations of prevailing notions as expressed in the poetry of his contemporaries. For example, 'Asleep' has been compared with poems by Rimbaud, Swinburne and Milton, but it may also be possible to detect deliberate references to that most public of poems celebrating heroes and glory, 'Into Battle'. Grenfell's happy warrior is at one with nature:

> The fighting man shall from the sun
>   Take warmth, and life from the glowing earth;
> Speed with the light-foot winds to run,
>   And with the trees to a newer birth.

The earth Grenfell celebrates is 'warm with Spring, / And with *green grass*'. Owen's dead soldier is also at one with nature, rotting into the landscape, which is wintry and cheerless, swept by 'these rains, these sleets of lead / And the winds's scimitars'. The corpse's

> thin sodden head
> Confuses more and more with the low mould,
> His hair being one with the *grey grass*.

The fields in which he lies are not 'warm with Spring', but 'finished' and strewn with rusty wire. Grenfell writes of his soldier that:

> All the bright company of Heaven
> Hold him in their high comradeship,

[244]

and that 'Night shall fold him in soft wings'. Owen cast doubts upon so comforting a transformation:

> Whether his deeper sleep lie shaded by the shaking
> Of great wings, and the thoughts that hung in stars,
> High pillowed on calm pillows of God's making,
> Above these clouds . . .
>
> Who knows? Who hopes? Who troubles? Let it pass!
> He sleeps. He sleeps less tremulous, less cold,
> Than we who wake, and waking say Alas!

The comforting illusion produced by the euphemism 'asleep' is rejected in this stark contrast, but, as a final twist, Owen suggests that at least the rotting corpse is out of the War. In another poem Owen also challenges the idea of the dead merging in some animistic way with nature. Whilst the reference is to Shelley's 'Adonais', 'Into Battle' and 'The Soldier' provided Owen with two contemporary versions of this theme:

> 'I shall be one with nature, herb and stone,'
> Shelley would tell me. Shelley would be stunned:
> The dullest Tommy hugs that fancy now.
> 'Pushing up daisies' is their creed, you know.

Owen also comments upon 'The Soldier' in his 'Imperial Elegy', in which the 'corner of some foreign field' that conceals Brooke's 'richer dust' is expanded to a vast mass-grave for the thousands of dead:

> Not one corner of a foreign field
> But a span as wide as Europe;
> An appearance of a titan's grave,
> And the length thereof a thousand miles,
> It crossed all Europe like a mystic road,
> Or as the Spirit's Pathway lieth on the night.
> And I heard a voice crying
> This is the Path of Glory.

'The Paths of Glory', as Owen knew from Gray's 'Elegy', 'lead but to the Grave'.

[245]

Traditional Shakespearean trappings of warfare, which had been debased by Henley and Newbolt, are dispensed with in 'Spring Offensive':

> No alarms
> Of bugles, no high flags, no clamorous haste, –
> Only a life and flare of eyes that faced
> The sun, like a friend with whom love is done.

The traditional rewards of war, its much-vaunted decorations, become wounds in 'A Terre':

> I have my medals? – Discs to make eyes close.
> My glorious ribbons? – ripped from my own back
> In scarlet shreds. (That's for your poetry book).

There is little doubt here as to the sort of poetry book Owen has in mind. Traditional symbols such as Britannia the Mother debased the currency of motherhood for this devoted son. Of the illustrations to *War Poems from The Times*, Owen had written: 'Simpson's cartoons (*Britannias very much excepted*) are marvels.' Dominic Hibberd has suggested that a poem referred to by Owen as 'Brittannia' (sic) was probably the lines now known as 'The Kind Ghosts'. Britannia, or similar personifications of England, was frequently addressed in patriotic poems and also appeared on recruiting posters. The call 'England awake!' is futile, Owen suggests; Britannia is at best asleep and indifferent, at worst a Medea figure:

> She sleeps on soft, last breaths; but no ghost looms
> Out of the stillness of her palace wall,
> Her wall of boys on boys and dooms on dooms.
>
> She dreams of golden gardens and sweet glooms
> Not marvelling why her roses never fall
> Nor what red mouths were torn to make their blooms.
>
> The shades keep down which well might roam her hall.
> Quiet their blood lies in her crimson rooms
> And she is not afraid of their footfall.

[246]

> They move not from her tapestries, their pall,
> Nor pace her terraces, their hetacombs,
> Lest aught she be disturbed, or grieved at all.[1]

The platitudes about honour which drove men to war are reflected in 'S.I.W.':

> Patting goodbye, doubtless they told the lad
> He'd always show the Hun a brave man's face;
> Father would sooner him dead than in disgrace, –
> Was proud to see him going, aye, and glad.

The soldier cannot stand the experience of war and shoots himself in the mouth:

> With him they buried the muzzle his teeth had kissed,
> And truthfully wrote the mother, 'Tim died smiling'.

The metrically stressed 'truthfully' bitterly explodes the cliché which follows it. Other men, Owen realised, joined up for other reasons:

> Someone had said he'd look a god in kilts,
> That's why; and maybe, too, to please his Meg,
> Aye, that was it, to please the giddy jilts
> He asked to join . . .
>   He thought of jewelled hilts
> For daggers in plaid socks; of smart salutes;
> And care of arms; and leave; and pay arrears;
> Esprit de corps; and hints for young recruits.
> And soon, he was drafted out with drums and cheers.

And soon, the legs of which he had been so proud were amputated. Dominic Hibberd has remarked upon the irony of the final line of 'Disabled' which

---

[1] Compare this with the verses contributed anonymously to the *Elizabethan* in March 1918: 'Britannia Regards Her Sleeping Sons' '(School-boys of the OTC). Written after reading the 'Pro Patria' columns of the *Westminster School Magazine*': 'And now – ah! now the night's long shadows fall; / And like soft infants in the darkness strayed / Fearful because no homely voices call, / In Nature's bed your forms are lonely laid. / Rest! Rest! sweet sons; nor heed a mother's weeping: / 'Tis but to see my boys so soundly sleeping.'

echoes a recruiting poster. Indeed, the *Weekly Dispatch* published a photomontage in November 1914 in which a soldier standing over a wounded comrade looks to a football crowd and asks: 'Will they *never* come?' In Owen's poem the disabled man's repeated question, 'Why don't they come?' refers to the nurses who look after him and should be arriving to wheel him away from the park back to an institution. It seems likely that another item in a newspaper also lies behind this poem. Jessie Pope's 'The Beau Ideal' was first published in the *Daily Mail* and reprinted in her volume *More War Poems* (1915). This poem is well-meaning and (despite appearances) unironic, but the jaunty callousness of the final line might well have roused Owen's anger. It concerns a girl called Rose whose ideal had been 'Belvidere Apollos'; in the wake of the War, her tastes have changed:

> To-day the sound in wind and limb
> Don't flutter Rose one tittle.
> Her maiden ardour cleaves to him
> Who's proved that he is brittle,
> Whose healing cicatrices show
> The colours of a prism,
> Whose back is bent into a bow
> By Flanders rheumatism.
>
> The lad whose troth with Rose would plight,
> Nor apprehend rejection,
> Must be in shabby khaki dight
> To compass her affection.
> Who buys her an engagement ring
> And finds her kind and kissing,
> Must have one member in a sling
> Or, preferably, missing.

Jessie Pope embraced the whole public-school ethos, as can be seen by the epigraphs concerning chivalry and playing the game quoted earlier. Such clichés may also have been gained from other sources. Owen was at Craiglockhart with Second Lieutenant J.B. Salmond, who was a sub-editor on the *Mail* and a contributor to the *Boy's Own Paper*. He had helped Owen when the poet was editor of the hospital's magazine, *The Hydra*, by negotiating with printers. No doubt Owen became acquainted with sporting stories and notions of playing the game through Salmond; indeed, he outlined a story which he headed: 'BOP stories for magazines'. (These notes have never been published; one wonders what sort of story Owen could write that would hold any appeal for the BOP, or any other boys' magazine.) Owen wrote to his mother about Salmond in August 1917; 'Disabled' was written in October of the same year, at the same time as 'Dulce et Decorum Est'. Given these influences it may not be entirely fanciful to see a pun upon the 'colours' awarded to sportsmen, and upon athletics races, in the following line:

> He's lost his colour very far from here,
> Poured it down shell-holes till the veins ran dry,
> And half his lifetime lapsed in the hot race
> And leap of purple spurted from his thigh.[1]

It was also in August 1917 that Owen first read *The Old Huntsman* and nervously introduced himself to the book's author. His immediate reaction was to write a poem in Sassoon's style, later recast as 'The Dead-Beat'. The collaboration with Sassoon upon 'Anthem for Doomed Youth' is well documented. Jon Stallworthy has detected an echo from the preface to a popular anthology in the first line of this poem. The editor of *Poems of To-Day* (1916 edition) states that the subjects of the contents are chiefly history, the Earth (which combines a mystical appreciation of England with a celebration of its natural beauty) and 'Life itself'. 'But there is no arbitrary isolation of one theme from another; they mingle and interpenetrate throughout to the music of Pan's flute, and of Love's viol, and the Bugle-call of Endeavour, and the passing-bell of Death'. This anthology was aimed specifically at children, intended to introduce them to contemporary poetry, much of it lushly Georgian. However, lurking like grit in the cream of pastoral nostalgia are such poems as Newbolt's 'He Fell Among Thieves', 'Vitaï Lampada' and 'The Volunteer'; Binyon's 'England' and 'For the Fallen, 1914'; and Brooke's 'The Dead' and 'The Soldier'. The reader's attention is particularly drawn to the works (and the example) of Brooke: 'Most of the writers are living, and the rest are still vivid memories among us, while one of the youngest, almost as these words are written, has gone singing to lay down his life for his country's cause.'

---

[1] The poem contains a great deal of world-play: 'jilt', for example is a slang word for a flighty girl, but also, by extension, for someone who throws over a lover. Owen also puns upon 'arms' (weapons/limbs) in the lines already quoted, where the sportsman, now 'sewn short at elbow', recalls that 'care of arms' was one of the attractions of enlisting.

However, it is to Jessie Pope that Owen addressed his condemnation of the public-school ethos in 'Dulce et Decorum Est'. Early drafts of this poem were subtitled 'To Jessie Pope etc.' and 'To a certain Poetess'. For popular home-front poets the combatant was a figure who was either motivated by an exalted sense of self-sacrifice, or a jaunty young chap who laughed off the 'discomforts' of war, unobtrusively courageous, indomitably cheerful. Owen stands against this from the very first statement of his 'Preface': his poetry is 'not about heroes'. For Owen, the soldier is a passive, suffering creature who does little, but has things done *to* him. The soldiers 'die as cattle' or are sacrificed by Old Men that they might save the obstinate ram of pride. At best they are martyrs, not the individual saints who went willingly to their deaths for their beliefs, but those who were rounded up and slaughtered like early Christians at a Roman festival. They are shot at, blown up, blinded, dismembered and gassed, and their particular agonies are graphically described, just as early painters depicted the bloody facts of martyrdom. In "Dulce et Decorum Est" Owen sets the horrors of a gas-attack and its effect upon one soldier against a heritage of received ideas about the glory of dying for one's country. Gas was one of the new weapons which showed in a most dramatic way that notions of warfare as an honourable occupation, notions derived from a Classical past, were no longer relevant. Earlier drafts of the poem's final twelve lines emphasise both the youthful beauty of the victim and the guiltiness of propagandist poets:

> If in some smothering dreams you too could pace
> Behind the waggon that we flung him in,
> And watch the white eyes writhing in his face,
> His hanging face, *tortured for your own sin*;
> If you could hear, at every jolt, the blood
> Come gargling from the froth-corrupted lungs,
> *And think how, once, his head was like a bud,*
> *Fresh as a country rose, and keen, and young,* –
> My friend – you would not tell with such high zest
> To children ardent for some desperate glory,
> The old Lie: Dulce et decorum est
> Pro patria mori.

The first of the cancelled lines (printed here in italics) was replaced at some cost to the force of the poem. 'Tortured for your own sin' is metrically clumsy, but the final reading, 'like a devil's sick of sin', has one foot too many and is the worst line in the poem. The image is inexact, and fantastical compared to the description of the man 'guttering, choking, drowning' and 'the white eyes writhing in his face'. It may also be questioned whether the comparison between an innocent victim and a sin-sated devil is at all appropriate. 'Your sin' is the sin of those, like Jessie Pope, who peddled outworn clichés about military glory to a young and naïve audience. The cancelled couplet was replaced by a further description of the effects of gas[1] upon the soldier:

> Obscene as cancer, bitter as the cud
> Of vile, incurable sores on innocent tongues.

Owen sacrifices the rather sentimental image of the soldier's head as it once was and the emphasis upon his youth and ardour. Instead there is the implied comparison between the 'innocent tongues' spotted with sores and the malicious tongues of those who blithely spoke of the sweetness and decorousness of dying for one's country.

Owen also pointed up the difference between an academic study of Classical texts and virtues and the reality of life as a soldier in the twentieth century in a poem variously known as 'Bold Horatius' and 'Schoolmistress', which was probably written out of his experience at Tynecastle Secondary School, where he taught whilst convalescing at Craiglockhart. Whilst Owen taught the boys *Hiawatha*, the mistress in this poem teaches 'Bold Horatius' from Macaulay's *Lays of Ancient Rome* (1842), a volume of ballads about Classical endeavour, to which were added in the 1848 edition poems about more recent military history, including the Armada.[2] Owen told his mother that his teaching was 'one of the most humanly useful things I am doing now', in marked contrast to the education of 'the tender younglings' of the battalion when he rejoined his regiment in Scarborough: 'I have been "approached" on the subject, but I shall not consent to lecture on militarian subjects. The scheme either comes of a desperate feeling that the race is going to perdition intellectually or else it is a Jesuitical movement to catch 'em young, & prepare them for the Eucharist of their own blood'. Owen attacks the unnamed, perhaps merely representa-tional, schoolmistress as follows:

[1] Phosgene gas did indeed corrupt the lungs, destroying alveoli, and producing a liquid in which the victim quite literally drowned.

[2] Amongst other projects Macaulay was instrumental in bringing English educational methods to India whilst he was on the Supreme Council in the 1830s. These were to replace traditional oriental education with a Western, Classical one. Owen had read 'Bold Horatius' during his second term at Shrewsbury Technical School in 1907.

Having, with bold Horatius, stamped her feet
And waved a final swashing arabesque
O'er the brave days of old, she ceased to bleat,
Slapped her Macauley back upon the desk,
Resumed her calm gaze and her lofty seat.

Then, while she heard the classic lines repeat,
Once more the teacher's face clenched stern;
For through the window, looking on the street,
Three soldiers hailed her. She made no return.
One was called 'Orace whom she would not greet.

This cruel and disturbing poem, drafted whilst he was revising 'Dulce et Decorum Est', is indicative of Owen's concern with education and the War. The Horatius in question is not the poet, but Publius Cocles Horatius, the Roman soldier who held a bridgehead against the whole of an invading army, and was thus a byword for Classical valour and patriotism, celebrated in *The Aeneid* and elsewhere. The callous briskness of the teacher, who declaims the poem stirringly but without much thought ('swashing'; the sheep-like 'bleat') is condemned for her inability to make a connection between Classical feats of bravery and the modern common soldier whose courage and suffering so impressed the poet. She has a 'lofty seat', both literally (upon the raised dais in the classroom) and metaphorically (her patrician disdain towards the soldiers). Her attitude towards the poem she has been reading is emphasised by the archaic and poetic 'O'er' and the intolerable cliché which follows it: 'the brave days of old'. The pupils repeat the lines of the poem, imbibing a tradition which is intended to inspire them, and 'catch 'em young', but is quite out of touch with modern warfare. The contemporary Horatius, an aitch-dropping private, may be pitched against enormous odds, but is unlikely to acquit himself so well, and will certainly not have a bronze statue erected to him in any temple by a grateful politician, as happened to Publius Cocles.

When war was declared Owen was teaching English at the Berlitz School in Bordeaux. He then stayed with various French families, coaching them in English. In December 1914 he joined a family of English boys who had been stranded in France by the War. Their aunt was looking for a tutor for them until they were able to rejoin their fellow-pupils at Downside, 'a *Public* school' as Owen explained to his mother, clearly impressed. 'In spite of their speaking French at will', Owen reported, 'they are all from top to toe, English schoolboys. The jargon they kept up was delicious for me to hear. Their good aunt questioned me about these weird words and their meanings, not having the faintest notion of what means "clout", "topping", etc., etc.' Owen was to teach the boys until the following September, whilst their aunt, father and headmaster attempted to decide whether or not the Channel was safe to cross. Owen's Latin and Greek were not good enough and 'a public-school man' was called in to teach the boys Classics. Eventually Owen accompanied the boys to Britain and despatched the two older ones to Downside. They continued to keep in touch both there and when they were transferred to Stonyhurst, another Catholic public school. In April 1918 Owen learned that Johnny was about to leave school. 'He must be a creature of killable age by now,' he reflected glumly. He was one of the people Owen wanted to receive a volume of his poems 'not about heroes'.

Owen's concern for the de la Touche boys and for his pupils at the Tynecastle school was similar to that he felt for the men in his command. Early in the War he had been particularly outraged by the shelling of English ports by the Germans: 'When I read that a shell fell into a group of sixteen schoolboys and killed fifteen, I raved,' he told his mother. He was later to rave against the insidious indoctrination of schoolboys with old Lies. He had himself fallen victim to them, producing early in the War a Housmanesque ballad:

> O meet it is and passing sweet
>   To live in peace with others,
> But sweeter still and far more meet
>   To die in war for brothers.
>
> Far days are yet left for the old
>   And children's cheeks are ruddy,
> Because the good lads' limbs lie cold
>   And their brave cheeks are bloody.

Experience of war brought about a complete refutation of such notions. In a letter accompanying 'Dulce et Decorum Est', Owen explained the title to his mother: 'The famous Latin tag means of course *It is sweet* and meet to die for one's country. *Sweet! and decorous!*' Perhaps he was recalling with shame this earlier poem. This letter was written at a period when he was producing some of his best work. A glance at his letters and at Jon Stallworthy's biography shows the events and influences that were acting upon him during this productive period. There was the meeting with Sassoon (whose 'How To Die' – 'With due regard for decent taste' – was written at Craiglockhart); working with Salmond; teaching at Tynecastle; rejoining his regiment at Scarborough; friendship with the brilliant public-school Classicist, Bainbrigge; and reading Barbusse's *Under Fire*. No wonder that he was to castigate his cousin, Leslie Gunston, for writing a poem entitled 'Hymn of Love to England'. 'I am composing "Hymns of Hate"', he wrote. Whilst his poems were never as much hymns of hate as those of Sassoon, there was passion, as well as compassion, in his work. His outrage was of a different order than Sassoon's, rebelling against a tradition which he had imbibed at one remove. It is altogether fitting that 'the old Lie' should have received its death-blow at the hands of a Grammar School boy.

PART THREE

[7]

The View from the Cloisters

We don't forget – while in this dark December
We sit in Schoolrooms that you know so well,
And hear the sounds that you so well remember,
The clock, the hurrying feet, the Chapel bell;
Others are sitting in the seats you sat in,
There's nothing else seems altered here – and yet
Through all of it, the same old Greek and Latin,
    Be sure we don't forget.
      C.A. Alington, Headmaster of Eton

FOR the majority of public-school boys in August 1914 the principle concern was that the War would not last long enough for them to obtain their commissions and rush off to the Front. It was considered, as it had been when the Boer War started, that it would all be over by Christmas. Anthony Eden was assured by his OTC platoon commander that there simply wasn't enough money to keep the War going and that the City would not allow it to continue beyond a few days.[1]

Not everyone's motives for hoping that the War would last for some time were entirely honourable. Robert Graves counted upon hostilities continuing until at least October, thus delaying his entry to Oxford. The pressure upon pupils to go to University, never very strongly exerted, was now completely relaxed. Conformity deterred those who might have preferred to complete their education rather than have marched off to glory. Some, like Edmund Blunden, were 'allowed' to continue studying for the entrance examination, thus

[1] An estimation of the cost of the War, published shortly after the Armistice, put Britain's expenditure at £8,700,000,000.

[257]

delaying their training by a year. However, by the end of the first year of the War the universities were very sparsely populated. Not a single Wykehamist was sent to Oxford for the academic year beginning in the autumn of 1915. By this time 531 of the 549 boys who had left the school since 1909 had enlisted.

Boys not in (military) uniform returned to their schools for the new academic year in September 1914 to find their small worlds considerably altered. Many of the younger members of staff had joined up with the enthusiasm of their pupils, and old men who had been sent into retirement with speeches and presentations years before were dragged back to the classrooms. Some, like Mr Chips, responded to this call with 'holy joy'. Other men who were debarred by health from joining the forces responded with rather less enthusiasm. In need of a job, Aldous Huxley gloomily wrote to his brother that: 'Of the more repulsive solutions, two main ones appear: (a) To disseminate mendacity in our Great Modern Press; (b) To disseminate mendacity in our Great Modern Public Schools.' After a brief spell at Repton amidst colleagues he described as 'a set of Calibans', he went to Eton. His appalling sight (partially the result of inefficient medical care at the school when he was a pupil there) made it difficult to see what the boys were doing and so to exercise control. On top of this he complained that the pay was very bad, and when the opportunity arose at Easter 1919 he resigned with considerable relief.

S.P.B. Mais recalls 'The Beginning of a War Term' in 1915, when those 'too old, too young, or too decrepit to fight [were] going back to preserve the continuity of Winchborough [i.e. Sherborne] traditions, stirred by the example of our faithful dead to do our little best to keep England's honour untarnished, her shield of glory bright.' Despite this stirring ideal, Mais confesses that young masters such as himself have to put up with 'the staff left on the agents' books' who hobble out of retirement in order to criticise modern educational methods and 'openly deride their younger (and, incidentally, senior) colleagues'. Another type of temporary master inflicted upon schools was the Aldous Huxley model: 'the very young, much-bespectacled, physically unfit, but intellectually brilliant scholar', more suited to University teaching. His lessons are above the heads of his pupils and he is unable to keep control over his classes. The third class of temporary master is one Mais is bound to approve: the wounded veteran. 'Armless, legless, disabled permanently as a soldier, such a man may yet make a magnificent schoolmaster . . . Boys quite naturally reverence a man who has actually been face to face with death and narrowly missed it.' Mais suggests that such a man will be able

[258]

to maintain discipline and will prove invaluable to the OTC: 'Your fight is not yet over, O soldier-hero! Come once more into the lists; your physical battles have made you finer men than we are; come among us and share the spiritual conflict . . .' This makes one think of nothing so much as Evelyn Waugh's Captain Grimes who can keep order in class because the boys believe that he lost his leg in the War, rather than under a tram in Stoke-on-Trent.

Mais's view of his profession is absurdly inflated, of course,[1] but there is no doubt that the drain on manpower was felt very badly at the schools and more so as the War dragged on. Some schools even had to resort to women teachers, a suggestion which prompted a page of arch cartoons in *The Captain*, with a mortar-boarded cutie thanking the Senior Prefect with a kiss. Amongst the many disillusions suffered by H.E. Bates, arriving at Kettering, was that 'masters who had become soldiers had been replaced with what I can only describe as females'.

Although it appears that Marlborough did not have to resort to such extreme measures, the Master confessed to his prefects that 'owing to the calls made upon younger members of staff by the military authorities, the staff was growing rapidly weaker.' Prefects were expected to help out, although often there were few enough of them. 'The school was a different place', Alec Waugh recalled of Sherborne in September 1914. 'There was scarcely a boy over eighteen left; and not so very many over seventeen and a half. Most of those who were, were waiting for their commissions to come through.' Some pupils found the mantle of authority falling unexpectedly upon their shoulders: 'In the same way that Kitchener has called up his reserves, I have called up you', Nowell Smith told some of his pupils. 'I do not suppose that in the ordinary course of events any of you would have been prefects, but in the same way that, in the army, captains become colonels overnight, so you have been raised to a position of authority. I know that you will prove worthy of it.'

Whilst some people recalled that the War made little difference to life at boarding school, particularly at prep school, the evidence suggests that the War was a constant presence, lurking in classroom and corridor. At some schools the casualty lists were already up when the boys returned for the new term in September 1914, and they lengthened as the term wore on. Boys whose fathers or older brothers were killed often wore black arm-bands. Although the bereaved were accorded respect by their fellow-pupils, teachers often berated

[1] Perhaps Sherborne promoted this. One of Mais's colleagues, A.H. Trelawney-Ross was exempt from war service because of a heart complaint and so decided, '*as I could not kill Germans, I must try to build up Englishmen.*'

the newly-orphaned for not living up to the standards set by their hero-fathers. For boys the loss of a father was a case of 'bad luck', Christopher Isherwood recalled, and the crêpe-marked child would be excused the rough-and-tumble of the playground. If he wanted to lose himself in ragging, he simply removed his jacket. For teachers, however, a dead father was a useful stick with which to beat a troublesome pupil. The effect of this was often scarring. Isherwood began to reject the image of his father as a Dead Hero and with it he rejected all sense of duty this figure was supposed to instil. The effect upon his younger brother, Richard, was even worse:

> I did so hate being everlastingly reminded of him when I was young. Everybody kept saying how perfect he was, such a hero and so good at everything. He was always held up as someone you could never hope to be worthy of, and whenever I did anything wrong, I was told I was a disgrace to him . . . I used to simply loathe him.

Over fifty years later Richard was astonished to read his father's letters and discover the real man behind the hated icon.

Casualties amongst Old Boys were reported in detail and at length in school magazines, usually under headings such as '*Pro Patria*' with a cross or heavy black border. Etonian deaths were recorded in the *Chronicle* under the heading '*Etona Non Immemor*' and to make sure that this was the case casualties were posted on a notice board. At Marlborough these notices were painted in gold lettering. At Rugby the Chapel bell rang out at noon every day, all work stopped, and pupils were instructed to think of those Old Boys who were serving at the Front. Many people recall the reading out, usually in chapel, of the latest additions to the Roll of Honour. Usually impious boys began to find the services moving, especially when the uniforms of Old Boys mingled with those of present pupils. *The Eton College Chronicle* reported that:

> In these times Chapel on Sundays, especially in the evening, is an impressive sight, and one not easily forgotten by those who see it, whether they are boys or masters, or the knot of khaki which always assembles in the Ante-Chapel round the door, waiting to be given places inside.

Anthony Eden was one of those Etonians and remembered 'deeply moving intercession services' at the time when the casualties of Ypres were mounting. 'It was uncanny to look across Chapel to the back row opposite and realise that within six months probably half the boys there would be dead', G.A.N. Lowndes recalled of Marlborough.

School magazines also published commemorative verses about the dead, ranging from the Greek elegiacs of Ronald Knox in the *Salopian* to such simple sentiments as this anonymous verse from the *Eton Chronicle*:

> To A.H.B.
> October 21, 1914
>
> At the head of your Highland men,
> Charging the terrible wood,
> With only one thought in your dear old head,
> To die as a soldier should.[1]

Individual boys were sometimes commemorated before their names got lost amidst the ever-growing Rolls of Honour. Mrs Veitch presented Westminster with a challenge cup for the highest batting average each season in memory of her son, an excellent sportsman who had been featured amongst 'Prominent School Cricketers' in the 1914 volume of *The Captain*, had been in the Football XI, and was killed on the Somme exactly two years after the outbreak of the War. At Sherborne, Trelawney-Ross renamed dormitories in his House after Old Boys killed in action.

The death of a master, who might be thought to be setting an example by enlisting, was even more dramatic than that of an Old Boy. The first public-school master to be killed was Lieutenant A.J.N. Williamson of Highgate School, on 22 September 1914. This was reported in the *Times Educational Supplement* and taken up rather late, but with considerable effect, by *The Captain* in March 1915, which printed a picture of the teacher and emphasised his sporting prowess. In case readers missed the point, a paragraph later in the Editorial headed 'The Public Schools and the War' proclaimed:

> Everybody recognises the fact that the spirit of discipline and sportsmanship inculcated in our schools is bearing rich and glorious fruit on the stern fields of duty, and everyone knows that many of the most stirring and heroic deeds chronicled in the war redound to the credit of young officers whose schooldays ended but a few months ago.

[1] The *List of Etonians Who Fought in the Great War MCMXIV-MCMXIX* includes Second Lieutenant A.H. Blacklock of the Argyll & Sutherland who left Eton in 1913.

When George 'Hoj' Fletcher, an Old Etonian master who had taught at Shrewsbury and his old school, was killed, the reverberations were considerable. The whole front page of *The Eton College Chronicle*, bordered in black, was devoted to news of his death: 'An Eton Master killed fighting for his country, and for us; such a thing has never happened before: it crowns our many glories.' A poem published in a later edition of the *Chronicle* kept his name, and example, bright:

> Swiftly you won your uttermost desire,
> Dream-lover, lover of Eton, heart of fire.
> You served the School and England, and abide
> Safe, with the flag you saved, and satisfied.

The reference to the flag is literal as well as metonymic, since Fletcher not only saved the Flag by dying for England, but also crawled out between the lines in an act of bravado to recapture a French flag which the Germans had hung from a tree. The flag was sent back to Eton as a souvenir, and the deed was thought to be just the sort of stunt to impress and inspire schoolboys, however foolhardy it might appear to posterity. A fellow-officer said: 'He ought to have been given the VC and a court-martial; but it was worth doing. Nothing delighted and inspirited the Tommies more.' Fletcher had kept in touch with Shrewsbury, which he had left for Eton in 1913, and extracts from his letters were published in *The Salopian*, as were letters from other masters who were serving. There is a separate memorial at the school to Fletcher and the five other masters who were killed in the War. Fletcher wrote to his former colleagues exhorting them to enlist. He was killed shortly afterwards and it was this that made the 'Two Men', Evelyn Southwell and Malcolm White, enlist. When Southwell told his class of Fletcher's 'death and his last feat', he wrote to Fletcher's father, 'their answer was – what else would you have? – a loud burst of clapping.' To his own father, Southwell wrote: 'You will have read the news of Fletcher's death. I think you will agree with me that the matter is now closed. I must go and take his place.' White was similarly inspired, writing to Fletcher's father: 'I am leaving to take a regular commission this term. If I go out to Flanders, I hope I may catch some of [George's] spirit and show one hundredth part of his courage.'

School magazines were also crammed with appeals of one sort or another. Etonians who had already donated £163 5s. 5d. to the French soldiers in March 1915, were urged to attend a concert given by Clara Butt at the school, proceeds of which would be donated to the same cause. At Shrewsbury £11 18s. 1d. was collected by Philip Bainbrigge, one of the masters and a friend of Wilfred Owen, and presented 'with a delicate touch of appropriate-ness, in a "Navy Cut" box' to the Emergency Committee of the Navy League. They also supplied their adopted regiment, the King's Shropshire Light Infantry, with tobacco and matches. Cricket bats and games strip were also parcelled up and sent to the Front. Old Boys Societies donated large sums to the three Public Schools' Hospitals which were administered by the Red Cross and the St John's Fund. As a spur to Old Etonian subscribers it was pointed out that twelve of the first eighty patients at α Hospital in Park Lane were OEs. The initial donation from the schools raised £9,400, enough to run all three hospitals for one year. Another appeal was launched for motor ambulances, which cost some £400 each. A circular was sent to Old Salopians one Friday night, and Monday's post brought in £250, followed by another £300 on the Tuesday. The Old Salopians were soon to offer the War Office a second ambulance. The first one, a 35-h.p. Renault, bore 'a brass plate with the School Arms and the inscription: The Gift of Old Salopians. *Floreat Salopia.*' It was driven by the Revd E.M. Cooke OS of the Shrewsbury Mission in Liverpool. Similar ambulances were provided by Harrow and Marlborough.

During the holidays boys not involved in OTC exercises were urged to apply to the Cavendish Association for voluntary work with the Boy Scouts and the YMCA, or collecting books and clothes for refugees. Mais devotes an entire chapter of *A Public School in War Time* to 'The Holiday Task'. He writes that teachers set an example by 'giving up their much-longed-for weeks of rest in order to be of some service to the nation.' Sherborne masters apparently rushed off to all parts of the country at the end of term: the chaplain to a munitions factory (hardly suitable work for a man of the cloth, one would have thought), the music-master to 'YMCA Tents', and 'housemasters with big families' to harvest camps. According to Mais, public-school masters were to be found working as railway porters and even down the mines. One wonders whether men fit enough for such jobs might not also be fit enough to be in the trenches. Mais has a vision of a socialist utopia arising from the amateur interference of decrepit schoolmasters in the industrial workings of the nation:

We of the public schools have held only too long aloof from the life of the country. Now, through the agency of war, will the Cavendish Association be able to point to us and say, 'Did I not always tell you so? Does not salvation come through Personal, Social, Christian Service?' The mingling of all classes in this common endeavour will make for a better understanding between classes.

Perhaps such exhortation and example was necessary. At Westminster in 1918 there seems to have been as little enthusiasm for the Summer Harvest Camp as there had been for the OTC Camp in 1914. However, after a protest in the *Elizabethan* at the lack of numbers, enthusiasm (or a sense of duty) increased and the magazine was able to report 'a distinct step in our efforts towards helping the country in the matter of harvesting'. Since during the previous summer Westminsters had spent their time in Devon being shown the theory of harvesting, rather than practising it, this is unsurprising. Any failure of achievement in 1918 could be safely put down to the 'lack of co-operation or organising skill on the part of the farmers', who were occasionally at a loss as to how best to employ fifty public-school boys for three periods of three weeks.

Debating societies spent a great deal of time arguing about the War. Amongst the motions debated at Westminster during the first term of the War were that 'the Kaiser is responsible for the present War' (defeated 6–10),[1] that 'this House approves the conduct of the Government during the present crisis' (carried 11–10), that 'the bombardment of unfortified towns and the indiscriminate sowing of mines is unjustifiable' (carried 11–9), that 'it will be disastrous to the world when Arbitration takes the place of War' (carried 11–7), and that 'this war will cause a much-needed artistic revival' (lost by acclamation). A popular motion, debated frequently, concerned the need for conscription (carried 11–9 at Westminster in 1915). Elsewhere there were debates about the Dardanelles expedition, rationing, industrial compulsion and press censorship.

Lectures also reflected the crisis. At Shrewsbury the pupils were addressed on 'Patriotic Poetry', 'Some Medical Aspects of the War' (a talk which concluded with 'a few patriotic and popular slides which were enthusiatically applauded'), 'Explosives', 'The Geography of the Western Front' and 'Naval Tactics'. Visiting speakers came to spread propaganda and to recruit. In February 1915 Hilaire Belloc spoke on 'The Progress of the War', in April Conan Doyle (still giving the lead) lectured on 'Some Battles of the War', and Bonar Law was the guest speaker at Speech Day that summer. At St Peter's, York pupils were subjected to W. Rhys Roberts's lecture upon 'Patriotic Poetry, Greek and English', first delivered to the students of Leeds

[1] It was felt that the Kaiser was a feeble puppet and that his ministers were responsible for the War.

University to mark the 500th anniversary of the Battle of Agincourt in 1915. At Westminster Rear Admiral Sir R.F. Phillimore KCMG, CB, MVO, RN, OW, 'on the invitation of the Headmaster . . . said a few cheery words to the school and asked that His Majesty's Navy might get more support from Westminster than it does at present'.[1]

Further cheery words filled the correspondence columns of the schools' magazines. Editors asked for any letters from Old Boys serving at the Front. Few of those published bear much relation to the sort of letters Wilfred Owen wrote to his mother. The response to the experience of trench warfare was not disillusion, but usually that of cheerful stoicism, or elegiac platitudes about the noble death of a fellow Old Boy. Such complacence often infuriated other men in France who came across copies of their school magazines. In December 1915, F.H. Keeling, Rupert Brooke's Fabian friend who had insisted upon joining the ranks in spite of a Classical education at Winchester and Trinity College, Cambridge, complained that the school magazine had published:

some rot from some blithering correspondent who, I suppose, drives about comfortably in GHQ motor-cars and thinks it is a wonderful thing to come under shell fire, to the effect that all the troops are comfortably housed for the winter in nice warm huts. This sort of thing makes men sweat out here. I don't grumble at a tent with a coke-fire (when coke is available) even in the coldest weather; but it is a bloody shame to deceive the public at home and say we are in comfortable huts when we aren't.

Particularly popular with editors were letters which told of boys from the same school meeting by chance at the Front. Three Old Westminsters 'finding themselves herded together in what the natives are pleased to call a railway carriage' discussed 'res collegii' and then wrote to the *Elizabethan* about it. By the end of the year two of the three had been killed. One correspondent wrote 'with some diffidence' about a fellow OW 'because the paragraphs of eulogy that appear with absolute precision in most school magazines on the dead condemn themselves by their sentimental universality as in most cases obviously untrue'. However, the panegyric that follows merely suggests that someone who was '*Not* popular, *not* distinguished in athletic or intellectual ability, *not* striking except in a personality of extraordinary obstinacy and endurance', and

---

[1] In July 1915 of the 1,089 OWs serving only 76 were in the Navy. The Navy tended to attract boys from crammers and special colleges. The Army and the dashing new RFC held more appeal for public-school boys.

moreover blind in one eye, was nonetheless utterly reliable and a good soldier. Some correspondents clearly saw it as their duty to recruit amongst their former classmates. R.M. Neill wrote to the *Elizabethan* urging Westminsters to join the Royal Flying Corps: 'Any sportsman will realise that, apart from fighting, there is absolutely nothing to touch flying as a sport . . . It is the public schoolboy who very often makes the best pilot, and age is of no account whatsoever'. Six weeks after writing this letter, Neill was dead, killed in action whilst his call was being read by former school-fellows.

Further stern stuff was delivered in magazine editorials. The *Salopian*'s editor took refuge in orotund vagueness:

It is well, before we have lost, as the term advances, our true sense of the proportion existing between us and the outside world, to consider, though it is a hard task, how stupendous the events of the last month have been. For we are like people in a room on the top floor of a lofty building. The room, it is true, is large and airy and prosperous-looking; but from the crowded streets below rises the ever-growing hum of a seething multitude. Nations are being moulded in the fires of war, but all that comes up to us is a faint murmur, made rhythmical and soothing by the distance. Yet the fact that in those streets are many, battling for their existence and for something more, should make us wish to part the smoke-clouds and, seeing things as they are, give them the best assistance and sympathy we may.

Similar intimations of Great Events were expressed in the *Elizabethan* of February 1915. Although, unlike schools in the countryside, Westminster had no military camp nearby, Westminsters:

live well within range of the War Office, and the Victoria Tower stands like a sentinel over the Abbey and her children . . . Even the sombre cloisters have their awakenings; there was a time when the giants of old would do valiant battle in the milling green but more fearsome than that is the sight of some grave prebend in the uniform of Chaplain to the Forces.

And so on.

Any divergence from the straight, patriotic line was liable to have disastrous consequences, as Edward Lyttelton, headmaster of Eton, found out. Lyttelton was eccentric, but also something of an innovator, and thus respected in some quarters. The school even tolerated his bold idea of inviting a member of the unemployed to address the pupils in 1905. However, attitudes hardened during the War, and a sermon delivered at St Margaret's, Westminster in

March 1915, in which he suggested that there should be a negotiated peace, caused an outcry. Lyttelton was sincere, but neither an intellectual nor a statesman, and a wiser man would have kept his unfashionable ideas to himself. Like Arnold, he wanted to see a truly Christian society, governed according to Christian principles. The Christian principles in operation in 1915 were fighting the good fight and laying down one's life, not the application of Christian charity on a vast scale, starting with the inter-nationalisation of Gibraltar as a gesture of good faith. March 1915, in the wake of the costly battle of Neuve-Chapelle,[1] was not the time to suggest a negotiated peace. The press accused Lyttelton of being pro-German, claiming that his sermon had been quoted with glee in German newspapers. Headlines proclaimed: 'Flood of Protest', 'Letting the Germans Off Lightly' and 'Public Wrath'. In 1915 the Headmaster of Eton was in a position of influence and trust unimaginable today and, like royalty, was not supposed to enter into political debate. It was Lyttelton's failure to recognise this which condemned him, as the most succinctly damning letter in *The Times*, written by a Winchester master, made clear:

> He has sinned both against his country and his school . . . he has sinned against his school because he has broken the unwritten law that headmasters should put the good of their school before their own personal feeling and avoid the expression of opinion on matters of public policy which may shock the parents of their boys or diminish the confidence which their masters and the school should feel towards them. I write as one who has been an Englishman for more than seventy years and a public-school master for more than forty.

However much Lyttelton protested, he had been tried and found guilty by the press. It was surely the hand of Northcliffe which lay behind the mischievous placing of the following news item at the bottom of *The Times*'s Letters Page filled with correspondence from Lyttelton and his critics: 'GERMAN MEASLES AT ETON. Owing to an outbreak of German Measles, Eton College broke up yesterday instead of to-morrow.'

Lyttelton held on for a year, but the publicity given to the prosecution of his German maid upon a trumped-up charge of spying was the final straw and Lyttelton tendered his resignation in April 1916. His enemies did not conceal their jubilation. The following item appeared in a magazine and is preserved, unidentified, in the Eton College Library:

[1] Some sixteen Old Etonians died in the course of this battle.

Dr Lyttelton has resigned, and soon Eton will know him no more. Elaborate comment is needless. But it is no use pretending that his eleven years' reign was a success, or that he was any more popular at Eton than he was at his former job at Haileybury. Lyttelton is an odd person with odd, uncomfortable ideas in which he is, to give him his due, perfectly sincere. But he doesn't understand the management of the human boy, and no headmaster has ever got himself into more scrapes. The Beagles, the famous expulsion case, food fads, and, finally, the let's-love-the-Kaiser attitude were a series of deadly nails in the Lytteltonian coffin.[1]

Naturally there was a considerable increase in the activities of the Corps now that there was a definite end in view. Any sneers about 'playing at soldiers' rapidly vanished. During the 1914 summer holidays headmasters at all the schools received two circulars from the War Office 'begging, in effect, that Junior OTCs should be kept together and promising future employment'. This was not easy since many of the adults who had trained boys in the OTC had enlisted during the vacation or had been called away to train 'real' soldiers. The Westminster Corps had put its rifles 'at the disposal of the Queen's Westminsters, the Royal Fusiliers, and the London Scottish' and had to parade twice without arms, 'but we expect from now to have our rifles again as usual', they confidently predicted in October 1914. However, it was reported in the next issue of the *Elizabethan* that the OTC had been forced to return 90 per cent of its serviceable rifles, leaving them with 92 weapons for 260 cadets. Thus the keenness of the 109 new recruits during the first few weeks of the autumn term was thwarted by the very department that was 'begging' that the OTC should be kept running. Efforts were made at Shrewsbury to finish the new rifle-range, which was opened in November 1914, although without much landscaping of the surrounding area in evidence. One wag writing in the *Salopian* complained of the mud in the area of the building, but felt that it was a good preparation for the trenches. Mais recorded that there was no need for compulsion since every boy was now eager to join the OTC. Even the milksops and muffs could be usefully employed as morse or semaphore signallers.

Preparatory schools were also caught up in the spirit. At Elstree the school paraded with wooden rifles. At Oldfield, the headmaster was too old for active

[1] A headmaster who *was* pro-German was Cecil Reddie of Abbotsholme. The outbreak of war did nothing to quench his admiration for England's enemy; numbers fell as patriotic parents removed their sons. By the time he finally resigned (in 1927) only two pupils were left.

service but nonetheless 'volunteered for a para-military Home Guard and very formally fell himself in every morning, sloped arms, and marched himself off, in his grey uniform, to the station to guard munitions at Poole'. One of his pupils recalled the deleterious effect upon the school of this sense of patriotic duty: 'His absence, only partially compensated for by one invalid master, meant a very limited male staff and a consequent lack of discipline amongst the boys'. A ferocious boy scout troop was the school's equivalent of a corps. When the school donkey wandered into a nearby army camp, boys pursued it, all the while saluting bewildered officers. 'My arm ached from all the saluting involved, which I may say got little response,' one boy remembered. It must have been with considerable relief that he left Oldfield for the Downs School in the Malverns, a Quaker foundation where pupils were 'isolated . . . from the prevailing war psychosis' and were taught by conscientious objectors. The headmaster annoyed some of the non-Quaker parents by intoning '*Pax melior bellum*' rather than '*Dulce et decorum est pro patria mori*' during Latin classes.[1]

However, such schools were an exception. More representative was St Edmund's School at Hindhead where pupils such as Auden and Isherwood were subjected to 'rousing speeches about the honourable actions going on in Europe in defence of Decency' given by the headmaster. The school magazine reported the activities of the corps and published a poem in which Isherwood parodied Lewis Carroll in the cause of anti-Hun feeling: '"You are old, Father William," the Crown Prince said . . .'. Boys hung around a Canadian army camp in the hope of collecting a complete set of cigarette cards which depicted, with some poignancy one imagines, 'Gems of Belgian Architecture'. The Canadians had dug a trench-system across the common and boys on their Sunday walk were encouraged to jump across them by the masters in charge. 'Perhaps they wanted to bring home to us something of the physical reality of war,' Isherwood suggested.

If so, they certainly succeeded, as far as I was concerned. Many of the trenches were seven or eight feet deep; it made me dizzy to look down into them. And though there were plenty of places I could jump across, they seemed alarmingly wide to me, with my short legs. We also played hide and seek in them. This was fun. But, one day, I got temporarily lost and

---

[1] At Leighton Park, a Quaker public school, '"Pacifism" was never greatly stressed', but there was no OTC. Instead, boys were sent off to 'help elderly folk cultivate their vegetables' and dig allotments.

experienced some of the terror of the trench-labyrinth which Robert Graves and other war writers have described.

This was not, perhaps, the sort of preparation at which the schools aimed.

Despite an increase in the activities of the OTC, games were still played with much vigour and the parallels between rugby football and war were frequently emphasised. A writer in the *Elizabethan* saluted two boys who were leaving to enlist (one of whom was to be killed) with the assertion that they would 'no doubt distinguish themselves as much on the battlefield as they have done on the football and cricket fields, where they took a lion's share in making [Ashburnham's House] pre-eminent in sport.' 'There is a greater game than cricket to be played through the coming months,' the *Salopian*'s editor warned, 'and a few are going (indeed a few have already gone) to play the game on another ground than the Common.' The rush to enlist often left sports teams severely depleted; at 'Fernhurst' games were no longer up to the exacting standards of 'the Bull': 'I never saw such slackness. What good do you imagine you men will be in the trenches, if you can't last out a short game of rugger like this?' 'Slackness' was much at issue: 'There have been many signs lately that seem to betray a growing slackness up Fields, a steady falling-off in the interest which should be accorded to games,' the *Elizabethan* rumbled in November 1915. What was to be done about this 'pitiful lack of enthusiasm'? It was necessary to emphasise the importance of games, which are 'an integral part, and no unimportant one, of that system which has produced the men who are so lightheartedly[1] and efficiently officering our armies.' Games should not 'interfere with military duty', but like everything else should be pursued with: 'Ten times more zeal than usual, with ten times more energy, with ten times more conviction . . . let us put our whole soul into a grimmer and more exacting game.' 'Vitaï Lampada' was frequently evoked, as was Wellington's famous remark, in order to justify the continuance of public-school sport. A speaker in a debate at Shrewsbury spoke for the majority when he 'defended footballers with great eloquence and told the house that a love of sport had made England what it was. This war is being won on the playing-fields of our public schools even as Waterloo had been won on the playing-fields of Eton.'

If some boys appeared to be unpatriotically listless on the games fields this

---

[1] Allhusen countered this sort of stuff on an angry sheet inserted in his manuscript book of memoirs. He wrote that there was 'none of the light-heartedness of story-books and Special Correspondents. How could we be irresponsible when men's lives were in our keeping, or light-hearted when our friends were going to be killed?'

was hardly surprising. Food, never a cause for celebration, rapidly got worse and there was less of it since both meat and bread rose in price almost immediately. 'Little slices of chilled meat, a small quantity of doubtful bread, and a few spoonfuls of sugar – these had to last a week,' William Plomer wrote of Rugby. 'I can remember working all the morning on a winter's day, then sitting down to a little slop of bony boiled fish and a dab of watery custard, and then working again, going out for a long run in the afternoon, and working again at night.' Rugbeians were allowed an extra lie-in of thirty minutes each morning by way of compensation for this inadequate and revolting diet, but Plomer felt that 'semi-starvation and puberty and too much form-work by artificial light' permanently damaged his eyesight. 'The food was appalling and meat was mostly grey matter in aspic which we were convinced was jellyfish', recalled one boy who was at prep school during the War. 'The margarine tasted like train oil and we all had diarrhoea.' Another boy remembered 'endless lentil', but was lucky enough to have this occasionally supplemented by the eggs of fantail pigeons, which his school, Leighton Park, allowed him to keep, and goat's milk. Within a year food prices had risen by around 32 per cent and conditions grew steadily worse. By the autumn of 1916 prices had increased by 65 per cent, with individual items such as sugar (two thirds of which had formerly been imported from Germany and Austria) going up by as much as 163 per cent. This was felt particularly at schools where a sweet pudding was often the only compensation for an otherwise disgusting meal. Some schools had strokes of good fortune. At Elstree Preparatory School the cook came to the headmaster in tears because the sugar supply had been exhausted. The headmaster drove to Whitehall to see the Sugar Controller personally. To his surprise two sacks of the precious commodity were loaded into the boot of his car; the Controller happened to be an Old Elstree Boy.

Loyal citizens such as Lieutenant Colonel A.C. Borton JP, whose diary of the Great War was published in 1973, ploughed up lawns in order to plant potatoes. 'That I should live to see it,' he exclaimed. 'Yet it had to go.' The schools were less keen to put their land at the service of the country. Games-fields that could have yielded large crops of vegetables continued to be lovingly maintained, the hallowed turf apparently considered more important as a training ground for future officers than a market garden. The Board of Agriculture found it necessary to write to the schools at the beginning of 1917, asking for the 'maximum amount of ground to be cultivated'. Amidst its vast tracts Marlborough managed to find five spare acres. Three acres of water meadows behind the chapel were planted with cabbages and a further two acres were dug for potatoes.[1] In February 1917 the prefects held a meeting to discuss the problems arising from Lord Davenport's new food regulations. Since there was no spare labour, the prefects had been asked by the new headmaster, Dr Cyril Norwood, to 'solicit the help of the school'. It was decided that the cabbage patch should be divided into plots, each of which was allocated to individual houses for cultivation. Ten boys per plot were to work (out of school hours) in half-hour shifts. The potatoes needed less attention and it was felt that the task of weeding could be left to junior boys. This even distribution of labour was abandoned during haymaking in the summer, since it was felt that the task should be completed as quickly as possible. The strongest boys in each house were recruited.

Six resolutions concerning voluntary rationing were put forward and passed by the prefects. Housemasters, however, apparently found some of these restrictions rather severe and only half of them came into practice. These were that no food parcels should be received by boys from their parents; the Marlborough tuck shops and grocers were placed out of bounds after 12.30 pm; and 'brewing'[2] in studies could only take place between 4.00 and 6.30 pm and should not involve 'the consumption of meat or fish in any form'. The draconian measure of banning bread at lunch, and sugar altogether, were felt to be unreasonable and unnecessary, and the threat issued to Knapton's shop that if it did not restrict its 'output for the consumption of the College' it would be put 'out of bounds on all occasions' (and presumably out of business very rapidly) was considered unwise. At the beginning of the autumn term unrestricted brewing was once again allowed, but eggs were banned. In October a rule preventing boys from eating on the premises of the tuck shops was rescinded in order to 'prevent the nuisance of boys being found eating in the street'. In January 1918 tea and margarine had become short and boys were not allowed to buy these commodities in the shops. Eggs were once more allowed, as were sausages. Amidst all these complicated and constantly changing rules it is unsurprising that indiscipline was reported to be rife in the school. There must have been considerable relief at the beginning of the autumn term in 1918 when it was decided that since rationing had become universal, Marlborough's self-imposed regulations were unnecessary and thus abolished.

[1] A photograph of Etonians (one of them in tails) digging up the famous 'Mesopotamia' appeared in a newspaper with the inevitable caption: '*The Playing Fields of Eton – 1917*'.

[2] 'Brewing' was a means by which boys supplemented the school diet with food of their own, prepared and consumed in their studies.

Elsewhere boys were urged in the columns of the school magazines to 'EAT LESS BREAD'. Those who failed to heed this warning were dealt with severely. The unfortunate Billy Bunter was marched around Greyfriars with a notice pinned to his corpulent body: 'The Prize Hog. This animal has been caught helping the Germans by wasting food supplies'. This incident, unlike most of those dreamed up by Charles Hamilton, was not entirely fanciful. At St Edmund's preparatory school the young W.H. Auden was seen taking a second slice of bread and margarine: 'Auden, I see, wants the Huns to win,' a master announced. An even worse disgrace befell Auden's fellow-poet, Stephen Spender who, with some other boys, ate more bread than he was allowed. Hearing of this, the housemaster, in an alarming abdication of responsibility, proclaimed: 'These boys are worse than huns, they're FOOD HOGS. I'm not going to try and discover the culprits. I leave it to the remainder of you to do what you like with them. I outlaw them.' Spender laconically recalls: 'Some boys tied pieces of rope round my arms and legs and pulled in different directions.' Those boys who managed to look well-fed without breaking food restrictions were considered a splendid advertisement for their school's diet. Henry Green, a naturally chubby lad, recalls being paraded before prospective parents, 'thumped and fingered like fat stock at a show'. Another boy who appeared to be gaining weight was also held up for admiration by his headmaster's wife ('Come and look at our prize cherub!'). It was later discovered that food poisoning was responsible for his appearance.

In spite of restrictions and new barbarities, the view from the cloisters was one of unbounded optimism as far as the authorities were concerned. The War was kept before the pupils in the classroom, on the playing-fields and on the drill-square. Casualties were a reminder of the cost of war, but each death was represented as an inspiriting example of the public-school ideal reaching its apotheosis. Even those whose school careers had been undistinguished had proved themselves, and vindicated the system, on distant battlefields. The voices of those who demurred were effectively silenced, or simply went unheard. Sorley's tart letters remained in manuscript until after the War. Nowell Smith declined to publish Waugh's defence of *The Loom of Youth* in the pages of *The Shirburnian*. Sassoon's protest went unrecorded in the columns of *The Marlburian*.

However, the atmosphere of the schools during the War certainly had an effect upon those who were too young to fight. Some, like Isherwood, felt that they had been deprived of the maturing experience of taking part in the War. They were forever divided from their elders by this. Isherwood admits to having made a cult of the public-school system compounded of pastiche scenes from traditional school stories. Gradually, with the assistance of fellow-Reptonian Edward Upward, the image of the public school evolved into a grotesque fantasy world which the two boys called 'Mortmere'. A similar process of evolution was taking place in the minds of other young men who were to become the representative writers of the 'Thirties. For Auden, the prep- and public-school world contained elements of Norse sagas, elements which were incorporated into the early plays he wrote in collaboration with Isherwood. More sinisterly, he was to claim that: 'The best reason I have for opposing fascism is that at school I lived in a Fascist state.' This was a particular reference to a system of honour which was in operation at his public school, Gresham's. It has been plausibly claimed that Orwell drew up his painful memories of a War-time prep school in order to create the totalitarian society he depicts in *Nineteen Eighty-Four*. There is a sense that all these writers had suffered the shock of seeing the complacency which had characterised their secure childhoods cruelly exposed; they achieved maturity dispossessed.

The chasm which had opened up between the generations, and had been emphasised in the poems of Owen and Sassoon, certainly helped to shape the political attitudes of the 'Thirties writers. The old men who had apparently sacrificed the young were symbols of a conservative and oppressive authority. Stephen Spender was to recall that his circle's espousal of communism was directly related to the descriptions of the bond between officers and men which they had found in the poetry of Sassoon and Owen. For Isherwood and Upward 'Wilfred' joined 'Kathy' (Mansfield) and 'Emmy' (Brontë) as guiding spirits.

For these men the values of the public schools seemed irrelevant to a post-War world. Had they taken part in the War they might have found some use for their moral education, but denied this chance they felt both cheated and obscurely guilty. To a certain extent they were as obsessed with their schooldays as previous generations had been, but viewed them with irony or contempt rather than with devotion. Before the War, the title given by Orwell to his reminiscences of prep school would have been taken at face value, but few people of his generation would write of their education '*Such, Such Were the Joys*'.

[8]

Armistice?

I

> He belonged, in fact, to the Breed; the Breed that had always existed in England, and will always exist till the world's end . . . Just now a generation of them lie around Ypres and La Bassée; Neuve Chapelle and Bapaume. The graves are overgrown and the crosses are marked with indelible pencil. Dead – yes; but not the Breed. The Breed never dies . . .
>
> *'Sapper'*

EVEN before the War had ended committees had been set up all across the country to raise money for memorials to the dead of the schools. In February 1917 a letter appeared in *The Times* signed by Lord Landsdowne, Lord Curzon, Arthur Balfour and others proposing a memorial at Eton. The College itself donated £10,000 and the headmaster gave £1,000. Leading OEs set a fine example, with Rosebery giving £1,000, and Curzon, Lascelles and Philip Sassoon giving £500 each. Initial donations ranged from £100 to £1,000, whilst a circular from the Provost was sent to every single (surviving) Old Etonian. The final memorial, a bronze frieze running along one side of Founder's Quad, crammed with the names of the 1,157 Old Boys who died in the War, is an impressive reminder of the price paid by the schools for their enthusiastic idealism.

Not all schools had as many to commemorate or as many wealthy Old Boys as Eton, but everyone seems to have given according to his means. Westminster proposed a memorial in July 1917; by December it had raised £4,500. At Marlborough a pamphlet was published listing donations ranging from 2s.6d. (from the celebrated botanist, W. Keble Martin, who had served as a chaplain at the Front) to several gifts of £500. The total raised was £19,240 13s. 4d.

There was considerable disagreement concerning the form these memorials should take, a problem depicted in R.F. Delderfield's *To Serve Them All My Days*, in which the advanced, young, working-class teacher, Powlett-Jones (a veteran of the War), presses for science laboratories rather than a conventional memorial. Most schools raised enough money to satisfy several suggestions, many of them investing excess funds in order to provide bursaries for the education of the sons of Old Boys killed in action.[1] Apart from the innumerable statues, plaques, windows and halls, the dead were also commemorated in new libraries, museums, classrooms, gymnasiums, playing-fields,[2] sports pavilions, armouries, drill-halls, swimming pools, science laboratories, sanatoriums, dining-halls, galleries and staircases. Chapels were enlarged, organs replaced, plate added to, screens, choirstalls and electric lighting installed. The bursar at Giggleswick got a new office, whilst the headmaster of Trent College had a new house built, with a garden and four acres of land.

The vastly elaborate memorial at St George's, Harpenden incorporated 'silk flags with the initials and regimental crests of each of the Dead, worked by their families', whilst in a pavilion to the dead of Merchant Taylor's, names were 'carved by relatives as an everlasting memorial, and will not be exhibited publicly'. If anything, memorials at colonial schools were even more elaborate and bizarre. A bronze group at the Diocesan Church of England Grammar School in Geelong was 'symbolic of the triumph of Youthful Heroism over Evil' and incorporated figures of soldiers, Youth and 'the Germanic purpose of war' (an immense bird). At Brisbane Grammar there was a four-volume Golden Book, illuminated by the headmaster's daughter, which was kept in a crystal cabinet in the library, a captured German field-gun (presented by the Commonwealth Government), and 'a complete German Field Telephone'.

Whatever the diversity of the memorials, the message was the same from St Andrew's, Aurora to St Lawrence's, Ramsgate. In the words of Field Marshal Lord Plumer, speaking at the memorial service at Charterhouse, the War was: 'a complete vindication of the English Public-School training in enabling inexperienced soldiers to take responsible posts successfully'. The Archbishop of York, speaking at Rossall, agreed with the Field Marshal:

---

[1] A suggestion that this munificence should be extended to the daughters of Old Westminsters was firmly resisted.

[2] An Old Westminster wrote from the trenches to suggest that since 'the fields of Westminster were but a stepping-stone to the Field of Honour . . . a proportion of the fund . . . should be reserved for the furtherance of sport.' If his wish was not granted, his spirit was shared. Innumerable speeches were made at dedication ceremonies in which the battlefield was compared with the games-pitch.

We must never let the mist of disillusionment blind our eyes to the greatness of the light that shone upon our English life. The generation since the War has need to be reminded of that heritage of trust and of honour, into which they have entered. I shall always think that the spirit of our Public Schools rose to its highest power in the flame of sacrifice which lit up those fateful years. These English boys must merit the famous words of Pericles, 'They fled from shame, but with their bodies they endured the battle, and so in a moment, at the supreme moment of their fortune, passed from the place, not of their fear but of their glory.' If the old place of the Public School and University men is passing, their sun is setting in splendour on the fields of France and Flanders.

To pretend that 297 Old Rossallians (including J.R. Ackerley's elder brother, decapitated by a shell whilst lighting his pipe) found the supreme moment of their fortune dying in the trenches suggests mists other than those of disillusionment. However, speaker after speaker at dedication ceremonies uttered similar sentiments. Loyalty to the Old School, self-sacrifice, playing the game, attaining the Grail – every single cliché of the public-school ethos was presented as if newly minted.

As with the speeches, so the memorials themselves enshrined the ideals which one might have thought had been shot to tatters during the War. St George was a popular figure, appearing upon pedestals, in windows and in tapestries. Etonians were used as models for the faces of the figures in a tapestry woven by Morris & Co. for Lower Chapel which depicted the boyhood of this saint. Other chivalric figures include King Arthur and his knights: the wall painting at St George's, Harpenden in memory of the seven Captains of School depicts 'Sir Galahad coming upon a procession of the Guilds, Crafts and Husbandmen issuing from a cathedral'. To emphasise the chivalric heritage of which the dead had become a part, the Revd C. Harris's setting of John Arkwright's 'The Supreme Sacrifice' was frequently sung at memorial and dedication ceremonies:

> O valiant hearts, who to your glory came,
> Through dust of conflict and through battle-flame;
> Tranquil you lie, your knightly virtue proved,
> Your memory hallowed in the Land you loved.[1]

[1] This is a happier choice than that made at the City of Oxford School. It does not seem particularly apposite for the recently and violently bereaved to sing the jaunty: 'Let us with a gladsome mind/Praise the Lord for He is kind./For His mercies aye endure/Ever faithful, ever sure.'

The Classics were frequently quoted, including the notorious *Dulce et decorum est* . . . (Bristol Grammar, Newcastle Royal Grammar and the Hereford Cathedral School). Pericles was invoked as frequently as playing-fields. The Greek inscription upon the King's Wimbledon memorial is translated: 'Theirs is the prize of fair-garlanded death', a sentiment which inevitably recalls Blunden's ironic appropriation of Keats's 'Ode on a Grecian Urn' ('And all her silken flanks with garlands drest') in his sonnet 'Vlamertinghe'. Simonides is quoted at St Peter's, York, recalling W. Rhys Roberts's lecture; elsewhere are consolatory phrases which sound better in Latin, but do not add up to very much: '*Bene mori semper vivere*' (It is good to die so as to live forever) and '*Mors est janus vitae*' (Death is the gateway of life).

Clearly ceremonies of dedication were not the occasion for discussing the rights and wrongs of a war, the cost of which was being counted personally by the congregation. However, there is no doubt that the Dead were to be a permanent example to the Living. At Aldenham, Rossall, Marlborough, Uppingham, Malvern, Lancing, Mill Hill and other schools, speeches were made exhorting the audience to follow in the footsteps of those who had been killed. 'Do thou likewise' was the essence of such addresses. Even prep schools were not immune. Like many other schools, Durnford, in Dorset, produced an elaborate memorial book to their Dead. Published in 1924, it is prefaced by a quotation from Sir John Smythe's account of the 'Men in Flanders 1589–90', which is intended to emphasise the continuity of the happy yeoman warrior down the centuries. It contains brief biographies of the two masters and fifty-one Old Boys who had been killed: 'Their story is not graven on stone over their native earth, but lives on far away, without visible symbol, woven into the staff of other men's lives. For you now it remains to rival what they have done.' Within fifteen years the opportunity would arise.

Whilst we may deplore many of the sentiments expressed, the fact that they may have eased the grief of the bereaved is a vital mitigating factor. And yet there was an alternative. 'All a poet can do today is warn', wrote Owen. 'That is why the true poets must be truthful.' In spite of the fact that there was no OTC at Leighton Park, the Quaker school near Reading, twenty-eight of its Old Boys were killed in action. The memorial board is inscribed with the simple, neutral statement: 'They died for great ideals'. The school designated a Place of Remembrance, which neither required, nor received, an official opening. Here 'duty is drawn to the duty of those now living, so as to prevent war in future.'

II

After the War there was also an armistice between the schools and their critics; perhaps it was felt that some deference was due to the high proportion of public-school men who had died: some twenty per cent of all those who had served.[1] Circumstances demanded something unequivocally in favour of the schools, something like Ernest Raymond's *Tell England* or Beverley Nichols's *Prelude*. Nichols was later to claim that he loathed every minute of his time at Marlborough, but this is not the impression he gives in his engagingly soppy novel, published whilst he was still an undergraduate in 1920. At first Paul hates the discomfort of school life at 'Martinsell' which comes as a rude shock after his soft upbringing by his glamorous, widowed mother. More interested in dancing than in games ('It wasn't as if the [cricket] ball were attractive, or as though one could sport with it delicately when one had caught it.'), Paul is not the sort of lad best suited to the rigours of a War-time public school. However, he soon adapts, is taken up by an older boy and falls in love with one of his contemporaries. Although there are debates amongst sophisticated Sixth Formers about education, the system is praised in spite of its faults. *The Loom of Youth* is given an expected trouncing, and Paul leaves school to enlist and serve with distinction in France, where he is killed. The novel ends with Paul's last letter to his friend at Martinsell:

> But when all's said and done, it's Martinsell, Martinsell, Martinsell, that I long for, Martinsell that somehow − I don't know how − has given me strength and power and has made me love. I don't know whether its system be right or wrong, but it is Martinsell that has made me come out here and fight, and has guided me right all along.

Most people seemed to agree, including Ian Hay, for whom Nichols worked on a propaganda tour of America immediately after the War:

---

[1] The overall percentage of serving officers killed in action was about 13.5 per cent, compared with 10 per cent amongst the ranks. At Downside, Fettes and Glenalmond the figure was 23 per cent, whilst at Loretto and Harrow it rose to 27 per cent.

For officers, Britain turned to her public schools . . . When the great call came, those young Armies of ours were officered, without difficulty, by many thousand competent cadets furnished by this system. They were pathetically young; but they possessed two priceless qualifications: they knew their job, and they played the game. They never asked men to go where they would not go themselves. So, children though they were, their men followed them everywhere. There are not many of them left now.

This is from the revised (1921) edition of *The Lighter Side of School Life*, a collection of sketches, first published in October 1914. This genially uncritical volume, with its notorious final sentence ('If this be mediocrity, who would soar?'), was followed by the similarly anodyne *The First Hundred Thousand*. It will come as no surprise to anyone who has read these books that Hay was involved with recruiting during the War before he moved to the Ministry of Information in 1916.

Tell England never questions 'whether the system be right or wrong', but is a straightforward paean to 'Kensingtowe' and a lament for the boys who were killed in the War. It is subtitled 'A Study in a Generation', and it is Padre Monty, the army chaplain serving with the book's heroes at Gallipoli, who provides the title:

> 'Tell England –' You must write a book and tell 'em, Rupert, about the dead schoolboys of your generation –
> > 'Tell England, ye who pass this monument,
> > We died for her, and here we rest content.'

Rupert Ray, who had previously found these lines 'rather swish', is now 'unable to conquer a slight warming of the eyes at the words', spoken as the ship steams away from the Peninsula where his friend, Edgar Doe, lies buried. Unlike Owen's projected book of poems, *Tell England* was intended to be in every sense consolatory. Its last pages are supposedly written on the eve of Rupert's death in the last days of the War:

> I cannot bear to think of my mother's pain, if to-morrow claims me. But I leave her this book, into which I seem to have poured my life . . .
> Oh, but if I go down, I want to ask you not to think it anything but a happy ending. It will be happy, because victory came to the nation, and that is more important than the life of any individual . . .

[280]

The novel ends with Rupert's last thoughts, thoughts which sum up the attitude of the grieving schools immediately after the War:

> I may be whimsical tonight, but I feel that the old Colonel was right when he saw nothing unlovely in Penny's death; and that Monty was right when he said that Doe had done a perfect thing at the last, and so grasped the Grail. And I have the strange idea that very likely I, too, shall find beauty in the morning.

Although, to adapt Orwell, it is sodden in the worst illusions of 1914, and Padre Monty has not improved with passing time, *Tell England* is even today a moving novel. Competent rather than inspired, it is nonetheless irradiated by a sincerity that prevents it from becoming as sentimental as *Prelude*. Raymond, like Masefield, served in Gallipoli, and he too managed to salvage something from that catastrophe. The book's commercial success was no doubt a result of this sense that the sacrifice had been worthwhile. It was printed fourteen times during its first year of publication (1922) and six times during 1923. There was a new impression every year until 1931.

By this time the brief armistice between the schools and their critics had been destroyed. The elegiac tone of Raymond's attempt to *Tell England* had been replaced by the raucous sounds of Robert Graves saying *Goodbye to All That*. Graves was not the only author to link and criticise the public schools and the War; Richard Aldington, C.E. Montague and Einar O'Duffy added their voices. A wave of anger and bitterness broke in 1926 with a spate of novels and memoirs in which the authors' days as schoolboys and subalterns were recalled in a jaundiced frame of mind. As the first War memoirs began to appear, in which honour and idealism were depicted floundering in the filth of the Western Front, voices were once again raised against the schools in which such illusions were bred.

III

Since the days of Thomas Arnold, the public schools had always served a political purpose. Arnold's wish to reform the schools arose from his wish to reform society and provide responsible leaders worthy of their position in order to safeguard the stability of society. The spread of the schools in Arnold's wake owed something to his idealism, but was also similarly motivated. The schools were opened up to the rising plutocracy in order to ally the bourgeoisie with the threatened landed classes; if they had risen from the lower classes, might not they side with them against the upper classes? The only way to maintain supremacy was to invite potential competitors to become allies, and education provided a less distasteful way than marriage of forging links between old and new money.

Once the middle class had been absorbed, there still remained the problem of an increasingly isolated and potentially rebellious working class. Indeed, mission work began in the 1860s in response to rioting in the West End. Much of this work was done by men like Thomas Hughes, whose gift for proselytism can be judged from the success of *Tom Brown's Schooldays*. The further involvement of the universities and public schools in mission work was prompted by further riots in 1886. Like their fellow-missionaries in Africa and other countries, these men working in the East End and the Industrial North combined charity with proselytism; it was not only the Gospel of Christ that was being propagated. The notion of a 'natural gentleman', smart young working-class recruits to the ethos of their social superiors, was one that allied respectability with subjugation. There is little doubt that much missionary work was entirely altruistic and achieved a great deal for the poverty-stricken urban population. However, there was also a sense that one result of such good work was a latent colonisation.

Just how far the working classes had become impregnated by the mores of the public schools can be seen in the new respectability cadet corps brought to the army. Previously looked on askance as the refuge of rogues, the army began to be seen as a worthy occupation. This idea was also propagated in the magazines which were beginning to circulate amongst the newly-literate population. At first the magazines demonstrated certain virtues in action; later the tone became distinctly militarist, a process which reached a climax with the papers of the Amalgamated Press. The combination of all these elements fired the population of young men with the sort of ideals and enthusiasms which could be harnessed in the event of a major international war involving civilian volunteers.

It may be argued that the working classes had their own codes of solidarity and idealism which found expression in the trade union movement. Certainly the 'Pals' Battalions raised in the north of England were self-generating and displayed a loyalty and patriotism that had working-class roots. However, it is significant that the unions were not recognised as a potential means of recruitment. The reason is simple. The trade union movement, which had been gaining in strength in the years leading up to 1914, had been striving for improvement in workers' conditions independently of, and in opposition to, the patronage of the upper and middle classes. The division between employer and worker was not one likely to be of use in the formation of an army. What was required was the deference of one class to another, an acknowledgement by the potential ranks of the 'natural' superiority of the potential officers. This was in stark contrast to the aspirations of the trade union movement. Indeed, at the beginning of the War, the Government spent much time bargaining with the unions in order to keep the wheels of industry turning. Such was the enthusiasm for the War that men who were needed for the manufacture of armaments had rushed off to the recruiting offices. The unions were appealed to in order to *discourage* men from enlisting. As the casualties mounted and more men were required in the forces, the Government had cause to regret its earlier policy. The introduction of conscription in 1916 was staunchly opposed by the unions; the TUC voted against the Military Service Bill by an overwhelming majority. It might be said that the only way the propagandists appealed to the working classes through the channel of their own culture was by suggesting that they followed the lead of their footballing heroes.

The officer class had been indoctrinated within the public schools with a set of ideals and notions of leadership which could be very easily exploited in a war. Boys had not been trained for the army explicitly; this had been a social rather than a military education. However, the formation of the OTC was a more frank preparation for war. It meant that the War Office now had a direct stake in the schools and was in frequent communication with headmasters in order to encourage boys to enter the forces as a career or to consider joining volunteer forces once they had left school. In order to entice pupils, emphasis was placed upon field days and camps at which exciting pitched battles between rival schools could take place. Mais's account of the jolly romps at Sherborne during the War, with 'dead' subalterns allowed to warn other platoons about enemy positions, demonstrates how little similarity such exercises bore to the reality of trench warfare. Machine-guns might not have been invented as far as the OTC was concerned.

Whilst it might be argued that the 'moral' preparation within the schools was as outmoded and redundant as the military one, it must be stressed that a large number of combatants were sustained by their belief in the ideals for which they imagined they were fighting. In spite of circumstances which provoked scepticism amongst the less devout, the majority of young officers seem to have maintained their faith throughout the War. The schools and their ethos exacted a loyalty which seems to have been virtually unshakeable. The reflections of Paul Bäumer and the other young soldiers of *All Quiet on the Western Front* do not display the same constancy. They blame their teachers for misleading them:

> For us lads of eighteen they ought to have been mediators and guides to the world of maturity, the world of work, of duty, of culture, of progress – to the future. We often made fun of them and played jokes on them, but in our hearts we trusted them. The idea of authority, which they represented, was associated in our minds with a greater insight and a more humane wisdom. But the first death we saw shattered this belief. We had to recognise that our generation was more to be trusted than theirs. They surpassed us only in cleverness. The first bombardment showed us our mistake, and under it the world as they had taught it to us broke in pieces.

The very things which destroy Bäumer's faith strengthen that of Edgar Doe in *Tell England*:

> If I'd never known the shock of seeing sudden death at my side, I'd have missed a terribly wonderful thing. They say music's the most evocative art in the world, but *sacré nom de Dieu*, they hadn't counted the orchestra of a bombardment. That's music at ten thousand pounds a minute. And if I'd not heard that, I'd never have known what it is to have my soul drawn out of me by the maddening excitement of an intensive bombardment.

Lying on his death-bed, shot in stomach and shoulder, Doe reflects: 'If I'd known when I started that it would end like this – I'd have gone through with it just the same.' The supposition that had combatants known what the War would be like, the majority of them would have gone through with it just the same, does not excuse the indoctrination of a generation with old lies about the moral value of war. It is no disrespect to the dead to regret that many of them fought and died for all the wrong reasons. That during the course of the War many individual acts demonstrated a kind of chivalry does not mean that the War was about chivalry. That men dribbled footballs towards the enemy trenches does not mean that the War was a game. That men died for an ethos does not mean that the ethos was worth dying for.

[284]

Sources

A Note on Sources

These notes give the sources of all material which is quoted. Rather than disfigure the text with numbers, I have simply listed references by page number and in order. Quotations are identified, whenever possible, by author or title; occasionally it has been necessary to use a brief extract. Books are referred to by author; full details are recorded in the Bibliography. In cases where I have quoted from more than one book by the same author, I have added a shortened form of the title: e.g. 'Brooke.*Letters*' and 'Brooke.*Poems*'. In the case of Owen's poetry, I have benefitted from all the editions listed in the Bibliography, but all references are to the Hogarth Press edition, edited by Jon Stallworthy (1985).

In the following notes, '*ECL*' refers to papers from the College Library at Eton, including the Loder and A.C. Benson collections; '*MCL*' refers to manuscript material in the Marlborough College Library; '*Sherborne*' refers to the two volumes of letters and press cuttings relating to *The Loom of Youth*, which Alec Waugh donated to his old school's library. I was refused permission to quote from, or even identify, a number of papers in the Department of Documents at the Imperial War Museum. In consequence I have had to paraphrase certain passages and these are designed in the following notes simply as '*IWM*'.

Epigraphs – Raymond p. 168; quoted Kernot p. 106.

INTRODUCTION

I:

15 Brittain – Panichas pp. 371–2.

II:

16 Grenfell – Mosley p. 245.
Casualty figures – Gardner p. 214 and Kernot *passim*.

17 Owen – 'Futility' in Owen.*Poems* p. 135.
Bullets – Hornung, quoted Hicks, p. 45.

III:

18 Seccombe – Waugh.*Loom* (1917) pp. 12–13.

19 Creed – *The Country House* (Heinemann 1907), quoted Hicks p. 5

20 Mack – Mack p. 305.
Health & Strength – March, 1919, *Sherborne.*
Lyttelton – *Contemporary Review*, Dec. 1917, pp. 658–664.
Dartmouth – *Spectator*, 29.12.17.

21 Browne – Browne pp. 21–4.
Loom – Waugh.*Loom* p. 251.
footnote – quoted Ollard p. 90.

22 Waugh – Waugh.*Early Years* p. 104.
Sassoon – Sassoon.*Diaries 1915–18* p. 177.
Gollancz – Gollancz.*My Dear* p. 32.

23 Gollancz – Gollancz.*More* pp. 178,170.

24 Gollancz – *ibid* p. 299.

IV:

24 Osborn – Osborn.*Muse* p. xx.

25 Waugh's critic – quoted Waugh.*Early Years* p. 118.
Sorley – Sorley.*Letters* p. 262.
Osborn – Osborn.*Muse* p. v.

26 Talbot Kelly – Talbot Kelly p. 18.
Osborn – Osborn.*New* p. 4.
Adcock – Adcock pp. 34–5.
Mackintosh – 'Recruiting' in Mackintosh. *War.*

27 Brooke – Brophy, et al. p. 135.
Brittain – Panichas p. 370.

PART ONE

CHAPTER ONE:
SCHOOLS FOR SUBALTERNS

1: Answering the Call

31 *Elizabethan* – *Elizabethan* XIV.17.
Mais – Mais pp. 9–10.

32 *Punch* – *Mr Punch's History of the Great War* (1919) p. 51, reproduced Cadogan & Craig p. 93.

33 Old Suttonian – Kernot p. 103.
Figures – Haste p. 50; Marwick p. 15; Winter.*Death's* p. 29; Liddell Hart p. 31.

34 'young gentlemen' – Middlebrook p. 16.

35 Winchester – Nichols.*Anthology* pp. 32–3
Sorley – Sorley.*Letters* p. 16.
2,000 vacancies – *History UPS* p.14.
Chapman – Chapman, G. p. 13.

36 Sherston – Sassoon.*Fox-Hunting* p. 306.
Nettleton – Nettleton p. 15.
Waugh – Waugh.*Early Years* p. 74.
Sorley – Sorley.*Letters* pp. 241, 254.
Willey – Panichas p. 324.

37 Graves – Graves.*Goodbye* p. 78.

38 Eden – Eden pp. 65, 68.

39 Sherriff – Panichas pp. 136–7.
Hall – interviewed in *Lions Led by Donkeys* (Channel 4 documentary 9.11.85.).
Davies – Birkin pp. 222–3.

2: The Clarendon Commission

40 Higgins – quoted Mack pp. 8–9.

41 Clarendon on commissioners – quoted Chandos p. 323.
Report – Vol. I pp. 44, 56, quoted Mack p. 38.

42 Classroom failure – *ibid* p. 34.

43 Cheltenham – quoted Morgan p. 3.
footnote – Waugh.*Early Years* p. 54.

3: A Legend and a Legacy

44 Provost – quoted Strachey.*Eminent* p. 177.

46 Silhouettes – Kinglake p. 220.
Testimony – quoted Chandos p. 220.
Arnold's letter – Stanley Vol. I p. 218.

47 'It is not necessary' – quoted Bamford p. 73.
'I never disguise' – Stanley Vol. I p. 248.

48 Stanley – quoted Chandos pp. 259–60.

49 Brooke – Hughes Pt I Ch. 6 p. 110.

50 Squire Brown – *ibid* Pt I Ch. 4 p. 65.

51 footnote – Lancaster p. 603.

52 Scaife – Vachell pp. 12, 270, 273.
Arnold – quoted Strachey.*Eminent* p. 182.

4: Training for Empire

55 Cory – quoted Ollard pp. 69–70.
Warre – *The Times*, 29.6.00 – 3.1.01 *passim*.
Survey – quoted Gardner p. 206.
footnote – Wilkinson pp. 23–4.

56 Newbolt – Newbolt.*My World* p. 165.

57 Newbolt – *ibid* pp. 164–5, 166, 73.
Twymans – Newbolt.*Twymans* pp. 81–2.

58 Newbolt – Newbolt.*My World* pp. 62–3.
footnote – Leslie p. 59 and *passim*; Powell in Greene pp. 150–1.

59 *Stalky* – Kipling pp. 212–3.

60 Minchin – Minchin p. 129.

61 Minchin – *ibid* pp. 43, 48, 44.

5: Being Prepared

61 *Salopian* – XXXIX.21.

62 Debates – *Salopian* XXXI.4, XXXIII.11; *Elizabethan* XIV.19; *Marlburian* XXXV.537, XLV.677.
Henley – 'The Song of the Sword' in Henley.*Song*.

63 Rossalian – *TES* 6.10.14.
Harrow – Fox p. 59.
Old Etonian – 'O.E.' pp. 53–4.

64 Rugby – Teignmouth-Shore p. 68.
Circular – *ECL*.
Elizabethan – *Elizabethan* XIV.15., XIV.16.

65 Shrewsbury – West p. 150.
Sherborne – Mais p. 8; Waugh.*Loom* pp. 34–5.
Marlborough – Harling p. 7; *Captain* Vol. XXI p. 985; Nichols.*Prelude* pp. 98–101; Sorley.*Letters* p. 84.

66 Beacon School – Pound p. 15.
Fox – Fox p. 59.
Rosebery – Newsome p. 35.
Jones – *Captain* August 1907.

67 Roberts – Pound p. 16.
Blunden – Panichas p. 25.
Eton – *ECL*.
Mais – Mais p. 14.

68 *Captain* – *Captain* December 1915.
Blunden – Panichas p. 25.
footnote – *Salopian* XXXIV.3.

CHAPTER TWO:
A NOBLE TRADITION?

69 Nottingham – quoted Kernot p. 180.

1. The Best House of the Best School in England

71 Brooke – Hughes Pt I Ch. 6 pp. 110–112.

72 Brooke – *ibid* Pt I Ch. 6 p. 113.

75 Robertson – Mack p. 143.
76 Coke – Coke p. 306.

2. The Great Game
77 *Lear* – I. v; II.ii.
78 Tom Brown – Hughes Pt II Ch. 8
pp. 321–2.
Oppidan – Leslie p. 83.
79 Lyttelton – Geoffrey Madan, quoted
Ollard p. 90.
Almond – *Loretto Register* (1929),
quoted Mangan pp. 55–6.
81 Lewis – Lewis, C.S. p. 85.
Loom – Waugh.*Loom* pp. 53–4.
82 Vachell – Vachell pp. 251–2, 258,
257, 250, 261.
Baxter – Drummond p. 16.

3. Youth, Death and the Classics
85 Clarendon – quoted Mack p. 27.
Commissioners – *Report* Vol. I
pp. 23–4, quoted Mack p. 34–5.
86 Classics masters – Wilkinson p. 65;
Mack p. 314.
87 *Oppidan* – Leslie p. 72.
Loom – Waugh.*Loom* p. 102.
Kitchener – Howson pp. 162–3.
Powell – Powell p. 62.
David Blaize – Benson p. 295.
Elegiacs – Mackail p. 6.
88 Cory – Professor Munro, quoted
Ollard p. 60.
Connolly – Connolly pp. 235, 239.
footnote – 'Fernhurst', Waugh.*Loom*
p. 16; Jones, L.E. *Boyhood* p. 214.
89 Mackail – Mackail p. 38.
90 Cheltenham – Morgan p. 5.
Mackail – Mackail p. 39.
91 footnote 1 – Welldon p. 3.
footnote 2 – quoted Birkin p. 196;
Barrie.novel pp. 167, 170, 171, 172;
Barrie.play p. 128; Grenfell, quoted
Pound p. 194.
92 Grenfell – quoted Mosley p. 68.
Cleotes – trans. Mackail p. 161.

Connolly – Connolly p. 271.
Bassington – Saki.*Complete* p. 579.
Brooke – Brooke.*Poems* pp. xi–xii.
93 Brooke – Brooke.*Letters* p. 525.
Barrie – quoted Birkin p. 205.
Barrie – quoted Birkin p. 175.
Housman – Housman.*A Shropshire
Lad* XXIII.
footnote – Waugh.*Ronald Knox*
p. 59.
94 Barrie on *A Shropshire Lad* –
Cynthia Asquith's *A Portrait of
Barrie* (1959), quoted Birkin p. 262.
Housman sales – Graves, R.P.
p. 119.
Mackail – Mackail pp. 64–5.
Orwell – Orwell.*Inside* pp. 20–22.
Auden – Auden pp. 332.
Brooke – quoted Hassall p. 94.
95 Sorley – Sorley.*Letters* pp. 48–50.
'Fernhurst' – Waugh.*Loom* p. 244.
Rieu – Homer, pp. xvi, xviii.
Mackail – Mackail pp. 68–9.
96 Mackail – *ibid* pp. 69–70.
Powell – Powell p. 62.
97 *Oppidan* – Leslie pp. 101–3, 264,
266.
footnote – *Iliad* XVI, Homer
p. 306.
98 Sermon – Vachell pp. 314–5
footnote – Raymond p. 299.

4: Public-School Paladins
100 Arthur's father – Hughes Pt II
Ch. 2 pp. 215, 217.
101 Fisticuffs – *ibid* Pt II Ch. 5 p. 253.
102 Newbolt – Newbolt.*Happy Warrior*
p. vii.
103 Benson – *Diary*, ed. Percy Lubbock
(1926), quoted Ollard p. 93.
Oppidan – Leslie pp. 210–11.
104 Sidney – Kernot p. 162.
Skrine – Skrine pp. 58, 56.
105 Norwood – *The English Tradition in
Education* (John Murray 1929) p. 19,

quoted Barnett p. 27.
Orwell – 'The Lion and the
Unicorn' in Orwell.*Collected* Vol. 2
p. 90.

5: Passing the Love of Women
105 Hunt – *Autobiography* (1850)
Ch. IV, quoted Reade p. 61.
106 Disraeli – Disraeli Ch. IX p. 46.
Rendall – quoted Graves.*Goodbye*
p. 39.
107 Astute charge – Waugh.*Loom*,
Preface p. 12.
Sturgis – Sturgis pp. 158–9.
108 Reddie – Holroyd pp. 58–60.
Strachey – Strachey.*By Himself*
p. 82.
Hill – Vachell p. 100.
109 *David Blaize* – Benson pp. 84, 30,
166, 175, 226, 228.
110 Wilde – Hyde p. 201.
Brooke – Brooke.*Letters* pp. 46, 54.
111 Brooke – *Ibid* p. 59.
Scott-Moncrieff – *New Field* Vol. 2
No 9 (Pageant Number 1908).
Grudging admission –
Waugh.*Loom*, Preface p. 12.
112 Waugh – Waugh.*Early Years* p. 51.
Sexual mores – Lewis Chapter 6,
p. 89 *ff.*; 'Prefects' Book', *MCL*;
Gathorne-Hardy pp. 178–9; Devine,
Sherborne.
113 *Tell England* – Raymond pp. 23,
41–2.
Hill – Vachell pp. 221, 254.
114 *Hill* – *ibid* pp. 129–30, 135–6.

CHAPTER THREE:
SPREADING THE WORD

1: The School Story
116 Lunn – Lunn p. 43.
Sphere – 28.2.14. *ECL*.
117 footnote – Leslie p. 216.
118 Hughes – Hughes Pt I Ch. 6
pp. 112–3.

119 Hughes – *ibid* Pt I Ch. 6 p. 113.
Lunn – Lunn pp. 253, 5.
Sassoon – Sassoon.*Old* pp. 194,
231.
120 Bates – Greene pp. 23, 24–5.
'natural and English' – Hughes
Pt II Ch. 5 p. 271.
121 *Hill* – Vachell p. 233.
122 'vindictiveness' – Hicks p. 81.
124 *Fifth Form* advertisements – quoted
Howarth p. 57.
'The strong' – quoted Cox p. 46.
Hutchinson – quoted Cox p. 20.
'truly Christian' – quoted Cox
p. 49.

2: Boys' Magazines
126 Orwell – Orwell.*Inside* p. 203.
127 Muggeridge – Inglis p. 108.
footnotes – Turner pp. 164–5, 163,
220.
128 Roberts – *The Classic Slum* (1971),
quoted Carpenter, K. p. 57.
Stables – *BOP* (1888), quoted Cox
p. 68.
A Narrow Escape – *BOP*, April
1880.
129 footnote – Cox p. 76.
130 Conan Doyle – quoted Howarth
pp. 108–9.
131 'Makes Britons' – *Chums* 13.9.05.
132 Sandy – *Chums* 20.6.14, 11.4.14.
133 Harrovian father – quoted Turner
p. 113.
Evening News – quoted Brendon
p. 21.
134 Aircraft research figures –
Winter.*First* p.18.
Haig – quoted *ibid* p. 11.
'Will my readers' – quoted Turner
p. 193.
135 'The Invasion of England' – quoted
ibid p. 194.
'aimed from the first' – quoted *ibid*
p. 126.

'our huge possessions' – quoted *ibid* p. 195.

136 Larkin – 'MCMXIV' in *The Whitsun Weddings* (Faber & Faber 1964).
Greenwell – Greenwell. p. *xxi*.

137 Pistol Troop – Waugh.*Little* pp. 61–2.

3: Sounding Bugles

137 footnote – Ferguson pp. 25–6.

138 footnote – *Salopian* XXXIX.21.

139 Press comments – reprinted in the back of the volume.
'nothing if not' – quoted Howarth p. 87.

140 Russell – quoted Vansittart p. 29.

4: Missionaries
Unless otherwise indicated, details of the Eton Mission are from Carter.

141 'with the weapons' – Hughes Pt II Ch. 5 p. 253.

142 Ashbee – Crawford p. 20.
Church Reformer – June 1888, quoted Chapman, M. p. 6.

143 Bushell – Bushell pp. 125–6.
Lunn – Lunn pp. 105, 223.

144 'beastly Socialist' – *ibid* p. 224.
Sorley – Sorley.*Letters* pp. 20, 25, 43, 42, 43.
Eton Mission – *Eton Mission Ball Programme.*
Newbolt – quoted Howarth p. 9.

145 Church Lads' Brigade – quoted Girouard p. 252.

146 Company report – *Elizabethan* XV.20 (December 1918).
'Play-up!' – *Scouting for Boys* (1909 ed.) p. 267, quoted Springhall p. 58.

147 *Punch* cartoon – reproduced in Springhall.
When William – Saki.*Complete* p. 813.

PART TWO

CHAPTER FOUR:
NOW, GOD BE THANKED

Epigraph – 'The Dead' in Brooke.*Poems* p. 7.

1: Anglo-Saxon Attitudes

151 Epigraph – *Through the Looking-Glass* by Lewis Carroll (1871), Ch. VII.

152 Sorley – Sorley.*Letters* pp. 222, 230, 246, 227–8.

153 Sorley – *ibid* p. 263.
Brooke – Brooke.*Letters* pp. 632–3.

154 Brooke – to Frances Cornford, quoted Hassall p. 277.
Wren – quoted Howarth p. 122.
Brooke – 'Peace' in Brooke.*Poems* p. 5.

155 *Star* – quoted Hassall p. 516.
Osborn – Osborn.*New* p.60.
Sorley – Sorley.*Letters* p. 249.
Osborn – Osborn.*New* p. 59.
Sorley – Sorley.*Letters* p. 41.
Adcock – Adcock pp. 9, 209.

156 Sorley – 'What You Will', *Marlburian* 10.7.13.; Sorley.*Letters* pp. 102, 99, 110–1, 221, 259, 253.

157 Sorley – 'Two Sonnets – II' in Sorley.*Collected* p. 88; 'When you see millions of the mouthless dead' in *ibid* p. 91; Sorley.*Letters* pp. 245, 257.

2: The University & Public Schools Brigade

158 Epigraph – *History UPS* p. 111.
Letter to *Times* – *ibid* p. 15.

159 'Height' – *ibid* p. 24.
Spectator – *ibid* p. 17.
War Office submission – *ibid* pp. 17–18.
Kitchener – quoted *ibid* p. 21.

'Old Boys' – quoted *ibid* pp. 24–5.
160 'soldierly appearance' – *ibid* p. 29.
'under men' – *ibid* p. 30.
'consideration' – *ibid* p. 55.
161 *Morning Post* – quoted *ibid* pp. 60–1.
Richards – Richards p. 154.
Hiscock – Hiscock pp. 11, 20

CHAPTER FIVE:
OFFICERS AND MEN

1: Gentlemen and Players
163 Graves – Graves.*But It Still* p. 245.
164 'by reading the letters' – *IWM*.
165 Talbot Kelly – Talbot Kelly p. 22.
Greenwell – Greenwell p. 27.
Fourth of June dinner – *IWM*.
166 Woodroffe – Salopian XXXIV.14.
Guards officer – *IWM*.
Pte Miller – Nevill, *IWM*.
Etonian officer – *IWM*.
footnote – Letter to author from
Mr Anthony Bond.
167 Manning – Manning p. 59.
'What it was' – Sherriff in Panichas
pp. 154, 139, 154, 152, 139.

2: A Body and a Soul, Entire
168 Training manual – War
Office.*Instructions*.
169 'Do you know' – Graves.*But It Still*
p. 245.
Ackerley – Ackerley.*My Father*
p. 50.
170 Cunnington, Cutting – Nevill,
IWM.
Richards – Richards p. 227.
171 Richards – *ibid* pp. 227–8, 271.
173 Sassoon – Sassoon.*Diaries 1915–18*
p. 100.
Telegram – quoted Richards p. 271
Sassoon – Sassoon.*Diaries 1915–18*
pp. 229.
Soldier to Sassoon – quoted *ibid*
p. 270.

Sassoon – *ibid* pp. 261, 274–5, 277–
8.
'Can I forget' – *ibid* p. 278.
174 Owen – Owen.*Letters* pp. 580, 521,
570, 571.

3: Comrades in Arms
175 Read – Panichas p. *vi*.
Aldington – Aldington pp. 30–1.
Hiscock – Hiscock p. 33.
176 Hiscock – *ibid* pp. 85, 26, 106–7.
177 Blythe – Blythe pp. 188, 180.
Manning – Manning p. 217.
Richards – Richards p. 254.
Jacobs – Nevill, *IWM*.
178 Graves – Graves.*Goodbye* p. 164.
Sassoon – Sassoon.*Diaries 1915–18*
p. 45.

4: Another Kingdom
178 Liddell Hart – Panichas p. 102.
footnote – Chapman, G. p. 110.
180 'But now your country' – 'Your
King and Country Want You' by
Paul A. Rubens.
Soldiers' parody – quoted Walsh
p. 21.
183 de Sola Pinto – Panichas p. 78.
184 'Apropos' – Sassoon.*Diaries 1920–22*
p. 34.
'the pride of women' –
Sassoon.*Diaries 1915–18* p. 121.
Lady Brassey – quoted *ibid* p. 166.
'fashionable young woman' –
Sassoon.*Infantry* p. 188.
'Life is so wonderful' –
Sassoon.*Diaries 1915–18* p. 172.
185 'Unsusceptible' – Sassoon.*Infantry*
pp. 188–9.
Graves – Graves.*Goodbye* p. 23.
Macmillan – Macmillan.*Oxford*
pp. 27–8.
186 Raleigh – Sherriff & Bartlett p. 70.
Sassoon – Sassoon.*Diaries 1915–18*
p. 94.

5: Greater Love
Epigraph – *op. cit.*, p. 221.
187 Fussell – Fussell p. 284.
Graves – Graves.*In Broken* pp. 63,
319.
footnote – Owen.*Letters* p. 582.
188 'were designed' – Sassoon.*Siegfried's*
p. 68.
190 Graves – Graves.*In Broken* pp. 50–1;
Graves.*Goodbye* p. 23.
191 'One draft' – Stallworthy.*Wilfred
Owen* p. 230.
footnote – 'Beauty' in Owen.*Poems*
p. 180.
192 footnote – 'Two Loves', quoted
Hyde pp. 200–1.

6: All About Heroes
Epigraph – Owen.*Letters* p. 511.
193 'poetic crush' – Fussell p. 289.
'a quiet' – Graves.*Goodbye* p. 217.
Owen on Sassoon – Owen.*Letters*
pp. 485, 486.
footnote 2 – 'Drop me a name':
Observer, 25.3.79.
194 'one word' – Owen.*Letters* p. 489.
'Know that' – *ibid* p. 505, 506.
'like school exercises' –
Sassoon.*Siegfried's* p. 59.
195 'a tale of Harrow' – Owen.*Letters*
p. 535.
'I wish' – *ibid* p. 506.
'there issued' – *ibid* p. 571.
'The best piece' – *ibid* p. 570.

CHAPTER SIX:
THE VIEW FROM THE FRONT

1: A Distant Prospect
Epigraph – Vaughan p. 6.
196 Sassoon – Sassoon.*Old* p. 206.
Edmonds – 'Edmonds' p. 11.
197 Greenwell – Greenwell pp. 45, 11,
38.
Baker – Housman, L. p. 36.

Anderson – *ibid* p. 30.
Nichols – Nichols.*Anthology*
pp. 61–2.
198 'would never understand' – Sherriff
& Bartlett pp. 59, 131.
Beverley Nichols –
Nichols.*Unforgiving* p. 33.
Robert Nichols – Nichols.*Anthology*
p. 44.
199 Gilbert – Gilbert p. 44.
'People used' – Sassoon.*War Poems*
p. 15.

2: An Awfully Big Adventure
Epigraph – Raymond p. 275.
200 Lewis – Lewis, C. pp. 15, 71, 133.
Briscoe – Briscoe p. *v*.
201 Bortons – Borton pp. 202, 203, 44,
61.
Nichols – Nichols.*Anthology* p. 50.
Vaughan – Vaughan p. 116.
Guardsman – *IWM*.
Jones–Housman, L. p. 159.
202 White – Howson p. 256.
Vaughan – Vaughan p. 121.
Sassoon – Sassoon.*Diaries 1915–18*
pp. 51, 68, 50–1, 67.
Kendle – Sassoon.*Infantry* pp. 50–1,
65.
203 Peter Pan – Barrie. play p. 91.
Remarque – Remarque p. 5.

3: For School, King and Country
Epigraph – quoted Kernot p. 80.
203 Jones – Jones, P. p. 2.
204 Muggeridge – Inglis p. 109.
Southwell – Howson p. 187.
205 telegram – *ibid* p. 89.
'The thoughts' – West p. 118.
Southwell – Howson p. 53, 110,
72, 120, 189, 294, 301.
White – *ibid* pp. 89, 137, 133, 244,
255.
206 White – *ibid* p. 256.
Madan – Madan pp. *xiv*, *xvi*, *xviii*.

207 Gillespie – Osborn.*New* p. 122.
'a very beautiful thing' – quoted
Kernot p. 28.
Bishop of Salisbury – *ibid* p. 110.
Old Etonian – Rayner-Wood
p. 108.
Elizabethan – Elizabethan XIV.25.
Salopian – Salopian XXXIV.12.
Rayner-Wood – Rayner-Wood
pp. *v*, 99.

208 Rayner-Wood – *ibid* pp. 81, 117,
viii, 131.
Anson – *ibid* p. 104.
Murray – *IWM*.
Provost – *Eton Chronicle* 10.6.15.

209 Cavan – *ibid* 14.6.17.
Basra – *Letters* p. 40.
Etonian telegrams – *Eton Chronicle*
10.6.15, 8.6.16, 29.6.16, 7.6.17,
21.6.17.
'The Fourth of June . . .' – *ibid*
10.6.15.
Old Marlburian dinner – *List*.
Old Salopians – *Salopian*
XXXIV.8.
Anson – Rayner-Wood p. 104.

210 *Eton Chronicle* – Eton Chronicle
11.3.15.
Rayner-Wood – Rayner-Wood
p. 53.
Jones – Jones, P. p. 2.

211 Old Salopians – *Salopian* XXXV.2,
XXXIV.15.
'anonymous boy' – *Letters*. pp. 48,
49.
4: *Our Team in Khaki*
Epigraph – 'Cricket – 1915' in
Pope.*More*.

211 Winter – Winter.*Death's* p. 66.

212 '500,000 men' – Haste p. 59.
'We've watched you' – 'Your King
and Country Want You' by Paul
A. Rubens.
'Men of Millwall' – Haste p. 60.
Rifle Brigade – Macdonald.*Somme*
p. 319.

Vaughan – Vaughan p. 15.

213 Alcock – Nevill, *IWM*.
'wild cheer' – Middlebrook p. 87.
Carver – Nevill, *IWM*.
Unwin – *ibid*.
Christmas card – *ibid*.
footnote 1 – Middlebrook,
Appendix 5, pp. 330–1.

215 Loos – Fussell p. 27.
Beersheba – Borton p. 137.
Pound – Pound p. 47.
Osborn – Osborn.*Muse* pp. *vi–vii*.
Wilkinson – *ibid* p. 210.
'So short a time' – *Eton Chronicle*
14.10.15.

216 Bain – Mangan pp. 255, 263, 264.
Bain on Sorley – Sorley.*Letters*
p. 64.

217 'This Pavilion' – quoted Kernot
p. 30

5: *Dying in their Glory*
Epigraph – 'On the Lacedaemonian
Dead at Plataia', trans. Mackail.

217 Brooke – Brooke.*Letters* p. 660.

218 Brooke – *ibid* pp. 662, 668. 'The
Old Vicarage, Grantchester' in
Brooke.*Poems* p. 54.

219 Shaw-Stewart – Cooper p. 137.
Kelly – Hassall p. 512.
'And Priam' – Brooke.*Poems* p. *cli*.
'Yes, you are' – Mosley p. 239.
'The thought' – *ibid* p. 263.

220 'At the moment' – *ibid* p. 265.
Asquith – *ibid* p. 265.
Baring – Osborn.*New* p. 283.
'a memorial' – Evan Charteris,
quoted Mosley p. 266.
Osborn – Osborn.*New* pp. 283–4.

221 Osborn's epitaph – *ibid* p. 311.
Falls – Panichas p. 235.
West – West, A.G. pp. 5–6.
Adam – Housman, L. p. 22.
'in every pocket' – Nichols.*Anthology*
p. 29.

Shropshire Lad sales – Graves, R.P. pp. 174–5.
Owen – 'Arms and the Boy' in Owen.*Poems* p. 131.

222 Fussell – Fussell p. 282.
Graves – Graves.*In Broken* p. 57.
Loos casualties – Pound p. 233.

223 Shaw-Stewart – quoted Cooper p. 160.

224 Sherston – Sassoon.*Infantry* pp. 90–1, 93.
'Gibson is a ghost' – Sassoon.*Diaries 1920–22* p. 73.
Herbert – 'R.B.' in Osborn.*Muse* p. 128.

225 'Doubtless the Romans' – *Spectator* 16.2.18.
'naked cribs' – quoted Fussell p. 181.
Simonides – trans. Mackail p. 70.
Lee – *Spectator* 29.12.17.
Martin – Middlebrook p. 86.

226 'his love of Homer' – Osborn.*New* p. 256.
Epitaph – Middlebrook p. 249.

6: Good-bye to Galahad
Epigraph – 'St George and the Dragon' in Pope.*More*.

227 *Gallipoli* – Masefield.*Gallipoli* pp. 34–5.
Ian Hamilton – quoted Liddle p. 217.

228 Masefield on Hamilton – Masefield.*Letters* p. 141.
'not as a tragedy' – Masefield.*Gallipoli* p. 3.
'That insane move' – Masefield.*Letters* p. 288.
Gilbert – Gilbert pp. 1, 2.

229 Gilbert – *ibid* pp. 3, 5–6, 8, 9–10, 12–13, 62–3.

230 Gilbert – *ibid* pp. 63–4, 66, 127–8, 224–5, 103, 171, 235, 153.

231 Grenfells – quoted Pound pp. 191, 167.

Danway – *ibid* p. 87.
Herbert – Fitzherbert p. 2.

232 Osborn – Osborn.*New* p. 6.
Adcock – Adcock p. 10–11.
Roos and Croft – *Elizabethan* XV.6, XIV.26.
Nichols – quoted Lehmann.*English Poets* p. 33
Sassoon – 'Letter to Robert Graves' in Sassoon.*War Poems* p. 130.

233 Brooke – Brooke.*Letters* pp. 662–3, 668, 667.

234 Churchill – quoted Brooke.*Poems* pp. *clviii–clix*.
Monro – quoted Hassall p. 520.
Hamilton – quoted Girouard p. 286, Pound p. 121.

235 Newbolt – Newbolt.*Happy Warrior* Preface.

236 Newbolt – Newbolt.*Tales* pp. 248–9.
Lewis – Lewis, C. p. 45.
Newbolt – Newbolt.*Tales* p. 249.
Briscoe – Briscoe pp. 101, 59.

237 Richards – Richards p. 224.
'once I sought' – 'The Poet as Hero' in Sassoon.*War Poems* p. 61.
'unconvincing operations' – Sassoon.*Fox-Hunting* p. 250.

238 Sassoon – *ibid* pp. 268, 286, 304.
'I used to say' – Sassoon.*Diaries 1915–18* p. 52.
'how England' – 'The Giant-Killer', *ibid* p. 56.

239 Jones – Jones, D. p. *xi*.

240 Fussell – Fussell pp. 144, 147.
Chapman – Chapman, G. p. 13.

241 Middlebrook – Middlebrook p. 123.
Little Mother – quoted Graves.*Goodbye* p. 189

7: The Old Lie Exposed
Epigraph – Housman, L. pp. 299–300.

243 'any gentleman' – Owen.*Letters* p. 341.

'I deliberately' – *ibid* p. 285.
'This book' – Owen.*Poems* p. 192.

244 'Asleep' – *ibid* p. 129.

245 'I shall be one' – 'A Terre' in *ibid*
p. 156.
'An Imperial Elegy' – *ibid* p. 177.

246 'Spring Offensive' – *ibid* p. 169.
'A Terre' – *ibid* p. 155.
'Simpson's cartoons' – Owen.*Letters*
p. 355.
Hibberd – *Wilfred Owen* (Writers
and Their Work series 1975) p. 35.
'The Kind Ghosts' – Owen.*Poems*
p. 158.

247 'S.I.W.' – *ibid* pp. 137–8.
'Someone said' – 'Disabled' in *ibid*
pp. 152–3.
Hibberd – 'Some Contemporary
Allusions in Poems by Rosenberg,
Owen and Sassoon' in *Notes and
Queries* August 1979.
footnote – *Elizabethan* XV.16.

248 *Weekly Dispatch* – 22.11.14.

249 'B.O.P. stories' – Stallworthy.*Wilfred
Owen* p. 201.
'He's lost' – 'Disabled' in
Owen.*Poems* p. 152.
Stallworthy – Stallworthy.*Wilfred
Owen* p. 216.
'The editor of *Poems*' – *Poems of To-
day*, Prefatory Note.

250 'Dulce et Decorum Est' –
Owen.*Poems* p. 117; variations in
Day Lewis edition p. 56.

251 'one of the most' – Owen.*Letters*
p. 496.
'I have been "approached"' – *ibid*
p. 516.

252 'Schoolmistress' – Owen.*Poems*
p. 116.
'a *Public* school' – Owen.*Letters*
p. 302.
'In spite of' – *ibid* p. 300.

253 'a public school man' – *ibid* p. 334.
'he must be' – *ibid* p. 544.

'When I read' – *ibid* p. 310.
'O meet it is' – Stallworthy.*Wilfred
Owen* pp. 104–5.
'The famous Latin' – Owen.*Letters*
p. 501.

254 Owen to Gunston – *ibid* p. 510.

PART THREE

CHAPTER SEVEN:
THE VIEW FROM THE CLOISTERS

Epigraph – 'To the School at War',
Salopian XXXIV.6.

258 Wykehamists – Pound p. 151.
'Mr Chips' – Hilton p. 93.
Huxley – quoted in Bedford p. 65.
Mais – Mais pp. 1, 112, 113, 116.

259 Mais – *ibid* p. 118.
Bates – Greene p. 25.
Marlborough – 'Prefects' Book',
MCL.
Waugh – Waugh.*Early Years*
p. 57.
Nowell Smith – *ibid* p. 58.
footnote – Trelawney-Ross p. 17.

260 'I did so hate' – Isherwood.*Kathleen*
p. 357.
Eton Chronicle – *Eton Chronicle*
11.3.15.
Eden – Eden p. 62.
'It was uncanny' – *Marlburian* Lent
1966.

261 'To A.H.B.' – *Eton Chronicle*
14.10.15.
'Everybody recognises' – *Captain*
15.3.15.

262 'An Eton Master' – *Eton Chronicle*
25.3.15.
'Swiftly you won' – *ibid* 1.7.15.
'He ought' – *ibid* 25.3.15.
Southwell and White – Howson
pp. 45, 43, 38.

263 Bainbrigge – *Salopian* XXXIV.5.
Mais – Mais pp. 122–3.

264 Westminster – *Elizabethan* XV.19.
Debates – *Elizabethan* XIV.17, 18,
19 and *passim*.
Lectures – *Salopian* XXXIV.6.8.9.
265 Westminster – *Elizabethan* XV.17.
Keeling – Housman, L. p. 160.
Old Westminsters – *Elizabethan*
XV.3, 2.
266 Neill – *ibid* XV.10.
Salopian – *Salopian* XIV.20.
Elizabethan – *Elizabethan* XXXIV.1.
267 'He has sinned' – *Times* 31.3.15.
'GERMAN MEASLES' – *ibid*.
268 'begging in effect' – *Elizabethan*
XIV.17.
269 'volunteered' – Letter to author from
G.W. Cadbury.
Downs headmaster – Letter to
author from R.L. Steynor.
St Edmund's – Fryer pp. 48–9.
Isherwood – Isherwood.*Exhumations*
p. 169.
footnote – Letter to author from
F.H. Gillett.
270 *Elizabethan* – *Elizabethan* XIV.17,
27.
Salopian – *Salopian* XXXIV.11, 10.
271 Plomer – Greene p. 139.
'The food was appalling' – Letter to
author from G.W. Cadbury.
'endless lentil' – Letter to author
from F.H. Gillett.
Food prices – Marwick p. 161.
Borton – Borton p. 161.
'maximum amount' – 'Prefects'
Book', *MCL*.
272 Marlborough – *ibid*.
273 Bunter – Turner pp. 240–1.

Auden – Carpenter p. 17.
Spender – Greene p. 185.
Green – Green pp. 18–19.
Another boy – R.L. Steynor.
274 Auden – Greene p. 17.

CHAPTER EIGHT:
ARMISTICE?

I:
Epigraph – 'Sapper' p. 43.
All details of War Memorials are
from Kernot.
276 Plumer – quoted Kernot p. 138.
footnote 2 – *Elizabethan* XV.18.
277 'We must never' – quoted Kernot
pp. 94–5.
footnote – *ibid* p. 61.
278 'Their story' – Cotton.
Owen – Owen.*Poems* p. 192.

II:
279 Nichols – Nichols, B.*Prelude* pp.
74–5, 291.
footnote – Maclean.*Great War*
p. 17.
280 'For officers' – Hay.*Lighter*
pp. 220–1.
'If this be' – Hay. *ibid* p. 220.
Tell England – Raymond pp. 314,
273, 319.
281 'I may be whimsical' – *ibid*
p. 320.

III:
284 Baumer – Remarque p. 14.
Doe – Raymond pp. 275, 296.

Bibliography

Books are listed in their first editions; where other editions have been used for the purposes of quotation, the publisher (if different) and date follow in square brackets.

I Manuscript sources

Diaries and letters of: D. Allhusen, A. Gibbs and W.P. Nevill. (All kept in the Department of Documents at the Imperial War Museum). Also other papers in the Department, identified 'IWM' in source notes.

Correspondence relating to *The Loom of Youth* donated to Sherborne School by Alec Waugh.

Letters to the author from G.W. Cadbury, F.H. Gillett, D. More and R.L. Steynor.

'The Eton Mission, Hackney Wick, 1880–1891'. Unpublished ts. by W.M. Carter (1934). (Eton College Library).

'Memories of the Downs School 1916–1919'. Unpublished ts. by R. Lestor Steynor (1980).

II Archives

Eton College (College Library)
Marlborough College
Sherborne School
Shrewsbury School
Westminster School

III Newspapers and Periodicals

The Boys' Own Paper   *The Captain*
The Champion   *Chums*
The Contemporary Review   *The Elizabethan*
The English Review   *The Eton College Chronicle*
The Illustrated War News   *The Marlburian*
The New Field   *The Phoenix*
A Public School Looks at the World   *The Salopian*
The Spectator   *Stand*
The Times   *The Times Educational Supplement*
The Times Literary Supplement   *Young England*

IV Books

ACKERLEY, J.R. *My Father and Myself.* The Bodley Head 1968 [Penguin 1971].
— *The Prisoners of War.* Chatto & Windus 1925.
ADCOCK, A. ST J. *For Remembrance.* Chatto & Windus 1918 [rev. 1920].
ALDINGTON, R. *Death of a Hero.* Chatto & Windus 1929.
All Can Help: A Handbook for War-Time. Duty & Discipline Movement 1914 [rev. 1915].
ARNOLD, T. – see Stanley, A.P.
ASHLEY-COOPER, F.S. *Eton v. Harrow at the Wicket.* St James Press 1922.
AUDEN, W.H. *Forewords and Afterwords.* Faber & Faber, 1973.

BADGER, A.B. *The Public Schools and the Nation.* Robert Hale 1944.
BAGNOLD, E. *A Diary Without Dates.* Heinemann 1918.
BAMFORD, T.W. *Thomas Arnold.* Cresset Press 1960.
BARING, M. *Poems: 1914–1917.* Martin Secker 1918.
BARNETT, C. *The Collapse of British Power.* Eyre Methuen 1972.
BARRIE, J.M. *Peter and Wendy.* Hodder & Stoughton 1911 [Penguin 1967, as *Peter Pan*].
— *Peter Pan.* Hodder & Stoughton 1928.
BEDFORD, S. *Aldous Huxley: A Biography. Vol I.* Chatto & Windus and Collins 1973.
BENSON, E.F. *David Blaize.* Hodder & Stoughton 1916.
BERGONZI, B. *Heroes' Twilight.* Constable 1965 [Macmillan 1980].
BIRKIN, A. *J.M. Barrie and the Lost Boys.* Constable 1979.
BLUNDEN, E. *Undertones of War.* Richard Cobden-Sanderson 1928 [Penguin 1937].
BLYTHE, R. *The View in Winter.* Allen Lane 1979 [Penguin 1981].

BORTON, A.C. *My Warrior Sons* [ed. Guy Slater]. Peter Davies 1973.

BRADFORD, E.E. *The New Chivalry and Other Poems.* Kegan Paul 1918.

BRENDON, P. *Eminent Edwardians.* Secker & Warburg 1979.

BRISCOE, W.A. *The Boy Hero of the Air.* Humphrey Milford and OUP 1921.

BRITTAIN, V. *Testament of Youth.* Gollancz 1933 [Virago 1978].

BROOKE, R.C. *The Collected Poems* [ed. with Memoir E. Marsh]. Sidgwick & Jackson 1918.

— *The Letters* [ed. G. Keynes]. Faber & Faber 1968.

— *The Prose* [ed. C. Hassall]. Sidgwick & Jackson 1956.

BROPHY, B., LEVEY, M. & OSBORNE, C. *Fifty Works of English Literature We Could Do Without.* Rapp & Carroll 1967.

BROPHY, J. & PARTRIDGE, E. *The Long Trail: Soldiers' Songs and Slang 1914–18.* Revised ed. André Deutsch 1965.

BROWNE, M. *A Dream of Youth.* Longmans, Green & Co. 1919.

BUSHELL, W.F. *School Memories.* Philip Son & Nephew 1962.

CADOGAN, M. & CRAIG, P. *Women and Children First.* Gollancz 1978.

CARPENTER, H. *W.H. Auden: A Biography.* George Allen & Unwin 1981.

CARPENTER, K. *Penny Dreadfuls and Comics.* Victoria & Albert Museum 1983.

CARRINGTON, C. – see 'Edmonds, C.'

CHAPMAN, G. *A Passionate Prodigality.* Ivor Nicholson & Watson 1933 [MacGibbon & Kee 1965].

CHAPMAN, M. *St Mary of Eton with St Augustine, Hackney Wick (The Eton Mission): A History 1880–1980.* Privately printed n.d.

CHANDOS, J. *Boys Together.* Hutchinson 1984.

CLOUGH, A. *A Choice of Clough's Verse* [ed. M. Thorpe]. Faber & Faber 1969.

COKE, D. *The Bending of a Twig.* Chapman & Hall 1906.

CONNOLLY, C. *The Enemies of Promise.* Routledge & Kegan Paul 1938 [Penguin 1961].

COOPER, D. *The Rainbow Comes and Goes.* Rupert Hart-Davis 1959.

COTTON, V.E. [ed.] *Durnford Memorial Book of the Great War, 1914–1918.* Medici Society 1924.

COX, J. *Take a Cold Tub, Sir!* Lutterworth Press 1982.

CRAWFORD, A. *C.R. Ashbee, Architect, Designer and Romantic Socialist.* Yale Press 1985.

DELDERFIELD, R.F. *To Serve Them All My Days.* Hodder & Stoughton 1972.

DESBOROUGH, E. *Pages from a Family Journal, 1888–1915.* Eton College 1916.

DISRAELI, B. *Coningsby.* Henry Colban 1844 [Ward Lock & Co. 1892].

[DRUMMUND, H.] *Baxter's Second Innings.* Hodder & Stoughton 1892.

EDEN, A. *Another World*. Allen Lane 1976.

'EDMONDS, C.' *A Subaltern's War*. Peter Davies 1929 [Ikon 1964].

ELLIS, J. *Eye-Deep in Hell*. Croom Helm 1976 [Fontana 1977].

Eton Mission Annual Report, December 1914.

Eton Mission Ball Programme, 1951.

Etonians Who Fought in the Great War MCMXIV–MCMXIX. Medici Society 1921.

EWART, G. [ed.] *Forty Years On – An Anthology of School Songs*. Sidgwick & Jackson 1969.

FARRAR, F.W. *Eric, or Little by Little*. Edinburgh 1858.

— *St Winifred's*. Edinburgh 1862.

— [ed.] *Essays on Liberal Education*. Macmillan 1867.

FERGUSON, J. *The Arts in Britain in World War I*. Stainer & Bell 1980.

FITZHERBERT, M. *The Man Who Was Greenmantle*. John Murray 1983.

FOX, A. *Public School Life: Harrow*. Sport & General Press Agency 1911.

FRASER, G.MCD [ed.] *The World of the Public School*. Weidenfeld & Nicolson 1977.

FRYER, J. *Isherwood*. New English Library 1977.

FUSSELL, P. *The Great War and Modern Memory*. OUP 1975.

GARDNER, B. *The Public Schools*. Hamish Hamilton 1973.

— [ed.] *Up the Line to Death*. Methuen 1964.

GATHORNE-HARDY, J. *The Public School Phenomenon*. Hodder & Stoughton 1977 [Penguin 1979].

GILBERT, V. *The Romance of the Last Crusade*. D. Appleton & Co., New York 1924.

GIROUARD, M. *The Return to Camelot*. Yale 1981.

GOLLANCZ, V. *More For Timothy*. Gollancz 1953.

— *My Dear Timothy*. Gollancz 1952.

— *Reminiscences of Affection*. Gollancz 1968.

— & SOMERVELL, D. *Political Education at a Public School*. William Collins 1918.

— *The School and the World*. Chapman & Hall 1919.

GRAVES, R. *But It Still Goes On*. Jonathan Cape 1930.

— *Fairies and Fusiliers*. Heinemann 1917

— *Goodbye to All That*. Jonathan Cape 1929; revised ed. Cassell 1958 [Penguin 1960].

— *In Broken Images* [ed. Paul O'Prey]. Hutchinson 1982.

GRAVES, R.P. *A.E. Housman: The Scholar-Poet*. Routledge & Kegan Paul 1979 [Oxford 1981].

GREEN, H. *Pack My Bag*. Hogarth Press 1940.

GREENE, G. [ed.] *The Old School*. Jonathan Cape 1934.

GREENWELL, G. *An Infant in Arms*. Lovat Dickson & Thompson 1935 [Allen Lane 1972].

GROSSKURTH, P. *John Addington Symonds*. Longmans 1964.

GURNER, R. *I Chose Teaching*. J.M. Dent 1937.

GURNEY, I *Collected Poems* [ed. P. Kavanagh], OUP 1982.

— *War Letters* [ed. R.K.R. Thornton]. Carcanet 1983 [Hogarth 1984].

HAIG-BROWN, A.R. *The OTC and the Great War*. Country Life 1915.

HARCOURT, L.V. *An Eton Bibliography*. Swan Sonnenschein & Co. 1898.

HARDY, H.H. *Public School Life: Rugby*. Sport & General Press Agency 1911.

HARLING, W.F. [ed.] *Marlborough College: The Corps 1860–1960*. Marlborough College 1960.

HARRIES, M, & S. *The War Artists*. Michael Joseph 1983.

HASSALL, C. *Rupert Brooke*. Faber & Faber 1964 [1972].

HASTE, C. *Keep the Home Fires Burning*. Allen Lane 1977.

HAY, I. *The First 100,000*. W. Blackwood & Son 1915.

— *The Lighter Side of School Life*. T.N. Foulis 1914 [revised ed. 1921].

HENLEY, W.E. *For England's Sake: Verses and Songs in Time of War*. David Nutt 1900.

— *The Song of the Sword, and Other Verses*. David Nutt 1892.

— [ed.] *Lyra Heroica*. David Nutt 1892.

HESSE, H. *The Prodigy*. [trans. W.J. Strachan]. Peter Owen 1961 [Penguin 1973].

HEWISON, R. *Under Siege*. Weidenfeld & Nicolson 1977.

HICKS, W.R. *The School in English and German Fiction*. Soncino Press 1933.

HILTON, J. *Good-bye, Mr Chips*. Hodder & Stoughton 1934.

HISCOCK, E. *The Bells of Hell Go Ting-a-Ling-a-Ling*. Arlington Books 1976 [Corgi 1977].

A History of Elstree School. Privately printed 1978.

The History of the Royal Fusiliers "U.P.S.". The Times 1917.

HOLMES, R. *Firing Line*. Jonathan Cape 1985.

HOLROYD, M. *Lytton Strachey: The Unknown Years*. Heinemann 1976.

HOMER *The Iliad* [trans. E.V. Rieu]. Penguin 1950.

HONEY, J.R. de S. *Tom Brown's Universe*. Millington Books 1977.

'HOOD, J.' *The Heart of a Schoolboy*. Longmans, Green & Co. 1919.

HORNUNG, E.W. *Fathers of Men*. Smith, Elder & Co. 1912.

HOUSMAN, A.E. *A Shropshire Lad*. Kegan Paul 1896.

HOUSMAN, L. [ed.] *War Letters of Fallen Englishmen*. Gollancz 1930.

HOWARTH, P. *Play Up and Play the Game*. Eyre Methuen 1973.

HOWSON, H.E.E. [ed.] *Two Men: A Memoir*. Oxford 1919.

HUGHES, T. *Tom Brown's Schooldays*. Macmillan 1857 [Simpkin Marshall n.d.].

HURD, M. *The Ordeal of Ivor Gurney*. OUP 1978.

HYDE, H.M. *The Trials of Oscar Wilde*. Penguin 1962 [Dover 1973].

INGLIS, B. [ed.] *John Bull's Schooldays*. Hutchinson 1961.

ISHERWOOD, C. *Exhumations*. Methuen 1966 [Penguin 1969].
— *Kathleen and Frank*. Methuen 1971.

JAY, P. [ed.] *The Greek Anthology*. Allen Lane 1973.
JONES, D. *In Parenthesis*. Faber & Faber 1937 [rev. ed 1978].
JONES, L.E. *An Edwardian Youth*. Macmillan 1956.
— *A Victorian Boyhood*. Macmillan 1955.
JONES, P. *War Letters of a Public-School Boy*. Cassell 1918.

KERNOT, C.F. *British Public Schools' War Memorials*. Roberts & Newton 1927.
KINGLAKE, A. *Eothen*. London 1844 [Methuen 1948].
KIPLING, R. *Stalky & Co*. Macmillan 1899 [1908].

LANCASTER, M.-J. *Brian Howard: Portrait of a Failure*. Anthony Blond 1968.
LANGGUTH, A.J. *Saki: A Life of Hector Hugh Munro*. Hamish Hamilton 1981.
LEHMANN, J. *The English Poets of the First World War*. Thames & Hudson 1981.
— *Rupert Brooke: His Life and His Legend*. Weidenfeld & Nicolson 1980.
LEJEUNE, A. & LEWIS, M. *Gentlemen's Clubs in London*. Macdonald & Jane 1979.
LESLIE, S. *The Oppidan*. Chatto & Windus 1922.
Letters of an Old Etonian, July 1914 – January 1917. Blackwell 1919.
LEWIS, C. *Sagittarius Rising*. Peter Davies 1936 [Penguin, revised ed. 1977].
LEWIS, C.S. *Surprised by Joy*. Geoffrey Bles 1955.
LIDDLE, P. *Men of Gallipoli*. Allen Lane 1976.
LIDDELL HART, B. *History of the First World War*. Faber & Faber 1934. [Enlarged, revised ed. Pan 1972].
List of Donations for the Marlborough College War Memorial. Privately printed 1918.
LUNN, A. *The Harrovians*. Methuen 1913.

MACDONALD, L. *The Roses of No Man's Land*. Michael Joseph 1980.
— *Somme*. Michael Joseph 1983.
— *They Called It Passchendaele*. Michael Joseph 1978.
MACK, E.C. *Public Schools and British Opinion Since 1860*. Columbia University Press 1941.
MACKAIL, J.W. *Select Epigrams from the Greek Anthology*. Longmans, Green & Co. 1890 [Rev. ed. 1906].
MACKINTOSH, E.A. *A Highland Regiment*. John Lane 1917.
— *War the Liberator*. John Lane 1918.
MACLEAN, A.H.H. *Public Schools and the Great War 1914–19*. Edward Stanford 1923.
— *Public Schools and the War in South Africa*. Edward Stanford 1903.
MACMILLAN, H. *Oxford Before the Deluge*. Macmillan 1984.
— *The Winds of Change*. Macmillan 1966.

[MACNAGHTEN, H.] *Eton Letters, 1915–1918. By a House Master.* Spottiswoode, Ballantyne & Co.

MADAN, G.. *The Notebooks of Geoffrey Madan.* [ed. J.A. Gere & J. Sparrow]. OUP 1981 [1984].

MAIS, S.P.B. *A Public School in War Time.* John Murray 1916.

MANGAN, J.W. *Athleticism in the Victorian and Edwardian Public Schools.* CUP 1981.

MANNING, F. *The Middle Parts of Fortune.* Peter Davies 1977 [Granada 1977].

MARSH, E. [ed.] *Georgian Poetry 1916–1917.* The Poetry Bookshop 1918.

MARSHALL, B. *George Brown's Schooldays.* Constable 1946.

MARWICK, A. *The Deluge.* Macmillan 1965 [Revised ed. 1973].

MASEFIELD, J. *Gallipoli.* Heinemann 1916.

— *Letters from the Front 1915–17.* [ed. Peter Vansittart]. Constable 1984.

MIDDLEBROOK, M. *The First Day on the Somme.* Allen Lane 1971 [Penguin 1984].

MINCHIN, J.E. *Our Public Schools.* Sonnenschein 1901.

MONRO, H. *Collected Poems.* Richard Cobden-Sanderson 1933.

MUNRO, H.H. — *see* 'Saki'.

MORGAN, M.C. *Cheltenham College: The First Hundred Years.* Richard Sadler Ltd. 1968.

MOSLEY, N. *Julian Grenfell.* Weidenfeld & Nicolson 1976.

MOTTRAM, R.H. *The Spanish Farm Trilogy, 1914–1918.* Chatto & Windus 1927.

MURRAY, F.E. *A Catalogue of Selected Books from the Private Library of a Student of Boyhood, Youth and Comradeship.* F.E. Murray 1924.

MUSIL, R. *Young Törless* [trans. E. Wilkins & E. Kaiser]. Secker & Warburg 1955.

NEWBOLT, H. *The Book of the Happy Warrior.* Longmans, Green & Co. 1917.

— *Clifton Chapel and Other School Poems.* John Murray 1908.

— *Later Life and Letters.* Faber & Faber 1942.

— *My World as in My Time.* Faber & Faber 1932.

— *Tales of the Great War.* Longmans, Green & Co. 1916.

— *The Twymans.* Blackwood 1911.

NETTLETON, J. *The Anger of the Guns.* William Kimber 1979.

NEWSOME, D. *Godliness and Good Learning.* John Murray 1961.

NICHOLS, B. *Father Figure.* Heinemann 1972.

— *Prelude.* Chatto & Windus 1920.

— *The Unforgiving Minute.* W.H. Allen 1978.

NICHOLS, R. *Ardours and Endurances.* Chatto & Windus 1917.

— [ed.] *An Anthology of War Poetry 1914–1918.* Nicholson & Watson 1943.

OGILVIE, V. *The English Public School.* Batsford 1957.

'O.E.' *Public School Life: Eton.* Sport & General Press Agency 1910.

OLLARD, R. *An English Education.* Collins 1982.

ORWELL, G. *Collected Essays, Journalism and Letters*. 4 Vols. [ed. S. Orwell & I Angus]. Secker & Warburg 1968 [Penguin 1970].
— *Inside the Whale and Other Essays*. Penguin 1962.
OSBORN, E.B. *The New Elizabethans*. The Bodley Head 1919.
— [ed.] *The Muse in Arms*. John Murray 1917.
OWEN, H. *Journey from Obscurity; Vol III: War*. OUP 1965.
OWEN, W. *Collected Letters* [ed. H. Owen & J. Bell], OUP 1967.
— *The Collected Poems* [ed. C. Day Lewis] Chatto & Windus 1963.
— *The Poems* [ed. J. Stallworthy]. Hogarth 1985.
— *Wilfred Owen: The Poems* [ed. J. Silkin]. Penguin 1985.

PANICHAS, G. [ed.] *Promise of Greatness*. Cassell 1968.
PARSONS, I. [ed.] *The Men Who March Away*. Chatto & Windus 1965.
PILKINGTON, E. *An Eton Playing Field*. Edward Arnold 1896.
Poems of To-Day. The English Association and Sidgwick & Jackson 1915.
POPE, J. *Jessie Pope's War Poems*. Grant Richards 1915.
— *More War Poems*. Grant Richards 1915.
— *Simple Rhymes for Stirring Times*. C.A. Pearson 1916.
POUND, R. *The Lost Generation*. Constable 1964.
POWELL, A. *Infants of Spring*. Heinemann 1976.
[*To Keep the Ball Rolling* (1 vol. ed.). Penguin 1983].

QUAYLE, E. *The Collector's Book of Boys' Stories*. Studio Vista 1973.
QUIGLY, I. *The Heirs of Tom Brown*. Chatto & Windus 1982.

RAYMOND, E. *Tell England*. Cassell 1922. [Pocket ed. 1928].
RAYNER WOOD, A.C. *Twenty Years After*. Spottiswoode, Ballantyne & Co. 1939.
READ, H. *Collected Poems*. Faber & Faber 1946.
READE, B. *Sexual Heretics*. Routledge & Kegan Paul 1970.
REED, T.B. *The Cock House at Fellsgarth*. Religious Tract Society 1893.
— *The Fifth Form at St. Dominic's*. Religious Tract Society 1887.
REILLY, C. [ed.] *Scars Upon My Heart*. Virago 1981.
REMARQUE, E.M. *All Quiet on the Western Front*. Putnam & Co. 1929 [Triad/Granada 1977]
RICHARDS, F. *Old Soldiers Never Die*. Faber & Faber 1933 [Anthony Mott Ltd. 1983].
ROBERTS, W. RHYS. *Patriotic Poetry, Greek and English*. John Murray 1916.
ROBBINS, K. *The First World War*. OUP 1984.
ROGERS, T. *Rupert Brooke: A Reappraisal and Selection*. Routledge & Kegan Paul 1971.
ROSE, J. *The Case of Peter Pan*. Macmillan 1984.
ROSENBERG, I. *The Collected Works*. [ed. I. Parsons]. Chatto & Windus 1979.

'SAKI'. *The Complete Works*. The Bodley Head 1980.
— *Reginald*. Methuen 1904.
— *The Unbearable Bassington*. John Lane 1912.
— *When William Came*. John Lane 1913.
'SAPPER'. *Mufti*. Hodder & Stoughton, 1919.
SASSOON, S. *Diaries 1915–1918*. [ed. R. Hart-Davis]. Faber & Faber 1983.
— *Diaries 1920–1922*. [ed. R. Hart-Davis]. Faber & Faber 1981.
— *Memoirs of a Fox-Hunting Man*. Faber & Faber 1928.
— *Memoirs of an Infantry Officer*. Faber & Faber 1930.
— *The Old Century*. Faber & Faber 1938.
— *Sherston's Progress*. Faber & Faber 1936.
— *Siegfried's Journey*. Faber & Faber 1946.
— *The War Poems*. [ed. R. Hart-Davis]. Faber & Faber 1983.
— *The Weald of Youth*. Faber & Faber 1942.
SCOTT-MONCRIEFF, C.K. [trans.] *The Song of Roland*. Chapman & Hall 1919.
SEELEY, J.R. *The Expansion of England*. Macmillan 1883.
SHERRIFF, R.C. *Journey's End: A Play in Three Acts*. Gollancz 1929.
— & BARTLETT V. *Journey's End: A Novel*. Gollancz 1930.
SILKIN, J. *Out of Battle*. OUP 1972.
— [ed.] *The Penguin Book of First World War Poetry*. Penguin 1979.
SKRINE, J.H. *Pastor Agnorum*. Longmans, Green & Co. 1902.
SMITH, T. D'ARCH *Love in Earnest*. Routledge & Kegan Paul 1970.
SOMERVELL, D. *see* Gollancz, V.
SORLEY, C.H. *Collected Poems* [ed. J. Moorcroft Wilson]. Cecil Woolf 1985.
— *Letters* [ed. W.R. Sorley]. CUP 1919.
— *Marlborough and Other Poems*. CUP 1916.
SPRINGHALL, J. *Youth, Empire and Society*. Croom Helm 1977.
STALLWORTHY, J. *Wilfred Owen*. OUP and Chatto & Windus 1974.
— [ed.]*The Oxford Book of War Poetry*. OUP 1984.
STANLEY, A.P. *The Life and Correspondence of Thomas Arnold*. Ward Lock 1844. [John Murray 1880. 2 vols].
STEERS, H.D. *The Officers' Training Corps Year Book and Diary*. Forster, Green & Co. 1913.
STRACHEY, L. *Eminent Victorians*. Chatto & Windus 1918 [Phoenix Library 1928].
— *Lytton Strachey by Himself* [ed. M. Holroyd]. Heinemann 1971.
STURGIS, H.O. *Tim*. Macmillan 1891.
SYMONDS, J.A. *Memoirs* [ed. P. Grosskurth]. Hutchinson 1984.

TALBOT-KELLY, R.B. *A Subaltern's Odyssey*. William Kimber 1980.
TAYLOR, A.J.P. *The First World War*. Hamish Hamilton 1963.
TEIGNMOUTH-SHORE, W. *Public School Life: Westminster*. Sport & General Press Agency 1910.

Index

School Tarts, 112
Scott, Sir Walter, 104
Scott-Moncrieff, C.K., 111, 232;
  'Evensong and Morwesong', 111
The Scout, 147
Seaman, Owen, 152
Seccombe, Thomas, 18–19, 21
Sedburgh, 206
Seeley, J.R., *The Expansion of England*, 54
self-sacrifice, theme of, 26, 99, 104, 112,
  228, 277
Shakespeare, William, 137, 239, 243, 246;
  Henry V, 101, 137 &n, 154, 230, 235
Shaw, George Bernard, 156
Shaw-Stewart, Patrick, 218, 219, 221,
  223–4
Shelley, P.B., 244, 245
Sherborne, 21, 31, 36, 43n, 53, 65, 112,
  144, 145, 207, 258 &n, 259, 261, 263,
  283
Sherriff, R.C., 39, 159, 167, 171, 242;
  Journey's End, 164, 167, 169, 185–6, 198
Sherston, George *see* Sassoon, Siegfried
The Shirburnian, 273
Shrewsbury, 16, 17, 61–2, 68n, 76, 88,
  103, 262, 263, 270; New House, 204,
  206; Rifle Corps (OTC), 65, 268;
  wartime lectures, 264
Shrewsbury Mission, Liverpool, 143, 146,
  263
Shrewsbury Technical School, 243, 251n
Sidney, Sir Philip, 103–4, 232, 234
Simonides, 96, 99, 217, 225, 235, 278
Simpson's cartoons, 246
Sixth Formers, 47, 48, 70, 74, 87, 110, 121
Skrine, J.H., *Pastor Agnorum*, 104
Smith, Nowell, 259, 273
Smith, William Alexander, 145
Smythe, Sir John, 'Men in Flanders
  1589–90', 278
Snow, Captain, 37–8
Sola Pinto, Vivian de, 173, 183
'The Soldier', *see* Brooke, Rupert
Soldier Poet, concept of, 22, 26, 232–5;
  see also war poets

Somervell, David, 22–3, 24
Somme, Battle of the (1916), 25, 134,
  161, 169, 177, 186, 196, 202, 204, 207,
  212, 213–14, 224, 225–6, 232, 237,
  241, 261
Sons of Britannia, 129
Sorley, Charles, 35, 36, 37, 70, 95, 144,
  151, 152–3, 154, 155–7, 216–17, 234;
  'All the Hills and Vales Along', 155
  Marlborough and Other Poems, 155;
  'Whom We Therefore Ignorantly
  Worship', 152
The Souls, 92, 219–21, 231
Southwell, Evelyn, 204–6, 210, 262
Spectator, 20, 159, 225
Spender, Stephen, 193n, 273, 274
Spenser, Edmund, *The Faerie Queen*, 101,
  104, 239n
Sportsmen's Battalions (Royal Fusiliers),
  162
Stables, Dr Gordon, 128
Stallworthy, Jon, 191, 249, 253
Stanley, A.P., 45, 48–9, 53, 57; *Life and
  Correspondence of Thomas Arnold*, 49
Sterling, Robert, 206
Stonyhurst school, 253
Stowe, Harriet Beecher, *Uncle Tom's
  Cabin*, 129
Strachey, Lytton, 108, *Eminent Victorians*,
  53
Strato, 89
Stuart-Young, J.M., 187
Stubbes, Philip, *Anatomy of Abuses*, 77
Sturgis, H.O., *Tim*, 107–8, 187
suffragettes, 179
Summer Camps, OTC, 31–2, 63, 64,
  67, 264
Summer Harvest Camp, 236, 264
Sutherland, Private David, 171–2
Swinburne, A.C., 55; 'Before the Mirror',
  191
Symonds, Dr, 48
Symonds, J.A., *Memoirs*, 106n
Szczepanski, Paul von, *Spartanerjünglinge*,
  123

Printed in Great Britain
by Amazon.co.uk, Ltd.,
Marston Gate.